Items should be returned on or before the last date shown below. Items not already requested by other borrowers may be renewed in person, in writing or by telephone. To renew, please quote the number on the barcode label. To renew online a PIN is required. This can be requested at your local library.
Renew online @ www.dublincitypubliclibraries.ie
Fines charged for overdue items will include postage incurred in recovery. Damage to or loss of items will be charged to the borrower.

Leabharlanna Poiblí Chathair Bhaile Átha Cliath
Dublin City Public Libraries

Baile Átha Cliath
Dublin City

Leabharlann Shráid Chaoimhín
Kevin Street Library
Tel: 01 222 8488

Date Due	Date Due	Date Due
	1 2 NOV 2019	

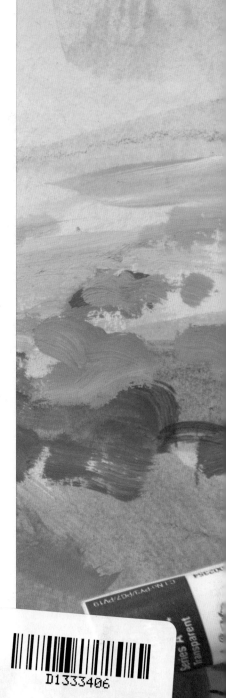

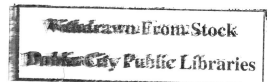
HOW TO DRAW AND PAINT
FIGURES &
LANDSCAPES

HOW TO DRAW AND PAINT
FIGURES &
LANDSCAPES

• Expert techniques and 70
exercises and projects shown
in over 1700 illustrations

• Produce lively studies in oil,
acrylic, gouache, pen and ink,
pencil, charcoal and pastels

VINCENT MILNE, ABIGAIL EDGAR
& SARAH HOGGETT

LORENZ BOOKS

This edition is published by Lorenz Books,
an imprint of Anness Publishing Ltd,
108 Great Russell Street,
London WC1B 3NA;
info@anness.com

www.lorenzbooks.com; www.annesspublishing.com

If you like the images in this book and would like to investigate
using them for publishing, promotions or advertising, please visit
our website www.practicalpictures.com for more information.

© Anness Publishing Ltd 2015

A CIP catalogue record for this book
is available from the British Library.

Publisher: Joanna Lorenz
Senior Editor: Felicity Forster
Photographer: Martin Norris
Designer: Nigel Partridge
Production Controller: Pirong Wang

PUBLISHER'S NOTE
Although the advice and information in this book are believed
to be accurate and true at the time of going to press, neither
the authors nor the publisher can accept any legal responsibility
or liability for any errors or omissions that may have been made
nor for any inaccuracies nor for any loss, harm or injury that
comes about from following instructions or advice in this book.

Contents

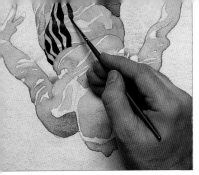

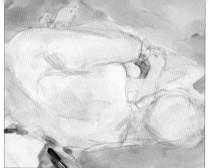

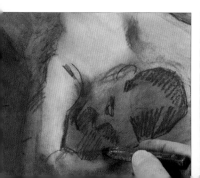

Introduction

This practical volume provides a thorough introduction to everything you need to know about drawing figures and landscapes – from nudes and portraiture to buildings and stunning scenes of the natural world. Capturing the beauty and tranquility of landscapes and the people living in it is an engrossing challenge, and this book will provide the techniques and help you to produce artworks to be proud of.

Drawing people

There is a long-established tradition of drawing and painting the nude in Western art, from prehistoric times, when cave dwellers first used mineral pigments to create their simple representations of hunters and their prey, through the idealized marble sculptures of ancient Greece to the beautifully observed anatomical studies of great Renaissance artists such as Michelangelo and Leonardo da Vinci, and right up to the present day. Portraiture, too, has gone through many styles and changes over the

▶ The central placing of the head and the solemn outward gaze impart a sense of strength and dignity to the image.

▼ Drawing the figure in a set time frame is a good way to study the human form.

▶ Working in three colours is an excellent way to model form. Here, areas of the light paper are uncovered, while the light and dark tones are achieved by shading with white and black.

centuries, from formal portraits intended as much to flatter the subject and show off a patron's wealth as to capture a realistic likeness, to 'warts and all' portraits that seek to convey, or lay bare, the character and personality of the sitter.

For many amateur artists, being able to produce good portraits and life drawings is the ultimate goal. Wouldn't it be lovely to be able to paint one's

family and friends? At the same time, however, the subject is viewed with a certain amount of trepidation.

Paintings of people are expected to be a true, almost photographically accurate, likenesses. "It doesn't even look like him" is probably the most common criticism of a portrait – and a critique like that could well put you off life drawing for good. In the face of that, perhaps it's understandable that many decide to play it safe and stick to less contentious subjects such as still lifes and scenes of holiday destinations.

If you'd like to have a go at drawing and painting people, the sections on drawing nudes and portraits provide an excellent and thorough introduction to everything you need to know.

Naturally, your own models may look very different to those who have sat for the projects in this book, and you will have your own ideas on compositions, room settings and so on – but don't be put off by that. You can learn a lot from the artists who have contributed to this book, and gain from their experience.

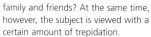
▲ Charcoal encourages bold drawing and can give a dramatic effect.

▼ A grey-green colour is a traditional choice for underpainting portraits, as it helps to establish a contrast between shadow areas and warmer highlights.

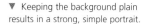
▲ Less is very often more! If you're new to life drawing, keep the background plain so that you can focus on the figure, resulting in a strong, simple portrait.

▼ Keeping the background plain results in a strong, simple portrait.

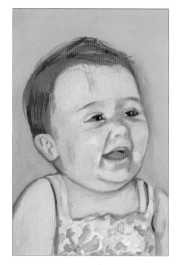

◄ Landscapes may be realistic, subdued, vivid or stylized – depending on the scene, time of day and the artist's style.

How to use this book

All the artists who have contributed to this book have many years' experience of drawing and painting. They work in a range of media, and their styles range from highly detailed, almost photo-realistic renditions to looser, expressive interpretations that explore the artist's personal and emotional response to the scene before his or her eyes. Even if a project is in a medium you do not normally use or in a style that does not particularly appeal to you, studying the way the artist has tackled the subject will give you invaluable insights that you can use in your own work. You may choose to copy the projects exactly, as a technical exercise to help you master new techniques or media; alternatively, you can use them as a starting point for your own explorations. However you use them, they will add to your growing understanding of the technical aspects of drawing and painting and enrich your awareness of the choices open to you as an artist.

The book also sets out some of the technicalities of drawing through a series of tutorials, touching on a range of topics from very simple anatomy,

Drawing landscapes

Along with life drawing, landscapes are one of the most popular of all subjects for artists – and with good reason. From high mountain peaks to lush valley floors, raging torrents to calm ponds, sylvan oases to arid deserts, the natural world is infinitely varied and endlessly fascinating. Man-made landscapes, too – whether they be remote, picturesque villages perched on a hillside or urban settings in which old and new are intriguingly juxtaposed – can have tremendous visual appeal.

Despite its popularity, however, landscape drawing and painting has its own particular challenges. The vagaries of the weather mean that working in situ is often simply not feasible. Even when you are able to take your sketchbook and paints out on location, the quality and direction of the light are constantly changing, shadows come and go, and colours and tones can appear different from one minute to the next. Out of necessity, many artists are obliged to work at least part of the time from photographs.

There is, however, no substitute for experiencing the landscape for yourself, even if all you do is make a few quick reference sketches. You will produce a far better result by painting a landscape that you have actually visited, where you have been able to explore different viewpoints and pick out the essentials of the scene for yourself, than by working from a photo of a place you have never been to.

◄ Learning how to apply paint, pencil or charcoal and blend for atmospheric effect is essential for landscape artists.

▼ Capturing the tranquillity of a scene with reflective water is a great exercise in observation and composition, and can create a vibrant piece of art.

measuring and proportions to hands and feet, and facial hair. Here you will find guidance on specific subjects such as lighting and weather conditions, clouds, trees, foliage, and moving water.

To get the most out of this book, work consistently through the spreads, take your time and try out the exercises and projects at a pace that suits you. If you need to spend longer or go back and repeat any sections, do so to gain fuller understanding and greater mastery. Alternatively, if you are more experienced and there are specific aspects that you feel you need a little help with or you simply want to experiment with different media, dip into the book as a refresher course whenever you need to.

What comes after that? Well, it's up to you! The old adage 'practice makes perfect' really holds true in drawing and painting. Practise when you can – and don't wait until you have the time to create a full-scale life study, or you will never get started. Artists' sketchbooks are crammed full of studies made whenever they have got a few minutes to spare, and, whether they are preparatory sketches for a larger work

or practice exercises to sharpen observational skills, the time this work takes is always valuably spent.

Drawing and painting is an unending voyage of discovery. Every person is different and every scene is different; even shapes and relationships within the same pose may alter slightly as the work progresses, keeping you on the alert and making you continually reassess things. And this is what makes these subjects so fascinating to study.

▲ Aerial and linear perspective are essential for creating a sense of depth and distance.

▶ Close study of the effects of light and shadow can produce interesting results in any medium.

▼ This rendition of a waterfall in full spate conveys the atmosphere and mood of the scene rather than capturing every leaf and twig in great detail.

Materials

If you are new to drawing and painting, you may well find the choice of materials on offer completely bewildering.

This chapter sets out the pros and cons of each medium, and provides practical information on everything from selecting paper and brushes to priming and stretching canvases, so that you can make an informed choice about what is really essential.

Start with a selection of good-quality materials, adding new items as and when you need them. Think, too, about whether you are going to be working in the studio or outdoors, on location: you may well need a lighter, more portable kit for field work.

It is also worth trying out media that you might not previously have considered. If you love the luminosity of watercolour for portraying the fleeting effects of light, for example, why not see if you can create a similar effect with soft pastels? If you have mastered the art of applying layer upon layer of coloured pencil to create delicate, detailed figure studies, why not experiment with a looser, freer style for big, bold panoramas in oils or acrylics? Varying your approach will keep your work fresh by giving you new creative and technical challenges.

Monochrome media

For sketching and underdrawing, as well as for striking studies in contrast and line, there are many different monochrome media, all of which offer different qualities to your artwork.

A good selection is the foundation of your personal art store, and it is worth exploring many media, including different brands, to find the ones you like working with.

Pencils

Pencils are graded according to hardness. 9H is the hardest down to HB and F (for fine) and then up to 9B, which is the softest. The higher the proportion of clay to graphite, the harder the pencil. A selection of five grades – say, a 2H, HB, 2B, 4B and 6B – is adequate for most purposes.

Soft pencils give a very dense, black mark, while hard pencils give a grey mark. The differences can be seen below – these marks were made by appying the same pressure to different grades of pencil. If you require a darker mark, do not try to apply more pressure, but switch to a softer pencil.

H

4H

F

6B

3B

B

Water-soluble graphite pencils

There are also water-soluble graphite pencils, which are made with a binder that dissolves in water. Available in a range of grades, they can be used dry, dipped in water or worked into

with a brush and water to create a range of watercolour-like effects. Water-soluble graphite pencils are an ideal tool for sketching on location, as they offer you the versatility of combining linear marks with tonal washes. Use the tip to create fine details and the side of the pencil to cover large areas quickly.

Graphite sticks

Solid sticks of graphite come in various sizes and grades. Some resemble conventional pencils, while others are shorter and thicker. You can also buy irregular-shaped chunks and fine graphite powder, and thinner strips of graphite in varying degrees of hardness that fit a barrel with a clutch mechanism.

Graphite sticks are capable of making a wider range of marks than conventional graphite pencils. For example, you can use the point or edge of a profile stick to make a thin mark, or stroke the whole side of the stick over the paper to make a broader mark.

Charcoal

The other monochromatic drawing material popular with artists is charcoal. It comes in different lengths and in thin, medium, thick and extra-thick sticks. You can also buy chunks that are ideal for expressive drawings. Stick charcoal is very brittle and powdery, and is great for broad areas of tone.

Compressed charcoal is made from charcoal dust mixed with a binder and fine clay and pressed into shape. Sticks and pencils are available. Unlike stick charcoal, charcoal pencils are ideal for detailed, linear work.

As with other powdery media, drawings made in charcoal should be sprayed with fixative to hold the pigment in place and prevent smudging.

Thick charcoal stick

Thin charcoal stick

Pen and ink

With so many types of pens and colours of ink available, not to mention the possibility of combining linear work with broad washes of colour, this is an extremely versatile medium and one that is well worth exploring. Begin by making a light pencil underdrawing of your subject, then draw over with pen – but beware of simply inking over your pencil lines, as this can look rather flat and dead. When you have gained enough confidence, your aim should be to put in the minimum of lines in pencil, simply to ensure you've got the proportions and angles right, and then do the majority of the work in pen.

Inks

The two types of inks used by artists are waterproof and water-soluble. The former can be diluted with water, but are permanent once dry, so line work can be worked over with washes without any fear of it being removed.

They often contain shellac, and thick applications dry with a sheen. The best-known is Indian ink, actually from China. It makes great line drawings. It is deep black but can be diluted to give a beautiful range of warm greys.

Water-soluble inks can be reworked once dry, and work can be lightened and corrections made. Don't overlook watercolours and liquid acrylics – both can be used like ink but come in a wider range of colours.

Waterproof ink

Water-soluble ink

Liquid acrylic

Dip pens and nibs

A dip pen does not have a reservoir of ink; as the name suggests, it is simply dipped into the ink to make marks. Drawings made with a dip pen have a unique quality, as the nib can make a line of varying width depending on how much pressure you apply. You can also turn the pen over and use the back of the nib to make broader marks. As you have to keep reloading with ink, it is difficult to make a long, continuous line – but for many subjects the rather scratchy, broken lines are very attractive.

When you first use a new nib it can be reluctant to accept ink. To solve this, rub it with a little saliva.

Nibs

Dip pen

Sketching pens, fountain pens and technical pens

Sketching pens and fountain pens make ideal sketching tools and enable you to use ink on location without having to carry bottles of ink.

Technical pens deliver ink through a tube rather than a shaped nib, so the line is of a uniform width. If you want to make a drawing that has a range of line widths, you will need several pens with different-sized tubular nibs.

Sketching pen

Bamboo, reed and quill pens

The nib of a bamboo pen delivers a 'dry', rather coarse line. Reed and quill pens are flexible and give a subtle line that varies in thickness. The nibs break easily, but can be recut with a knife.

Rollerball, fibre-tip and marker pens

Rollerball and fibre-tip pens are ideal for sketching out ideas, although finished drawings made using these pens can have a rather mechanical feel to them, as the line does not vary in width. This can work well as an effect.

By working quickly with a rollerball you can make a very light line by delivering less ink to the nib. Fibre-tip and marker pens come in an range of tip widths, from super-fine to calligraphic style tips and also in a wide range of colours.

Coloured drawing media

Coloured pencils contain a coloured pigment and clay, held together with a binder. They are impregnated with wax so that the colour holds to the support with no need for a fixative. They are especially useful for making coloured drawings on location, as they are a very stable medium and are not prone to smudging. Mixing takes place optically on the surface of the support rather than by physical blending, and all brands are inter-mixable, although certain brands can be more easily erased than others; so always try out one or two individual pencils from a range before you buy a large set. Choose hard pencils for linear work and soft ones for large, loosely-applied areas of colour.

Water-soluble pencils

Most coloured-pencil manufacturers also produce a range of water-soluble pencils, which can be used to make conventional pencil drawings and blended with water to create watercolour-like effects. In recent years, solid pigment sticks that resemble pastels have been introduced that are also water-soluble and can be used in conjunction with conventional coloured pencils or on their own.

Wet and dry ▼
Water-soluble pencils can be used dry, the same way as conventional pencils.

Conté crayons and pencils

The best way to use Conté crayons is to snap off a section and use the side of the crayon to block in large areas, and a tip or edge for linear marks.

The pigment in Conté crayons is relatively powdery, so, like soft pastels and charcoal, it can be blended by rubbing with a finger, rag or torchon. Conté crayon drawings benefit from being given a coat of fixative to prevent smudging. However, Conté crayons are harder and more oily than soft pastels, so you can lay one colour over another, letting the under-colour show through.

Conté is also available in pencils, which contain wax and need no fixing (setting); the other benefit is that the tip can be sharpened to a point.

Conté crayons ▼
These small, square-profile sticks are available in boxed sets of traditional colours. Drawings made using these traditional colours are reminiscent of the wonderful chalk drawings of old masters such as Michelangelo or Leonardo da Vinci.

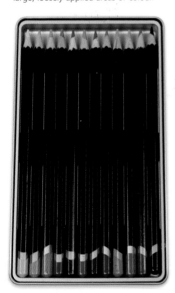

Huge colour range ▲
Artists who work in coloured pencil tend to accumulate a vast range in different shades – the variance between one tone and its neighbour often being very slight. This is chiefly because you cannot physically mix coloured pencil marks to create a new shade (unlike watercolour or acrylic paints). So, if you want lots of different greens in a landscape, you will need a different pencil for each one.

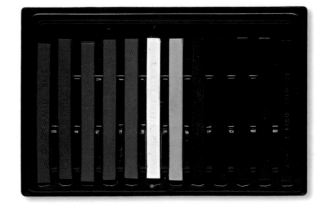

Conté pencils ▼
As they can be sharpened to a point, Conté pencils are ideal for drawings that require precision and detail.

Pastels

Pastel work is often described as painting rather than drawing as the techniques used are often similar to techniques used in painting. Pastels are made by mixing pigment with a weak binder, and the more binder used the harder the pastel will be. Pastels are fun to work with and ideal for making colour sketches as well as producing vivid, dynamic artwork.

Soft pastels

As soft pastels contain relatively little binder, they are prone to crumbling, so they have a paper wrapper to help keep them in one piece. Even so, dust still comes off, and can easily contaminate other colours nearby. The best option is to arrange your pastels by colour type and store them in boxes.

Pastels are mixed on the support either by physically blending them or by allowing colours to mix optically. The less you blend, the fresher the image looks. For this reason, pastels are made in a range of hundreds of tints and shades.

As pastels are powdery, use textured paper to hold the pigment in place. Spray soft pastel drawings with fixative to prevent smudging. You can fix (set) work in progress, too – but colours may darken, so don't overdo it.

Box of pastels ▼
When you buy a set of pastels, they come packaged in a compartmentalized box so that they do not rub against each other and become dirtied.

Hard pastels

One advantage of hard pastels is that, in use, they do not shed as much pigment as soft pastels, therefore they will not clog the texture of the paper as quickly. For this reason, they are often used in the initial stages of a work that is completed using soft pastels. Hard pastels can be blended together by rubbing, but not as easily or as seamlessly as soft pastels.

Oil pastels

Made by combining fats and waxes with pigment, oil pastels are totally different to pigmented soft and hard pastels and should not be mixed with them. Oil pastels can be used on unprimed drawing paper and they never completely dry.

Oil-pastel sticks are quite fat and therefore not really suitable for detailed work or fine, subtle blending. For bold, confident strokes, however, they are perfect.

Oil-pastel marks have something of the thick, buttery quality of oil paints. The pastels are highly pigmented and available in a good range of colours. If they are used on oil-painting paper, they can be worked in using a solvent such as white spirit (paint thinner), applied with a brush or rag. You can also smooth out oil-pastel marks with wet fingers. Oil and water are not compatible, and a damp finger will not pick up colour.

Oil pastels can be blended optically on the support by scribbling one colour on top of another. You can also create textural effects by scratching into the pastel marks with a sharp implement – a technique known as sgraffito.

Oil pastels ▼
Less crumbly than soft pastels, and harder in texture, oil pastels are round sticks and come in various sizes.

Pastel pencils

The colours of pastel pencils are strong, yet the pencil shape makes them ideal for drawing lines. The pastel strip can be sharpened to a point, making pastel pencils ideal for describing detail in drawings that have been made using conventional hard or soft pastels.

Pastel pencils ▼
Available in a comprehensive range of colours, pastel pencils are clean to use and are ideal for linear work.

Watercolour paint

Watercolour paints are available in two main forms: pans, which are the familiar compressed blocks of colour that need to be brushed with water to release the colour; or tubes of moist paint. The same finely powdered pigments bound with gum arabic solution are used to make both types. The pigments provide the colour, while the gum arabic allows the paint to adhere to the paper, even when diluted.

It is a matter of personal preference whether you use pans or tubes. The advantage of pans is that they can be slotted into a paintbox, making them easily portable, and this is something to consider if you often paint on location. Tubes, on the other hand, are often better if you are working in your studio and need to make a large amount of colour for a wash. With tubes, you need to remember to replace the caps

immediately, otherwise the paint will harden and become unusable. Pans of dry paint can be rehydrated.

Tubes of paint ▼
Tubes of watercolour paint are available in different sizes. It is worth buying the larger sizes for colours that you think you will use frequently. Keep the caps tightly sealed and rinse spilt paint off the tubes before storing them.

Grades of paint

There are two grades of watercolour paint: artists' and students' quality. Artists' quality paints are the more expensive, because they contain a high proportion of good-quality pigments. Students' quality paints contain less pure pigment and more fillers, and are usually available in a smaller range of colours than artists' quality paints.

If you come across the word 'hue' in a paint name, it indicates that the paint contains cheaper alternatives instead of the real pigment. Generally speaking, you get what you pay for: artists'

quality paints tend to produce more subtle mixtures of colours.

The other thing that you need to think about when buying paints is their permanence. The label or the manufacturer's catalogue should give you the permanency rating. In the United Kingdom, the permanency ratings are class AA (extremely permanent), class A (durable), class B (moderate) and class C (fugitive). The ASTM (American Society for Testing and Materials) codes for light-fastness are ASTM I (excellent), ASTM II (very good)

and ASTM III (not sufficiently light-fast). Some pigments, such as alizarin crimson and viridian, stain more than others: they penetrate the fibres of the paper and cannot be removed.

Finally, although we always think of watercolour as being transparent, you should be aware that some pigments are actually slightly opaque and will impart a degree of opacity to any colours with which they are mixed. These so-called opaque pigments include all the cadmium colours and cerulean blue.

Judging colours

It is not always possible to judge the colour of paints by looking at the pans in your palette, as they often look dark. In fact, it is very easy to dip your brush into the wrong pan, so always check before you put brush to paper.

Even when you have mixed a wash in your palette, appearances can be deceptive, as watercolour paint always looks lighter when it is dry. The only way to be sure what colour or tone you have mixed is to apply it to paper and let it dry. It is always best to build up tones gradually until you get the effect you want. The more you practise, the better you will get at anticipating results.

Appearances can be deceptive ▼
These two pans look very dark, almost black. In fact, one is Payne's grey and the other a bright ultramarine blue.

Test your colours ▼
Keep a piece of scrap paper next to you as you work so that you can test your colour mixes before you apply them.

Gouache paint

Made using the same pigments and binders found in transparent watercolour, gouache is a water-soluble paint. The addition of *blanc fixe* – a chalk – gives the paint its opacity. Because gouache is opaque you can paint light colours over darker ones – unlike traditional watercolour, where the paint's inherent transparency means that light colours will not cover any darker shades that lie underneath.

The best-quality gouache contains a high proportion of coloured pigment. Artists' gouache tends to be made using permanent pigments that are light-fast. The 'designers' range uses less permanent pigments, as designers' work is intended to last for a short time.

Characteristics of gouache

All of the equipment and techniques used with watercolour can be used with gouache. Like watercolour, gouache can be painted on white paper or board; due to its opacity and covering power, it can also be used on a coloured or toned ground and over gesso-primed board or canvas. Gouache is typically used on smoother surfaces than might be advised for traditional watercolour, as the texture of the support is less of a creative or aesthetic consideration.

If they are not used, certain gouache colours are prone to drying up over time. Gouache does remain soluble when dry, but dried-up tubes can be a problem to use.

Certain dye-based colours are very strong and, if used beneath other layers of paint, can have a tendency to bleed.

Work confidently ▲
Gouache remains soluble when it is dry, so if you are applying one colour over another, your brushwork needs to be confident and direct: a clean, single stroke, as here, will not pick up paint from the first layer.

Muddied colours ▲
If you scrub paint over an underlying colour, you will pick up paint from the first layer and muddy the colour of the second layer, as here.

Wet into wet ▲
Like transparent watercolour paint, gouache paint can be worked wet into wet (as here) or wet on dry.

Removing dry paint ▲
Dry paint can be re-wetted and removed by blotting with an absorbent paper towel.

Change in colour when dry ▼
Gouache paint looks slightly darker when dry than it does when wet, so it is good practice to test your mixes on a piece of scrap paper – although, with practice, you will quickly learn to make allowances for this.

Wet gouache paint

Dry gouache paint

Gouache paint

Oil paint

There are two types of traditional oil paint – professional, or artists', grade and the less expensive students' quality. The difference is that artists' paint uses finely ground, high-quality pigments, which are bound in the best oils and contain very little filler, while students' paints use less expensive pigments and contain greater quantities of filler to bulk out the paint. The filler is usually *blanc fixe* or aluminium hydrate, both with a very low tinting strength.

Students' quality paint is often very good and is, in fact, used by students, amateur painters and professionals.

The range of colours is more limited but still comprehensive, and each tube of paint in the range, irrespective of its colour, costs the same. Artists' quality paint is sold according to the quality and cost of the pigment used to make it. Each colour in the range is given a series number or letter; the higher the number or letter, the more expensive the paint. Various oils are used to bind and make the paint workable; linseed, poppy and safflower oil are the most common. The choice of oil depends on the characteristics and drying properties of the pigment being mixed.

Working "fat over lean" ▲
The golden rule when using oil paint is to work 'fat' (or oily, flexible paint) over 'lean', inflexible paint that contains little or no oil.

Tubes or tubs? ▼
Oil paint is sold in tubes containing anything from 15 to 275ml (1 tbsp to 9fl oz). If you tend to use a large quantity of a particular colour – for toning grounds, for example – you can buy paint in cans containing up to 5 litres (8¾ pints).

Glazing with oils ▲
Oils are perfect for glazes (transparent applications of paint over another colour). The process is slow, but quick-drying glazing mediums can speed things up.

Drawing with oils ▶
Oil bars consist of paint with added wax and drying agents. The wax stiffens the paint, enabling it to be rolled into what resembles a giant pastel.

Mixing colours with oils

Colour mixing with oils is relatively straightforward, as there is no colour shift as the paint dries: the colour that you apply wet to the canvas will look the same when it has dried, so (unlike acrylics, gouache or watercolour) you do not need to make allowances for changes as you paint. However, colour that looks bright when applied can begin to look dull as it dries. This is due to the oil in the paint sinking into a previously applied absorbent layer of paint below. You can revive the colour in sunken patches by 'oiling out' – that is, by brushing an oil-and-spirit mixture or applying a little retouching varnish over the affected area.

Water-mixable oil paint

Water-mixable oil paint is made using linseed and safflower oils that have been modified to be soluble in water. Once the paint has dried and the oils have oxidized, it is as permanent and stable as conventional oil paint. Some water-mixable paint can also be used with conventional oil paint, although its mixability is gradually compromised with the more traditional paint that is added.

Alkyd oil paints

Alkyd oil paints contain synthetic resin but are used in the same way as traditional oil paints and can be mixed with the usual mediums and thinners.

Alkyd-based paint dries much faster than oil-based paint, so it is useful for underpainting prior to using traditional oils and for work with glazes or layers. However, you should not use alkyd paint over traditional oil paint, as its fast drying time can cause problems.

Acrylic paint

Acrylic paint can be mixed with a wide range of acrylic mediums and additives and is thinned with water. Unlike oil paint, it dries quickly and the paint film remains extremely flexible and will not crack. The paint can be used with a wide range of techniques, from thick impasto, as with oil paint, to the semi-transparent washes of watercolour. Indeed, most of the techniques used in both oil and watercolour painting can be used with acrylic paint. Acrylic paints come in three different consistencies. Tube paint tends to be of a buttery consistency and holds its shape when squeezed from the tube. Tub paint is thinner and more creamy in consistency, which makes it easier to brush out and cover large areas. There are also liquid acrylic colours with the consistency of ink, sold as acrylic inks.

You may experience no problems in mixing different brands or consistencies, but it is always good practice to follow the manufacturer's instructions.

◀ **Liquid acrylics**
Liquid acrylics are the consistency of writing ink.

Tubs ▶
Acrylic paint in tubs stores easily.

Tubes ▶
Acrylic paints in tubes are convenient to carry and use with a palette.

Characteristics of acrylic paint

Being water soluble, acrylic paint is very easy to use, requiring only the addition of clean water. Water also cleans up wet paint after a work session. Once it has dried, however, acrylic paint creates a hard but flexible film that will not fade or crack and is impervious to more applications of acrylic or oil paint or their associated mediums or solvents.

Acrylic paint dries relatively quickly: a thin film will be touch dry in a few minutes and even thick applications dry in a matter of hours. Unlike oil paints, all acrylic colours, depending on the thickness of paint, dry at the same rate.

Mediums and additives ▲
A wide range of mediums and additives can be mixed into acrylic paint to alter and enhance its handling characteristics.

Extending drying time ▲
The drying time of acrylic paint can be extended by using a retarding medium, which gives you longer to work into the paint and blend colours.

Covering power
Acrylic paint that is applied straight from the tube has good covering power, even when you apply a light colour over a dark one, so adding highlights to dark areas is easy.

Texture gels ▲
Various gels can be mixed into acrylic paint to give a range of textural effects. These can be worked in while the paint is still wet.

Adhesive qualities ▲
Many acrylic mediums have very good adhesive qualities, making them ideal for collage work– sticking paper or other materials on to the support.

Glazing with acrylics ▲
Acrylic colours can be glazed by thinning the paint with water, although a better result is achieved by adding an acrylic medium.

Shape-holding ability
Like oil paint, acrylic paint that is applied thickly, straight from the tube, holds its shape and the mark of the brush as it dries, which can allow you to use interesting textures.

Palettes

The surface on which an artist arranges colours prior to mixing and applying them to the support is known as the palette. (Somewhat confusingly, the same word is also used to describe the range of colours used by a particular artist, or the range of colours found in a painting.) The type of palette that you use depends on the medium in which you are working, but you will undoubtedly find that you need more space for mixing colours than you might imagine. A small palette gets filled with colour mixes very quickly and it is a false economy to clean the mixing area too often: you may be cleaning away usable paint or mixed colours that you might want to use again. Always buy the largest palette practical.

Wooden palettes

Flat wooden palettes in the traditional kidney or rectangular shapes with a thumb hole are intended for use with oil paints. They are made from hardwood, or from the more economical plywood.

Before you use a wooden palette with oil paint for the first time, rub linseed oil into the surface of both sides. Allow it to permeate the surface. This will prevent oil from the paint from being absorbed into the surface of the palette and will make it easier to clean. Re-apply linseed oil periodically and a good wooden palette will last for ever.

Wooden palettes are not recommended for acrylic paint, however, as hardened acrylic paint can be difficult to remove from the surface.

Holding and using the palette ▼
Place your thumb through the thumb hole and balance the palette on your arm. Arrange pure colour around the edge. Position the dipper(s) at a convenient point, leaving the centre of the palette free for mixing colours.

White palettes

Plastic palettes are uniformly white. They are made in both the traditional flat kidney and rectangular shapes. The surface is impervious, which makes them ideal for use with either oil or acrylic paint. They are easy to clean, but the surface can become stained after using very strong colours such as viridian or phthalocyanine blue.

There are also plastic palettes with wells and recesses, intended for use with watercolour and gouache. The choice of shape is entirely subjective, but it should be of a reasonable size.

White porcelain palettes offer limited space for mixing. Intended for use with watercolour and gouache, they are aesthetically pleasing but can easily be chipped and broken.

Wooden palette ▲
Artists working with oil paints generally prefer a wooden palette. Always buy one that is large enough to hold all the paint and mixes that you intend to use.

Slanted-well palette ▲
This type of porcelain palette is used for mixing gouache or watercolour. The individual colours are placed in the round wells and the paint is mixed in the rectangular sections.

Disposable palettes

A relatively recent innovation is the disposable paper palette, which can be used with both oils and acrylics. These come in a block and are made from an impervious parchment-like paper. A thumb hole punched through the block enables it to be held in the same way as a traditional palette; alternatively, it can be placed flat on a surface. Once the work is finished, the used sheet is torn off and thrown away.

Paper palette ▲
Disposable palettes are convenient and make cleaning up after a painting session an easy task.

Stay-wet palette

Intended for use with acrylic paints, the stay-wet palette will stop paints from drying out and becoming unworkable if left exposed to the air for any length of time. The palette consists of a shallow, recessed tray into which a water-impregnated membrane is placed. The paint is placed and mixed on this membrane, which prevents the paint from drying out. If you want to leave a painting halfway through and come back to it later, you can place a plastic cover over the tray, sealing the moist paint in the palette. This prevents the water from evaporating and the paint from becoming hard and unusable. The entire palette can be stored in a cool place or even in the refrigerator. If the membrane does dry out, simply re-wet it.

Stay-wet palette ▶
This type of palette, in which the paint is mixed on a water-impregnated membrane, prevents acrylic paint from drying out. If you like, you can simply spray acrylic paint with water to keep it moist while you work.

Containers for water, solvents and oil

Although a regular supply of containers, such as empty jam jars, can be recycled from household waste and are just as good as a container bought for the purpose, several types of specially designed containers are available from art supply stores.

Among the most useful are dippers – small, open containers for oil and solvent that clip on to the edge of the traditional palette. Some have screw or clip-on lids to prevent the solvent from evaporating when it is not in use. You can buy both single and double dippers, like the one shown on the right. Dippers are useful when you want to work at speed.

Dipper ▼
Used in oil painting, dippers are clipped on to the side of the palette and contain small amounts of oil or medium and thinner.

Improvised palettes

For work in the studio, any number of impermeable surfaces and containers can be used as palettes. Perhaps the most adaptable is a sheet of thick counter glass, which you can buy from a glazier; the glass should be at least ¼in (5mm) thick and the edges should be polished smooth. Glass is easy to clean and any type of paint can be mixed on it. To see if your colours will work on the support you have chosen to use, slip a sheet of paper the same colour as the support beneath the glass.

Aluminium-foil food containers, tin cans, glass jars, paper and polystyrene cups also make useful and inexpensive containers for mixing large quantities of paint and for holding water or solvents. Take care not to put oil solvents in plastic or polystyrene containers, though, as the containers may dissolve.

Additives

Artists working with oils and acrylics will need to explore paint additives, which help attain various textures and effects in their work. Although oil paint can be used straight from the tube, it is usual to alter the paint's consistency by adding a mixture of oil or thinner (solvent). Simply transfer the additive to the palette a little at a time and mix it with the paint. Manufacturers of acrylic paints have also introduced a range of mediums and additives that allow artists to use the paint to its full effect. Oils and mediums are used to alter the consistency of the paint, allowing it to be brushed out smoothly or to make it dry more quickly. Once exposed to air, the oils dry and leave behind a tough, leathery film that contains the pigment. Different oils have different properties – for example, linseed dries relatively quickly but yellows with age so is only used for darker colours.

A painting medium is a ready-mixed painting solution that may contain various oils, waxes and drying agents. The oils available are simply used as a self-mixed medium. Your choice of oil or medium will depend on several factors, including cost, the type of finish required, the thickness of the paint being used and the range of colours.

There are several alkyd-based mediums on the market. They all accelerate the drying time of the paint, which can help to considerably lessen the waiting time between each application of paint. Some alkyd mediums are thixotropic; these are initially stiff and gel-like but, once worked, become clear and loose. Other alkyd mediums contain inert silica and add body to the paint; useful for impasto techniques where a thick mix of paint is required. Discussing your work with an art stockist will help you decide which additives you need.

Oils

There are a great many oils and thinners available. The more common ones are listed below.

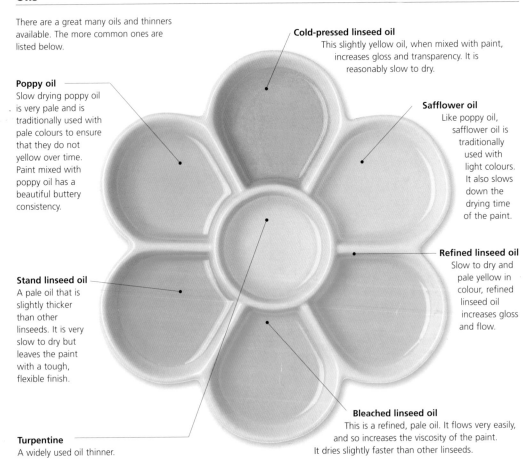

Cold-pressed linseed oil
This slightly yellow oil, when mixed with paint, increases gloss and transparency. It is reasonably slow to dry.

Poppy oil
Slow drying poppy oil is very pale and is traditionally used with pale colours to ensure that they do not yellow over time. Paint mixed with poppy oil has a beautiful buttery consistency.

Safflower oil
Like poppy oil, safflower oil is traditionally used with light colours. It also slows down the drying time of the paint.

Refined linseed oil
Slow to dry and pale yellow in colour, refined linseed oil increases gloss and flow.

Stand linseed oil
A pale oil that is slightly thicker than other linseeds. It is very slow to dry but leaves the paint with a tough, flexible finish.

Bleached linseed oil
This is a refined, pale oil. It flows very easily, and so increases the viscosity of the paint. It dries slightly faster than other linseeds.

Turpentine
A widely used oil thinner.

Thinners

The amount of thinner that you use depends on how loose or fluid you want the paint to be. If you use too much, however, the paint film may become weak and prone to cracking.

Turpentine
Turpentine is the strongest and best of all the thinners used in oil painting. It has a very strong smell. Old turpentine can discolour and become gummy if exposed to air and light. To help prevent this, store it in cans or dark glass jars.

White spirit
Paint thinner or white spirit is clear and has a milder smell than turpentine. It does not deteriorate and dries faster than turpentine. However, it can leave the paint surface matt.

Oil of spike lavender
Unlike other solvents, which speed up the drying time of oil paint, oil of spike lavender slows the drying time. It is very expensive. Like turpentine and white spirit, it is colourless.

Low-odour thinners
Various low-odour thinners have come on to the market in recent years. The drawback of low-odour thinners is that they are relatively expensive and dry slowly.

Citrus solvents
You may be able to find citrus thinners. They are thicker than turpentine or white spirit but smell wonderful. They are more expensive than traditional thinners and slow to evaporate.

Liquin
Liquin is just one of a number of alkyd painting mediums that speed up drying time considerably – often to just a few hours. It also improves flow and increases the flexibility of the paint film. It is excellent for use in glazes.

Acrylic additives

Acrylic paints dry to leave a matt or slightly glossy surface. Gloss or matt mediums can be added, singly or mixed, to leave the surface with the desired finish. A gloss surface tends to make colours look brighter.

Gloss and matt mediums ▶
Both gloss (top) and matt (bottom) mediums are relatively thin white liquids that dry clear if applied to a support without being mixed with paint. Matt medium increases transparency and can be used to make matt glazes, but as a varnish can deaden colour. Gloss will enhance the depth of colour.

Flow-improving mediums

Adding flow-improving mediums reduces the water tension, increasing the flow of the paint and its absorption into the surface of the support.

One of the most useful applications for flow-improving medium is to add a few drops to very thin paint, which can tend to puddle rather than brush out evenly across the surface of the support. This is ideal when you want to tone the ground with a thin layer of acrylic before you begin your painting.

When a flow-improving medium is used with slightly thicker paint, a level surface will result, with little or no evidence of brushstrokes.

The medium can also be mixed with paint that is to be sprayed, as it assists the flow of paint and helps to prevent blockages within the spraying mechanism.

Retarding mediums

Acrylic paints dry quickly. Although this is generally considered to be an advantage, there are occasions when you might want to take your time over a particular technique or a specific area of a painting – when you are blending colours together or working wet paint into wet, for example. Adding a little retarding medium slows down the drying time of the paint considerably, keeping it workable for longer.

Gel mediums

With the same consistency as tube colour, gel mediums are available as matt or gloss finishes. They are added to the paint in the same way as fluid mediums. They increase the brilliance and transparency of the paint, while maintaining its thicker consistency. Gel medium is an excellent adhesive and extends drying time. It can be mixed with various substances such as sand or sawdust to create textural effects.

The effect of modelling paste ▼
Modelling pastes dry to give a hard finish, which can be sanded or carved into using a sharp knife.

The effect of heavy gel medium ▼
Mixed with acrylic paint, heavy gel medium forms a thick paint that is useful for impasto work.

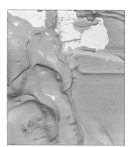

Paintbrushes

Oil-painting brushes are traditionally made from hog bristles, which hold their shape well and can also hold a substantial amount of paint. Natural hair brushes are usually used for watercolour and gouache, and can be used for acrylics and fine detail work in oils, if cleaned thoroughly afterwards.

Synthetic brushes are good quality and hard-wearing, and less expensive than either bristle or natural-hair brushes. However, they can quickly lose their shape if they are not looked after and cleaned well.

Cleaning brushes

1 Cleaning your brushes thoroughly will make them last longer. Wipe off any excess wet paint on a rag or a piece of newspaper. Take a palette knife and place it as close to the metal ferrule as possible. Working away from the ferrule towards the bristles, scrape off as much paint as you can.

2 Pour a small amount of household white spirit (paint thinner) – or water, if you are using a water-based paint such as acrylic or gouache – into a jar; you will need enough to cover the bristles of the brush. Agitate the brush in the jar, pressing it against the sides to dislodge any dried-on paint.

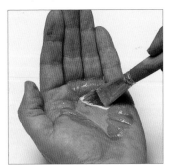

3 Rub household detergent into the bristles with your fingers. Rinse in clean water until the water runs clear. Reshape the bristles and store the brush in a jar with the bristles pointing upward, so that they hold their shape.

Brush shapes

Brushes for fine detail ▶
A rigger brush is very long and thin. It was originally invented for painting the straight lines of the ropes and rigging on ships in marine painting – hence the rather odd-sounding name. A liner is a flat brush which has the end cut away at an angle. Both of these brushes may be made from natural or synthetic fibres.

Wash brushes ▶
The wash brush has a wide body, which holds a large quantity of paint. It is used for covering large areas with a uniform or flat wash of paint. There are two types of wash brush: rounded or 'mop' brushes, which are commonly used with watercolour and gouache, and flat wash brushes, which are more suited for use with oils and acrylics.

Flat brushes ▼
These brushes have square ends. They hold a lot of paint, which can be applied as short impasto strokes or brushed out flat. Large flat brushes are useful for blocking in and covering large areas quickly. Short flats, known as 'brights', hold less paint and are stiffer. They make precise, short strokes, ideal for impasto work and detail.

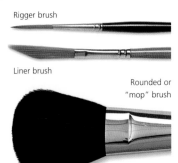

Rigger brush

Liner brush

Rounded or "mop" brush

Flat wash brush

Round brushes ▼
These are round-headed brushes that are used for detail and for single-stroke marks. Larger round brushes hold a lot of paint and are useful for the initial blocking-in. The point on round brushes can quickly disappear, as it becomes worn down by the abrasive action of the rough support. The brushes shown here are made of natural hair.

Large flat brush

Short flat brush

Large round brush

Small round brush

Other paint applicators

Brushes are only part of the artist's toolbox. You can achieve great textual effects by using many other types of applicator, from knives to rags.

Artists' palette and painting knives

Palette knives are intended for mixing paint with additives on the palette, scraping up unwanted paint from the palette or support, and general cleaning. Good knives can also be found in DIY or decorating stores.

You can create a wide range of marks using painting knives. In general, the body of the blade is used to spread paint, the point for detail and the edge for making crisp linear marks.

Regardless of the type of knife you use, it is very important to clean it thoroughly after use. Paint that has dried on the blade will prevent fresh paint from flowing evenly off the blade. Do not use caustic paint strippers on plastic blades, as they will dissolve; instead, peel the paint away.

Steel knives ▲
A wide range of steel painting and palette knives is available. In order to work successfully with this method of paint application, you will need several.

Plastic knives ▲
Less expensive and less durable than steel knives, plastic knives manipulate watercolour and gouache paints better than their steel counterparts.

Paint shapers

A relatively new addition to the artist's range of tools are paint shapers. They closely resemble brushes, but are used to move paint around in a way similar to that used when painting with a knife. Instead of bristle, fibre or hair, the shaper is made of a non-absorbent silicone rubber.

Foam and sponge applicators

Nylon foam is used to make both foam brushes and foam rollers. Both of these are available in a range of sizes and, while they are not intended as substitutes for the brush, they are used to bring a different quality to the marks they make.

Sponge applicators and paint shapers ▶
Shapers can be used to apply paint and create textures, and to remove wet paint. Foam rollers can cover large areas quickly. Sponge applicators are useful for initial blocking in.

`Natural and man-made sponges
With their pleasing irregular texture, natural sponges are used to apply washes and textures, and are invaluable for spreading thin paint over large areas and for making textural marks. They are also useful for mopping up spilt paint and for wiping paint from the support in order to make corrections. They are especially useful to landscape artists. Man-made sponges can be cut to the desired shape and size and used in a similar fashion.

Alternative applicators

Paint can be applied and manipulated using almost anything. The only limitations are set by practicality and imagination. The tool box and cutlery drawer are perhaps a good starting point, but you will no doubt discover plenty of other items around the home that you can use. Cardboard, pieces of rag, wood, wire wool and many other seemingly unlikely objects can all be – quite literally – pressed into service.

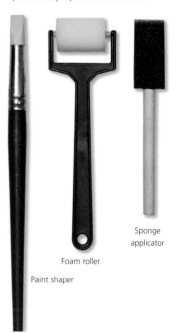

Sponge applicator

Foam roller

Paint shaper

Supports

A 'support' is the name for the surface on which a drawing or painting is made. It needs to be physically stable and resistant to deterioration from the corrosive materials used, as well as the atmosphere. It should also be light enough to be transported easily. Importantly, choose a support with the right texture for the media, marks and techniques you intend to use.

Drawing papers

Drawing papers vary enormously in quality and cost, depending on whether the paper is handmade, machine-made or mould-made. The thickness of a paper is described in one of two ways. The first is in pounds (lbs) and describes the weight of a ream (500 sheets). The second is in grams (gsm), and describes the weight of one square metre of a single sheet. Sheets vary considerably in size.

Many papers can also be bought in roll form and cut to the size required. You can also buy pads, which are lightly glued at one end, from which you tear off individual sheets as required. One of the benefits of buying a pad of paper is that it usually has a stiff cardboard back, which gives you a solid surface to lean on when working on location and means that you don't have to carry a heavy drawing board around with you. Sketchbooks have the same advantage.

The most common drawing paper has a smooth surface that is suitable for graphite, coloured pencil and ink work. Papers intended for use with watercolour also make ideal drawing supports. These papers come in three distinctly different surfaces – HP (hot-pressed) papers, which are smooth; CP (cold-pressed) papers, also known as NOT, or 'Not hot-pressed' papers, which have some surface texture; and rough papers which, not surprisingly, have a rougher texture.

Art and illustration boards are made from cardboard with paper laminated to the surface. They offer a stable, hard surface on which to work and are especially useful for pen line and wash, but can also be used with graphite and coloured pencil. They do not buckle when wet, as lightweight papers are prone to do, and are available in a range of sizes and surface textures, from very smooth to rough.

Coloured paper ▲
The main advantage of making a drawing on coloured paper is that you can choose a colour that complements the subject and enhances the mood of the drawing. Coloured papers can be used with all drawing media.

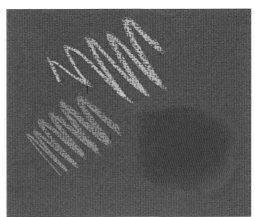

Pastel papers ▲
Papers for use with pastels are coated with pumice powder or tiny cork particles that hold the pigment and allow for a build-up of colour. They are available in a range of natural colours that complement the pastel shades.

Preparing your own surfaces

It is both satisfying and surprisingly easy to prepare your own drawing surfaces. Acrylic gesso, a kind of primer that is used to prepare a surface such as canvas or board when painting in oils or acrylics, can also be painted on to paper to give a brilliant white, hard surface that receives graphite and coloured pencil beautifully.

To make a surface that is suitable for pastels, you can mix the gesso with pumice powder. You can also buy ready-made pastel primer.

To create a toned or coloured ground, simply tint the gesso by adding a small amount of acrylic paint to it in the appropriate colour.

Painting papers

Papers for use with paints need to be carefully chosen. Some hold paint well, other papers are textured or smooth, and of course there are many different shades – all these factors will affect your final artwork.

Canvas paper and board ▶

Artists' canvas boards are made by laminating canvas – or paper textured to look like canvas – on to cardboard. They are made in several sizes and textures and are ideal for use when painting on location. However, take care not to get them wet, as the cardboard backing will disintegrate. They can also be easily damaged if you drop them on their corners. They are ready sized and can be used for painting in both oils and acrylics.

Paper and illustration board

Although best suited to works using water-based materials, paper and illustration board, provided it is primed with acrylic primer, can also be used for painting in oils.

Watercolour papers provide ideal surfaces for gouache work. The papers are found in various thicknesses and with three distinct surfaces – rough, hot-pressed (which is smooth) and NOT or cold-pressed, which has a slight texture. Watercolour boards tend to have either a rough or a hot-pressed surface. Illustration board tends to be very smooth and is intended for use with gouache and linework.

Tinted papers ▼

Although they are sometimes frowned upon by watercolour purists, tinted papers can be useful when you want to establish an overall colour key. Ready-made tinted papers are a good alternative to laying an initial flat wash.

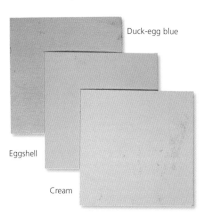

Duck-egg blue

Eggshell

Cream

Oil and acrylic papers

Both oil and acrylic papers have a texture similar to canvas and sheets can be bought loose or bound together in blocks. Although they are not suitable for work that is meant to last, they are perfect for sketching and colour notes.

Stretching paper for watercolours

Papers come in different weights, which refers to the weight of a ream (500 sheets) and can vary from 90lb (185 grams per square metre or gsm) to 300lb (640gsm) or more. The heavier the paper, the more absorbent. Papers that are less than 140lb (300gsm) in weight need to be stretched before use.

1 Dip a sponge in clean water and wipe it over the paper, making sure you leave no part untouched. Make sure a generous amount of water has been applied over the whole surface and that the paper is perfectly flat.

2 Moisten four lengths of gum strip and place one along each long side of the paper. (Only gummed brown paper tape is suitable; masking tape will not adhere.) Repeat for the short edge of the paper. Leave to dry. (In order to be certain that the paper will not lift, you could staple it to the board.)

Canvas

Without doubt, canvas is the most widely used support for both oil and acrylic work. Several types of canvas are available, made from different fibres. The most common are made from either cotton or linen, both of which can be purchased ready stretched and primed to a range of standard sizes (although there are suppliers who will prepare supports to any size) or on the roll by the yard (metre) either primed or unprimed. Unprimed canvas is easier to stretch.

Cotton duck ▼

Cotton duck has a more regular (some people might say more mechanical) weave than linen. It is also less expensive than linen.

Linen canvas ▼

Linen canvas is made from the fibres of the flax plant, *Linum usitatissimum*. The seeds of the plant are also pressed to make linseed oil, used by artists. Linen canvas is available in a number different textures and weights, from very fine to coarse. The fibres are stronger than cotton fibres, which means that the fabric is less likely to sag and stretch over time.

Stretching canvas

Canvas must be stretched taut over a rectangular wooden frame before use. For this you will need stretcher bars and wooden wedges.

Stretcher bars are usually made of pine and are sold in pairs of various standard lengths. They are pre-mitred and each end has a slot-in tenon joint. Longer bars are morticed to receive a cross bar (recommended for large supports over 75 x 100cm/30 x 40in).

1 Tap the bars together to make a frame. Arrange the canvas on a flat surface and put the frame on top. Staple the canvas to the back of the frame, ensuring it stays taut.

2 Tap wooden wedges lightly into the inside of each corner. These can be hammered in further to allow you to increase the tension and tautness of the canvas if necessary.

Priming canvas

Canvas is usually sized and primed (or, increasingly, just primed) prior to being worked on. This serves two purposes. The process not only tensions the fabric over the stretcher bars but also (and more importantly in the case of supports used for oil) seals and protects the fabric from the corrosive agents present in the paint and solvents. Priming also provides a smooth, clean surface on which to produce work.

In traditional preparation, the canvas is given a coat of glue size. The most widely used size is made from animal skin and bones and is known as rabbit-skin glue. It is available as dried granules or small slabs. When mixed with hot water the dried glue melts; the resulting liquid is brushed over the canvas to seal it.

Increasingly, acrylic emulsions are used to size canvas. Unlike rabbit-skin glue, the emulsions do not have to be heated but are used diluted with water.

The traditional partner to glue size is an oil-based primer. Lead white, which is toxic, together with titanium white and flake white, are all used in oil-based primers. To penetrate the canvas the primer should be the consistency of single cream; dilute it with white spirit (paint thinner) if necessary.

Traditional primer can take several days to dry, however; a modern alternative is an alkyd primer, which dries in a couple of hours.

Primers based on acrylic emulsion are easier to use. These are often known as acrylic gesso, although they are unlike traditional gesso. Acrylic primer should not be used over glue size, but it can be brushed directly on to the canvas. Acrylic primers can be used with both oil and acrylic paint, but oil primers should not be used with acrylic paints.

Primer can be applied with a brush or a palette knife. With a brush the weave of the canvas tends to show.

If you want to work on a toned ground, add a small amount of colour to the primer before you apply it. Add oil colour to oil primer and acrylic colour to acrylic primer.

Boards

Several types of wooden board make good supports for oil and acrylic work. Wood gives off acidic vapours that are detrimental to paint (for an example of how wood products deteriorate with age, think how quickly newspaper yellows). The solution is to prime the board with acrylic gesso, or glue canvas to the surface; a technique known as marouflaging. There are three types of board in common use: plywood, hardboard (masonite) and medium-density fibreboard (MDF). Plywood is made up of a wooden core sandwiched between a number of thin layers of wood glued together. Hardboard is a composite panel made by hot pressing steam-exploded wood fibres with resin, and is less prone to warping than solid wood or plywood. MDF is made in the same way, with the addition of a synthetic resin. It has a less hard and glossy face side than standard dense hardboard. All these boards come in a range of sizes. If used at a size where they begin to bend, mount rigid wooden battens on the reverse to reinforce them.

Priming board

Wood was traditionally sized with rabbit-skin glue and then primed with a thixotropic primer in the same way as canvas; nowadays, most artists use ready-made acrylic primer or acrylic gesso primer, which obviates the need for sizing. Acrylic primer also dries much more quickly.

Before you prime your boards, make sure they are smooth and free of dust. You should also wipe over them with methylated spirits to remove all traces of grease.

Using a wide, flat brush, apply primer over the board with smooth, vertical strokes. For a very large surface, apply the primer with a paint roller. Allow to dry. When it is dry, rub the surface of the board with fine-grade sandpaper to smooth out any ridges in the paint, and blow or dust off any powder. Apply another coat of primer, making smooth horizontal strokes and again allow to dry. Repeat as many times as you wish, sanding between coats.

Covering board with canvas

Canvas-covered board is a light painting surface that is useful when you are painting on location. It combines the strength and low cost of board with the texture of canvas. You can use linen, cotton duck or calico, which is cheap. When you have stuck the canvas to the board let it dry for two hours in a warm room. Prime the canvas with acrylic primer before use.

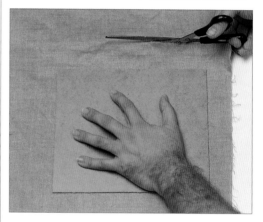

1 Arrange the canvas on a flat surface. Place the board on the canvas. Allowing a 5cm (2in) overlap all around, cut out the canvas. Remove the canvas and using a wide, flat brush, liberally brush matt acrylic medium over the board.

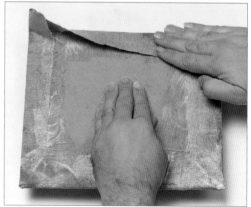

2 Place the canvas on the sticky side of the board and smooth it out with your fingertips, working from the centre outwards. Brush acrylic medium over the canvas to make sure that it is firmly stuck down. Place the board canvas-side down on an bowl so that it does not stick to your work surface. Brush acrylic medium around the edges of the board. Fold over the excess canvas, mitring the corners, and brush more medium over the corners to stick them firmly.

Art essentials

There are a few other pieces of equipment that you will probably find useful in your painting, ranging from things to secure your work to the drawing board and easels to support your painting, to aids for specific painting techniques.

Boards and easels

The most important thing is that the surface on which you are working is completely flat and cannot wobble as you work. If you use blocks of watercolour paper, then the block itself will provide support; you can simply rest it on a table or on your knee. If you use sheets of watercolour paper, then they need to be firmly secured to a board. Buy firm boards that will not warp and buckle (45 x 60cm/18 x 24in is a useful size), and attach the paper to the board by means of gum strip or staples.

It is entirely a matter of personal preference as to whether or not you use an easel. There are several types on the market, but remember that watercolour paint is a very fluid liquid and can easily flow down the paper into areas that you do not want it to touch. Choose an easel that can be used flat and propped at only a slight angle. The upright easels used by oil painters are not really suitable for watercolour painting.

Table easel ▶
This inexpensive table easel is adequate for most artists' needs. Like the box easel it can be adjusted to a number of different angles, allowing you to alter the angle to suit the technique you are using. It can also be stored neatly.

Portable box easel ▼
This easel includes a handy side drawer in which you can store all you need for a day's location work, as well as adjustable bars so that it can hold various sizes of drawing board firmly in place. Some easels can only be set at very steep angles, which is unsuitable for watercolour, so do check before you buy.

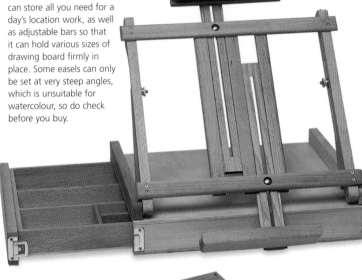

Other useful items

Various pieces of equipment come in handy, including a scalpel or craft (utility) knife: the fine tip allows you to prise up pieces of masking tape that have become stuck down too firmly without damaging the paper. You can also use a scalpel to scratch off fine lines of paint – a technique known as sgrafitto. Paper towel is invaluable for cleaning out paint palettes and lifting off or softening colour before it dries.

As you develop your painting style and techniques, you may want to add other equipment to the basic items shown here. You will probably assemble a selection of props, from bowls, vases and other objects for still lifes, to pieces of fabric and papers to use as backgrounds. Similarly, you may want to set aside pictures or photographs that appeal to you for use as reference material. The only real limit to what you can use is your imagination.

Eraser ◄
A kneaded eraser is useful for correcting the pencil lines of your underdrawing, and for removing the lines so that they do not show through the paint on the finished painting.

Masking tape and masking fluid ▲
One of the basic techniques in watercolour is masking. It is used to protect areas of the paper you want to keep unpainted. Depending on the size and shape of the area you want to protect, masking tape and masking fluid are most commonly used. Masking tape can also be used to secure heavy watercolour paper to a drawing board.

Gum arabic ▲
Adding gum arabic, a natural substance also called gum acacia, to watercolour paint increases the viscosity of the paint and slows down the drying time. This gives you longer to work. Add a few drops of the gum arabic to your paint and stir to blend. Gum arabic imparts a slight sheen on the paper, and increases the intensity of the paint colour.

Sponge ▲
Natural or synthetic sponges are useful for mopping up excess water. Small pieces of sponge can be used to lift off colour from wet paint. Sponges are also used to apply paint.

Gum strip ◄
Gummed brown paper strip is essential for taping stretched lightweight watercolour paper to a board to ensure that it does not buckle. Leave the paper stretched on the drawing board until you have finished and the paint has dried, then simply cut it off, using a scalpel or craft (utility) knife and a metal ruler. Masking tape is not suitable for this purpose.

Mahl stick ▲
This rod of wood (bamboo) with a soft leather ball at one end can be positioned over the work and leant on to steady the painting hand and protect your work from being smudged.

Varnishes

Used on finished oil and acrylic paintings, varnishes unify and protect the surface under a gloss or semi-matt sheen. Here are some of the most widely used.

Acrylic matt varnish
Synthetic varnishes can be used on oil and acrylic paintings. The one shown here dries to a matt finish.

Wax varnish
Beeswax mixed with a solvent makes the wax varnish that is often used on oil paintings. The wax is brushed over the work and allowed to stand for a short time. The excess is then removed with a rag and the surface buffed. The more the surface is buffed, the higher the resulting sheen.

Acrylic gloss varnish
This synthetic varnish dries on acrylic paintings to a gloss finish.

Retouching varnish
If there are parts of your oil painting that look sunken, with dull looking paint, retouching varnish can be used at any time while the work is in progress to revive problem areas. Both damar and mastic thinned with solvent can be used as retouching varnish.

Damar varnish
For use on oil paintings, damar varnish is made from the resin of the damar tree, which is found throughout Indonesia and Malaysia. The resin is mixed with turpentine to create a slightly cloudy liquid. The cloudiness is caused by natural waxes in the resin, and clears as the varnish dries. Damar does yellow with age, but it is easy to remove it and replace it with a fresh coat. The varnish dries very quickly.

Nudes

From ancient times up to the present day, drawing, painting and sculpting the naked human form has held a fascination for artists. This chapter looks at both the male and the female nude and explores a range of poses.

The chapter begins with a series of lessons on the technical aspects of drawing and painting people followed by a gallery of nude drawings and paintings by professional artists. Studying the work of other artists to see how they've tackled a particular subject is always illuminating,and you should take every opportunity to do so – particularly the works of the great masters, such as Leonardo, Michelangelo, Rubens and Rembrandt.

After the gallery is a series of quick sketches and detailed step-by-step projects for invaluable practice in all the major media, which you should try to fit into your day often. You can copy the projects exactly if you wish, but it's even better to use them as a starting point for your own explorations.

Measuring and proportions

No matter what subject you're drawing or painting, you need take careful measurements so that the relative sizes of different elements are correct. You also need to check continually as you work to make sure that you keep the proportions true to life. After a while, you'll find that this becomes second nature – but if you're a beginner, it's important to make a conscious effort to measure and check everything before you put it down on paper. Remember, too, to make your initial marks quite light so that you can make adjustments if need be. Even experienced artists find that they need to make revisions – and this is particularly true in portraiture and life drawing, where the position of the model will inevitably shift slightly during the course of the pose.

Taking measurements
Choose a unit within your subject against which you can measure everything else. That unit can be anything you like – the width of the eyes, the length of the nose, the distance between the bridge of the nose and the chin, for example.

With this method, it's absolutely vital that you keep your arm straight, so that the pencil remains a constant distance from the subject. Close one eye to make it easier to focus, and concentrate on looking at the pencil rather than at your subject.

The subject ▶
Here, the subject is a small statue, but the principle remains the same whatever you are drawing.

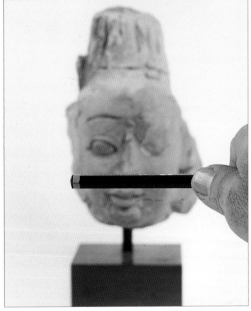

1 Close one eye and, holding a pencil at arms' length, measure the chosen section of your subject – here, the distance from the forehead to the chin. Align the top of the pencil with one end of the section you are measuring and move your thumb up or down the shaft of the pencil until it is level with the other end of the distance being measured.

2 Then transfer this unit of measurement to the paper. The unit of measurement is relative to the scale of your drawing. You will need to double or treble the ratio. Next, use the same unit of measurement to compare the size of other parts of the subject. Here, the distance across the widest part of the statue is the same as the measurement taken in Step 1.

The proportions of the human body

Artists have tried for centuries to define the proportions of the human body, but in reality proportions vary from one individual to another just as features vary. However, the head is a standard 'unit of measurement' that is often used in assessing proportions. Generally speaking, the average adult is roughly seven and a half heads tall. The height of his or her head fits seven and a half times into the total height of the body. It is important to stress that these proportions are average. Nonetheless, if you know the 'norm', you will find it easier to assess how far your model conforms to or departs from it.

Children, however, are another matter. In babies, the head takes up a larger proportion of the whole and a young baby's total height may be only about four times the height of the head, with about three-quarters of the height being the head and abdomen. The limbs then grow dramatically in the early years; by the age of three, the legs make up about half the total height.

Although the head is a standard and accepted unit of measurement, you can use anything you choose. For example, in a sitting pose the head may be seen in perspective, which will make it difficult to use it as a unit against which to judge other parts of the body. In a portrait where the model's hand supports the chin, for example, you could compare the length of the head to the hand. Or you could look at the length of the forearm in relation to the thigh. The important thing is that you check and measure sizes as you work.

If we look at further sub-divisions, more general guidelines emerge. In a standing figure, the pubic area is just below the mid-point of the body; the legs make up nearly half the total height. If the hands are hanging loosely by the sides, they will reach the mid-point of the thighs, while the elbows will be roughly level with the waist. When you're drawing or painting the figure, look for alignments such as this to check that you're placing limbs and features correctly. You can also put in 'landmarks' such as the nipples as guides, although there is no substitute for repeated and careful measuring.

There are also some differences in body shape between the sexes. Men's shoulders are generally wider than women's and their legs longer. A female pelvis is wider at the top.

General proportions ▼
See how proportions change with age. In this sketch, the adult male figure is seven-and-a-half heads tall and the woman is just over seven heads. The boy is just over six heads tall; the young child is just over four heads, while the baby is just under four – so his head takes up a much larger proportion of his total height than it does in adults.

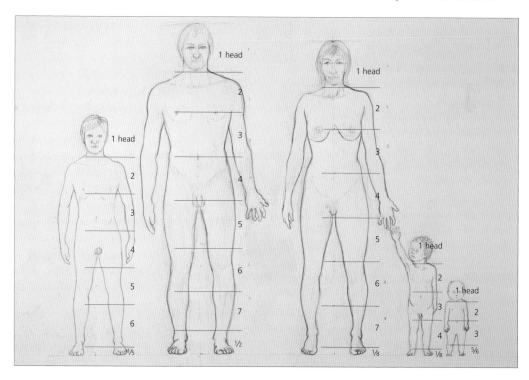

Simple anatomy

Beginners often make the mistake of trying to draw or paint every detail that they see, rather than deciding what is really important in a pose. You don't need to capture every crease in the skin or every bony protuberance – but if you understand something of what's happening beneath the surface, you will find it easier to pick out the essentials. For artists, the most important bones are those that are visible near the surface of the skin. Divide the body into sections; spine, shoulder blades, rib cage, bones of the arms and hands, pelvis (hips), and the bones of the legs and feet.

The spine
The spine, or vertebral column, is the most important support structure in the body. People often tend to think of it as being a fairly rigid, straight structure, so you may be surprised by how much it curves. In a normal upright posture there are four curves, which correspond to the different sections of the spine and describe a double S-shape: viewed from the side, the cervical vertebrae (the vertebrae in the neck) curve outwards; the thoracic vertebrae, which support the ribs, curve inwards; the lumbar vertebrae, which link to the pelvis, curve outwards again; and the vertebrae in the coccyx curve inwards. When you're analyzing a standing pose, the way the spine curves is critical. People often overlook the curve in the vertebrae of the neck, in particular, which makes the head jut forwards.

In a relaxed, reclining pose, the weight of the model will be supported by the pelvis, so the spine will sag or gently curve under the pull of gravity. In most models you will clearly see a depression running down the centre of the back, which shows you the position of the spine. Look at the protruding bones of the scapula and pelvis to help work out the balance of the pose.

The body's flexibility depends on the movement of the spine, so the next thing to look at is how the spine attaches to the shoulder girdle, rib cage and pelvis.

The shoulders
Making up the shoulder girdle are the scapula, or shoulder blade (a triangular-shaped bone that lies on the back of the thorax, the collarbone or clavicle, and the acromion, which is the outermost shoulder bone. When drawing or painting the nude, look for the bony upper edge of the scapula as this indicates the tilt of the shoulders.

The rib cage
The bones that form the rib cage are suspended from the thoracic vertebrae. The rib cage, inside which are vital organs such as the heart, liver and lungs, is wider at the bottom than at the top. Viewed from the front or side, the individual bones and overall shape of the rib cage can be clearly seen in thin individuals, although in many people a layer of fatty tissue makes them less obvious.

The pelvis
Attached to the base of the spine is the pelvis. Women tend to have a wider pelvis than men. The portions that jut outwards are known as the iliac crests and, from both the front and back view, these are useful 'landmarks' to watch out for. From the back you can also see the two small dimples of the rather grandly named 'posterior superior iliac spines': these, too, are useful landmarks, as they indicate the tilt of the pelvis.

The arms
Now let's consider the upper limbs. The long bone of the upper arm is the humerus. The upper half of the humerus is almost cylindrical, but it flattens and widens in the lower half, near the elbow. There are two main bones in the forearm – the radius and the ulna – and these cross over one another as you rotate your hand. The ulna, in particular, is prominent at both the elbow and the wrist and provides a useful point against which you can judge the position of other features.

The hands
In the hand, look for the joints across the back of the hand and the fingers (the metacarpals and phalanges), as they help you establish the different planes of the hand.

The legs
The hip bone juts out beyond the edge of the pelvis. The femur, or thigh bone, is the longest bone in the body. In the lower leg, the two main bones are the fibula and the tibia (shin bone). The patella, or knee cap, is prominent, as are the bones on the inside and outside of the ankle (the knobbly base of the tibia and fibula).

Bones visible beneath the skin ▼
In thin models with little fatty tissue you will probably be able to see many of the major bones of the body. Below, the underlying skeletal structure is highly evident at the point where the muscle in the neck (the sternocleidomastoid muscle) meets the collarbone and at the bony protrusions of the sternum and rib cage.

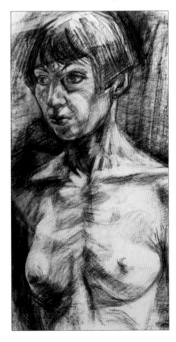

The skeleton ▶
This is a slightly stylized sketch of the main bones of the skeleton that you need to be aware of as an artist.

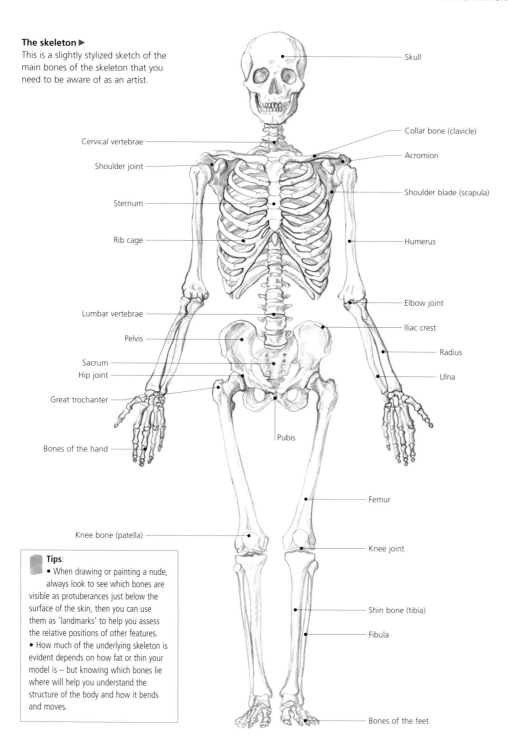

Skull

Collar bone (clavicle)

Acromion

Cervical vertebrae

Shoulder joint

Shoulder blade (scapula)

Sternum

Rib cage

Humerus

Elbow joint

Lumbar vertebrae

Iliac crest

Pelvis

Radius

Sacrum

Hip joint

Ulna

Great trochanter

Bones of the hand

Pubis

Femur

Knee bone (patella)

Knee joint

Tips:
• When drawing or painting a nude, always look to see which bones are visible as protuberances just below the surface of the skin, then you can use them as 'landmarks' to help you assess the relative positions of other features.
• How much of the underlying skeleton is evident depends on how fat or thin your model is – but knowing which bones lie where will help you understand the structure of the body and how it bends and moves.

Shin bone (tibia)

Fibula

Bones of the feet

The muscles

As with the bones of the skeleton, muscles are of interest to artists only insofar as they affect the surface of the body, and naturally we see them more prominently in people of an athletic build. Nonetheless, it is still useful to have a basic knowledge of the main muscle groups and how they work. You can convey the effect of muscles on surface form through careful use of tone. Try copying illustrations of the muscles from books on anatomy so that you get an understanding of the direction in which the muscles run and the range of movements that they allow; in doing so, you will be better able to create a sense of movement and tension in your work.

So what are the muscles that can we see under the surface – and how do they contribute to the movement, postures and shapes of the body?

Muscles of the back and torso

The **platysma** covers the shoulder girdle, the neck and the lower part of the face. It is only evident in extreme expressions of anguish or pain.

The **sternocleidomastoid** is the most prominent muscle in the front of the neck. It is one of the muscles that turns and bends the head to the side.

The dominating muscles of the back are the **trapezius** muscles – large triangular muscles attached to the back of the skull and the vertebrae. They cover the back between the shoulder blades and also extend over the shoulder to join the clavicle (collarbone) at the shoulder joint. They stabilize the shoulder girdle and move the shoulder blade and clavicle.

The **deltoid** muscle covers the shoulder and is attached to the bones of the shoulder girdle and humerus. It flexes and rotates the arm.

The **infraspinatus**, **teres major** and **teres minor** muscles cover the scapula and are visible between the deltoid and the latissimus dorsi. They rotate the arm and lift the arm backwards.

The **latissimus dorsi** covers a large area of the lower back and wraps around the side of the trunk to create the back fold of the armpit. It is thin, so the underlying bones are usually visible. It brings the shoulder blades together, pulls the shoulders down and back and lowers the raised arm.

The **pectoralis major** is the chest muscle. It lowers the raised arm, abducts and rotates the arm inwards, and lowers the shoulder forwards. It helps with respiration and forms the front fold of the armpit.

The **serratus anterior** lifts the ribs, moves the shoulder blades and enables elevation of the arm.

The **external oblique** lies on the side of the trunk and is part of the superficial abdominal musculature. It flexes and rotates the trunk.

The **gluteus maximus**, **gluteus medius** and **minimus** form the buttocks. The gluteus maximus functions when we climb or stand from a sitting position. It extends and rotates the hip joint and stabilizes the pelvis. The gluteus medius rotates, flexes and abducts the upper hip. The **tensor fasciae latae** flexes the hip joint, stabilizes the femur and rotates the leg.

The stomach muscles, the **rectus abdominis**, run down from the lower ribs through the centre of the body to the pubis. Look for this line when drawing a figure from the front, as it is a useful central axis that you can use as a guideline. It flexes the trunk and supports the internal organs.

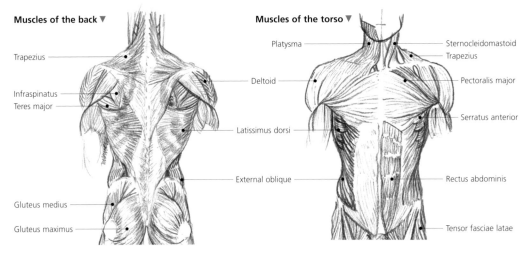

Muscles of the back ▼

Trapezius

Infraspinatus
Teres major

Gluteus medius

Gluteus maximus

Muscles of the torso ▼

Platysma

Deltoid

Latissimus dorsi

External oblique

Sternocleidomastoid
Trapezius

Pectoralis major

Serratus anterior

Rectus abdominis

Tensor fasciae latae

Muscles of the arms

When the palm of the hand is facing forwards, the muscles in the front of the arm are flexors (they bend the arm), while those at the back are extensors (they straighten the arm). In the upper arm, the **biceps** flexes and rotates the limb. Located under the biceps, the **brachialis** flexes the elbow. The **triceps** extends the lower arm at the elbow and moves the shoulder blade.

In the lower arm there are three groups of forearm muscles, which act upon the bones of the forearm, wrist and fingers. They are named as extensors, flexors or abductors and are shown individually on the sketches. Three muscles move the thumb; three extensors are in the back of the hand; and there are ten muscles in the palm.

Muscles of the leg

The **biceps femoris, semitendinosus** and **semimembranosus** (commonly known as the hamstrings) are superficial flexor muscles in the rear of the thigh. They extend the hip joint, flex the knee joint and rotate the leg.

The **gracilis** muscle arises in the pubis and extends into the tibia. When the thigh is abducted, it is visible at the back of the knee along with the semitendinosus and sartorius.

The **sartorius** runs from the iliac spine and diagonally across the thigh, into the tibia. It flexes the knee and rotates the leg.

The quadriceps femoris group is made up of the **rectus femoris, vastus intermedius, vastus medialis** and **vastus lateralis**. They all extend the

knee joint. The rectus femoris also flexes the upper leg at the hip joint.

The **tibialis anterior** and **extensor digitorum longus** are surface muscles on the front of the leg; the tendons run into the foot.

The **peroneus longus** and **brevis** run along the side of the leg; the tendons run through to the ankle.

The triceps surae is a muscle group at the back of the leg and is composed of the **soleus** and the **gastrocnemius**. These muscles lift the weight of the body when we are standing on our toes, as well as when we are standing or walking. The soleus tendon at the back of the leg and heel is called the **Achilles tendon**. The gastrocnemius lifts the heel and flexes the knee joint.

Muscles of the arm ▼

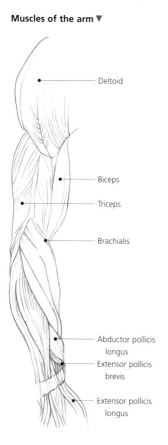

Deltoid

Biceps

Triceps

Brachialis

Abductor pollicis longus

Extensor pollicis brevis

Extensor pollicis longus

Muscles of the front of the leg ▼

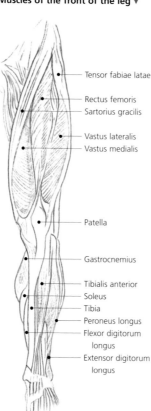

Tensor fabiae latae

Rectus femoris
Sartorius gracilis

Vastus lateralis
Vastus medialis

Patella

Gastrocnemius

Tibialis anterior
Soleus
Tibia
Peroneus longus
Flexor digitorum longus
Extensor digitorum longus

Muscles of the back of the leg ▼

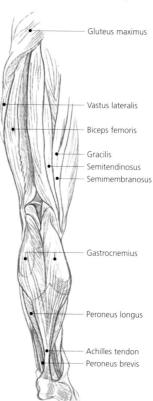

Gluteus maximus

Vastus lateralis

Biceps femoris

Gracilis
Semitendinosus
Semimembranosus

Gastrocnemius

Peroneus longus

Achilles tendon
Peroneus brevis

Balance and movement

Maintaining our balance is something that we do instinctively most of the time: our bodies naturally make tiny adjustments as we move to prevent us from falling over. When you're drawing or painting, however, things don't come quite so readily! It's all too easy to produce something in which the figure looks as if it's leaning to one side.

Establishing balance

You need first of all to determine the 'line of balance' of the pose – and the way to do this is to drop an imaginary plumb line down to the point on the ground where the weight of the body falls. The line that you choose depends on the angle from which you're viewing

the figure: from the front, start from the hollow space at the base of the neck, between the collarbones; from the side, take a line down from the ear hole; from the back, take a line down from the base of the neck. Hold a pencil or brush vertically in front of you, aligning with one of these points; the weight-bearing point should intersect that vertical line. Draw this line lightly in the early stages of your work for reference.

If the model is standing with all his or her weight on one leg, the weight-bearing point will be the arch of the foot that carries the weight. It's more likely, however, that the weight will be unevenly distributed, as it is not comfortable to stand with all your weight on one leg; in this case the weight-bearing point will be in between the feet. Even if the model is leaning to one side or bending over, this will apply.

Knowing the shapes of the main bones of the skeleton will also help you to establish the balance of the pose. Look for the bones that lie near the surface of the skin. From the back, the shoulder blades show the shoulders' angle and the depressions of the posterior superior iliac spines reveal the pelvic tilt. The twist of the spinal column is also useful. From the front, the tilt of the shoulders and pelvis show the torso position, while the collarbones show the angle of the shoulders.

The muscular support around the skeleton creates a system of tension within the body. Muscles form pairs. When one contracts, the other relaxes and stretches – and this enables the body to maintain balance. If the weight is on the right foot, then the upper body will shift over this leg to maintain balance and the shoulder girdle will tilt down to the right; the pelvis will then tilt to the left. If a model extends his or her arm upward, the lower leg will lift back to balance it. Look for these movements in every pose. When opposing muscles are in equal tension, the body is still; when the tensions are unequal, the body moves.

Weight on one foot ▲
Here the weight is mainly on one foot, with a little of it taken by the hand resting on the table. The balance line, or imaginary plumb line, starts at the centre of the base of the neck and runs through to the centre of the weight-bearing foot.

Weight distributed between the feet ▲
Here, the model's weight is more evenly distributed, but there is still more weight on her left foot than on her right. Consequently, the balance line falls nearer the left foot – the one that is maintaining the balance.

Weight on the right leg ▶
Here, the weight is more on the model's right leg than on her right arm. The balance line runs through the centre of the weight-bearing leg. The shoulders and hips slope in opposite directions to maintain the balance of the body.

Weight taken by the arms ▼
In this pose, very little weight is taken by the feet, so the balance line falls some way outside them.

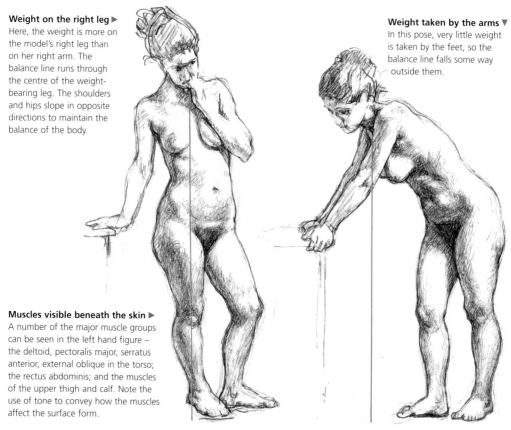

Muscles visible beneath the skin ▶
A number of the major muscle groups can be seen in the left hand figure – the deltoid, pectoralis major, serratus anterior, external oblique in the torso; the rectus abdominis; and the muscles of the upper thigh and calf. Note the use of tone to convey how the muscles affect the surface form.

Portraying movement

Balance and movement are closely interrelated: balance is a matter of arresting the movement of the body, while movement occurs when the body's natural point of balance is upset. Often, the only way we know that a figure in a painting is moving is because we know that the pose could not be held without the figure falling over: the artist has 'frozen' a split second in time, as in a still photograph.

Looking at still photos is a good way of analyzing how a figure is moving – but don't rely too heavily on them as reference sources as there's a danger that your drawings and paintings will look very static. You're also more likely to simply copy what's there instead of really thinking about how the body is moving. Try drawing from life, instead.

Start with a relatively slow movement, such as someone walking, and try to analyze the repeated motions that occur, jotting down small marks until you feel you've got the rhythm of the movement fixed in your mind. Gradually move on to faster motions – running, dancing – perhaps even drawing from the television or a DVD. As they say, practice makes perfect!

The moving form ▶
To depict the figure in motion, you need to use a medium that actively discourages detail. This figure has been drawn with a brush and diluted Chinese ink, with a few deft touches of charcoal line. The definition is minimal, yet the drawing is an elegant description of the fluid lines of body and arms.

The figure in perspective

Perspective sounds like a dauntingly technical term and (like anatomy) you will find books that go into a lot of detail, setting out complicated 'rules' and measuring systems. What it really boils downs to, however, is training yourself to observe accurately and put down on paper what you can actually see.

The important thing to remember is that forms appear larger or smaller depending where they are in relation to your viewpoint. This is one of the ways in which you can create an impression of scale and distance in your drawings and paintings and make things look three-dimensional.

Equidistant features ◄
In this sketch, the model is standing with her feet together, arms hanging straight by her side. Both hands look more or less the same length, as do both feet. This is because both hands and both feet are the same distance away from the viewer.

Features at different distances from the viewer ►
In this sketch, the model has brought a foot forward and has stretched out one arm as if to shake someone by the hand. The hand and foot that are nearest appear slightly larger than those that have not moved – even though they are, in reality, the same size.

One-point perspective

The first rule of perspective is that all parallel lines, when viewed from anywhere other than straight across your vision, appear to converge on the horizon. The point at which they converge is known as the 'vanishing point'. Vanishing points are always situated on the horizon line, which runs across your field of vision at eye level. If you are higher than your subject, then the vanishing lines will slope up to the horizon; if you are lower than your subject, they will slope down.

The same applies to a human figure viewed in perspective. If, for example, your model is lying on the floor with his or her head further away from you than the feet, then the head will appear to be compressed in length – a phenomenon known as foreshortening.

Contour lines on their own are not always enough to create a sense of volume, so think of the figure as being in a box. As the sides of a box run parallel to one another, this will make it easier for you to judge the degree of convergence.

Parallel lines converge ►
The artist has drawn a grid underneath the figure, as if the model is lying on a tiled floor. Our experience tells us that each square of the grid is the same size, but because the parallel lines of the grid are receding away from us towards the vanishing point above the forehead (on the horizon of our vision), the lines appear to converge – and hence the squares diminish in size the further they are from the viewer. Note, too, how the head is foreshortened as it is furthest away.

Two-point perspective

If you then change your viewpoint so that two sides of your model become visible, then you are dealing with what is known as two-point perspective. Imagine, then, that you're looking at a seated figure not from straight on but from slightly to one side. You can see one side of the body and something of the front – in other words, two major planes. In this scenario, two vanishing points come into play. The parallel lines of each plane converge at a different vanishing point. Those on the right converge at a vanishing point on the right; those on the left converge at a vanishing point on the left. As in one-point perspective, if you are higher than the subject the vanishing lines will slope up to the horizon; if you are lower than your subject, they will slope down.

If you're a beginner, you may find it easier to lightly enclose your subject in a box, so that you can see which features run parallel to the edges and assess where the vanishing point(s) could be placed. With practice, you'll be able to omit this stage.

Two vanishing points ▼
Here we can see two planes – the side and front. The parallel lines of each plane converge at a different vanishing point. To create a realistic impression of distance, you need to make the edges of the dais slope inwards towards the appropriate vanishing point. Similarly, features need to diminish in scale: note, for example, how the right foot appears smaller than the left foot because it is further away.

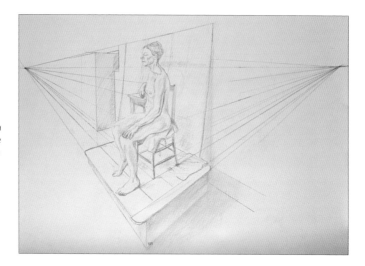

Multi-point perspective

In many compositions with more than one figure, in particular, the models will probably be arranged at different angles to each other and you may well see more than two major planes. It is possible (though time-consuming!) to plot all the vanishing points mathematically, but if you remember the basic principle – that each plane of each subject has its own vanishing point – and rely primarily on your own observations and on measuring one part of the body against another, then you will be well on the way to success. Practise your skills with one subject before moving on to multiple figures.

Foreshortened figure ▶
The head, body and limbs are seldom all viewed in profile, except in simple standing poses. When seen at a tangent, any element will appear diminished in length, or foreshortened, as it recedes away from you, while the width is little affected along the span. With extreme foreshortening, you can expect to see some overlaps: for example, a foreshortened head seen from above might show the chin overlapped by the nose.

From this viewpoint, the model's right shoulder appears much broader than the left – though they are, of course, the same size.

Viewed from a relatively high eye level, the torso appears shortened in relation to the model's legs.

Live models or photographs?

At some point, the question will arise of whether or not it is acceptable to work from a photograph or whether you should always work from life. There's no doubt that spending time with your model will enable you to pick up on all those quintessential little quirks and mannerisms – that sparkle in the eye, a tilt of the head or a particular stance – that make each one of us so individual. It also forces you to be aware of the fact that your model is a living, breathing person whose pose and expression will inevitably change as the sitting goes on; drawings and paintings made from photographs sometimes lack that sense of life, no matter how accurately observed the individual features are.

Models

If you hire a model yourself, there are some things you need to remember. Understandably, many models will be wary of posing for total strangers outside an art-school environment, particularly if you're asking them to pose in the nude. Make sure you tell them in advance exactly what the session will entail, how long it will last, say how many people will be involved and agree a fee. If they don't know you,

be prepared to provide references. If you want to hire a model privately, it's a good idea to contact one that you've already met in an official life-drawing class – then the model knows that you're a *bona fide* art student and you know that they've got useful life-modelling experience.

It's also very important to consider your model's comfort during the session. Check that they can hold the

pose you're asking them to adopt comfortably, and establish before you start how long they will have to hold that pose; even experienced models will probably need to stretch their legs after half an hour or so, and dynamic, twisting poses can only be held for a few minutes. If they're posing nude, make sure the room is warm and that they have somewhere private to change and undress. Give them a general indication of the pose that you want – for example, a standing pose with the upper body twisted – and then let them move around and settle into a pose that feels natural and comfortable to them.

Before you start painting, however, take time to really look at the pose. Ask yourself if the background complements or distracts; even a minor adjustment to the way a piece of fabric drapes can make a big difference to your composition. Think about the overall shape of the composition: are there strong lines in the pose that will help to lead the viewer's eye around the picture and look at the negative spaces in the pose.

Reclining pose ◄
A reclining pose is comfortable and easy to hold for a relatively long period of time.

Photographs

Sometimes, however, there really is no alternative: a photograph can capture a moments that you simply could not recreate in any other way. And for beginners, working with a live model for the first time can be quite intimidating. So never feel you have to apologize for working from photos; it's a great way of getting to grips with

things like measuring and creating a sense of light and shade. If you have the chance, however, do try to get some life-drawing experience. There are lots of good and inexpensive evening classes that provide the perfect opportunity to work in a professional atmosphere under the guidance of an experienced tutor. Alternatively, get

together with a group of like-minded friends and share the cost of hiring a model – or ask family members and friends if they'd be willing to pose for you. For quick sketches, especially when you're a complete beginner, you might also like to try drawing and painting yourself, by setting up a large mirror near your easel or work table.

Composition

In its simplest terms, 'composition' is the way you arrange the different elements of your drawing or painting within the picture space. Before you can do that, however, you have to decide on the picture space itself – the size and proportions of your paper or canvas.

Many artists opt for a format in which the ratio of the short side of the canvas to the longer side is 1 : 1.6 – the so-called 'golden rectangle', which evolved as an artistic ideal during the Renaissance. The golden rectangle is a safe bet, as it works horizontally and vertically, so suits many different subjects, but it is by no means the only option. A lot depends on your subject matter and on the effect and mood you want to create. Look at other artists' work and, if you see an unusual format, think about why the artist might have chosen it. An artist might, for example, choose a long, thin panoramic format for a landscape painting to emphasize the breadth of the landscape, or a square format for a portrait in order to fill the canvas with a dramatic painting of just the sitter's head.

Arranging elements within the picture space

Over the centuries, artists have devised various ways of positioning the main pictorial elements on an invisible grid around specific positions within the picture space. One of the simplest is splitting the picture area into three, both horizontally and vertically, which gives a grid of nine sections with lines crossing at four points. The theory is that positioning major elements of the composition near these lines or their intersections ('on the third') will give a pleasing image.

It is also important to lead the viewer's eye towards the picture's main centre of interest. You can do this by introducing lines or curves, real or implied, into the composition. A road leading up to your main subject is an example of a real line; an implied line might be a composition in which the artist has arranged throws or cushions in a curving line that leads the viewer's eye through to the subject, a reclining figure on a sofa.

Figure studies bring their own special compositional requirements. A central placing generally looks stiff and unnatural, as does a direct, face-on approach. Heads are usually placed off centre, with the sitter viewed from a three-quarter angle. More space is often left on the side towards which the sitter is looking. You also need to think about how much space to leave above the head. Too much and the head can appear pushed down; too little and it will seem cramped.

These are just a few of the compositional devices that have evolved over the years. The best way to learn about composition is to study other artists' work and try to work out how they have directed your eye towards the focal point of the image. You will gradually find that you can compose a picture instinctively – but if you're relatively new to painting, it really is worth taking the time to think about it, and even try sketching out different options, before you commit yourself and mark the canvas or paper.

Diagonal lines ▶
In this study of a seated female figure, the model's body creates a diagonal line which will help to lead the viewer's eye around the painting.

Gallery

This section displays a range of nudes in different media and styles, from rapid brush-and-wash drawings made in just a matter of minutes, which capture the essence of the pose with a few carefully placed strokes, to finely detailed paintings that explore the intricacies and subtleties of the human form in all its glory. Studying other artists' work is always a useful and revealing exercise, so try and see as many finished paintings as you can, either in books or museums, and examine them carefully and try to analyze what the artist achieved. Look at the direction and use of light and shade to create rounded, three-dimensional forms. Try to work out whether colours are warm or cool, and what effect this has. Think about the techniques that the artist has employed and consider what aspects you might be able to apply in your own work. Going beyond the technical aspects of drawing and painting, think about things like composition, lighting, and props, and how they contribute to the work as a whole. Everyone's taste differs and you will find your own favourites in this gallery, but even paintings that do not appeal to you can turn out to be surprisingly informative. The more you look at other people's work, the more you will learn – and the more you will be able to apply those lessons to your own work.

Composing with shapes ▶
In his pastel drawing, *Elly*, David Cuthbert has made an exciting composition by reducing detail to a minimum and concentrating on the interplay of shapes – the curves of the limbs counterpointing the more geometric shapes of the clothing and chair.

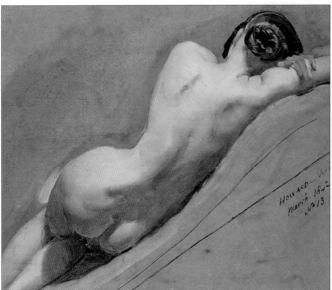

Muscle and bone structure ◀
The appeal of Edward Frost's *Life Study of the Female Figure* lies in the lovely, sinuous curves of the body. The underlying musculature and bone structure can be clearly seen and the subtle tonal transitions across the form have been painstakingly rendered. Note the cast shadows across the lower back and under the buttocks: these add interest to the composition and enhance the three-dimensional feel. The composition, with the figure cutting through the picture space from bottom left to top right, is unusual but adds a strong, dynamic element to an otherwise calm, static pose.

The standing figure ▲▼

In drawing or painting the human figure, it is vital to analyze the pose and to understand how the weight is distributed and how the whole body is affected by any movement. In these brush-and-wash drawings, James Horton captures beautifully both the swing of the body, and also its three-dimensional quality of mass and weight. Although these are intended as nothing more than quick sketches, note how effectively the artists has combined bold, linear marks (made using the tip of the brush as a drawing implement) with deftly placed washes in varying dilutions of ink to create modelling on the figure.

Rounded forms ▶

This simple pencil drawing by Elisabeth Harden concentrates on the rounded nature of the female form. The relaxed pose of the model and raised left leg are depicted in a flowing outline, with no sharp angles used at all. Note how fluently the artist has used the pencil here: always try to keep the pencil moving as you search out the forms in a drawing like this, so that you build up a momentum and a degree of fluidity in your lines and can make adjustments as necessary.

▶

Muscles visible beneath the skin ▲
The impressive thing about this pencil sketch, *Standing Figure*
by Vincent Milne, is the way that he has used tone to convey
how the muscles affect the surface form of the body. Note
how strong linear strokes, hatching and smudging have all
been used to good effect to create tones of different densities.

Light and shadow for modelling ◄
In *Standing Male Nude* by William Etty, the cast shadows
show the relief in the anatomy of the model. A deeper space
beyond the model is created by the contrast of dark shadow
against the bright light on his back and left leg. Another more
subtle contrast exists between the light on the red cloth and
the dark shadows of the right side of the model. Etty's skill
with oils explores the relationship between the muscle groups
of the back and legs. He observes how flesh colours change
in light and shadow and reveals the fine relief of the back
muscles in bright light and the heavier rounded volumes of
the lower limbs in strong tonal contrasts. The pose is
composed within two diagonals, running from each shoulder
down to the feet. The model puts his weight onto his left leg
and reaches forward with head bowed.

Brush-and-ink ▼
Both these drawings by Hazel Harrison
were done in under ten minutes, with
slightly diluted brown ink and a Chinese
brush. The method is excellent for quick
figure drawings and movement studies.

Drawing light ▲
Forms are described by the way in
which the light falls on them, so in life
drawing or portraiture it helps to have a
fairly strong source of illumination. In
Gerry Baptist's simple but powerful
charcoal drawing, the light comes from
one side, slightly behind the model,
making a lovely pale shape across the
shoulders and down the hip and leg.

Of course, we only read the white
paper as being a highlight area because
of the contrasting darks nearby.
Here, the shadows have been created
by wiping the side of the charcoal stick
across the paper, applying only minimal
pressure for the mid tones and much
more pressure for the really dark areas.
The artist has then softened these dark
areas by smudging the marks.

▶

Dramatic light ▶

Maureen Jordan has called her painting *In the Spotlight* and, as the title implies, the main subject is light rather than the figure itself, which is treated as a bold, broad generalization. She has applied the pastel thickly, working on textured watercolour paper, which allows a considerable build-up of pigment.

Directional strokes ▼

A classic combination of line and side strokes can be seen in this lively figure study, *Nude against Pink* by Maureen Jordan. Note how the artist has used the pastel sticks in a descriptive way, following the directions of the shapes and forms.

Painting flesh tones ▶

In *Seated Nude* Robert Maxwell Wood has chosen the paper wisely; it is almost the same colour as the mid tone of the model's flesh, which means he can allow the paper to show in the final painting and create a sense of lightness and airiness that could not be achieved by covering the entire paper with pastel pigment. This use of a coloured ground is a traditional technique in pastel and oil painting. Wood has used blending methods in places, but has avoided overdoing this, as it can make the image appear bland. Instead he has contrasted blends with crisp diagonal hatching and fine outlines made with the tip of the pastel to describe the fall of light on the head, neck and arms.

Vignetting technique ▲

James Horton has not attempted to treat the background or foreground in detail, concentrating instead on the rich, golden colours of the body in *Reclining Nude*. This vignetting method, in which the focal point of the picture is emphasized by allowing the surrounding colours to merge gently into the toned paper, is a traditional pastel-drawing technique. The method is also often used in photography, where the centre of a composition will be brightly lit or in clear focus, and the outer detail fading into dark or slightly out of focus.

Perspective and foreshortening ▶
Vincent Milne's *Reclining Nude* is a
simple but effective study in drawing
the figure in perspective. Note, for
example, how tiny the feet appear
compared with the hands. The
model's legs are raised, adding a
vertical element to the composition
and allowing the artist to
incorporate strong shading on the
side of the legs that is furthest away
from the light. Both these things
turn an otherwise straightforward
technical exercise into something
that is visually much more
interesting. Although the artist used
the same charcoal stick throughout
the drawing, note how varied the
marks are: fine linear detail in the
hands and feet, broad areas of mid
and dark tone put in using the side
of the stick, and dense, heavy
shadows that have been vigorously
scribbled in. Note, too, how blocking
in the background behind the
model's feet has the effect of both
creating a context for the scene and
focusing our attention on the figure.

Mood and tension ◀
In Harold Gilman's *Nude on a Bed* the
direct gaze is almost confrontational in
mood and the pose, in which the
model is hunched up hugging her
knees, also contributes to a feeling of
tension. The figure forms a rough
triangle within the picture space, the
base of the triangle being the diagonal
line of the blankets that runs upwards
from the bottom right corner. The
patterned wallpaper in the background
might well be overpowering had the
artist not left space to the right of the
model's head.

Quick sketches

Making a series of quick sketches – say, up to 10–15 minutes each – is a great way to start a life-drawing session. Think of the process as a series of loosening-up exercises, in much the same way as you would start a session in the gym with warm-up exercises. Try to work on a large scale, filling the paper with a single sketch and moving your whole arm rather than just your fingers. This will help to free up your hand and wrist, so that you can use your pencil or brush with bold, confident strokes; if you work on too small a scale, the likelihood is that you will tighten up and lose spontaneity.

Look at the angles of the hips and shoulders to assess the balance of the pose and, even though you're working quickly, remember to measure features in relation to others and look at how features interrelate. Make use of inverted triangles to check the alignment and positioning. Put in any light guide marks that you can. The process will encourage you to really look at your subject and assess the essentials of a pose. An added bonus is that the model does not have to pose for long.

Naturally, some media are better for quick sketches than others. Soft pastels and charcoal are wonderful, as you can use the side of the sticks for broad sweeps of colour and the tips for finer detail. Pencils and pen and ink are slower, as you have to use hatching to create mid and dark tones – but you could try diluting ink and applying it with a brush instead. If you've only got a few minutes, there simply isn't time to lay down delicate watercolour or acrylic washes and allow each one to dry before you move on to the next so, rather than trying to introduce a lot of colour, opt for tonal studies. Pre-mix a range of tones from one colour so that you can quickly put in the light, mid and dark tones. You can use very dilute oil paints in the same way. Tonal studies are a useful exercise in their own right, as they force you to think about light and shade and how to render a three-dimensional form on the flat surface of the paper or canvas.

Charcoal pencil, 3–4 minutes ▼
This sketch was made very quickly, as an exercise in seeing the figure as a series of geometric forms. The torso is basically a box shape with the front and one side plane clearly visible, while the model's left leg is made up of two interlocking cylinders. A curved line over the belly helps to imply its rounded shape. Faint construction lines indicate how the artist has checked the relative positions and angles of different features: the right nipple is almost directly above the navel, the left knee aligns with the tip of the right hip and the right shoulder slopes down at the same angle, parallel.

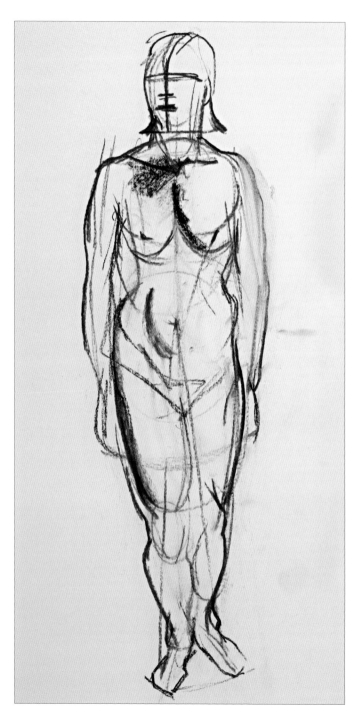

Charcoal pencil, approx. 5 minutes ◀
This is a very simple pose with the model standing almost square on to the artist's viewpoint. It does not make for a dynamic composition, but it is a good starting point if you're new to drawing the figure as it will give you practice in measuring and placing the limbs and other features correctly. Note how the artist has put in faint construction lines as a guide: a line through the central axis of the face establishes that the model's head is turned slightly to her right, while the nipples and navel form an inverted triangle. Even in a really quick sketch you can make the figure look rounded by using faint, curving lines within the form as well as contour lines around it.

Charcoal and white chalk, approx. 10 minutes ▼
Here you can see a faint diagonal line running up through the model's right leg right up to the base of the neck. This is a dynamic angle that gives the pose a sense of energy. The figure was drawn as a series of interlocking boxes, using the tip of a charcoal stick. Using the side of the stick, tone was then added to the figure and background and smudged with the fingertips. The highlights on the figure were put in with white chalk; lifting off charcoal using a torchon achieves the same result, but perhaps not so bright.

▶

Pen and ink, brush and ink, approx. 5 minutes ▲
The outline of the figure was made using a dip pen and ink, which gives a slightly irregular quality of line that is very appealing. Dilute sepia ink was then brushed on for the shaded areas of the body – a quick-and-easy way of implying the direction and intensity of the light and of making the figure look three-dimensional.

Charcoal and white chalk on toned ground, approx. 5 minutes ▶
Here, the artist has used both linear marks and the negative space around the figure to define her outline.
The raised arm, the tilt of the shoulders, the inner edge of the left leg and the outline of the right hip and buttocks are in fine charcoal stick. The shaded left-hand side of the body was blocked in with the side of the stick, then chalk was added around the edge, using the space outside the body to delineate the figure and differentiate it from the background. Chalk was also used for the highlights on the figure, telling us which direction the light is coming from. The lines of the skirting board and dado rail imply the room setting, albeit in the most minimal way, and establish the plane of the floor.

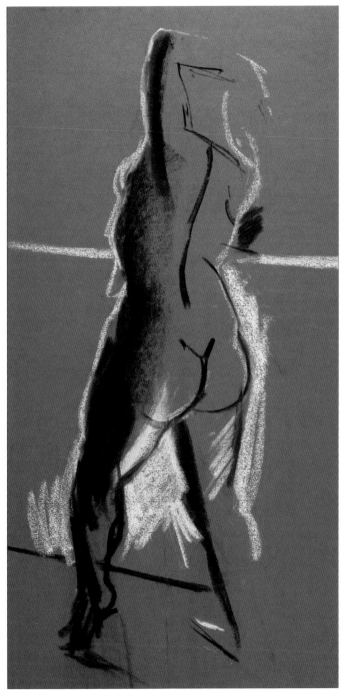

Brush and ink, 3–4 minutes ▲

For these two brush-and-ink sketches, the model was asked to adopt an 'action' stance, as if taking part in a fencing duel. With both arms and legs outstretched, these are not poses that can be held for long, but they are a useful means of studying the body in positions that are slightly out of the ordinary. In both sketches, the artist concentrated on establishing the geometric shapes of the limbs first, then added a little tone – as a light wash in the sketch on the right, and as hatching in the sketch on the left – to imply light and shade and introduce a subtle hint of modelling.

Pastel pencil, 3–4 minutes ▶

Here, the artist has put in a faint vertical line to check what aligns with what: you can see that the tip of the nose, the tip of the breast, the stomach and the tip of the right foot all touch this line, which helps establish the balance of the pose. Even with minimal shading, there is a sense that the figure is three-dimensional.

Half-hour pastel pencil sketch

If you're new to life drawing, you may be surprised at how tiring concentration and careful measuring can be! Work in relatively short bursts to begin with and remember to allow frequent breaks for you and your model. The sketch on these two pages took no more than about half an hour – but much detail has been captured in that short time.

This is a practice exercise in quickly grasping the essentials of the pose. Concentrate on careful measuring and assessing how each part of the body relates to the rest. A plain, undistracting background is ideal.

This is also an exercise in using tone for a three-dimensional impression. Only two pastel pencils were used, but

by looking carefully at the relative lights and darks, the artist has created a convincing study in which the fullness of the model's body is apparent.

Materials
- *Pastel pencils: yellow ochre, burnt umber*
- *Pastel paper*

The pose
The model was asked to pose with more of her weight on one foot, with her shoulder blades thrust back to emphasize the curve of her spine. A strong light positioned to the left and slightly behind the model helps to accentuate this. Placing the right arm behind the back creates a more interesting shape than simply letting it hang by her side.

1 Using a yellow ochre pastel pencil, begin to establish the main lines of the pose. Look for strong lines that you can use as a guide to checking the position and size of different parts of the body. The line of the shoulders in relation to the hips, the hollow of the spine and the negative space between the model's right arm and torso are good checkpoints.

> **Tip:** You may find you have more control over the pencil and can create more flowing lines if you hold it with your hand over the pencil, as in the photograph, rather than with your hand under the pencil as when writing.

2 Continue mapping out the pose, using contour rather than tone at this stage. Remember to look for geometric shapes that imply the three-dimensional form of the body – the cylinder of the legs and the box shape of the head, for example. Refine the shape of the arms, remembering to look for the different planes. Put in some of the contour lines that describe the creases in the skin – under the shoulders and at the point where the model's right arm bends at the elbow, for example. Restrict yourself to those lines that are structurally important, otherwise you'll lose the spontaneity of the drawing in a welter of detail. Remember you can use the lines to check the placements of other features.

3 Once you're happy with the placement of the different parts, you can begin to make the figure look more three-dimensional. Using a warmer burnt umber, begin to hatch in some of the darker tones on the back as well as along the shaded part of the left leg.

4 Put in some detail of the head – a simple indication of the features is sufficient. Put in the lines of the skirting board and dado rail; now check the perspective of the pose and that the feet are positioned correctly. Reinforce the outline of the left shoulder.

The finished sketch

Careful measuring, constantly checking each part of the body in relation to the rest, is one of the keys to success in figure drawing and painting; taking the time to assess tones so that you can make the figure appear three-dimensional is another. This sketch succeeds on both counts. Note also how the white of the paper stands for the lightest tones in the study – the background, the highlights on the figure, and the model's light-coloured hair, with only a few strands implying the direction of hair growth and the way the hair follows the shape of the cranium.

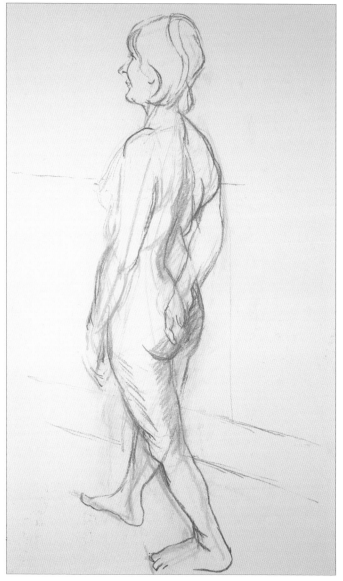

Half-hour charcoal sketch

Charcoal is a wonderful medium for quick sketches, as it can create both fine, strong linear marks and broad areas of shading. It is a good medium to draw poses that are difficult to hold for a long time. Leave the white of the paper blank for the brightest highlights.

The purpose of this sketch is to practise looking for balance lines within a pose. Look for any lines that you can draw in lightly between features to use as a guide. Drop lines (real or imaginary) down from the base of the skull or the lobe of the ear and see what other features intersect those lines. Look at where the left hip and position of the legs are in relation to the neck. Look at the relative angles of the hips and shoulder blades: is one higher or are they parallel to one another?

Remember that drawing any subject is a gradual process of refinement so don't fall into the trap of trying to be too detailed to begin with. Start with a few tentative marks and lines, then gradually build up the structures through a combination of contour lines, tone and shading.

Materials
- *Good-quality drawing paper*
- *Thin charcoal stick*
- *Kneaded eraser*

The pose
Here, much of the model's weight is on his left foot, but the 'balance line' falls between the feet rather than being entirely over the left foot. Placing his right hand on his hip thrusts his shoulder backwards and provides some tension and definition in the muscles of both the arms and the upper back. You can also use the negative space between the left arm and torso as a compositional aid.

1 Using a thin stick of charcoal, begin putting in tentative lines to establish the pose. Look for any lines and angles that you can use as a guide. Here, the artist has drawn lines of the spine, shoulders and the arms and legs.

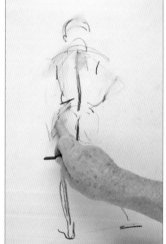

2 Continue mapping out the pose, then begin to strengthen your charcoal lines and also to block in some of the darkest areas of shade by smudging the charcoal as you start to build form. Keep measuring and checking throughout. Here, the artist has noticed that the left food is directly in line with the base of the skull.

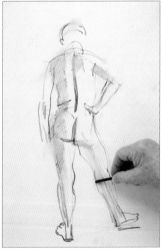

3 As you work, look at how shadows can help you create a sense of form. Draw in the arms looking at where the hands fall against the hips and thigh. Continue the shading down from the back and legs. Put in the feet and then the curve of the buttocks.

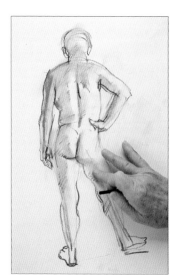

4 Continue shading, smudging any harsh lines to soften if necessary.

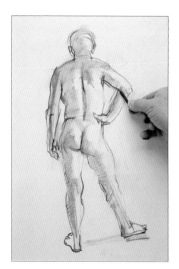

5 Using the tip of the charcoal stick add the linear marks of the hands, arms, head and the curve of the buttocks. Charcoal is a very powdery medium and it can be very easy to get smudges where you don't want them. Use a kneaded eraser to create crisp, bright highlights and clean off any dirty marks around your drawing.

The finished sketch
You may be surprised at how many different tones the artist has created from a single stick of charcoal, simply by varying the amount of pressure, smudging and lifting off pigment with an eraser to create the light-to-mid tones.

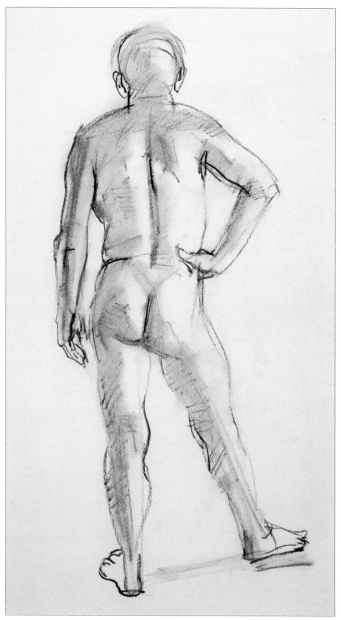

Watercolour and pastel pencil study

This two-hour project combines the linear quality of pastel pencils with soft watercolour washes. Watercolour is a slower medium to work in as, unless you are working wet into wet, you need to allow time for each layer to dry before you apply the next. Although this is not a highly resolved painting, it is nonetheless a little more elaborate than those on the previous pages. A straight-forward set-up such as this offers you the chance to place the figure in a recognizable context without having to worry about props.

A reclining pose is easy for the model to hold, which in turn makes life a lot easier for you as the artist: there is less chance of the model accidentally shifting position and thereby forcing you to make adjustments to your basic underdrawing.

The sketch shown here took approximately two hours but you could, of course, spend more time on it and put more detail into both the figure and the surroundings. However, take great care not to overwork the painting or you may be in danger of losing the freshness and spontaneity of those lovely watercolour washes.

Materials
- *HP watercolour paper*
- *Pastel pencils: red, Naples yellow, burnt umber, raw sienna, lemon yellow, cerulean blue*
- *Watercolour paints: ultramarine blue, burnt umber, cadmium yellow, yellow ochre, cadmium red, cerulean blue, Venetian red*
- *Brushes: large mop, medium round*
- *Kitchen paper*

The pose

The way the model bent her legs provided an interesting composition as it threw the lower part of her legs into shadow. A lamp placed to the left of the sofa provides some directional lighting and casts shadows from the figure on to the sofa. The cushion under the head provides a splash of red that warms up the whole painting and counterbalances the blue throws.

1 Using a red pastel pencil, begin mapping out the pose. Don't try to put in any detail at this stage – just concentrate on measuring carefully so that you place the features correctly. Here you can see how the artist has used a combination of geometric shapes and faint guidelines, such as the central line through the torso and an inverted triangle between the nipples and navel.

2 Continue until your underdrawing is complete and you are confident that everything is in the right place. It's very easy to get the proportions wrong if you do not take careful, objective measurements. Because the pose is foreshortened, the right knee appears to be considerably larger than the head, so take your time and keep measuring and checking as you work.

3 Now move on to the watercolour stage. It's often helpful to define the figure by putting the negative shapes around it. Using a large mop brush, wash very dilute ultramarine blue over the sofa, carefully avoiding the figure. Put in the folds and the deepest shadows in the bright blue fabric. To paint in the grey throw along the front edge of the sofa, mix a greenish grey from ultramarine blue, burnt umber and cadmium yellow. Allow to dry.

4 Mix a very dilute wash of yellow ochre with a touch of cadmium yellow and, using a medium round brush, put in the mid tones on the body. Paint the shadow areas under the chin and breasts and the underside of the right arm and leg with a cool mix of cadmium yellow and ultramarine. For the warmer skin tones, drop on dilute cadmium red and allow it to spread, wet into wet. Paint the red cushion in the same colour.

5 Strengthen the colour of the blue throws by brushing on cerulean blue (for the lighter areas) and the greenish grey mixture from Step 3 (for the shadows), as appropriate. For the shaded areas on and between the legs, add Venetian red to the yellow ochre and cadmium yellow mix. Add a little ultramarine to the mix to make a greyish purple and touch in the facial details – the eyebrows, pupils, nostrils and the shadow under the chin.

6 Darken the mid tones on the skin and cushion with dilute cadmium red. Brush a very dilute wash of lemon yellow over the area above the sofa. Using pastel pencils, loosely scribble Naples yellow over the body. Put in the pubic hair in burnt umber and go over the mid tones with a raw sienna. Use a lemon yellow pencil for the hair, with cerulean blue for the shadows.

The finished painting

Although this is a relatively quick study, the different planes and curves of the body have been skilfully observed and painted. The cast shadows enhance the sense of light and shade. The background is minimal but it sets the figure in context, while the folds and creases in the fabric throw and cushion add visual interest to the scene.

Pen and ink sketch

This project uses a dip nib pen, and two tones of sepia coloured ink: sepia coloured water-soluble ink, and a waterproof peat brown coloured ink. The sepia is diluted to create a range of tones. Sketching and fountain pens are also good for sketching; they are inexpensive and readily available from art and craft suppliers. Obviously, if you make a mistake in ink, it is much harder to erase than a pencil mark. For this reason it is always a good idea to map out the main lines of your subject first –

either by making a very light pencil underdrawing or, as here, by making a series of dots in very diluted ink.

When you're setting up the pose, remember to look at the negative spaces around the figure as well as at the lines of the figure itself, as the spaces play an important part in the balance of the composition as a whole. This is particularly important in a deceptively simple composition such as this one, where there are not many other elements to consider.

In this sketch the artist has composed the picture so that the model's right hand is resting on his hip and his head is resting on his left hand. This places the figure centrally, allowing us to see the torso clearly.

Materials
- *Watercolour paper*
- *Ink drawing pen*
- *Water-soluble sepia ink*
- *Waterproof peat brown ink*
- *Medium round brush*

The pose
The way the model is positioned is reminiscent of the classical drawings and paintings of the 15th century. Look at how the negative spaces contribute to the composition.

> **Tip:** You can make an incredibly wide range of marks with an ink drawing pen, so it is worth making some practice 'doodles' to explore the possibilities.

1 Using the sepia ink, begin to map out the main areas using a series of tiny dots, this will help to establish the basic pose and position. Remember to think of the body as a series of geometric shapes and to look at the negative spaces around the figure as well as at the outline of the figure itself.

2 Using a brush dipped in water, add a wash to put in some of the shadow areas on the torso. You do not want this to be an entirely linear brush drawing, so try to make a conscious effort to alternate between putting in the contour of the figure and using tone to build up the form.

3 Start to draw in the right hand, dotting first, and reassess the position of the hand in relation to the other parts of the body, look at the line from the chin to the hand for example. Cross-hatch the darker tones and use the brush to gently wash over the cross-hatching marks to blend.

4 Continue to dot in the rest of the figure, touch in the nipples and collar bone. Touch in the eyes, eyebrows and hair. Add a little sepia wash to the nose and chin, carefully apply more tone to the shaded side of the model's face. Draw in the lines on the forehead.

5 Begin to dot out the legs, checking the position against the rest of the figure. Draw in the left supporting arm, and continue to alternate between dotting and wash. Because the underpainting is still slightly damp, you can simply drop the stronger ink on to the initial lines and allow it to flow naturally; this creates a slightly fuzzy line that is very appealing.

▶

Assessment time
The lines of the pose have been established and a little shading on the underside of the right arm, torso and on the right thigh has begun the process of conveying the form of the figure. It is important to get the position of the torso right first as it is crucial to this drawing. You can move on to reinforce and add tones to the lines that you have already put down.

6 Using the peat brown ink, cross-hatch the darker areas on the torso to give tone to this area. Use the brush to wash over the cross-hatching to soften the lines.

With just a small amount of light tone, the figure is already beginning to look three-dimensional.

Note how the body and legs form angles that hold this very simple composition together.

7 Using the tip of the brush and diluted ink, define the shape of the feet and apply more detail to the facial features. Roughly scumble in the shadows on the sofa, leaving the lightest parts of the sofa untouched.

8 Use the pen with the peat brown ink and define the shape of the figure, the eyes, the side of the nose, the neck muscles, and hatch or cross-hatch the darkest areas on the figure. This shading is what will make the figure look rounded and three-dimensional, so take the time to assess the relative tones carefully.

The finished painting

The artist has combined linear 'pen drawing' with dilute washes of tone to create a deceptively simple-looking sketch. Note how many different tones he has managed to create from just two inks. In a sketch as simple as this, the negative spaces are as important as the positives. They balance the composition and create interesting shapes within it that help to draw the viewer's eye around the picture. The shadow on the sofa has been put in for context. It also helps to anchor the figure and prevent it from looking as if it is simply floating in thin air. The strong diagonal lines of the figure draws the eye around the sketch.

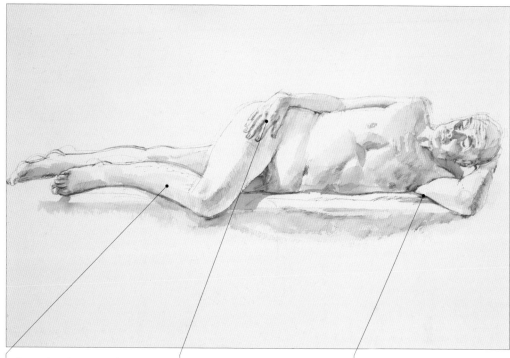

Dilute washes of ink create soft-edged areas of mid tone.

Ink pens are capable of producing very fine detail, where required.

For strong, linear marks, a waterproof ink has been used to define the figure.

Crouching male in pencil

The aim of this project is to practise using shading techniques to create modelling, and convey the three-dimensional form of the body.

Before you put pencil to paper, take time to really look at your subject and assess where the lightest and darkest areas are, as this is what will create the impression of three dimensions. In the pose shown here, for example, look at the model's right arm, leg and shoulders: look at where the light strikes them, and then gradually falls off. This means that your shading has to be equally gradual, with no hard-edged transition between tones.

With graphite pencils, you can create different tones simply by varying the amount of pressure you apply. You can also create darker areas of tone by drawing your hatching lines closer together – and lighter ones by spacing them further apart.

You also need to think about the direction of the hatching lines that you make. If all your hatching and cross-hatching lines run in the same direction, your drawing will take on a rather mechanical feel. Varying the direction of the hatching lines will help to give life to your drawing.

It's a good idea to make your hatching marks follow the shape of the form that they're describing. If you're drawing a rounded shape such as a buttock or breast, for example, make your hatching lines curved. Follow the shape of the form that you're drawing with both your eye and your hand and use the pencil to 'caress' the shape as you draw.

Try not to worry about any mistakes you may make. It is a good idea to leave any on the paper and to use these lines for reassessing.

Finally, remember to allow the white of the paper to stand for the very brightest highlights. This will give life and sparkle to your drawings.

Materials
• *Good-quality drawing paper*
• *5B pencil*
• *Kneaded eraser (optional)*

The pose
Position your model in front of a plain-coloured wall or backcloth. Place a light to one side, as side lighting gives good modelling and shows up the muscles, shoulder blades and the line of the spine. (You don't need specialist lighting: a standard lamp will do.) Here, the model is crouched down, slightly leaning forward over his right knee, making the curve of the back appear more prominent.

Tones
The artist used only one grade of pencil throughout this drawing – a 5B – simply varying the pressure to create different tones. It's better to do this than to keep switching from one pencil to another, as it allows you to maintain the flow of the drawing and also to improve your ability to manipulate the pencil to create different effects.

Tip: When you are looking at lines such as the angle of the shoulders, try mentally superimposing the hands of a clock on your subject and then working out what number the hands are pointing to. Here, for example, the line of the model's right shoulder is very slightly lower, at between 7 and 8 o'clock.

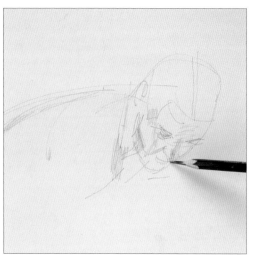

1 Using a sharp 5B pencil, very lightly map out the underlying geometric shapes, beginning with the shape of the head and the curve of the back. Look, too, for the angle of the shoulders in relation to the neck. Make your own initial marks very light so that they're barely there – just enough to show up on the paper and give you a starting point that you can build on.

2 Here, the artist starts to put in the facial features. Look at the diagonal line of the face with the line of the right arm, as this is a useful guide to positioning the figure.

3 Loosely indicate the shape of the ears. You can also start to put in some tone on the hair, using some simple cross-hatching. Your hatching lines should follow both the direction of hair growth and the contour of the form it's describing. Establish the line of the arm and right leg, noting where the arms are positioned in relation to the right knee and left foot.

4 Define the head and draw in the ear and hair line, adding shading below the nose and chin area and continuing to build up tones.

▶

Assessment time
The basic structure has been mapped out. The next stage is to begin putting in some more shading and to refine the whole figure in order to make the drawing look more rounded and three-dimensional.

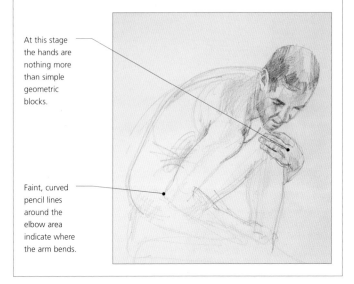

At this stage the hands are nothing more than simple geometric blocks.

Faint, curved pencil lines around the elbow area indicate where the arm bends.

5 Begin to develop the shadow lines on the right-hand side of the neck, and lightly hatch along the spine to indicate the areas of muscle and bone under the skin, curving the hatching lines to follow the form. Define fingers and build up tone on the hands.

6 Now move on to the feet: establish the basic block shape, and then refine this, cutting in with the pencil to reveal the planes of the toes. Paying close attention to which parts of the feet are in the light and which are in shadow will help you to achieve this.

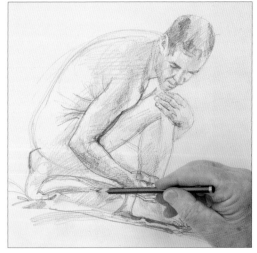

7 Continue shading across the whole drawing where necessary. Gradually increase your pressure on the pencil to achieve more depth of tone in the very dark areas, such as the underside edge of the right shoulder, arm and foot.

The finished drawing
Although the same pencil was used throughout this drawing, the artist has created an impressive and subtle range of tones through his careful use of hatching and cross-hatching. The shading follows the contours of the body and helps to imply the shapes of the muscles and bones that lie beneath the surface of the skin.

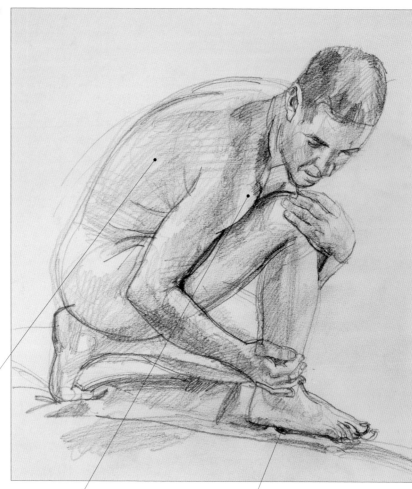

Note how the hatching in this area comprises a series of diagonal lines that echo the curve of the back.

The white of the paper stands for the most brightly lit areas and helps to give sparkle to the drawing.

Pressing heavily with the pencil conveys the very darkest tones.

Female figure in soft pastel

In addition to looking at the curves of the spine and the musculature of the body, this project gives you the chance to practise assessing skin tones. At first glance it might look as if the model's skin is very even in colour, but there are actually lots of different tones. This is due to the way light falls on the figure. When light hits a raised area such as the collar or shoulder bone, a shadow is formed on the opposite side, which is not in the light. The shadow area is darker in tone – it is these differences in tone that create the impression of a three-dimensional figure. Being able to assess tones accurately is the key to the success of your artwork.

Pastel drawings are often done on coloured paper, just as oil and acrylic paintings are often done on a toned ground. This enables you to start from a mid tone and work back to the darkest tones and up to the highlights. And as all these media are opaque, if you want to make adjustments later, you can apply a light colour on top of a dark one – something that is impossible in a transparent medium such as water-colour. It's also a good idea to allow some of the original paper colour to show through as a mid tone in the finished drawing, as this gives a more lively feel to the work.

Pastel papers come in a wide range of colours, from pale biscuit colours to deep, dark greens and reds. When choosing which colour of paper to use, look at the range of mid tones present in your subject; here, the mid tones of the model's skin are a rich, terracotta colour, which is almost identical to the paper colour that the artist selected.

When drawing skin in soft pastel, you can finger blend your marks to create a smooth skin texture – but take care not to lose the linear quality completely.

Materials
- *Terracotta-coloured pastel paper*
- *Soft pastels: mid brown, white, dark brown, pale blue, pale mauve, khaki brown, burnt umber*
- *Pencils: charcoal or black pastel*
- *Kneaded eraser*

The pose
This is a very simple pose, but the curving shapes are very appealing. Asking the model to turn her head to the left, so that her face can be seen in profile, prevents the picture from becoming too abstract and impersonal.

1 Working on terracotta-coloured pastel paper with a mid-brown soft pastel, sketch out the basic shape of the pose. Take careful measurements to ensure you get the proportions right. Look, in particular, for the line of the spinal column and the angle of the hips and shoulders.

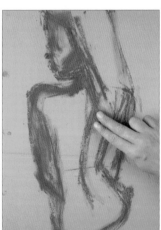

2 Establish the position of the eyes, nose and mouth. Blend the pastel marks on the paper with your fingers so that you begin to build up form and tone without adding too much pastel.

3 Using the side of a white pastel, begin to block in some of the white background to help define the figure. Use the tip of the pastel to put in some of the deep, sharp creases in the towel.

4 Using a darker brown pastel, put in some tones for the shadows under the chin, on the undersides of the arms and around the top of the towel. Use both the side and the tip of the pastel, depending on the kind of mark you need. Put some darker tones into the hair, following the direction of growth.

5 Stroke on some white highlights across the shoulder blades to begin to develop modelling on the back. Redefine the line of the spine. Then, using your fingertips, apply and blend some dark brown pastel over the muscle area below the shoulder blades (the latissimus dorsi, which wraps around the sides of the trunk) and gently wipe off some of the colour with a kneaded eraser to soften it and avoid the mark being too harsh and obtrusive.

6 Using a dark brown pastel, put in the darkest points of the facial features – the nostrils, mouth, eyebrows and eyelashes. Gently stroke a white pastel across the cheek for the highlight and put in the dark shadow under the cheekbone. Smudge the marks with your fingertips or a torchon, or wipe off colour with a kneaded eraser, if necessary, to soften the colour.

7 Using a white pastel, strengthen the line around the profile and the left shoulder so that the figure really stands out from the background. Because of the creases in the fabric, there are some shaded areas in the towel; lightly hatch them with a pale blue pastel. The blue is modified by the underlying white.

▶

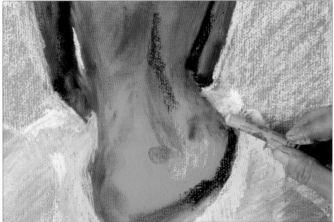

8 Apply pale mauve over the blue, so that you are alternating between cool (blue) and warm (mauve) tones. Alter the direction of your hatching to create variety and texture in your marks.

Tip: Leave some of the underlying tones and the terracotta colour of the paper showing through.

9 Apply more mauve over the left shoulder and the top of the buttocks, where there are some warm shadows. Hatch in the mid tones on the figure, using a khaki brown pastel.

10 Put more dark tones into the hair to build up both tone and texture. Use the same colour to put in the darkest skin tones on the undersides of the arms and between the arms and the torso.

11 For the mid-toned area on the left hip and buttock, use a warm brown or burnt umber. Also apply some burnt umber to the face to help build up the modelling, taking care to observe the light and dark areas very carefully.

Assessment time

Although the contrast between warm and cool colours has created a convincing sense of modelling on the figure, some minor adjustments are still required. The shadow on the left hip is too dark and the pastel marks need to be both lightened in colour and blended a little more. The shadow between the model's body and the top of the towel is also too heavy. But these are relatively minor details that can be fixed by hatching a lighter tone over the existing marks and finger blending the pastel. The biggest change that is required is in the background: at present, there is only a light covering of pastel on the paper. This needs to be intensified and blocked in more strongly. The very slight shadow that the model casts on the wall also needs to be added, to give the picture depth.

The background wall is very patchy in colour and too much of the underlying paper colour shows through.

The shape of the left breast needs to be defined more clearly.

These shadow areas are too dark and heavy.

12 Use a kneaded eraser to wipe off some of the colour and 'draw' in the shape of the left breast. Then apply a little burnt umber to the underside of the left arm, blending the colour with your fingertips, so that the paler-coloured breast stands out more clearly.

13 Using the side of a white pastel, block in the wall in the background. There is also a very faint cast shadow on the background wall to the right of the model. Put this in using the side of a pale blue pastel. It adds a little change of texture and provides a visual link to the cool, blue shadows in the towel.

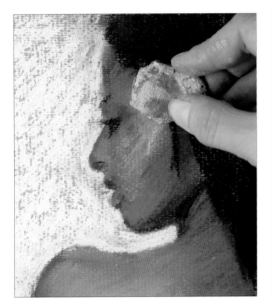

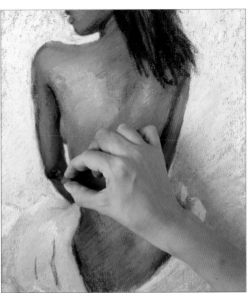

14 Some areas of the face have become rather too dark. Use a kneaded eraser to pull out a few highlights. With this particular model's coloration, you can take the colour right back to the original paper colour, which is virtually identical to the warm, highlit skin tones.

15 Hatch burnt umber over the left hip and blend the marks with your fingers to lighten the tone and soften the texture of this very dark shadow area. Using a dark brown pastel, strengthen the line between the left arm and the torso and create a little more modelling on the skin of the elbow.

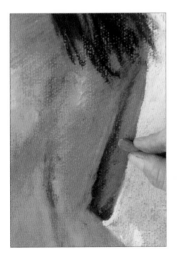

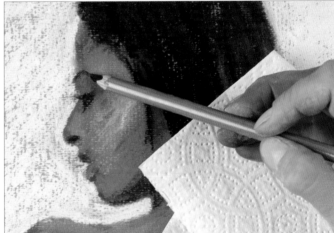

16 Even out the tones on the right arm, using a khaki brown pastel.

17 Use a charcoal or black pastel pencil to put in the fine line of the eyebrow and the nostrils. (Soft pastel sticks are too chunky for fine lines such as this, although you can try breaking one to get a sharp edge.)

Tip: Rest your hand on scrap paper as you work to prevent smudging other areas of your drawing. Keep the hand quite still and move the fingers.

The finished drawing

Through a combination of light hatching and finger blending, the artist has created subtle but effective shifts between light and dark tones, replicating the effect of light and shade on the body and creating a sense of form. With soft media such as pastel, the colour adheres to the raised bits of the paper but does not sit in the 'dips', creating a broken texture that gives the drawing great liveliness. The colour of the paper has also been utilized to good effect. Although the background is simple, it contains enough tonal variation to be visually interesting without detracting from the subject.

Shading and tonal contrasts are used to indicate different planes of the body: the left side is in shadow while the back is more brightly lit.

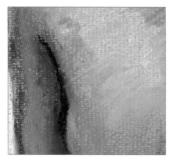

The hair is drawn using strong, broad strokes of black pastel, which conveys its texture and thickness well.

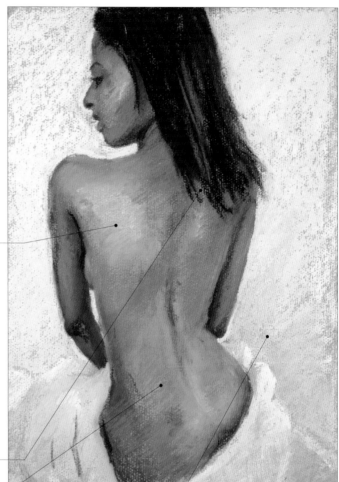

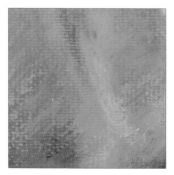

In places, the colour of the paper stands for the mid tones in the model's skin.

A hint of cast shadow on the background breaks up the monotony of the white wall.

Reclining nude in oils

The reclining nude – more particularly, the reclining female nude – is a classic subject in Western art.

There are a few practicalities to take into account – particularly if you are painting from life. First, make sure your model is comfortable: provide a sofa, blanket or other soft surface for her to lie on and make sure that the room is warm and free of draughts.

For the pose, it is often better to allow the model to settle into a position that feels natural than to tell her what pose to adopt. Although you can obtain interesting and dynamic paintings by directing the model to tense her muscles, such poses are difficult to hold.

This particular pose is easy to hold, even for a long period. The model's weight is evenly distributed along the whole length of her body and she is able to rest her head on her right forearm, cupping her hand around her head for extra support.

The differences in flesh tone need to be very carefully assessed in this project. Certain areas, such as the hands, the soles of the feet and the lower body, tend to be warmer in colour than others, because the blood vessels run closer to the surface of the skin. The upper body, on the other hand, is usually cooler in tone. However, one of the joys of painting in oils is that the paint remains soft and workable for a long time, so you can blend colours on the support as you work to create subtle transitions from one tone to another to show the way the body curves towards or away from the light source.

Materials
- Stretched canvas
- Rag
- Oil paints: cadmium orange, brilliant pink, raw sienna, cadmium red, cadmium yellow, brilliant turquoise, titanium white, ultramarine blue, lamp black, vermilion, cerulean blue
- Turpentine or white spirit (paint thinner)
- Drying linseed oil
- Brushes: selection of small and medium rounds, small or medium flat

The pose
One of the most interesting things about this particular model is the way in which her upper vertebrae and ribs are so clearly defined. The natural curves of her body create clearly defined areas of light and shade, which add interest to the composition. Note the masking tape on the blanket, outlining the model's pose. This enables the model to get back in the same position if she inadvertently moves during the session or has to take a break.

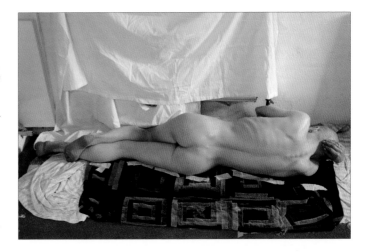

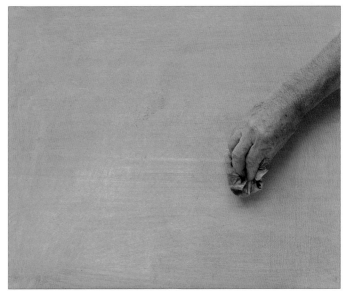

1 With a rag, spread cadmium orange paint evenly over the canvas, changing to brilliant pink in the top left. Leave to dry.

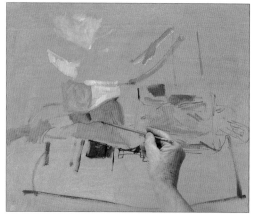

2 Using a medium round brush and raw sienna, 'draw' the edges of the blanket on which the model is lying and the dark shadow under her hips. Delineate the head, upper body and legs in cadmium red. The actual colours are not too important at this stage, as this is merely the underpainting, but warm colours are appropriate to the subject. Mix a range of warm flesh tones from cadmium yellow and cadmium orange and block in the warmest toned areas – the buttocks, the soles of the feet and the curve of the spine. Start putting in the main folds of the background cloth using mixtures of brilliant turquoise and titanium white.

3 Mix titanium white with a little ultramarine blue and block in some of the dark folds in the background cloth. Using a fine brush and cadmium red, loosely draw the head and supporting hand, reinforce the line separating the legs and indicate the angle of the hips.

> **Tip**: It is always important to remember the underlying anatomy of the pose, even when you are painting fleshy parts of the body where the shape of the bones is not visible.

4 Using green (mixed from titanium white, cadmium yellow and ultramarine blue) and a dark grey (mixed from ultramarine blue and raw sienna), start putting in the pattern of the patchwork blanket. Mix a pale blue-green from ultramarine blue and raw sienna and indicate the shadows under the ribs and the shaded part of the back. Note that this mixture is a complementary colour to the first flesh tones: shadow areas often contain a hint of a complementary colour.

5 Mix a pale orange from cadmium red, cadmium yellow and titanium white and begin putting in some of the paler flesh tones. Alternate between all the various flesh tones on your palette, blending them into one another on the support and continually assessing where the light and dark tones fall and whether the colours are warm or cool in temperature. Almost immediately, you will see that the body is starting to look three-dimensional.

▶

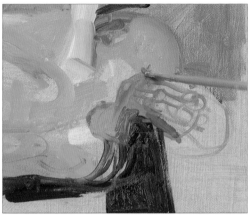

6 Continue working on the flesh tones. The highlights and shadows reveal the curves of the body: the backs of the thighs, for example, are in shadow and are therefore darker in tone than the tops of the buttocks, which are angled towards the light. Note the greenish tones on the upper body: the upper body is often noticeably cooler in tone than the lower body, perhaps because the blood vessels in this area are not so near the surface of the skin.

7 Block in the most deeply shaded areas of the white background cloth with a blue-biased mixture of ultramarine blue and titanium white. Use a slightly lighter version of this colour to paint the model's shaved head, allowing some of the ground to show through in parts as the colour of her scalp. Loosely draw the hand and fingers in cadmium red, indicating the joints in the fingers by means of rough circular or elliptical shapes.

Assessment time
Although the areas of warm and cool tone have been established, the figure still looks somewhat flat and one-dimensional. More tonal contrast is needed: spend time working out how you are going to achieve this. Remember to work across the picture as a whole rather than concentrating on one area – otherwise you run the risk of over-emphasizing certain areas and making them too detailed in relation to the rest, thus destroying the balance of the painting. At this stage it would be as important to work up the modelling on the calves and feet as make more progress on the torso.

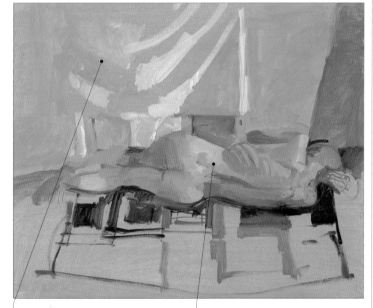

The broad areas of light and shade have been established – now you can refine this area.

There is not enough tonal contrast for the figure to look truly three-dimensional.

8 The cloth at the model's feet is draped to create interesting folds. Block in its shape loosely in a mixture of ultramarine blue and white, then put dark strokes of a darker grey or brown over the top to indicate the main folds. Begin putting in some of the mid tones in the background cloth, using mixtures of ultramarine blue and white as before.

9 Loosely paint the pattern of the patchwork blanket on which the model is lying, using broad strokes of the appropriate colour. Do not try to be too precise with the pattern: a loose interpretation will suffice. You should, however, note how the lines of the pattern change direction where the blanket is not perfectly flat.

10 Continue working on the blanket, gradually building up and strengthening the colours while keeping them fresh and spontaneous.

11 Redefine the fingers in cadmium orange and a little brilliant pink.

12 Darken the area around the head with a mixture of ultramarine blue, white and a little lamp black, so that the head stands out from the background. Work on the flesh tones, to improve the tonal contrast: the shoulder blade, for example, is lighter than the tones laid down so far, so paint it in a mixture of cadmium orange and white. Use the same colour to define the highlights on the top cervical vertebrae. The soles of the feet are very warm in colour; paint them in a mixture of cadmium red and vermilion.

▶

13 Now turn your attention to the background cloth, reinforcing the dark and mid-toned folds with a mixture of ultramarine blue, white and a tiny amount of cerulean blue – all the time assessing the tones of the cloth in relation to the overall scene rather than looking at it in isolation.

14 Use pure white for the brightest areas of the background cloth, changing to a smaller brush for the finest creases. Note how the folds vary in tone depending on how deep they are: use some mid tones where necessary to convey this.

15 Mix a dark green from ultramarine blue and cadmium yellow and reinforce the dark colours in the blanket. Use the same colour to strengthen the shadow under the model and give a sharp edge to the curve of her body. Brighten the light greens and pinks in the blanket; as the patchwork pattern is made up of straight strips of fabric, you may find that it helps to switch to a small or medium flat brush so that the lines of the pattern are straight and crisp-edged.

16 The triangular-shaped wedge of cloth on the right, just above the model's head, is too light and leads the viewer's eye out of the picture. Mix a mid-toned green and block it in, directing your brushstrokes upwards to avoid accidentally brushing paint on to the model's head.

The finished painting

The figure is positioned almost exactly across the centre of the picture – something that artists are often advised to avoid, but in this instance it adds to the calm, restful mood of the painting. The dark colours and sloping lines of the blanket and the folds in the background cloth all help to direct the viewer's eye towards the nude figure. The background cloth is painted slightly darker in tone than it is in reality: overly stark whites would detract from the figure.

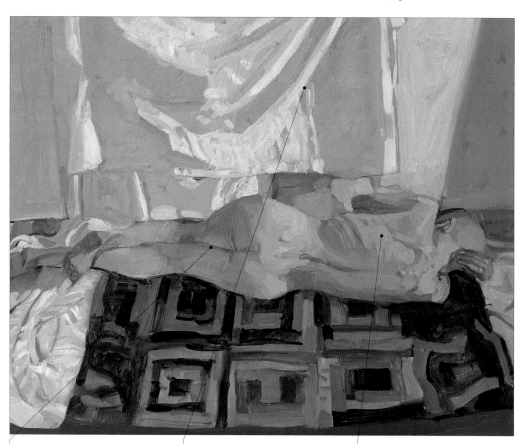

The legs are slightly bent: light and dark flesh tones show how some parts are angled into the light while others are shaded.

Careful assessment of tones is required in order to paint the white backcloth convincingly.

Skin is stretched taut over the ribs and upper vertebrae: subtle shading reveals the shape of the underlying bones.

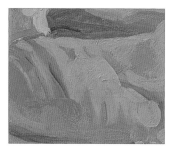

Male nude in charcoal and soft pastel

This project, made on grey pastel paper, combines charcoal (for the main lines and shading) and a cream-coloured soft pastel (for the highlights). Cream is a more sympathetic colour for the highlights in this drawing than white, which could look stark. The two media are used in the same way.

As the model's position is one that can quite easily be held for a long period, you have plenty of time to map out the essentials of the pose. It might be tempting to start by simply outlining the pose – but if you can imagine the skeleton of the body underneath the skin as you draw, and think of the body as a series of three-dimensional forms, you will undoubtedly find it much easier to get the shapes right.

Materials
- *Grey pastel paper*
- *Thin willow charcoal stick*
- *Kneaded eraser*
- *Soft pastel: pale cream*

The pose
This sofa provides support, making the pose easy to hold for a long time. Even so, it's a good idea to mark the position of the feet and hands with pieces of masking tape, in case the model moves. The back is slightly bent and the stomach is convex, creating interesting shading on the torso. Note the slight foreshortening: the legs are closest to the viewer and so appear slightly larger than they would if the model were standing up.

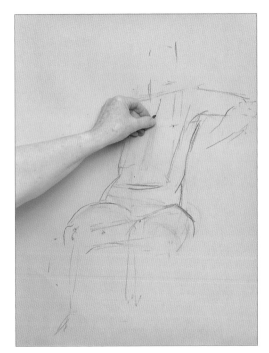

1 Sketch the figure using a thin stick of charcoal, making sure you allow space for the sofa on either side. Measure and mark where each part of the body is positioned in relation to the rest; the face, for example, is in line with the model's left knee. Also look at the slope of the shoulders and at where the elbow is positioned in relation to the chest.

2 Begin searching out the form, making angular marks that establish the three-dimensional shape of the head and torso. Put in faint guidelines running vertically and horizontally through the centre of the face to help you position the facial features. Lightly mark the shape of the sofa – the curve of the arm and the cushion behind the model.

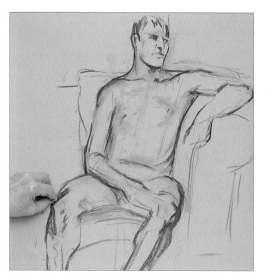

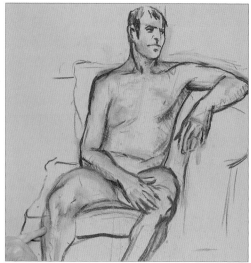

3 Once you've mapped out the basic composition, you can begin to strengthen the lines and put in the facial features in more detail. Draw the eyes, noting how the upper lids fold over the lower ones at the outer corners and how the line of the nose obscures the inner corner of the far eye. Roughly scribble in the hair line. Put in some shading under the chin, on the legs and arms, and on the left of the torso.

4 Using the tip of the charcoal, draw the muscle that runs diagonally along the side of the neck. This is a very strong, pronounced muscle and putting it in helps to emphasize the tilt of the head. Using the tip of your little finger, smooth out some of the shading on the torso and legs to create more subtle modelling. The figure is already beginning to look more three-dimensional.

5 Loosely scribble over the sofa, so that the figure stands out. Look at the negative shapes – the shape the sofa makes against the body – rather than at the body itself. This makes it easier to see if any adjustments need to be made to the outline of the body. Alter the direction of the hatching lines to make the different planes of the sofa more obvious.

6 Draw the model's left foot. (Try to think of it as a complete unit rather than a series of individual toes.) Shade one side, and indicate the spaces between the toes with very dark marks. Loosely scribble in the shadow cast on the base of the sofa by the model's legs, and hatch the different facets of the cushions.

7 Use a kneaded eraser to gently clean up and create more contrast between the lightest and darkest parts. Darken the spaces between the fingers and indicate the segments of the fingers to show how they articulate.

Assessment time
Assess the tonal contrast of the figure as a whole to see where more shading or highlights are needed. For example, the lower part of the torso is slightly shaded by the ribcage as the model slumps back on the sofa, and this area needs to be darkened.

The upper part of the torso is a little too bright.

More shading is needed on the model's left leg. At present it looks rather flat and does not show the muscle tone well.

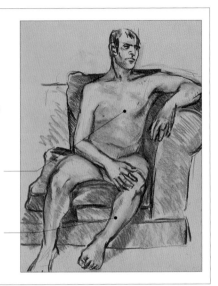

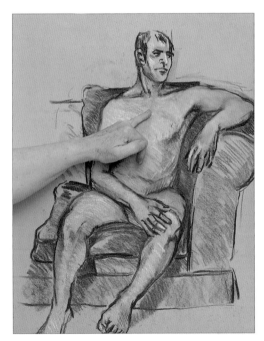

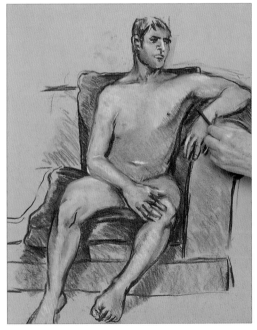

8 Using a very pale cream pastel, put in the highlights on the face, right arm and leg. (Cream is a more sympathetic colour for flesh tones than a stark white.) Even though the limbs are rounded forms, the highlights help to define the different planes. Blend the pastel marks with your fingertip.

9 Apply more charcoal shading on the lower part of the torso, again blending the marks with your fingertip. (Use your little finger for blending, as it is the driest part of the hand and the risk of smudging the charcoal is less.) Darken the sofa under the model's arm, so that he stands out more.

The finished drawing
Although this is not an overly elaborate drawing, it conveys the muscular nature of the model's body. The calves and thighs, in particular, are well developed (this particular model is a professional dancer). Subtle shading reveals the different planes of the body and the combination of dark, intense charcoal marks and soft pastel works well.

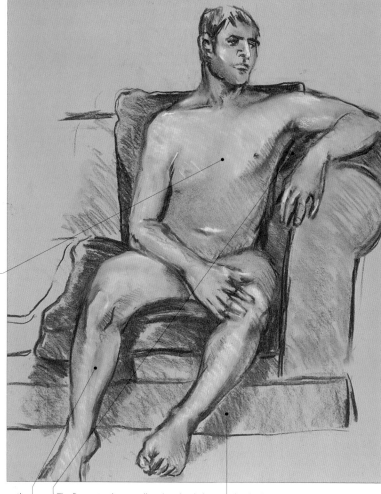

The pastel marks on the torso are blended to convey the smooth skin texture.

Note how effectively shading conveys the muscles in the calf.

The figure stands out well against the dark background of the sofa.

The shadow cast enhances the three-dimensional quality of the drawing.

Curled-up figure in watercolour

This project is about training your eye to see the figure as a whole shape, rather than as a torso with limbs appended. Ask your model to crouch on the floor or curl up, bringing their knees in towards the chest and perhaps wrapping their arms around their legs. Then look at the pose and decide what geometric shape it would fit inside – is it a square, a rectangle, a circle or some other geometric form?

Before you start to draw or paint the pose, lightly sketch the basic geometric shape on your paper or hold the shape in your mind's eye and make sure that the pose is contained within it. (It doesn't matter if some elements, such as a foot or hand, overhang the edge a little; it's the overall shape that's important.) Think of yourself as a sculptor using your pencil or brush to chisel shapes from a lump of marble.

Materials
- *HB pencil*
- *Heavy HP watercolour paper*
- *Watercolour paints: cobalt blue, alizarin crimson, viridian, cadmium yellow pale, Prussian blue, Venetian red, ultramarine blue*
- *Gouache paints: white*
- *Brushes: large flat, medium round, fine round*

The pose
Here, the artist selected a viewpoint slightly above the model, which allowed her to see over the model's shoulder to her bent legs and arms. (If her eye level had been level with the model's back she would have seen only the curve of the spine, which would have made for a less interesting composition.) The main light source was positioned in front of and above the model, so her upper leg and shoulder are brightly lit while her lower back is in shadow. The cool blues and greens of the cushions and throws were chosen to contrast with the warm tones of her skin.

1 Using an HB pencil, roughly sketch the pose. Here, the overall shape of the body is contained within a rectangle. Put in the main curve of the body, the angle of the shoulder, the head and the hands. The straight edges of the bed and cushion are also very useful guidelines.

2 Continue until you have all the points of reference that you need. Look for basic shapes. The hands and feet, for example, should be box shapes – don't be tempted to get into drawing the individual digits.

You should also indicate the different planes where the body turns from the light, such as the shoulder blades.

3 Mix a dilute wash of cobalt blue with a tiny bit of alizarin crimson. Using a large flat brush, put in the blue sheet. Use a mix of viridian and cobalt for the underlying colour of the striped blue cushion, and viridian and cadmium yellow pale for the green cushion. Add more yellow to the green mix and paint the bright green of the throw.

4 Wash in the colour of the blue background wall with a dilute mix of Prussian blue. Now wash a very dilute mix of Venetian red and cadmium yellow pale over the body, adding a little more red for the darker areas and remembering to leave the very brightest highlights untouched. Apply a very dilute wash of cadmium yellow pale to the hair.

5 Brush very dilute ultramarine blue, wet into wet, over the lower back, which is in deep shadow. Mix a bright green from viridian and cadmium yellow pale and, using a medium round brush, begin putting in the stripes of the patterned throw. Paint the deep turquoise colour of the throw using a mix of cobalt blue and viridian.

6 Mix a warm reddish brown from Venetian red and cadmium yellow pale and put in the mid tones of the hair. Apply cadmium red to the warmer, darker parts of the skin, such as the shoulder blades. Mix a dark brown from Venetian red and a little Prussian blue and put in the cast shadows under the hand and on the nape of the neck. Mix a dark green from viridian and a little yellow and put in the shadow under the green cushion. Put in the dark stripes and shadow under the striped blue cushion using ultramarine blue.

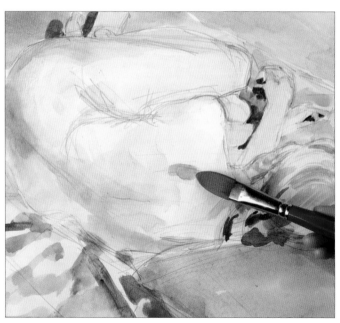

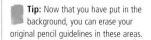
Tip: Now that you have put in the background, you can erase your original pencil guidelines in these areas.

7 For the cooler shadow on the lower left leg, use a mix of ultramarine blue and alizarin crimson. Use a paler version of this mix for the top edge of the left thigh. Paint the shadows cast by the feet in ultramarine blue. Using the reddish brown mix from the previous step, build up the warmer and darker tones on the skin – for example, the shadow under the shoulder blades, and on the left arm and thigh and the right knee.

▶

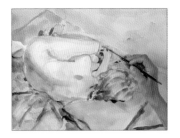

8 Continue building up the skin tones using the same reddish brown mix as before on the lower back. Using a fine round brush, apply the greens and blues of the throw and cushion right up to the edge of the figure to define it more sharply. Apply warm reddish browns where needed on the hands to create some modelling, cutting in with other colours for the negative shapes between the fingers. Carefully dot in the red nail varnish using cadmium red.

Tip: If the initial washes that you applied to the cushion have dried, dampen the area with a little clean water first (taking care not to lift off the underlying colour), so that the new paint spreads wet into wet – otherwise you may end up with rather harsh edges.

Assessment time
As this is intended to be a relatively quick and simple watercolour study, do not be tempted to overwork it, as you may destroy the clarity of the washes and lose the light and airy feel. Just take a few moments to look at the overall balance. Ask if there is sufficient light and shade on the body to make it look three-dimensional and if any more detail is required in the surroundings.

The hair merges into the nape of the neck and the cushion.

The foreground cushions look rather flat and need more tone.

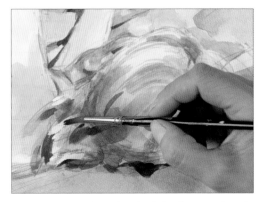

9 Mix cadmium yellow pale with a little white gouache and, using a fine round brush, carefully touch in some of the highlights on the tips of the hair.

10 Using a large round or mop brush and the viridian and cadmium yellow pale mix from Step 3, deepen the colour of the green cushion in the foreground and put in some folds in the fabric. This is the part of the picture that is nearest to us, and having a little more texture in the foreground can help to create a sense of scale.

The finished painting

Although this is a loosely painted, almost impressionistic interpretation of the pose, it has a liveliness and sparkle that are very appealing. The white of the paper also contributes to the feeling of liveliness. The trick with good watercolour painting is to achieve a combination of spontaneity and control – spontaneity in allowing the paint to flow and create lively mixes on the paper, and control in not allowing it to go where you do not want it to. Here, the artist has taken great care not to let any of the background colours spill over on to the body; at the same time, she has worked wet into wet to build up the skin tones and create a very realistic-looking impression of light and shade. Note how some of the pencil underdrawing shows through, the linear marks adding detail and enhancing the soft watercolour washes.

Wet-into-wet washes, built up layer by layer, have been used to build up areas of tone with no hard edges.

The pencil underdrawing adds a little linear detail and prevents the painting from looking too flat.

The cast shadows are a small but integral part of the composition, adding depth to the image.

Female figure in watercolour

You might imagine that posing a seated figure is somehow easier than posing a standing figure: surely all the model has to do is sit still! However, you need to create an interesting composition and make sure that your model can hold the pose in comfort.

A simple seated pose, with the model's back supported by the backrest of a chair or sofa, is certainly easy to hold – but it will not necessarily create a very dynamic picture. From virtually any angle, the model's midriff and thighs will be hidden from view. Viewed from the side, the chair or sofa may dominate your picture. Viewed from the front, the feet will be nearest to the artist and the rest of the body may then appear unattractively foreshortened.

Think about the overall line of the pose: do you want a strong diagonal line, as here, or a softer, more curving shape? Look for interesting angles in the composition: the negative shapes (that is, the spaces between different elements) are critical, as are the angles of the limbs. In the pose selected here, the model's right arm and left leg are bent, forming a zig-zagging line through the composition. Even quite small changes to the pose can make a very big difference to the overall effect, so ask your model to make minor adjustments until you arrive at something that you feel will create a strong composition.

The pose shown here is actually quite hard to hold for any length of time. Much of the model's weight is resting on her left arm, so regular breaks are essential. This is also a difficult pose for the model to resume exactly after a break, so be prepared to make minor adjustments as the painting progresses. Try to put down the basic structure relatively quickly, before the model needs to take a break.

Materials

- Heavy watercolour paper
- Watercolour paints: yellow ochre, ultramarine blue, vermilion, cerulean blue, alizarin crimson
- Brushes: medium round

The pose

The strong diagonal line of the body makes this a very dynamic pose. The bent right arm and left leg neatly counterbalance one another and form a line that zig-zags through the picture, while the triangular negative space between the model's left arm, torso and the cushion adds interest to the whole composition.

1 Mix a dilute wash of a neutral olive green from yellow ochre and ultramarine blue. Using a medium round brush, lightly draw in the main lines of the pose. As always, think of the body as a series of boxes rather than an outline. Use the tilt of the model's shoulders as a guideline to drawing the other elements and remember to look at the negative shapes as well as the positives.

2 Continue until you have mapped out the whole pose. The exact colours are not important, but keep them very pale for this 'underdrawing' and use colours that complement the skin tones you will be using.

3 When you're happy with the basic structure, add a little more ultramarine blue to the mix and refine the shape of the face and shoulders. Use a very dilute mix of the same colour to begin putting in the background. Use a little vermilion to lightly touch in the cushion on which the model is sitting, noting how the weight of her body pushes the edge of the cushion upwards. Apply a stronger wash of ultramarine blue for the fabric.

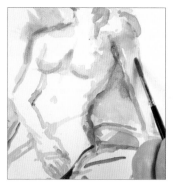

4 Lightly map in the position of the facial features, using the same blue-green mix as in the previous step for the eyebrows and eyes and a very dilute wash of vermilion for the shaded side of the nose. Mix a very dilute wash of cerulean blue and apply it to the background above the stool.

5 Mix a very dilute, cool purple from alizarin crimson with a tiny amount of ultramarine blue and lightly brush it on to the lower part of the breasts. Brush the same mix over the edge of the left arm, then drop in a little yellow ochre so that the colours blend wet into wet on the paper to create a warm, glowing skin tone.

6 Darken the hair with a mix of alizarin crimson and ultramarine blue. Do not try to put in every single strand, but make your brushstrokes follow the direction of the hair growth. Apply more blue to the background, pulling your brush away from the figure in a series of spiky strokes so that the colour does not bleed into the figure.

7 Carefully brush a little very dilute vermilion over the model's face, remembering to leave the very brightest highlights untouched. Using slightly darker versions of the previous mixes, brush a little colour on to the shaded side of the body – the model's left side.

8 Refine the facial details, using the bluish-purple mix for the eyes and vermilion for the nostrils, mouth and the dimple in the chin. Put more colour into the hair, using the same mix as in Step 6. Remember to leave some slight gaps for the highlights.

▶

Assessment time

The painting is taking shape well, and the character and detail are starting to come through. Some modelling has been created on the left-hand side of the model's body, but the other side of the body has been left largely untouched, even though this area is receiving a lot of light and consequently contains some bright highlights, for which you need to reserve the white of the paper. More tone needs to be added to the figure as a whole, to differentiate the light and shaded areas more clearly and give the figure some form. The stool on which the model is sitting needs to be painted in order to set the figure in context, and applying more colour around the model would help to differentiate her from the background, and frame her better. The skin tones also need warmth.

This area has received virtually no paint at all.

This area is in deep shadow and needs to be much darker in tone.

9 Using the same mixes as before – warm reddish purples and yellow ochre – build up the skin tones across the body as a whole, working wet into wet. Remember to leave the very brightest highlights untouched. Intensify the blue background and red cushion with stronger washes of ultramarine blue and vermilion respectively.

10 Strengthen the tones on the legs if necessary, so that they stand out from the background. Use yellow ochre to put in a suggestion of the wooden floorboards. This is quite a loose, impressionistic painting so do not attempt to put lots of detail into the surroundings: the figure should dominate the composition.

The finished painting

The main purpose of this study is to concentrate on the figure, and so the artist has put in just a suggestion of the background. However, the cool blue cloth acts as a foil to the warm colours of the skin and allows the figure to stand out. By paying attention to the light and dark areas and allowing the skin tones to blend wet into wet on the paper, the artist has created lively mixes that capture the effect of the light falling across the figure.

The edge of the arm is very brightly lit and has been left unpainted, so the background is essential in order for it to stand out.

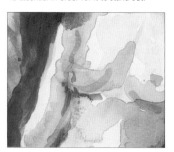

Although much of this area has been left unpainted, the cool, dark shadows under the breast convey the form.

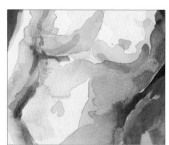

Lively, flowing brushstrokes and various colour mixes create an impression of the hair without putting in every single strand.

Seated figure in soft pastels

Once you've gained some experience of drawing and painting the figure against a plain backcloth, why not try including more of the setting in your picture? Often, just a hint of the surroundings – a rug on the floor, a vase of flowers or a book on a nearby table – is enough to create a sense of atmosphere. Props, such as the lily that the model is holding in this project, can also help create a 'story' – and, on a purely practical level, they give the model something to do with his or her hands. And strong, sculptural shapes like the lily can be used to cast interesting shadows, which you can use in your composition. Remember, however, that the figure should always remain the main focus of your painting. If you have a very complicated element in the background, such as wallpaper (or the rug in this scene), it's perfectly acceptable to simplify it in your painting and merely hint at the colours and pattern.

This project is worked in soft pastel, which is a wonderfully versatile medium. It allows you to make both strong, linear marks using the tip of the pastel and broad sweeps of colour using the side; you can also blend the marks with your fingers to create soft, smooth textures while still allowing several colours to mix optically on the paper.

Soft pastels come in a huge range of colours and there may be several shades of the same colour in a large set. The colour names may also vary from one manufacturer to another, so it can be hard to compare different brands; in fact, some brands have no colour names, only numbers. When choosing colours, be guided by your eyes.

If you have only a small set of pastels, white may be the only colour you have for the highlights. If this is the case, put down the highlight as white, and then apply another colour on top and blend in with your finger to create a pale tint.

Materials
- *Dark green pastel paper*
- *Soft pastels: various shades such as Naples yellow, pink, raw sienna, burnt umber, black, white, olive green*

The pose
The artist has included just enough of the room to provide a context for the pose without detracting from the figure. This is an easy pose for the model to hold, as her back is well supported. As the light is coming from the side, there are some fairly strong cast shadows on the sofa, which add interest to the composition. A few carefully chosen props – an open book, a lily and a couple of cushions and throws – complete the scene.

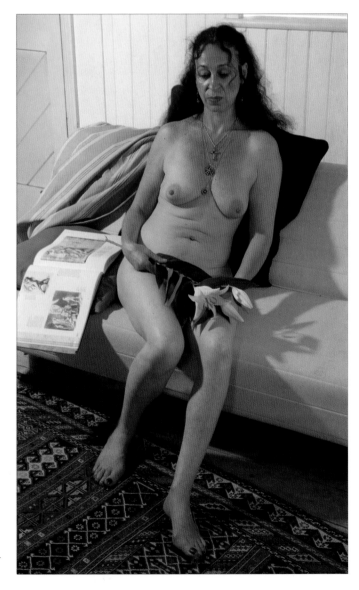

1 Establish the main lines of the pose and make sure that you can fit everything into the picture space. The first stages of a drawing are all about mapping out where features are in relation to each other. Here, for example, the right knee is almost directly below the right nipple. Put in the basic 'egg' shape of the head, which is slightly tilted here. Look for things like the relative size and angles of the feet, and think of the rest of the body as a series of geometric blocks to get the model's proportions right.

Tip: See if there's anything in the surroundings that you can incorporate in your first stage drawing as a guide to where things are placed. Here, for example, the artist has outlined the cushion behind the model's head and the triangle of light that breaks up the shadows cast on the sofa.

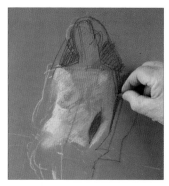

2 Begin to put down blocks of warm and cool colour as you work on your drawing. The right-hand side of the model's upper chest, for example, is very warm, but her left-hand side, which receives less direct light, is cooler in tone. There is quite a lot of reflected light on the breasts. Block in the cushion, as this will help to define the shape of the model's left arm.

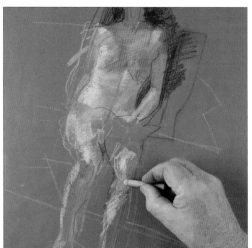

3 Continue working down the torso and legs, putting in the warm and cool tones. Don't try to be too precise at this stage: just establish the general shapes of the different areas.

Tip: Keep checking the proportions to make sure the body does not become too elongated and that you have left plenty of room for the feet.

4 Put in highlights around the face – for example, on the edge of the nose and on the model's right cheek and forehead – and on the shoulders, so that you start to develop the form. Establish the position of the facial features, without attempting to put in much detail at this stage. Gradually build up the flesh colours on the upper chest. Block in the dark cushion; this will help to define the edges of the figure without drawing a crisp, sharp line.

▶

5 Continue developing the modelling on the figure, looking all the time for the strong highlights and shadows that will reveal the form. Use a combination of short, linear marks that imply the muscle masses or bone structures beneath the skin (the rib cage, for example) and soft finger-blending for smooth areas such as the highlights above the right breast. Begin blocking in the shape of the lilies on the model's lap. (Use the dark green of the paper for the leaves in parts.)

6 Refine the facial features, looking for the highlights and shadows as before. Using the tip of the pastel, put in more of the general lines of the model's wavy hair.

Tip: If necessary, break your pastel stick to get a clean, sharp edge so that you can draw fine lines and details.

7 Roughly block in the striped throw and the sofa behind the model. As with the cushion in Step 4, this will help to define the edges of the figure. Note how the stripes on the throw change direction as the fabric folds and drapes.

8 Roughly draw in the open book beside the model. The white of the pages accents the turn of her wrist and emphasizes its shape. Begin putting in any cast shadows that you can see. The lily casts a shadow on the model's leg; put this in using a warm, reddish brown. Elsewhere on the legs, look for the highlights and shadows that delineate the calves.

9 Block in the dark shadow under the sofa, as well as the line of the rug on the floor.

10 Put in as much of the pattern of the rug as you wish, taking care not to allow the rug to overpower the rest of the drawing. The feet themselves should be drawn initially as simple geometric shapes before you attempt to put in any detail such as the individual toes. As always, create a sense of their form by looking for the lights and darks and the warm and cool areas; the instep of the right foot, for example, is very warm in tone, so use a relatively dark purple.

11 The cast shadows are a subtle but important part of the overall composition of this picture. Put in the shadow of the lily on the sofa using a pale, cool grey, and then the shadow that the body casts on the sofa using a dark green. You can smooth out and soften the pastel marks later if necessary – just block in the general shapes for now.

12 Using warm pinks, put in any missing highlights on the upper left arm and torso, where the bony protuberances of the collar and shoulder bones catch the light. This area receives much less light than the other side of the model's body, so you will notice that even the highlights are relatively dark in tone.

▶

Assessment time

With the exception of a few key highlights to really emphasize the bone structure, the drawing of the model is virtually complete. The light falling across the figure from the left creates lovely modelling. Although the artist has included no more than a suggestion of the patterned rug in the foreground, and has simply blocked in the background quite roughly, there is just enough detail around the model to add interest to the composition without detracting from the figure.

When creating your own life drawing projects you may choose to leave out personal jewellery, or indeed ask your model to wear a necklace or similar that you feel adds a certain 'personality' or colour to the pose. The blue jewellery has yet to be added to this drawing, and will add a contrasting cool highlight to the flushed, warm area beneath the model's throat.

Some highlights are missing on the clavicles.

The shadow cast by the lily could be strengthened a little to emphasize its shape.

13 Using a mid-toned olive green, block in the shaded front edge of the sofa, then blend the marks with your fingers. The parts of the sofa not in shadow were put in with a pale mauve. It's perfectly acceptable to use a little artistic licence for things like this; here, the artist felt that the mauve complemented the skin tones and was a more lively colour than the actual grey of the fabric.

14 Put in any final details and finishing touches such as the model's jewellery. Use white for the silver chains and green overlaid with a bright blue for the turquoise stones. Finally, put in any missing highlights on the neck and clavicle using a light raw sienna.

The finished drawing

Although the artist has included enough of the surroundings to create a sense of place, nothing is allowed to dominate the figure. Peripheral details such as the open book and the rug on the floor are put in only sketchily (although you could draw them in more detail if you wished). The strong side lighting has created interesting shadows that the artist has made an integral part of the composition. By carefully assessing the light and dark tones, the artist has created a convincingly three-dimensional portrayal.

The highlight area on the arm is broken up by the shadow cast by the left breast.

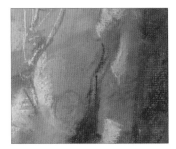

The open book lying beside the model contributes to the overall 'story', and suggests something about the subject.

A combination of linear marks and soft finger blending is used to convey the skin tones and the form of the figure.

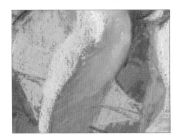

The cast shadow of the lily forms a graphic compositional element in its own right and breaks up an otherwise empty space.

Foreshortened male in oil bars

Drawing and painting the figure in perspective can make for a much more interesting pose than a standing or seated pose, in which the whole body is positioned at more or less the same distance from the artist.

In this pose, the model's head and torso appear considerably larger than his feet, simply because they are much closer to the artist. Plot exactly where each element of the figure goes before you begin drawing.

Your model will have to hold this pose for a considerable length of time, so make sure that he or she is aware of this before you begin. Here, the model was lying on a thin sheet on a hard wooden floor. Even the best and most experienced of models will have to take occasional breaks, so do whatever you can to ensure that the model can get back into the same position. For example, it's a good idea to put masking tape on the floor around the model's feet (and elbows, in this case) to use as a guide to get back into exactly the same position as before. You could also ask your model to focus on a specific point, such as a painting on the wall, so that they can redirect their gaze to this point when they resume the pose.

This drawing demonstrates a technique that the artist developed which uses a cloth and a little turpentine to blend the oil bar marks. Here, the artist has used only a few colours to give the painting a simple, monochrome feel that is very effective.

Materials
- *White paper*
- *Oil bars: yellow ochre, white, raw sienna*
- *Turpentine*
- *Cloth*
- *Graphite stick*
- *Small brush*

Tip
Keep your initial outlines rough as the paint can easily be covered over.

The pose
Ask your model to move around until he or she finds a pose that can be held relatively easily for a long period. Aim to get interesting angles and shapes within the composition: here, for example, the model initially stretched both legs out behind him in a straight line, but bending the right knee gave a much more dynamic shape to the pose, and having the model rest his head on his hands makes the pose seem natural and relaxed.

1 Using the yellow ochre oil bar, start to roughly draw the shape, keeping your movement loose. Look for features that line up, such as the right elbow and the right knee, as well as the clasped hands, right shoulder and the bulge of the left calf. Also, pay particular attention to the way the legs in this pose are very foreshortened.

2 Continue with the underpainting until you think you've got down any lines that you can use as guides. Using a cloth with a little turpentine, rub the oil bar lines that you've made so the lines blend together.

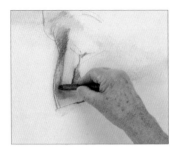

3 Use a graphite stick to begin to draw into the underpainting and start to map out the figure. Blend heavy marks with a cloth where needed.

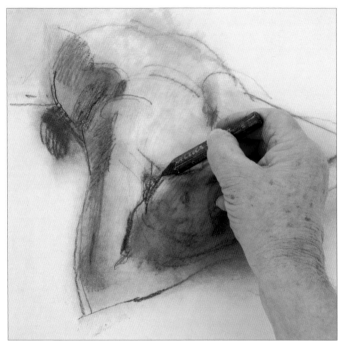

4 Draw in the head and facial features and blend with a cloth. Resist any temptation you may have to turn your head to look at the model's face: try to draw as you see it.

5 Use a yellow ochre oil bar to contine to draw the rest of the body shape. Use a raw sienna oil bar to map out the darker tones. Don't worry about getting all the colours just right at this stage. This is still the underpainting: you will be building up the colour and adjusting the tones gradually as the painting progresses. Use a graphite stick to shade the very darkest areas on the torso and underside of the arm.

6 Once you have a rough outline of the figure, start to block in the background colour. Here, the artist is using the black graphite stick to contrast the richness of the figure. Blend the graphite with a cloth and a little turpentine.

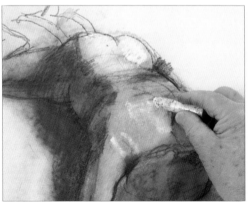

7 Use a white oil bar to add highlights to the lightest parts of the body, the buttocks and the shoulders. Again, smudge with a cloth and a little turpentine, then add a bit more white to the very lightest parts and gently smudge with your finger.

▶

Assessment time

All the underlying skin tones have been established. The final stages of the painting will be about making gradual adjustments, refining and improving on the modelling in order to make the figure look three-dimensional.

The highlights and shadows are evident, but the limbs do not look rounded.

The figure needs to jump out more from the background colour.

The facial features have been mapped out but more detailing is needed.

8 (Left) Start to build up the tones and shapes of the sheet, using the graphite stick. Draw in the folds and then smudge with a cloth and a little turpentine. Leave the lightest parts of the sheet for the highlights.

9 (Right) Next, give some definition to the head and face. Use the graphite stick to hatch shading to the hair and the darker areas of the face. Use the cloth to smudge and blend the hatching lines on the head and face to give a softer and denser feel.

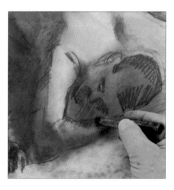

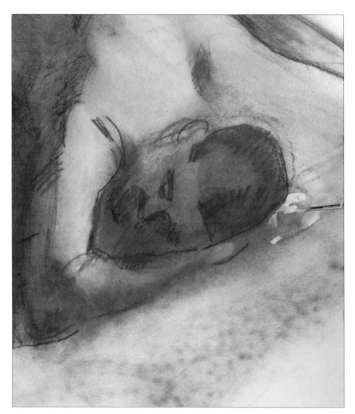

11 Mix some crushed yellow ochre oil bar with a little turpentine and paint on more lighter tones on the right area and the small of the back. This will give these areas more form and appear more rounded. Smudge the paint gently with your finger to blend.

12 Use the white liquid mixture from Step 10 to highlight the ear and hands. Add a little of the yellow ochre liquid mix from Step 11 to the mix to get a lighter tone to define the hands and arm more, blending any harsh lines where necessary.

10 Crush some white oil bar on a board and dip a small fine brush into a little turpentine then into the crushed white oil bar to make a liquid mixture. Start to paint on the hands and fingers, and add some highlights to the elbows, smudging the paint very gently with your finger.

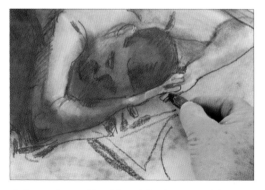

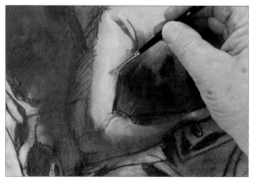

13 Use the graphite stick to define the arms and fingers. Draw in more folds in the sheet in front of the hands, smudging with a cloth and turpentine to blend.

14 On the arms, apply a little of the yellow ochre. Add white liquid colour mix to the upper part of the right arm, shoulders, back and ear to give more form.

▶

15 Use the graphite stick to define the legs and feet, then fill in the area between the legs, blending with the turpentine.

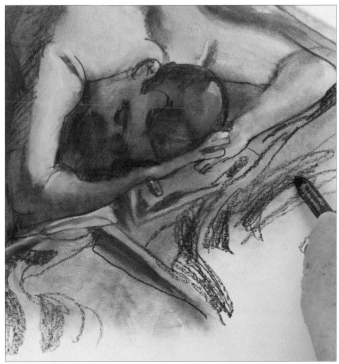

16 Continue to use the graphite stick to block in the darker areas around the torso.

17 Continue to draw in the folds in the background sheet with the graphite stick. You can keep the detail in the fabric loose as the main focus of this painting is the figure.

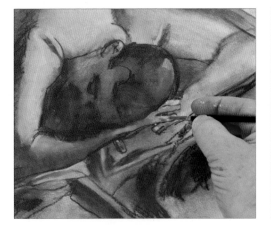

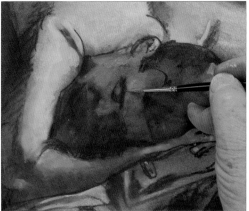

18 Use the white yellow liquid mix to highlight the hands and the lower arms. Blend the wet paint and soften the transition from one colour to another. Use the graphite stick to outline shapes where necessary.

19 Make final adjustments to the skin tones on the body. Here, the artist continues to highlight the forehead and cheeks to create a little more modelling on the face, blending the colours wet into wet with his fingers.

The finished painting

This delightfully monochrome painting concentrates attention firmly on the figure. The flesh tones are made up gradually through building up and blending layers of colour.

The textural quality of oil bars is also exploited here, with thick, impasto-like applications on the sheet. The darkness of the sheet adds to the warm yellows of the figure.

The sheet in the foreground is painted in more detail than that around the feet, creating an impression of distance.

The contrast of the lighter areas with the harsh outline makes the figure stand out from the background.

Modelling is created through subtle blends of colour and the juxtaposition of warm and cool tones.

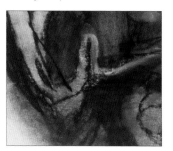

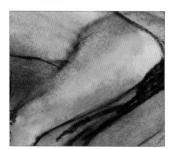

Standing male in Conté

This project uses Conté – an extremely versatile medium available in both pencil and stick form. The pencils are hard and sharp enough for you to be able to create crisp, linear detailing, yet soft enough for the marks to be smudged to create large areas of tone.

The aim of this project is to practise using shading techniques to create modelling, and convey the three-dimensional form of the body.

Before you put pencil to paper, take time to really look at your subject and assess where the lightest and darkest areas are, as this is what will create the impression of three dimensions. In the pose shown here, for example, look at the model's left arm and the curve of the spine down to the buttocks: there's a bright line of light highlighting these areas, then the light gradually falls off as the arm curves away from the light.

Materials
- *Good-quality drawing paper*
- *Conté pencils: yellow, yellow ochre, red brown, burnt umber*

The pose
Light slants across the figure. The model is standing in a relaxed, and thoughtful pose that is easy to hold. The purpose of this pose is to focus on the figure, so the background is left bare.

1 Draw a vertical line to start the figure. Using a pale yellow pencil, make the pelvic tilt and the corresponding shoulder tilt, then indicate where the head will be.

2 Draw in the vertical column. Think about the curve to the arch of the back. Don't worry about drawing in any outlines at this stage.

3 Draw a line straight down from the front of the forehead as this is useful to mark out where the shoulders should be. Draw in the shoulders and back, note that the shoulders are almost at a 45 degree angle.

4 Use yellow ochre pencil to draw the ear when you're happy with the position, and start to define the shapes. Note that the vertical line of the buttocks is quite far out. Add a little shading to give form to the darker areas.

5 Assess the vertical lines and the position of the head and shoulders in relation to them. Use a red brown pencil to add definition to the head and facial features, and start to add tone by shading in the darker areas.

6 Here, the artist is repositioning the body slightly to the right after reassessing the vertical lines. You can rub out any lines with your finger.

▶

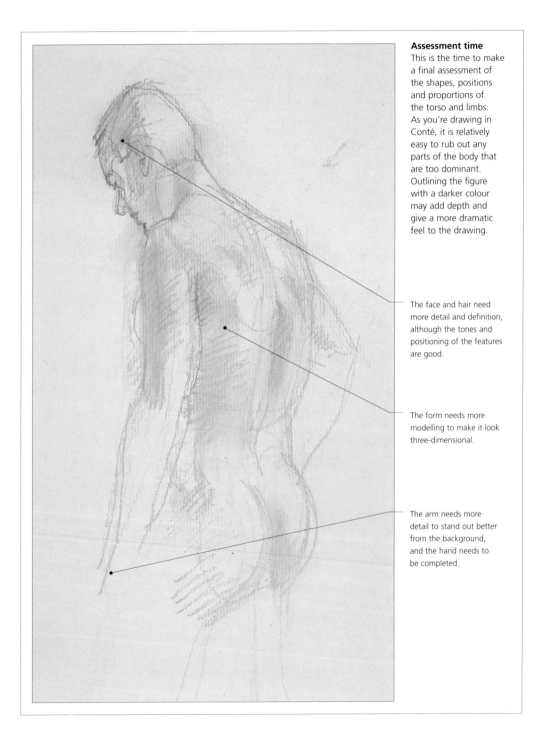

Assessment time
This is the time to make a final assessment of the shapes, positions and proportions of the torso and limbs. As you're drawing in Conté, it is relatively easy to rub out any parts of the body that are too dominant. Outlining the figure with a darker colour may add depth and give a more dramatic feel to the drawing.

The face and hair need more detail and definition, although the tones and positioning of the features are good.

The form needs more modelling to make it look three-dimensional.

The arm needs more detail to stand out better from the background, and the hand needs to be completed.

7 Use a red brown pencil to define the left arm and the outline of the back shading in the darkest areas.

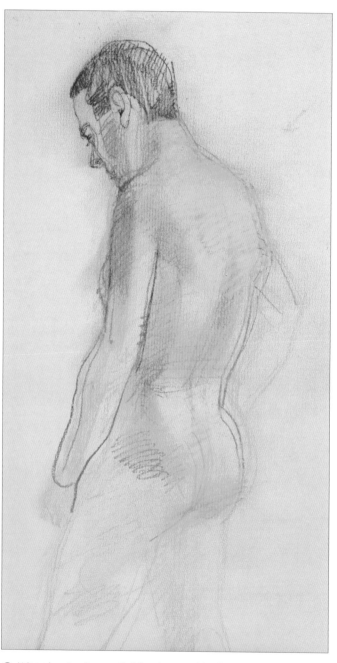

8 Use your finger to smudge the pencil marks on the back, so they blend together.

9 Using a burnt umber pencil, define the ear and head. Lightly hatch burnt umber for the darker tones of the hair following the direction of the hair growth. Outline the left arm and smudge with your finger where necessary.

▶

10 Lightly hatch yellow pencil over the light parts of the back so that you can begin to get a sense of light and shade.

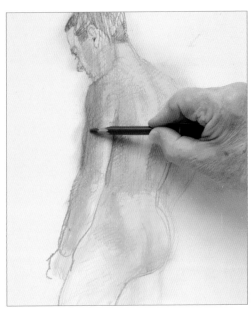

11 Use a red brown pencil to add tone to the back and neck. Define the buttocks and the left arm, smudging with your finger to soften any harsh lines.

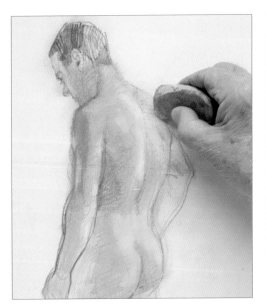

12 Use a kneaded eraser to pick out lost light, adding highlights to the spine and small of the back. Use yellow ochre pencil to add tone to the figure.

13 Use burnt umber pencil to reinforce the outline on the whole of the figure, hatching the very darkest areas on the left shoulder, buttocks, neck and back.

The finished drawing

Through skilful assessment of warm and cool tones, the artist has created a convincingly three-dimensional image and captured the intriguing play of light and shade on the figure. Conté is a wonderful medium for subtle transitions of tone and colour temperature. The shadows are an integral part of the composition, and the neutral background sets the figure off beautifully.

Linear detailing using the tip of the pencils which has a lovely organic feel.

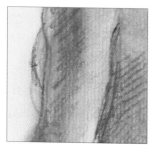

Hatching builds up areas of tone and gives a subtle mix of colour.

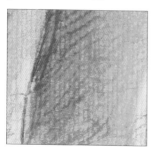

These light areas add to the modelling of the figure.

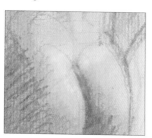

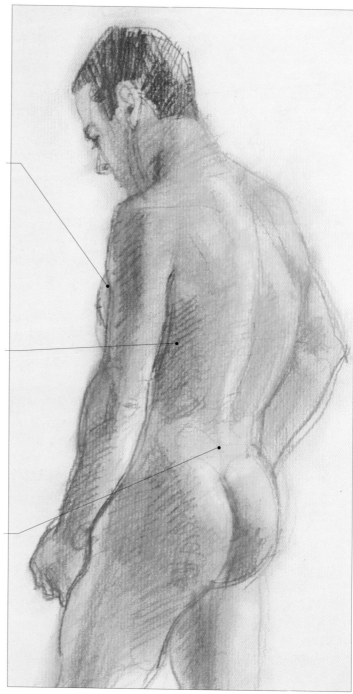

Foreshortened figure in soft pastel

We all have a preconceived idea of what the proportions of the human body are, but when you draw a foreshortened figure it becomes more important than ever to abandon these notions and make careful measurements. You must learn to trust your actual measurements and observations rather than rely on what you think you know.

To make precise measurements, it is absolutely vital that you remain in exactly the same place. If you move around, your viewpoint in relation to the model will change – and this will affect any measurements that you take. Do not start by trying to draw the whole outline; instead, put down light 'markers' to establish the extremities of the body – the top and bottom of the head, the outer points of the shoulders, the tip of the hand, the tilt of the knee and so on. It may not be obvious to others what these marks relate to, but if they mean something to you, that's fine.

Keep the setting and any props relatively simple. You have enough to contend with without having to worry about drawing complex surroundings. And remember that you can define your subject by what's around it, as well as by outline. If you are finding it too difficult to discern the exact shape of a particular part of the figure, shift your attention to the surroundings instead and draw the point at which they butt up against the figure.

Preliminary sketch

As a foreshortened pose is quite complex to draw, start by making a few quick sketches – no more than a couple of minutes each – to work out a composition that appeals to you.

Materials
- *Buff-coloured pastel paper*
- *Soft pastels: various shades of Naples yellow, burnt sienna, raw umber, white, pink, pale blue, pale green, grey*

The pose

In this pose, the model's feet are nearer the artist than her head, which means that her body is foreshortened; for example, compare the apparent length of the right arm with that of the right hip. The bed forms a diagonal line through the picture space, which makes a more interesting composition than simply looking straight down the full length of the bed. The throws and blankets have been kept deliberately simple in colour, so as not to distract from the model, but they add an interesting contrast in texture.

1 Begin by mapping out the composition, taking measurements and making sure that you can fit the whole figure on the paper. Look for strong lines within the pose that you can use as 'landmarks' – the line across the shoulders, for example, and the diagonal line of the crossed knee. Select colours that approximate to those in the finished drawing (pink where the head and arm come into contact with the striped throw, yellow for the other limbs and the outline of the body on the white throw), so that you can use them to keep track of where you are in the drawing.

2 Put in stronger marks to define bones beneath the skin such as the pelvic bones and the rib cage. Use warm and cool colours to differentiate the planes of the body. Here a cold grey has been used to block in the shape of the rib cage, with warmer yellows on the stomach and chest areas. The rib cage projects out to a greater depth than the head. Even if you can't see the outline clearly, remember its shape: rather like an upside-down basket, with the ribs curving down on either side of the central spine.

3 The upper right arm is very foreshortened: from this viewpoint, it appears roughly the same length as the line that runs down from the model's armpit to the body. Define the outer edge of the arm by using the colours of the striped throw around it. Within the arm, put in the main light and dark tones. Use a medium tone of burnt sienna for the dark areas on the outer and inner edges and Naples yellow for the lighter, more brightly lit areas, then smooth out the pastel marks using the tips of your fingers.

4 Move on to the central torso and look for the ridge of the pelvic bone, which is very pronounced. Note how the lines are angled here to indicate the different planes of the body. Roughly scribble in the hair in black pastel, using the overall shape to define the facial area. Establish the position of the facial features, and use a mix of warm and cool tones so that you begin to create a hint of modelling on the face.

Tip: Note the tilt of the head. When you draw this, it's important that you do not tilt your own head – otherwise the angle and tilt will be incorrect. Observe everything with your head in exactly the same position.

5 Look for any cast shadows that you can use to help build up the modelling on the figure. Here, for example, the right breast casts a strong shadow on the thorax. Put in some of the stripes in the throw behind the model's head, noting carefully where the stripes change direction.

▶

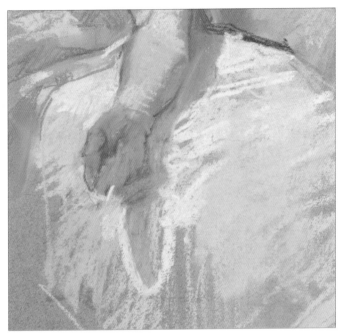

6 Begin to refine the shape of the model's right hand. Think of it as a geometric block rather than a series of individual fingers, and look for the warm and cool tones. The palm, for example, is cooler (yet darker) in tone than the fingers; it is drawn in a slightly bluer, more purple tone than the fingers. Put in the very bright highlight area of the lower arm in white pastel, making your hatching lines run across the forearm to imply its rounded form.

7 Roughly block in the white throw to establish the flat planes of the bed. Again, look for any cast shadows that may be helpful in the composition: here, the right arm casts a distinct shadow on the bed, so block it in with a pale, cool blue and blend the marks with your fingers to create a smooth area of tone.

8 Parts of the torso are very strongly lit. Use cool yellows and white to put in these highlit areas. There is a bright highlight line running along the model's right thigh. Put this in lightly in white and use it as a guide to the different planes of the leg. Much of the left leg, in contrast, is very dark, yet warm in tone: start by putting in the line of the shin in raw umber, then hatching over it.

9 Note how the left hand rests on and presses into the stomach: you can use the shape of the hand to imply the curve of the stomach. Think of the left hand as an overall shape, rather than drawing each finger individually. The fingers catch the light, while the back of the hand is in shadow. Pick out the individual highlights that catch the edge of each finger in a warm Naples yellow, and the remaining parts of the hand in warm shades of burnt sienna. The colours you use around the hand will also help to define it.

10 One side of the left leg catches the light and is warm in tone, while the other side is in shadow and is cool. Use a warm Naples yellow and a cool very pale blue to convey this. Note that a little of the left thigh is also visible from this angle; draw this in too. Now move back to the background: put in any stripes on the pink throw that are not obscured by the hair, and block in more of the white throw using the side of the pastel. Put in any folds and shadows on the white throw using a cool, pale blue or green.

11 Note that the right leg is not foreshortened, as it goes across the artist's line of vision. The left leg casts a dark shadow on the side of the right knee; block this in using a raw umber pastel. Use the highlight line along the centre of the model's right shinbone to help you define the form of the leg. Below it, use warm pinks, with burnt sienna on the foot. Above it, use cooler yellows. Define the feet, using Naples yellow, raw umber and burnt sienna, and put in the toe nails, noting how much of each nail is actually visible.

Assessment time
Here, the artist has toned down the very warm tones on the right leg by applying cool blue-greys on top of the initial warm tones. The colours mix optically on the paper, creating a lively sense of shimmering light. More minor adjustments are still required. Although the white throw should not dominate the drawing, here it is a little insubstantial: quite a lot of the original paper colour shows through. Some of the skin tones need to be adjusted in order for the different planes of the body to stand out more clearly. The only major problem here is the right arm, which is too foreshortened. It's a good idea to fix the drawing at this stage, so that you can incorporate stronger lines if necessary – but do remember to wait until the fixative has dried before going ahead and making any final changes.

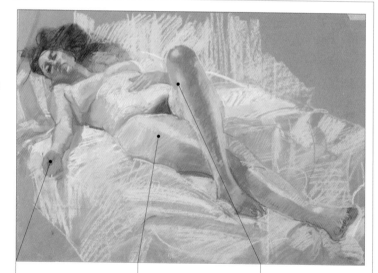

The right arm looks a little too foreshortened. The tips of the fingers should actually be more or less level with the left heel.

This area is too warm and uniform in tone. The colour looks rather matt. The torso, in contrast, is too cool in tone, and the colour between the hip and belly needs blending.

There is not a clear enough distinction between the lower leg and upper thigh.

12 With soft pastels, it is relatively easy to make changes, even in the later stages of a drawing. Here, the artist has redrawn the right arm, making it a little longer. This is the point at which you can also make a final check on the skin tones: because of the direction and angle of light, the right arm is relatively dark, so use warm siennas to strengthen the shaded underside of the arm and tone down the very bright highlights by applying yellow over the existing white.

13 The left hand has been drawn in greater detail than the rest: all you want to do is create the feeling of it resting on the surface of the model's stomach. By toning down the very bright yellow highlights on the fingers and evening out the tones, you can draw attention away from the fingers. The reflected light on the back of the hand is cooler than that on the group of fingers, so use a slightly bluer tone here to differentiate the planes of the hand.

14 The right hip receives a lot of direct light, so tone down the yellow by applying more white on top and blending the marks with your fingertips. This also has the effect of differentiating the different planes of the torso more clearly. To use a landscape analogy, if you think of the side of the torso and the flank as being a near vertical 'cliff', then the stomach is a more or less horizontal 'plateau' above them.

15 Using the side of the pastel, roughly block in the white wood panelling in the background. It's up to you how much detail you include in the surroundings, but make sure they do not dominate the portrait.

16 Adjust the skin tones, adding final highlights to the feet and calves and re-defining the shape of the ankles. Do this by bringing the pale surroundings right up to the ankle, not by darkening the line of the ankles.

> **Tip:** It's important to keep moving around the picture, between the figure and the background, in order to keep everything moving along at the same rate. This allows you to continually reassess one part of the drawing against another and adjust as necessary.

The finished drawing

Soft pastel allows you to make both strong, linear marks using the tip of the pastel and broad sweeps of colour using the side; you can also blend the marks with your fingers to create wonderfully soft, smooth textures, while still allowing several colours to mix optically on the paper. Here, the artist has exploited the potential of the medium to the full to create a lively drawing that shimmers with light. The foreshortening of the body and the contrasts between areas of light and shade have been meticulously observed. There is just enough background to enhance, not detract from, the figure.

The warm colour of the striped throw under the model's head frames and draws attention to her face. It also reflects some colour into the skin tones.

There is enough linear detail in the white throw to hint at the pattern and the cool blue shadows reveal that the fabric is slightly ruffled.

Note how the strong highlights and shadows along the shinbones help to define the different planes of the legs.

Portraits

Portraiture is sometimes perceived as being one of the most difficult subjects for artists. The truth is that, provided you train yourself to look and measure carefully, it's no more difficult than anything else; it's all based on keen observation. This chapter features a series of tutorials and a gallery of portraits by professional artists. You can study these finished works to see how they've approached a particular subject, which gives you the opportunity to see how artists working in a number of different media have tackled a range of portrait topics and challenges. This is followed by a series of quick sketches – a great way of grabbing a few minutes drawing practice when you are short of time. Finally, there are easy-to-follow and detailed step-by-step projects of people of all ages, from a young child to elderly subjects with a lifetime's experience. There are indoor and outdoor portraits, and there are smiling faces as well as more contemplative expressions – in short, something for everyone. Study these projects to find out how to undertake various challenges.

The head

One of the most common mistakes that beginners make when they are drawing a portrait is to try to put in too much detail in the very early stages. The most important thing to remember is that, as with any subject, you need to start by getting the basic shape right.

Although every head is different, and you have to learn to carefully observe your subject and measure the individual parts and the distances between them, it is nevertheless possible to set out some general guidelines that you can use as a starting point.

Start by practising viewing the head from straight on, to get used to looking at the general shape. From this angle the head is not a perfect circle, as often seen in children's drawings, but an egg shape, so begin with that.

Drawing the basic shape of the head

Draw this basic shape, keeping your initial marks quite light so that you can alter them if necessary. Build up the shape from the inside, making a series of curved marks that go around the shape and across it, so that you start to build up a three-dimensional sense of the form rather than a contour. In this way your hand is also working rhythmically, building up the shape without getting engrossed in the detail.

1 Start by drawing a series of curves.

2 Then add more spherical movements.

3 Add spheres and ovals for the features.

Positioning the facial features

Once you're used to the basic shape of the head, you can then begin to look at where the individual features of the face are positioned. Draw a line dividing the face from top to bottom, passing between the eyes, down the bridge of the nose, through the centre of the mouth and chin and through the neck. All the facial features are positioned symmetrically on either side of the face, so you can use this central line to check that you are placing them correctly.

Now lightly draw a series of lines across the face to mark the position of the facial features – the corners of the eyes, the top and bottom of the nose and the corners of the mouth. (Even the most experienced of artists often draw lines like this, which are known as 'construction lines', in the early stages of a portrait.) However, the exact positions will vary from one person to another, so careful measuring is essential.

General guidelines ▶

Although everyone's face is different, you can use these basic guides for assistance. Remember that these rules apply only when the head is viewed from straight on.

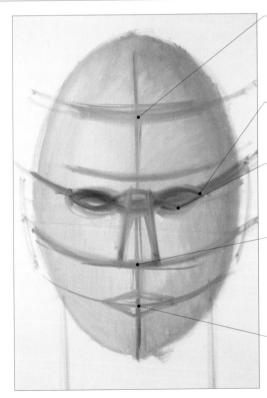

The hairline is the point at which the front plane of the face moves to the top plane of the skull.

The corners of the eyes are roughly level with the tips of the ears.

The base of the eye socket is located approximately halfway down the facial area.

The base of the nose is roughly halfway between the eyes and the base of the chin, and level with the lobes of the ears.

The mouth is less than halfway between the base of the nose and the tip of the chin.

The features in an inverted triangle

Another useful way of checking the position of the facial features is to draw an inverted triangle. There are two ways of doing this. You can either draw a horizontal line across to the outer corner of each eye and a line down from the corner of each eye to the chin (shown right, in blue) or alternatively, draw lines down from the outer corners of the eyes to the middle of the lips (shown right, in red). If the mouth extends beyond the side edges of the triangle, or the chin is below the apex, then you have probably positioned them incorrectly and need to re-measure – although, of course, people vary considerably, so you must judge with your eye as well.

Inverted triangles as construction lines ▶
In most people, all the facial features should be contained within these inverted triangles, so you can use them to check that you haven't made the mouth too wide or placed the chin too low down.

The head from different viewpoints

If you look at your sitter from above or below, then the relative positions of the features will alter. Measuring becomes even more important and you must train yourself to do this rather than rely on any prior knowledge of where the features are in relation to each other. Put in the central axis through the face, as before, then take careful measurements to establish where the features should be placed exactly – and keep measuring as you draw to ensure you are still on track.

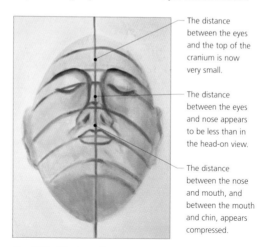

The tips of the ears are now above the level of the eyes.

The distance between the eyes and nose appears to be greater than in the head-on view.

The distance between the nose and mouth, and the mouth and chin, is very small.

The distance between the eyes and the top of the cranium is now very small.

The distance between the eyes and nose appears to be less than in the head-on view.

The distance between the nose and mouth, and between the mouth and chin, appears compressed.

Head tilted forwards ▲
When the head is tilted forwards – as it might be, for example, if your model is reading a book – you can see more of the cranium and less of the facial features.

Head tilted backwards ▲
When the model is looking up and his or her head is tilted backwards, you can see very little of the cranium. The lower part of the face, from nose to chin, takes up a larger proportion of the facial area.

▶

Making the head look three-dimensional

In addition to placing the facial features correctly, you also need to make the head look three-dimensional. To do this you need to create a sense of the major planes – the front, the sides, the top and the underside. No matter what subject you're drawing, a good principle is to try to think of it as a basic geometric shape – a sphere, a box, a cylinder or a cone. You will find that even the most complicated of subjects can often be looked at in this way. So think of the skull as a box. Draw (lightly) a box around the basic egg shape, noting where the different planes occur.

The number of planes that you see will vary depending on your viewpoint. From straight on, you see only one plane – the front. But if you look at the head from the side on and from the same eye level, you will see two planes – the side and the front. And if you look at the head from above or below, you will see three planes – the top (or underside), side and front.

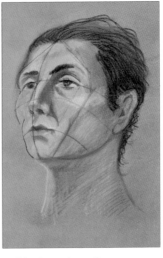

Drawing the major planes of the head

1 Draw the egg shape of the face inside a box and draw a central perpendicular and horizontal axis.

2 Now draw the box at different angles (but don't worry too much about the perspective at this stage). Depending on your viewpoint and the tilt of the head, you will see different planes and perhaps even different numbers of planes.

Visible planes depending on viewpoint ▲
In making this sketch, the artist was positioned slightly to one side of the model. As a result, we can see two major planes (the side and the front) and, as the model's head is tilted upwards, a suggestion of a third plane underneath. Marking the position of the different planes, however lightly, is a good idea for beginners.

Drawing the minor planes of the head

Up to now we've only looked at the very simple planes of the sides of the enclosing box. Within the head, however, there are many more planes that you need to capture. The nose is perhaps the most obvious, as it juts forward from the front of the box: it has four major planes – two sides, the top and the underside. But there are other less extreme planes, too – for example, within the forehead, across the cheekbones and under the chin. Try exploring your own face with your fingertips to see where these changes in plane, which define the underlying bone structure, occur. They are gradual but essential if you are to create a convincingly three-dimensional rendition of your subject.

Minor planes ▶
This sketch demonstrates breaking up the surface of the face into a number of different planes, depending on the underlying bone structure. Here we can clearly see the top plane of the head; the other major planes have been subdivided into smaller planes.

Using tone to create a three-dimensional impression

Up to this point, we've looked primarily at drawing the head using only line. Thinking of the head as a box, rather than a flat two-dimensional object, is the first step. Now you should begin to use tone – cross-hatching in pencil, shading with the side of a stick of charcoal or pastel, or applying a light wash in watercolour or acrylics – to create a sense of light and shade.

Changes in tone occur when the planes of the face and head change direction – for example, if your model is lit from the side, the side of the face nearest the light source will be light, while the side furthest away from it will be dark – and there will be a whole host of mid-tones in between.

The images here show a plaster-cast head of the French writer and philosopher Voltaire, lit from different directions. Where light falls directly on the subject, very little detail is discernible. But on the sides that are turned away from the light, strong shadows are formed – and these show up the muscle formation and bone structure, making the cast look three-dimensional.

Lit from the left, almost full profile ▼

Here, the light was positioned to the left of the plaster cast and slightly above it. As a result, the forehead is brightly illuminated: the artist left the paper untouched in this part of the drawing. On the left side of the head, (the right side as we look at the drawing), a mid-tone is used to draw deep shadows that reveal the sunken cheeks and indentations in the skull. The slab of the neck is drawn using a tone that is even darker, as virtually no direct light hits this part of the cast.

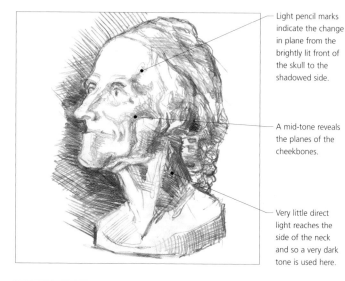

Light pencil marks indicate the change in plane from the brightly lit front of the skull to the shadowed side.

A mid-tone reveals the planes of the cheekbones.

Very little direct light reaches the side of the neck and so a very dark tone is used here.

Lit from left, almost full face ▲
Here, the cast was turned to show more of the face. The light is shining from the left, so everything on the other side of the rather prominent nose is in shadow.

Lit from left, three-quarters view ▲
Here the light was again positioned to the left – but slightly lower, almost level with the cast – and the cast was turned further to the right, emphasizing different features.

Lit from front, full face ▲
With the light in front and slightly to the right, the right side of the face is shaded. Note how the lighting flattens out the features: the cheekbones, in particular, look less angular.

The skull bones and muscles

You do not need to know the names of all the bones and muscles in the skull, but by knowing something of the skull's proportions, shapes and rhythms, you will have a much better understanding of how the flesh can reveal a true sense of the underlying form. If you have access to a model of a skull, draw it. If you do not, practise by referring to anatomy books.

The bones of the skull

The skull has both convex and concave surfaces. Convex forms protrude and are visible beneath the surface of the flesh at the brow, the cheeks and chin and jaw. The concave cavities are not visible on the surface: the eye sockets, for example, appear huge, but they are filled with the eyes and surrounding flesh of the eyelids.

Unlike most of the other bones in the body, the skull is not covered by large amounts of muscles and tissue – so the form of the head and face closely follow the form of the skull beneath. Once you know the general shape of the skull, you will then have some idea of the shapes to look for when drawing or painting the head – although the relative sizes, shapes and distances between different areas of the skull vary considerably from one person to another.

The structure of the skull ▼
The skull consists of only two separate parts – the mandible (or jawbone) and the cranium (which encloses the brain). Shown here are the bones that are most relevant to the artist. It is important to remember, however, that every individual's skull is slightly different. It is these differences that play an important part in making us recognizable as individuals.

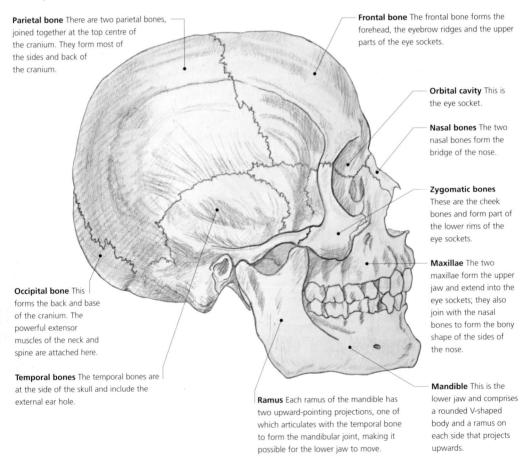

Parietal bone There are two parietal bones, joined together at the top centre of the cranium. They form most of the sides and back of the cranium.

Frontal bone The frontal bone forms the forehead, the eyebrow ridges and the upper parts of the eye sockets.

Orbital cavity This is the eye socket.

Nasal bones The two nasal bones form the bridge of the nose.

Zygomatic bones These are the cheek bones and form part of the lower rims of the eye sockets.

Maxillae The two maxillae form the upper jaw and extend into the eye sockets; they also join with the nasal bones to form the bony shape of the sides of the nose.

Occipital bone This forms the back and base of the cranium. The powerful extensor muscles of the neck and spine are attached here.

Temporal bones The temporal bones are at the side of the skull and include the external ear hole.

Ramus Each ramus of the mandible has two upward-pointing projections, one of which articulates with the temporal bone to form the mandibular joint, making it possible for the lower jaw to move.

Mandible This is the lower jaw and comprises a rounded V-shaped body and a ramus on each side that projects upwards.

The muscles of the head

In some areas of the head it is the muscles, rather than the bones of the skull, that determine the surface form. These muscles that move the facial features and give the face a range of expressions are known as the mimetic muscles. In most of the mimetic muscles, very little force is required. The muscles of mastication, which act on the mandible, are capable of exerting considerable force; the masseter is the most prominent of these.

The mimetic muscles ▼

Knowing a little bit about where the mimetic muscles occur and the effect that they have on the surface of the skin can help you to read and capture your model's mood and expression. For example, you will know which muscles are working to make a smile. Remember, when you create a portrait you are not just drawing or painting a face – you are trying to express a personality.

Orbicularis oculi Is concerned with blinking and closing the eyelid.

Levator labii superioris alaeque nasi Raises the nostrils and upper lip and slightly lifts the tip of the nose.

Zygomaticus major Lifts the corner of the mouth up and sideways.

Levator anguli oris Lifts the mouth upwards.

Masseter Lifts the mandible and closes the jaws.

Rissorius Works with the zygomaticus major to create the folds around the mouth when you laugh or smile.

Depressor labii inferioris Pulls the lower lip downwards.

Occipitofrontalis Moves the skin of the forehead and eyebrows.

Procerus Creates the fold in the top of the nose and wrinkles the bridge of the nose.

Nasalis Pulls the sides of the nose downwards and backwards.

Levator labii superioris Lifts and furrows the upper lip.

Orbicularis oris Closes and purses the mouth.

Depressor anguli oris Pulls the mouth downwards.

Mentalis Produces the horizontal furrow between the chin and lower lip.

Frowning man ◄

When you frown, the skin on your forehead wrinkles; the occipitofrontalis muscle, which is located just below the surface of the skin, enables this movement. The procerus creates the fold at the bridge of the nose. Also, the chin may lower; the mouth may pucker.

Laughing girl ▶

When you laugh or smile, your mouth stretches out to the sides; at the same time, deep folds are created on either side of the base of the nose; this is achieved through the movement of the rissorius and zygomaticus major muscles. The eyes and brow also move.

The facial features

Once you've mastered the position of the facial features, have a go at drawing each one by itself. In addition to giving you much-needed practice in observing and drawing what you see, this will also give you an insight into just how different people's appearances can be. The differences between one eye and its neighbour, the crookedness or straightness of the bridge of the nose or the fullness or thinness of someone's lips – all these are part of the individual's unique appearance. If you can't persuade anyone to pose for you, do a self-portrait or draw from photographs.

The eyes

The eyeball is a spherical form and it is important to make it look rounded. The way to do this, as with any rounded form, is to use light and dark tones to imply the curvature of the surface, which requires very careful observation on your part. The darks are strongest where the form comes forward, usually around the pupil. The upper eyelid generally casts a band of shadow across the upper part of the eye.

The highlights are strongest near the top of the iris, close to the pupil, as this is the zenith of the curvature of the eye. In oils, you can either let the darks dry first and then put in the highlight; alternatively, you can work wet into wet and put in the highlight in thicker paint with a rapid, light brushstroke. In watercolour, you need to leave a point of light, or use masking fluid to keep a spot of the paper white.

Another option with both oil and watercolour paint is to lift out the highlights.

The white of the eye is not pure white; it is often shadowed and may reflect a bright highlight. The eyelashes are larger and more visible on the upper lid than on the lower lid. Do not try to paint or draw every single eyelash; instead, put in a dark line to give an impression of eyelashes.

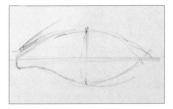

Central axis ▲
To start with, establish a central axis running through both eyes, so that you do not position one higher than the other. Establish the corners of each eye, measuring the space between the eyes.

The shape of the eye ▲
Then look at the shape of the individual eyes – how far open or closed are they? Draw the visible part of the iris; remembering that we rarely see the complete circle of the iris, as the upper lid usually obscures the top – especially in older people.

Shadows in the eye ▲
Pay attention to the lights and darks: the upper lids and eyelashes usually cast a shadow on to the eye. Here, a shadow is cast in the socket and underneath the brow. There is a faint bluish shadow in the eye, which accentuates the white.

The nose and nostrils

At first glance, the nose looks a rather complicated shape to draw, so simplify things by thinking of it initially as a matchbox turned on its side; this makes it easier to see the individual planes. The nose has four distinct planes – the bridge, two side planes moving from the bridge to the cheeks, and the plane underneath the tip of the nose where we see the dark of the nostrils.

On the lower nose there are so many changes in direction, from convex to concave, that it may be difficult to see the separate planes. The way that these convex and concave forms face into or away from the light source means that the nostrils always appear dark – but these contrasts in tone are relative to the other areas of shadow under the nose and on the upper lip. Take care

not to make them too dark and flat – look carefully at the colours and tones within the shadow.

Highlights usually appear at the edge where two planes meet, as at the junction between the bridge and side planes of the nose and on the tip of the nose. There will also be reflected mid-tones in the plane underneath, around the dark of the nostrils.

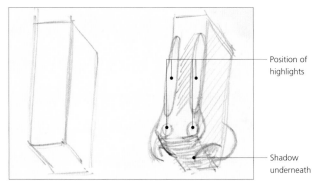

Position of highlights

Shadow underneath

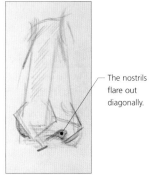

The nostrils flare out diagonally.

The shape of the nose ▲
Although the nose may have many curves and bumps within it, try to think of it as a box shape, like an upended matchbox, in which the individual planes – the two sides, the bridge and the underside – can be clearly defined.

The shape of the nostrils ▲
The nostrils have planes that catch the light and cast shadows. The dark part of the nostril should be considered as part of the underside of the nose.

Highlights ▲
Areas of light appear on the bridge, in the nostrils and at the end of the nose.

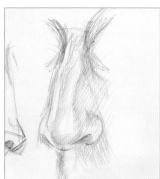

The planes of the nose ▲
Most people's noses change near this point on the bridge of the nose – the transition from bone to cartilage. Light reflects into the shadow under the nose and on the upper lip. Look very carefully: this is not solid shadow.

The mouth

Regardless of whether a person's lips are thin or full, they are pushed outwards by the teeth and follow the curve of the teeth – even though, from the front, the lips appear to be almost on a straight axis. The top lip often appears darker than the bottom lip because the plane of the top lip angles away from light above. (You can see this more clearly if you look at someone's mouth from the side.)

The philtrum is the groove of flesh in the upper lip, which gives the top lip its shape in the middle. This 'valley' of light and dark can be very useful with the right lighting: it signals direction and brings a sense of sculptural relief to an area that often has shadows cast by the nose.

Although you might think of the lips as a flat splash of colour across the lower half of the face, it's important to observe their shape – and, of course, that shape is affected by what lies beneath them.

The upper lip follows the groove of the philtrum, which descends from the nose. When we smile, the upper lip turns outwards and flattens against the teeth, and the philtrum changes shape.

If you make the line between the lips too dark, it can come forwards in the picture rather than recede, so look carefully at the tone of the two lips to see if the top lip overlaps the bottom one, in the centre below the philtrum.

Without lipstick, the lips are not necessarily different in colour to other colours in the face. Use the same colour for both lips, adjusting the tone as necessary. Usually the upper lip is darker than the bottom lip. There are also highlights in the lower lip; sometimes these can be created by using white, sometimes a totally different colour is required. A crimson mixed with yellow ochre or white in differing proportions usually gives a distinct lip colour. A darker colour in the lips may be an earth tone or a deeper purple.

Shape of the mouth ▼

There is a huge difference between the shapes of different people's mouths. To establish the shape, find the corners and use the philtrum in the upper lip to find the centre of the mouth.

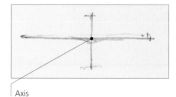

Axis

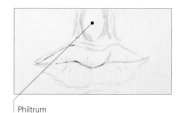

Philtrum

Lip shape and tone ▼

Lips are not a flat shape. Note how the upper lip overhangs the lower one. The top lip is darker than the lower one, as it slopes inwards, facing away from the light source.

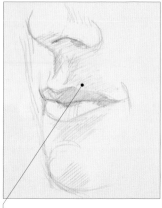

Light catches the edge of the upper lip

Folds around the mouth ▼

There is a faint line (in young people) or a deep fold (in older people) running from the nose around the mouth, dividing the mouth and cheek. The philtrum is also clearly visible: use contrasts of tone to make the recesses obvious. There may also be slight undulations below the lower lip. The folds around the mouth are more apparent in older people.

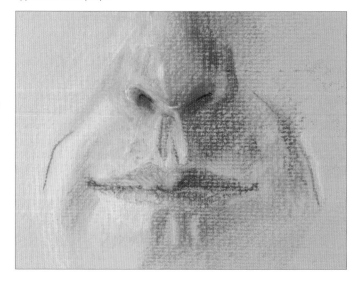

The ear

When you make studies of ears, make sure you work in strong light so that you can see the sculptural, shell-like, three-dimensional rhythms. Shadows give you the sense of the form of ears, especially in the interior. Try to model the form of the ear using light and dark tones.

To place the ear correctly, look to see where the ears align with other features such as the eyes or mouth, and look at the distance between the features. Start by taking a light diagonal line from the base of the lobe to the top of the ear to establish the length. The upper part of the ear is wider than the lower. Carefully observe the length of the lobe; it is longer in older people. Look at the shadow behind and below the ear and note how hair moves around the top and behind.

The interior of the ear always appears darker than the surrounding flesh – but if you make the interior of the ear too dark, you destroy the sense of where these recesses are and they jump forwards in the picture. Always look at the tonal contrasts – the amount of half tones and light that are around these darker areas.

Shape and structure of the ear ▼
Think of the ear as being like a seashell in the way that the outer ear spirals in to the centre. Look for the lights and darks in the different surfaces of the ear. The top of the ear and the ear lobe are the fleshiest parts and invariably appear lighter. The recesses of the inner part of the ear are in shadow.

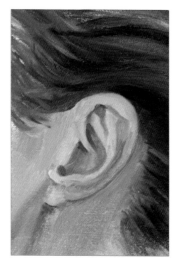

Examine your own reflection ▼
Look at your reflection in a mirror and see what shapes you can see in the ear. The shapes and angles will vary depending on your viewpoint. Note, for example, how the bony cartilage of the inner ear appears to jut out in this individual when he is viewed from this particular angle.

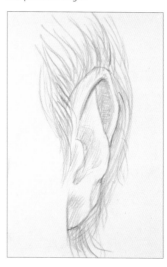

Shadows ▼
Look at the shadow underneath the lobe as this shaded area shows the relief of the ear.

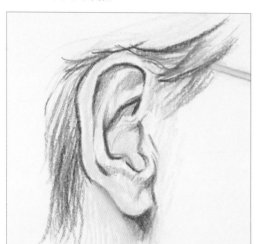

Hair around the ear ▼
Look at the way the hair falls around the ear: it may obscure the ear, but always remember the structure underneath.

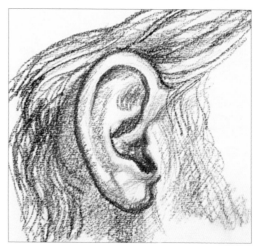

The hair

When drawing or painting hair, you must consider it as part of the head as a whole, rather than as a separate entity. Start by thinking about the overall shape and mass of the hair before you concern yourself with colour and texture. If someone has long, thin hair, it may hang down over the head, face and shoulders, showing the form underneath rather like a tight-fitting garment on the body. Big, curly hair, on the other hand, can almost double the volume of the head as a whole, and it can be hard to imply the shape of the cranium beneath.

Use the hair to help you search out the different planes within the head. Since the hair follows the contours of the scalp and therefore the different planes of the skull, even straight, very thin hair contains highlight and shadow areas as one plane changes direction into the next. Coarse, wavy hair may contain many transitions from light to dark as it undulates over the surface of the skull. Try to see hair as a series of blocks, rather than individual strands. These blocks reflect light in different ways, depending on the colour and type of hair. In straight, dark hair that clings closely to the scalp, the highlight may look like a bar of light; in wavy hair, each curl will have its own pattern of highlights and dark areas, so the highlights over the head as a whole will be much more fragmented.

The way that you convey these areas of light and shade depends, of course, on your choice of medium. A pencil drawing may include cross hatching to create different tones, erasing to lift out the highlights and lines illustrating the movement of strands or clumps of hair. If you are using soft pastels, use the side of the pastel for broad areas beneath any light strands and put in the lights on top as a final series of touches. You could also lightly brush or wipe a paper tissue over the broad areas to create softer effects.

If you are using oils or acrylics, you might choose to put in the darks first and use a rag (or a damp brush) to wipe them out, applying a lighter colour on

Wavy hair ▲

Here, the model's hair was pulled back over her scalp and tied up on the top of her head – but it still escapes in unruly waves! The bulk of the dark hair on the shaded side of her head was put in using the side of a charcoal stick, with bold, curling strands conveying the direction of hair growth. On the lighter side of her head, the artist left the original dark ochre colour of the paper showing through, just as he did in the mid-toned areas of the model's skin. You can also see some fleck of pinks and purples in the hair. You might think this is an unusual colour choice, but the artist selected them for their tonal values, rather than for their actual colour: they relate to the light and dark areas in the skin. Another reason for choosing them was that the model was from Hawaii and he wanted to create a sense of hot, tropical colours, just as Gauguin did so famously in his wonderfully vibrant paintings of Tahitian women.

top, making the subsequent layers thicker so that they do not merge with the underpainting. In watercolour, you normally work from light to dark so you need to establish the lightest tones first and then add the darks on top, allowing each layer to dry before the next.

Whatever medium you use, exploit the contrasts between warm and cool colours in order to convey the areas of light and dark within the hair. Hair picks up some reflected colour from its surroundings: you may see green/blue tones in blonde hair, hints of blue in black hair, and red or blonde in brown hair, depending on the light.

Sleek, shiny hair ▼

Here, the hair closely follows the contours of the scalp, but the artist has taken care to use different tones to convey the changes in plane. Note the blue highlights on the top of the head, for example, while the side nearest us is in shadow and is therefore darker in tone. A crimson purple oil paint serves as a mid-toned ground colour for the hair. The artist then applied a darker violet on top; with the addition of white, this same violet becomes a cool half light in the highlights in the back of the hair, behind the ear. The yellow background is reflected into the hair, so adding yellow ochre to the violet both lightens it and gives a complementary colour contrast which emphasizes the glossy quality of the hair.

Long flowing hair ▼

The key to drawing hair like this is to think of it not as a solid mass nor as a wild array of individual strands, but to aim for something in between: try to capture the general direction of hair growth without putting in every strand – and remember to look at how the hair follows the contours of the scalp. With charcoal and other monochrome media, you're limited to a small range of tones. Here, the mid tones are created by smudging the charcoal with the tip of a finger and the light tones by lifting off pigment with a torchon or kneaded eraser.

The hands and feet

Hands and feet are notoriously difficult to draw. One of the reasons for this is that people do not look at the hand or foot as a single unit; instead of being able to schematize the form into simple planes, they get too caught up in drawing details such as individual fingers and toes with too much prominence and tend to make them too big. Study them carefully until you are confident in your observational skills.

To find out about the basic anatomy, start by drawing your own hand or foot. Place your hand on paper, trace around the outline, and then 'fill in' the missing information – the veins, wrinkles of the knuckles and so on – using line. This gives a flat image. If you shine a light on your hand from the side, you will throw these details into relief; you can then describe the hand's surface using tone, which is much more interesting.

Schematize the shapes into simpler forms and define the planes. A clenched fist, for example, is a rough cube shape: there are four changes in plane on the back of the hand and fingers, plus two on the sides of the hand. Try to analyze the foot in the same way.

Then look at the surface anatomy – the veins, wrinkles, lines and folds. Flex your fingers or rotate your ankle and see how the tendons fan out. The tendons that you can see are the long tapering ends of the flexor muscles in the forearm (or, in the foot, the long tendons of the muscles running down the front of the lower leg). Look at how light catches the veins and wrinkles, but do not give them too much definition; if you make them too strong, they become too dominant and the sense of the form underneath gets lost.

The colour of hands and feet may also be different from other areas of the body. Hands are exposed to light, while feet are generally not exposed to the same degree. The skin's colour may also change because of its texture.

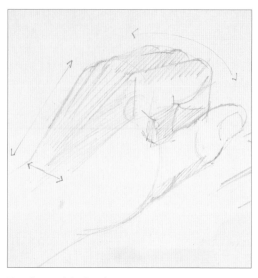

The planes of the hand ▲
Here we can see three main planes – the back of the hand, the side of the hand, and the section between the base of the fingers and the first knuckle. Tucked out of sight but implied, there are two further planes on the fingers – between the first and second knuckles, and the second knuckle and fingernail. Use tone to suggest the changes of plane: here, the brightest section is the side plane, with the back of the hand, and then the first segment of the fingers becoming progressively darker in tone as the planes turn away from the light source.

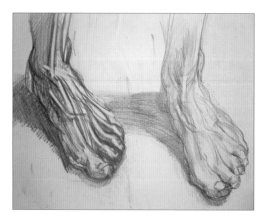

Visualizing forms under the surface ▲
Here you can see the muscles and tendons beneath the skin. The artist has used his knowledge of anatomy and studied the foot, shading in the raised and shadowed areas.

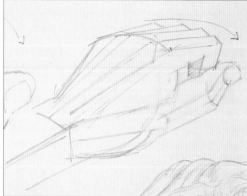

Underlying structure ▲
You may see the wrinkles and creases on your hand as a pattern of flowing lines, but don't forget that this is only the surface detail: what's more important is what lies underneath.

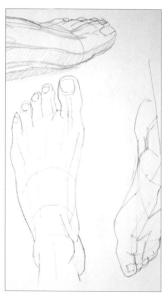

Cupped hands ▲

The different planes of the hands and fingers can be clearly seen, with subtle differences in tone (delineated with a flat brush) conveying the shape of the hands and the way the fingers curl around the coffee mug. The shadows cast on the mug by the fingers, as well as the highlights on the fingernails, reveal both the direction and the intensity of the light, while the dark, plain background allows the hands to stand out clearly. Note, too, how the amount of fingernail that is visible varies according to whether the fingers are angled towards or away from our view.

The planes of the feet ▲

These sketches show how the foot is broken down into a series of simplified planes. It is important to do this and to analyze the tones of the sections when you're depicting the foot, as it makes it easier for you to think of the whole unit and make it appear three-dimensional.

The palm and back of the hand ▲

The bony knuckles, tendons and veins are much in evidence on the back of the hand. Look at how they catch the light, as this will help you to convey their form and structure. Drawing the fleshy palm of the hand is a little more difficult, as there are fewer structures to guide you, but you will still see creases across the palm and around the knuckle joints that indicate the changing planes.

Creating light and shade ▲

In this charcoal sketch the highlights that convey the different planes of the feet and legs have been expertly created by wiping off charcoal with a kneaded eraser.

Colours and colour palettes

Although you may come across tubes of paint labelled 'flesh colour' in your art supplies store, in reality there is no such thing! Skin colour varies enormously from person to person and, of course, nobody's skin is a uniform colour all over. Take a look at your reflection in a mirror, or hold your hand up in front of you: you will soon see that, even on a relatively flat area, your skin colour actually contains many variations.

Things get even more complicated when we bring tone into the equation. Introducing tone is the main method artists use to make their subjects look solid and three-dimensional. A brightly lit area of skin will appear lighter in tone than one that is in shadow. In portraiture and figure painting, the transition from one plane to another – and hence from one tone to another – is often very subtle, and you need to be able to create a wide range of tones from every colour in your palette.

Mixing colours

Once you've selected your basic palette for a painting, it's a good idea to pre-mix a few tones, combining the same mixture of colours with different amounts of white (or water, in the case of watercolour) to achieve a light, mid and dark tone for each colour. You can then mix the subtle half tones around those main tones as required.

When mixing colours, use a large surface as a palette to prevent the colours from becoming muddied or jumbled. Try to begin and end with clearly defined tones and colours.

You can make any soft pastel lighter by adding white, but usually you will find such a huge range of ready-made colours in both soft pastels and coloured pencils that you do not necessarily need to darken or lighten them. However, it is worth experimenting to find out how different colours can mix optically on the paper.

Applying paint to the surface

However well you mix a colour on the palette, it will probably appear different when placed next to other colours on the support. If you are using a wet-into-wet technique (oils, acrylics, gouache and watercolour can all be used in this way), colours will mix into each other on the painting. You will need to be aware of this and work with a deft hand to prevent unwanted bleeds of colour.

If you are painting in layers and letting each colour dry, then the colour underneath will have an influence – a dark colour underneath will darken the top shade.

You can develop a painting in more opaque layers, putting thicker paint on thinner undercoats (the 'fat over lean' technique used in oil painting), then wiping off with a cloth or scraping through with a palette knife to create colour variations. Whatever technique you employ to apply paint, knowing how to use tonal values and warm and cool hues will help you control and evaluate the effects on the surface as they occur. The only way to know this is through practice.

Basic palette plus colour mixes for portrait opposite ▼
The basic palette shown below consists of the colours that the artist selected to make the portrait opposite. It is made up of just nine colours, which are shown down the left-hand side. Next to these colours you can see how each has been modified by combining it with one or more colours from the same basic palette. It's surprising how many different colours and tones you can create in this way.

Look at the painting and try to see where the different mixes occur. As you practise colour blending you will become adept at getting your tones right, even though at first it may seem a daunting element of portraiture. Just use scrap paper to experiment on before you colour your portrait.

Key

CGD	Chrome green deep	YO	Yellow ochre
TV	Terre verte	LY	Lemon yellow
BU	Burnt umber	U	Ultramarine
AC	Alizarin crimson	W	Titanium white
VR	Venetian red		

Pale skin, painted in oils ▼

In this oil portrait of a woman with very pale skin, the artist toned the canvas with a warm earth mix of Venetian red and yellow ochre, so that he could allow the same mix to show through for the hair and parts of the skin (in the forehead, for example). White was used to lighten the skin tones and crimson to create the darks, with the addition of blues to make bluish and purplish (cool and warm) grey where appropriate. (Note how the interplay of warm and cool tones in the flesh helps to create a sense of modelling.) Terre verte was used as a dark mid tone in the shadow under the chin. White was used as a pigment to give the flesh body and to lighten and make cooler the colour of the flesh.

The forehead has three tones – light in the middle (a warm hue – b), a mid-tone on the left (a warm hue – a) and a dark on the right in the shadow of the hair (c). In both the mid and dark tones, the coloured ground is visible through scumbled and wiped-off areas. The dark tone and colour of the hair in the shade (d) contrasts with a light ochre (e).

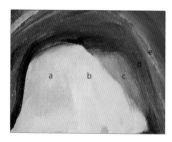

The background has a warm, dark grey (a) and a cooler, lighter colour (b), to contrast with the warm dark of the hair (c). The contrast helps focus the attention on the woman's face.

The jaw and neck are painted in two tones – a mid/light (a/c) and a dark (b). The mid-lights and dark tones are composed of green and brown/red contrasts to create a sense of volume.

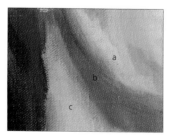

The side plane of the nose is a warm dark (a) composed of two hues. The profile of the nose is a cool, bright light (b). The whiteness of the light suggests natural daylight.

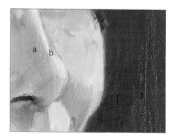

Assessing colours

When you're drawing or painting flesh, be it a portrait or a nude, you need to take into account two things: the actual colour of your model's skin and the effect of the light and surrounding colours on the model's skin. No two portrait situations are alike, so it's important that you make your observations with each model as carefully and as sympathetically as you can.

Beginners are often surprised to see how many colours artists discern (greens, blues, purples) in skin tones. It's impossible to be dogmatic about this, as it all depends on the particular lighting situation and the model, but often it's the interplay of warm and cool colours that makes a portrait really sparkle – so try using warm darks if you've got cool lights/mid tones – and vice versa.

Colour temperature

You also need to think about the relative warmth or coolness of colours. Colour temperature is important because of the way that warm colours appear to advance in a painting, while cool ones appear to recede. So in a portrait, areas that jut forwards, such as the nose, cheekbones and chin, have a contrast of warm and cool lights and mid tones. Highlights can be either warm or cool depending on the light source and the colour of the person's skin. You should have a warm and a cool version of each of the three primary colours – red, yellow and blue – in your palette, as this enables you to mix both warm and cool colours. Lemon yellow, for example, is cooler than cadmium yellow, while ultramarine blue is warmer than cerulean blue – so if you want to mix a cool green, mix it from a cool blue and yellow.

Basic palette plus colour mixes ▶
The palette for the opposite portrait is virtually identical to the one on page 56, with cadmium scarlet instead of the chrome green deep. Each colour has been modified by combining it with one or more colours from the same basic palette – but note how different some of the colours look on the coloured ground in the portrait.

Key
CS   Cadmium scarlet
TV   Terre verte
BU   Burnt umber
AC   Alizarin crimson
VR   Venetian red
YO   Yellow ochre
LY   Lemon yellow
U   Ultramarine
W   Titanium white

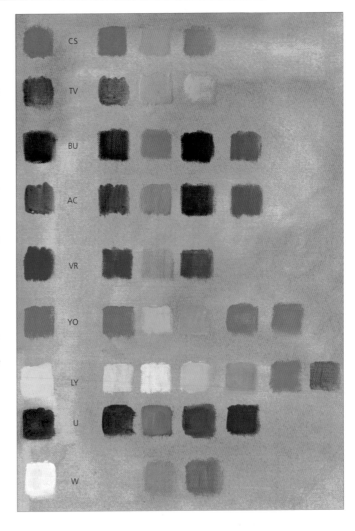

Dark skin, painted in oils ▼

This painting was also done on a toned ground; crimson was applied both thinly and thickly to create two different tones in the background. The thin ground colour on the right can also be seen as a mid tone in the face, giving the painting a liveliness that it might lack if the mid tones were painted in with more opaque colours. The basic skin tones are various mixtures of lots of yellow ochre, burnt umber and Venetian red with additions of white. The basic hair colour is a mixture of terre verte, ultramarine, burnt umber and crimson. Both warm and cool highlights can be seen, the warm highlight being a mixture of lemon yellow and white and the cool one a mixture of ultramarine with a hint of white.

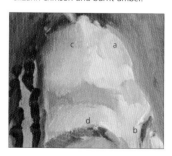

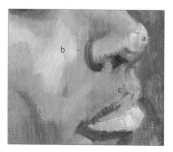

The forehead is in two planes – (a–b) and (c–d). (ab) has a range of cooler, light tones and (cd) a range of warmer mid and dark tones. The light tones are made from lemon yellow, white and a violet mixture. The warmer tones are a mixture of yellow ochre, alizarin crimson and burnt umber.

The end of the nose (a) has lights from pink, light blue, light green and lemon yellow and white. The objective was to have warm and cool lights next to each other. The cheek is a warm light (b) over a cooler green. A warm yellow ochre in the upper lip (c) overlaps the dark in the nostril.

Lemon yellow and white highlights (a) contrast with the mid tones at the end of the nose, which are composed of violet and Venetian red mixtures. The same highlight appears in the cheek (b), in contrast to a warm mid tone (yellow ochre) and a warm dark (Venetian red). Similar but slightly more subdued colours appear in the light side of the upper lip (c), with a warmer, darker Venetian red mixture on the opposite, darker side (d). Again, similar mixtures appear in the chin (e). The lips are a range of colours derived from alizarin crimson, with white and blue added to make light cooler violets mixed with ochre in the top lip. The bottom lip (f) is neat cadmium scarlet in the mid tone, with white for the lighter tone to show the fullness of the shape.

Light and shade

Light is a critical part of portraiture and figure painting: it is the contrast between light and shade, as the different planes of the head or body turn away from the light and into shadow, that enables artists to create a three-dimensional impression in their work. The four aspects of light that you need to consider are direction, quality (or intensity), colour and shadow.

Direction of light

First of all, think about where you are going to position your subject in relation to the light source. For beginners, the best direction is when the light is coming from just in front of and to one side of your subject – a set-up known as 'three-quarter lighting'. One side of your subject will be brightly lit, while the opposite side will be in shadow, making it much easier to distinguish the relative lights, darks and half tones. If the light is directly in front of your subject, it tends to 'flatten' the subject, making it harder to see the different planes and create that all-important sense of modelling. If the light is behind your subject it will create a 'halo' effect, again making it harder

to see the different planes. This is known as contre-jour lighting and is often used to good effect to create soft, romantic-looking images, so may be one of the many techniques you could work towards after you have become comfortable with working with three-quarter lighting.

Backlighting ▶
This technique can create lovely effects, silhouetting the figure, softening the colours and reducing the tonal contrasts. In this charming portrait of a mother and child, Geoff Marsters has exploited this kind of lighting to create a gentle and meditative mood that is entirely in keeping with the subject.

Quality of light

Light, both natural and artificial, varies considerably in quality or intensity. On a cloudy day, natural light may be very soft and diffused, whereas on a sunny summer's day it may be very bright and contrasty. Artificial light, too, can be used to cast a strong beam on to one specific place (think of a theatre spotlight), or diffused and spread over a wider area by being shone through a translucent material such as paper or fabric.

The time of day has an effect, too. Early in the morning and late in the afternoon, when the sun is relatively low in the sky, the light is at an oblique angle, which throws things into relief and creates good modelling; at midday, on the other hand, the sun is almost directly overhead, which tends to make things look flatter.

Midday light ◀
In Ian Sidaway's delightful portrait of a little girl looking at her reflection in a pool, the midday light is harsh and intense, bleaching out much of the detail on the child's hair and skin. The short shadow and still, unrippled water add to the sense of a sultry, hot noon. The darkening tones of grey on the stone surround of the pool give the image a sense of depth, while the warmth of the skin tones in the upper half of the image is balanced in the lower half by the rich, orangey-red of the goldfish, which contrasts with the cool blue dress.

Colour of light

Different kinds of light have distinct colour casts. Late afternoon sunlight, for example, often has a rich, warm glow, while fluorescent light has a pink or yellow tinge. Needless to say, these colour casts affect the colour of the objects that the light is illuminating.

Most of the time colour casts do not matter too much, as our eyes automatically adjust. It can, however, become a problem if you begin a painting in natural light and then, as the day progresses, turn on the artificial room lights to complete your work. If you've been using, say, cadmium yellow for highlights, those same highlights may appear much cooler under electric light, causing you to switch to the more acidic-looking lemon yellow. When you view your work in daylight again, the discrepancies will immediately become apparent. So be aware that this is a potential problem and try to keep the same kind of lighting throughout, even though this may mean that you need several painting sessions to complete your work.

Shadows

In addition to helping you create a three-dimensional impression, shadows can form an integral part of a painting in their own right and add a sense of drama to your work. Think, for example, of horror films, in which the shadow of the monster looms large on a wall before we ever see it in the flesh.

At the other end of the spectrum, dappled light playing on a figure can create constantly fluctuating shadows that suggest a soft, romantic mood. Even something as simple as the glazing bars on a window can cast shadows inside a room, which you can exploit as a compositional device. So although they're insubstantial, shadows are an important way of adding interest to your drawings and paintings.

Remember, however, that natural light is constantly changing and so shadows can change position, or even fade away completely, during the course of a painting session. It's a good idea to block them in, however lightly, at the start – or at least take a few photos to use as reference.

Shadow play ▼
The strong shadows cast on the wall behind the model add drama to this deceptively simple-looking, almost monochromatic portrait by Ian Sidaway.

Character and mood

Placing the flapping bird's wings so close to the edge of the frame enhances the sense of movement.

The use of complementary colours – here, red and green – is a good way of imparting a sense of vibrant energy to a painting.

The expression is one of sheer delight.

Exuberance ◄

In this painting by Ian Sidaway, the youthful exuberance of this little girl is evident from both her expression and from the energetic portrayal of the birds' flapping wings as they flutter upwards. The complementary colours – the red of the girl's sweater against the vivid green of the grass – also give the painting a sense of life and energy.

Capturing your subject's character and mood in a portrait involves bringing together many of the topics explored in the previous pages of this section, and is one of the most difficult and most rewarding challenges in portraiture. Individual features vary considerably from one person to another and of course you have to use all your technical skill as an artist to capture a good likeness. But portraiture involves much more than this: a good portrait should also capture something of the sitter's mood and personality. This will give the portrait meaning – for example, you could be making a statement about a particular time of the sitter's life or capturing an achievement or element of their personality that you (or the person commissioning the portrait) particularly admire.

Facial expressions, gestures and stance all play an important part in revealing a person's mood and, like individual facial features, these are things that you can capture through keen observation. Spend as much time as possible talking to your sitter and getting to know their expressions before you mark your paper. Laughter, frowns, open-eyed amazement – the muscle movements required to form these expressions all affect the surface form of the face. If your model is smiling, for example, the cheek muscles will pull the mouth wide; they also push up the lower eyelids, narrowing and sometimes completely closing the eyes. In a frown, on the other hand, the brows are pulled down, covering the upper eyelids and allowing the lower lids to drop. Look, too, at the teeth: generally we see much more of the upper teeth than the lower in a laughing expression or smile. In daily life we are very adept at detecting even slight muscular movements and reading the thoughts behind the resultant facial expressions. Combine these expressions with gestures – a shrug of the shoulders, upturned palms – and you can tell a lot about somebody's mood and temperament. Translating this into your artwork takes practice and patience but is one of the keys to successful portraiture.

Beyond this, you also need to make a series of aesthetic decisions. Some of these decisions are to do with composition – in other words, where you decide to place your subject in the picture space. In a conventional head-and-shoulders portrait, the figure is normally placed slightly off centre, with more space in front of them than behind; this creates a feeling of calm. If you feel a more confrontational mood is appropriate, however, you might choose a square format and a head-on view of the face, and place the head right in the centre of the picture space. Similarly, a profile view with the sitter's nose very close to the edge of the frame creates tension in the portrait.

You also need to think about what else to include in the portrait. Your choice of background will go some way to determining the mood of the portrait – so do you want a calm, pale background in a single colour or a lively, busy pattern? If you're painting a figure in a room setting, the items that you include can speak volumes about the sitter's interests and personality. Many great artists have taken this further, to include props or decor that are symbolic – think of the heraldic devices often present in portraits of aristocratic figures, for example. Every item included in the picture space is important in some way. While you may not be interested in symbolism, it is worth being selective about the props and background as they will affect the way your portrait is interpreted.

The way you light your subject affects the mood of the portrait. For a romantic portrait of a young girl, you might choose soft, diffused lighting or even position your sitter with window light

Sombre mood ▼

Portraiture involves more than simply achieving a likeness through correct observation of the shapes of noses, eyes and mouths. The best portraits give a feeling of atmosphere and express something of the sitter's character. In Karen Raney's *David* a sense of the sitter's melancholy and introspection is conveyed through the sombre colours of the clothing and background, and heavy, downward-sweeping brushmarks, as well as by the sitter's intense, yet inward-looking, gaze. The sitter seems to make direct eye contact with the observer, which is an important method by which a painting 'draws in' the viewer and encourages them to ask questions about the sitter's mood, the meaning of the painting, and about the feelings the artist wanted to evoke. Unlike the portrait on the opposite page, this painting evokes feelings of discomfort and curiosity.

Long, downward-dragging brushstrokes and the cool, muted colour of the background enhance the sense of melancholy.

The subdued expression and the direct, almost challenging, gaze say much about the sitter's mood.

The dark, blue-grey clothing matches the sitter's sombre mood.

coming from directly behind her, so that the colours are muted and detail is subdued. Harsh, strongly directional light can accentuate details such as wrinkles and expression lines in the face, which can work for some dynamic, 'action' or character portraits but may be too unflattering or stark for other subjects.

Finally, there are decisions to be made about your colour palette and the way you apply the paint. You might think that you just paint the colours that you see, but colour can be critical in evoking a mood so choose the spectrum carefully. Bright, hot shades generally create a lively mood, whereas sombre, muted shades give the opposite effect. Pick up on the colours that your sitter is wearing and use them elsewhere in the painting to reflect their mood. Of course, you can change the colours of the clothing to suit the mood of your portrait, if you wish.

Your brush and pencil strokes, too, can affect the atmosphere of the drawing or painting. Lively, vigorous strokes and thick, impasto work can create a feeling of energy, while soft washes, in which the brushstrokes are not really visible, can evoke a mood of calm. Generally, getting to know your sitter's personality will help you to decide the colours, techniques and strokes that will suit your portrait best and create an appropriate mood.

Gallery

From self portraits and studies of individuals to groups of two or more people in more complicated settings, this section features portraits in varying styles and media. Study them carefully for ideas and approaches that you can apply in your own work – and don't be tempted to dismiss something simply because it doesn't suit your own personal taste. You can learn as much from things you dislike as from things you enjoy.

Painting in monochrome ▶
In this unusual oil painting, *Self Portrait at 32 Years*, Gerald Cains has ruled out colour altogether, while using highly expressive brushwork. The effect is extraordinarily powerful. It can be a useful discipline to work in monochrome, as it helps you to concentrate on composition and tonal balance without the distraction of colour.

Plain background ▼
Ian Sidaway's initial work on *Lydia and Alice* was made using wet-into-wet washes and the features were then sharpened using wet on dry. Gum arabic was used in many of the mixes. This has the effect not only of intensifying the colour but also of making the washes more transparent. Gum arabic also makes dry paint soluble if it is re-wet, so you can wash off dry paint and make any necessary corrections – a very useful facility when painting portraits. The background is deliberately omitted to focus attention on the sitters.

Limited palette ▲

Working over a careful pencil drawing using wet-on-dry washes in *Sisters*, Ian Sidaway achieved harmony by using a limited range of colours. Interestingly, the two girls were painted at different times. The poses were carefully chosen so that the figures could be combined on the support. If you are doing a portrait from a photograph, the background elements can be altered or added to as you work. Alternatively, if you are painting someone in their environment, work on the background and setting at the same time as the figure to avoid the portrait looking as if it has simply been pasted in.

Form through colour ▶

As a general rule, the colours in shadows are cooler – that is, bluer or greener – than those in the highlight areas, and Gerry Baptist has skilfully exploited this warm/cool contrast to give solidity to the head in his acrylic *Self Portrait*. Note, too, how the different planes within the head are painted using simple blocks of colour rather than subtle transitions from one tone to the next – an approach that requires bold, confident brushwork. Although all the colours are quite heightened, they are nevertheless based on the actual colours of flesh, and the picture is successful in its own terms.

▶

Startling realism ▶
This portrait demonstrates the versatility
of the pencil to perfection. Here the
effect is almost photographic in its
minute attention to detail and texture,
and its subtle gradations of tone.

Outdoor setting ◀
Light is an important element in Timothy Easton's *The
Summer Read* and he has described the sitter more by
posture, clothing and general shape than by detailed
depiction of the features. With careful observation you will
find that it is perfectly possible to paint a recognizable
likeness without showing the face at all, just as you often
recognize a familar person from a distance by their posture.
The square format might seem a slightly unusual choice for a
portrait, but here the setting is as important as the sitter, who
occupies only a relatively small proportion of the picture
space. The table and chair virtually fill the entire width of
the picture space, with the flower border providing both
background colour and detail and a visual 'full stop'. The
viewer's eye is led around the image in a circular movement
from the sitter's head, around the table and back again.

Expressive use of watercolour ▶

At first sight, Ken Paine's expressive portrait *Amelia* might well be mistaken for an oil painting, but in fact it is watercolour with the addition of Chinese white. The artist made no initial pencil drawing, but started immediately with a brush and thin paint, gradually increasing the amount of white. The background is reduced to a minimum, very loosely painted, thus concentrating attention on the face.

Figure groups ▼

In landscape painting, a distant figure or group of figures is often introduced as a colour accent or an additional focus for the eye, but where figures form the whole subject, as in Sally Strand's charming *Crab Catch*, it is necessary to find ways of relating them to one another. Like many such compositions, this has an element of storytelling, with the boys sharing a common interest, but the artist has also used clever pictorial devices, notably the shapes and colours of the towel and bucket, to create a strong link between the two figures. The boys' absorbed expressions, and the fact that they are facing one another, also help to direct our attention to the centre of the scene – the contents of the bucket.

▶

Portrait of a group ▲

Figure groups are not the easiest of subjects to tackle in watercolour, as it is not possible to make extensive corrections, but Trevor Chamberlain's *Still-life Session at the Seed Warehouse* shows that in skilled hands there is nothing the medium cannot do. Each brushstroke has been placed with care and, although the artist has worked largely wet into wet, he has controlled the paint so that it has not spread randomly over the surface. The result it a fresh, lively painting with a wonderfully spontaneous feel. If you're attempting a subject like this, spend as much time as you can observing the scene before you commit brush to paper. Even though it may seem at first glance as though your subjects are continually moving, you'll find that when people are engrossed in an activity like this, they tend to revert to the same positions and postures; once you've recognized the essentials of each individual's 'pose', you'll find it much easier to set them down on paper.

Quick, expressive portrait in ink ▶

Pen and ink can achieve intricate and elaborate effects, but it is also a lovely medium for rapid line drawings. In this figure study *Girl in an Armchair*, Ted Gould has caught the essentials of the pose in a few pen strokes, sometimes superimposing lines where the first drawing was incorrect or where it needed clarifying.

Composing a figure study ▶

In a figure painting you must decide where to place the figure, whether or not to crop part of it, and whether you need to introduce other elements as a balance. Peter Clossick's *Helen Seated* gives the impression of spontaneity because it is so boldly and thickly painted, but it is carefully composed, with the diagonal thrust of the figure balanced by verticals and opposing diagonals in the background.

Painting children ▲

Painting an adult engaged in some typical pursuit can enhance your interpretation, but in the case of children it is a question of necessity; they seldom remain still for long, added to which they look stiff and self-conscious when artificially posed. In her delightful, light-suffused study of *Samantha and Alexis* (oil) Karen Raney has worked rapidly to capture a moment of communication between her two young subjects.

Form and brushwork ▶

As the human face and head are complex and difficult to paint, even before you have considered how to achieve a likeness of the sitter, there is a tendency to draw lines with a small brush. This is seldom satisfactory, however, as hard lines can destroy the form. In Ted Gould's *Sue* (oil), the features, although perfectly convincing, are described with the minimum of detail and no use of line, and the face, hair and clothing are built up with broad directional brushwork.

Using the paper colour ▶
In portraiture and figure work it is particularly important to choose the right colour of paper, especially if you intend to leave areas of it uncovered, as in Ken Paine's superb *Young Girl*. The painting is almost monochromatic, with the lights and darks built up from the mid-tone of the brown paper.

Freestyle in pen ▲
A fine fibre-tipped pen has been used for this self-portrait by Hazel Harrison, and the forms have been constructed in a spontaneous way, with the pen moving freely over the paper.

Symmetry ◀
One of the so-called 'rules' of composition is to avoid symmetry, but rules are made to be broken and Elizabeth Moore has deliberately flouted them in this unnamed portrait, to produce an oil painting that almost has the quality of an icon.

Building tonal structure ▶
Ken Paine exploits the directness and expressive qualities of pastel in his *Head of a Young Woman*. He works with great rapidity, usually beginning by building up the tonal structure with a monochrome "underpainting" made with broad strokes of short lengths of pastel. Linear definition and bright colour accents are left until the final stages. The coloured paper is still visible in areas.

Quick sketches

The only way to get better at drawing and painting is to practise, so try to get into the habit of sketching every day. All you need is a small notebook and a pen or pencil. Carry them around with you wherever you go and do a bit of 'people watching' when you've got a few minutes to spare – on the train or bus to work, in a café during your lunch break, even when you're waiting to collect the kids from school.

Before you embark on really detailed portraits, start by practising getting the features in the right places. Draw heads from different angles so that you get used to how the relative positions of the features change when the head is tilted.

Sketch profiles as well as faces viewed from directly in front and look at where the nose breaks the line of the cheek and at how much of the eye on the far side of the face is visible. Look for different planes within the head and face. Ask friends or family members to pose for you so that you get used to drawing lots of different people. You'll be amazed at how quickly your powers of observation improve.

In the sketches shown on these two pages, the construction lines have been exaggerated so that they show up more clearly. In your own sketches, use very light lines and marks. You can cover or erase these as your artwork develops.

Soft pastel, 15 minutes ▶
The central axis of the face runs down through the nose, but because the sitter's head is turned slightly to one side, we can see more on one side of this line than on the other. The features are contained within an inverted triangle that runs from the outer corners of the eyes to the centre of the lips (the philtrum), while the centre of the eye is in line with the outer corner of the mouth.

Dip pen and ink, 15 minutes ▲
As ink is indelible and virtually impossible to cover up if you make a mistake, the artist began by putting in tiny dots to mark the outer corners of the eyes and mouth and the nostrils. Note how large the area between the nose and chin appears in relation to the head as a whole when the head is tilted upwards like this.

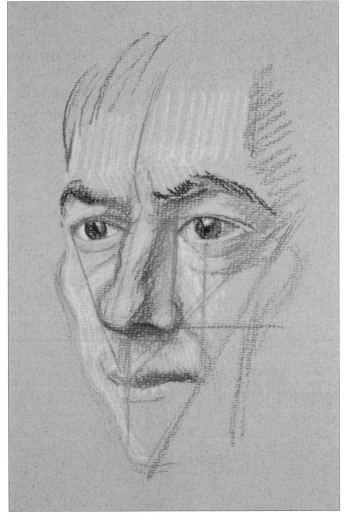

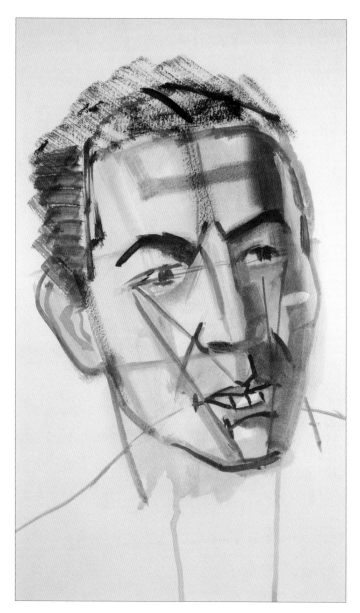

Charcoal, 10 minutes ▲
In this sketch the artist began by wiping the side of a stick of charcoal over the paper to create a broad area of tone, which he then softened by gently wiping with a paper tissue. On top of the basic 'egg' shape of the head, he has indicated the major planes of the face and cranium, as well as the hairline. Although this is intended as nothing more than an exercise in observation, making sketches like this is a good way of training yourself to look for the different planes of the head. Gradually, you'll find that you can use tone, rather than line, to express the transition from one plane to the next.

Acrylic, 15 minutes ▲
Here the artist roughly blocked in the shape of the face in yellow ochre paint to approximate to the skin tones, before adding the construction lines in a darker tone. Note how he established the underlying shape of the cranium before roughly scumbling on colour for the hair. He has also roughly marked in the major planes of the forehead and the side of the face, and applied a slightly darker tone to the shaded side of the sitter's face to create some sense of modelling.

▶

Make quick sketches – say 15 to 30 minutes – to train your eye to see subtle differences in tone in people's faces as the different planes turn towards or away from the light source. Look to see where the deepest shadows and the brightest highlights fall, and then try to assess the mid tones in between. Remember that there are many minor planes within the face and head, as well as major planes such as the sides of the nose. These minor planes – high or recessed cheekbones, furrows in the brow – are often what help you to capture the individuality of your sitter.

The way that you convey tone depends, of course, on the medium in which you're working. In pencil or pen and ink, you can use hatching or cross-hatching, making your hatching lines close together for dark tones and spacing them further apart for lighter tones. In charcoal and soft pastel you can create a broad area of tone by using the side of the stick, pressing hard for a very dark tone and applying less pressure for lighter areas – and of course in both these media you can wipe off pigment with a soft tissue or torchon to create lighter tones.

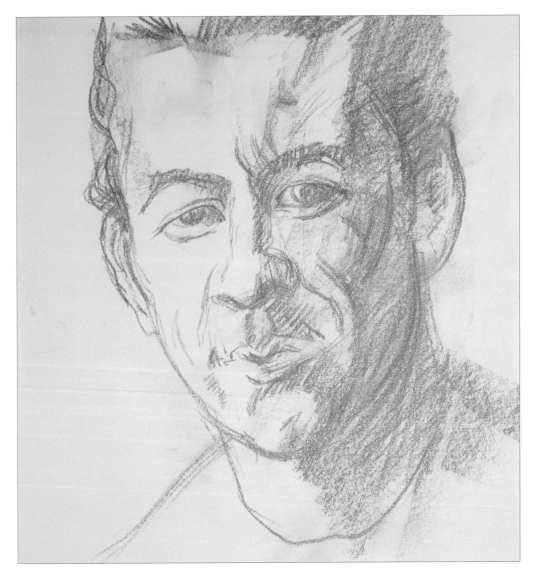

In watercolour, you can build up tones gradually, applying several layers of paint until you get the effect you want. In oils and acrylics, depending on the texture you want to create, you can either scumble the paint on quite roughly or apply it as a thin wash.

Remember that the colour of the support can play an important role, too. When working in soft pastels, artists often choose a coloured paper, while in oil and acrylic portraits it is accepted practice to tone the ground before you begin to paint. Select a colour that approximates to the mid tones in your subject, so that you can allow the colour of the ground to show through in the portrait. In watercolour sketches and drawings, you can allow the white of the paper to stand for the very brightest highlights. Letting the paper work for you in this way both speeds up the process and gives a feeling of spontaneity and light to your work.

Conté stick, 20 minutes ◄
Here, the sitter was lit very strongly from one side. On this side of the face, a few faint mid-tone lines convey the creases in the skin around the mouth and nose. On the shaded side of the face the artist created mid and dark tones in two ways: he hatched in small, precise areas such as the nose using the tip and the sharp edge of the square Conté stick and blocked in broad areas on the side of the face and neck with the side of the stick.

Acrylics, 15 minutes ◄
Using just two or three colours, the artist has created a wide range of tones. The white paper stands for the brightest highlights, while the lighter mid tones of the skin are a wash of yellow ochre. The mid and dark tones are varying dilutions of burnt umber, applied as a thin wash in some places and scumbled on more thickly and vigorously in the deep shadows on the side of the face and neck. Applying the paint with a flat brush has created a wide range of marks, from fine lines made by holding the brush almost vertically and using the tip, to broad areas of wash, as on the forehead.

Pastel pencil, 10–15 minutes ▲
In this sketch the buff-coloured pastel paper stands for the mid tones, with white pencil hatching being used for the highlights on the side of the face and neck and purple hatching for the shadows. Note how the density of the hatching varies depending on the depth of tone required, with lines drawn close together in the darkest areas (on the far side of the face and under the nose, for example) and spaced more widely in the hair.

The eyes, step by step

Before you embark on full-scale portraits, why not try making some small, quick sketches of individual features such as the eyes or mouth? Homing in on details like this is a great way of sharpening your powers of observation as it forces you to look really hard at shapes and tones. There are lots of undulations across the surface of the face that reveal the shape of the skull beneath and, whatever medium you work in, it's vital that you vary your flesh tones in order to convey these changes in surface form.

Structures such as the eyes and ears are particularly intricate and contain lots of tiny highlight and shadow areas that you need to render with great care. In addition to light and dark tones, remember to use both warm and cool mixes. Warm colours appear to advance,

while cool ones recede – and you can exploit this fact to make prominent features such as the nose come forward in the painting.

This demonstration was made in watercolour, which, because of its natural translucency, is a lovely medium for painting the reflective, liquid surface of the eye. Take care not to lose the white of the paper, as this is the lightest tone. The painting took about 45 minutes to complete.

Materials

- *Rough watercolour paper*
- *Watercolour paints: yellow ochre, alizarin crimson, ultramarine blue, burnt umber, cadmium red, cerulean blue*
- *Brushes: Fine round, large flat*
- *Kitchen paper*

The pose

A three-quarter profile was chosen for this sketch, as both eyes are visible and it gives you the chance to explore the way the eyes relate to the nose. Note how, from this angle, the bridge of the nose partially obscures the far eye.

1 Lightly brush the area of paper that you are going to use with clean water so that you can work wet into wet, without creating any hard-edged marks in the early stages. Establish the axis of the eyes and, using a fine brush, dot in the outer corners of the eyes to mark their position. Using a pale mix of yellow ochre and alizarin crimson, outline the almond shape of the eyes, the eyebrows and the line of the nose.

2 Using a grey mix of yellow ochre and ultramarine and short, spiky brush marks, paint in the eyebrows. Using a stronger version of the yellow ochre and alizarin mix, strengthen the line of the upper lids. Add a little ultramarine to the mix and, working wet into wet, put in the deep, recessed shadow around the inner corner of the near eye. Paint the irises using both burnt umber and ultramarine blue as appropriate, remembering to leave the white of the paper for the highlights.

3 Using a very dilute mix of cadmium red, paint the lower lids, leaving the edges white where they catch the light. Paint the dark shadows under and around the inner edge of the near eye in the yellow ochre and alizarin crimson mix. Mix a warm orangey red from yellow ochre and cadmium red and apply it over the upper edge of the upper lids. Use the same colour for the line of the nose.

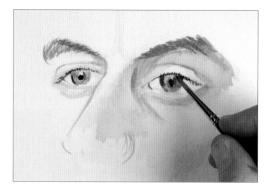

4 Brush the pale cadmium red and yellow ochre mix over the rounded socket of the near eye. Brush clean water over the cheek under the near eye, then drop the pale cadmium red and yellow ochre mix into it, wet into wet. Darken the yellow ochre and alizarin mix by adding ultramarine blue, then paint the line of the eyelashes, using short, spiky brush marks and dots. Use the same colour in the eyebrows.

5 For the shadow in the white of the eye, use a very pale cerulean blue. Dab it off almost immediately with kitchen paper so that there's only a tiny hint of colour. Apply a warm mix of yellow ochre and a little cadmium red to the far cheek, using a slightly darker version of the mix just under the eye. Using the yellow ochre, alizarin crimson and ultramarine mix from Step 2, model the shaded side of the nose, leaving the bridge of the nose (which is in the light) untouched.

6 Put in the nostrils with a deep cadmium red. Using a large flat brush, wash the yellow ochre and cadmium red mix over the near cheek and the warm areas on the side of the nose, modulating the blue mix applied in Step 5 and remembering to leave the highlights white.

The finished sketch
This sketch clearly shows the eyeballs as spherical forms in deep, recessed sockets. Note how much larger the sitter's left eye is than his right; although we tend to assume that both eyes are the same size and shape, they are often asymmetrical. Allowing the white of the paper to stand for the brightest highlights gives this little study real life and sparkle.

The ear, step by step

Just like any other human feature, ears can vary considerably from one person to another. Some people have long earlobes, while others have short ones. Some people have ears that stick out while others have ears that lie flat, close to the skull. The basic structure is the same in everyone, however – an outer and an inner fold, known respectively as the helix and antihelix, which lead around in a curve to the central cavity, or concha. Once you're aware of this structure, you're aware of what to look for. As always, it's the contrast between light and dark tones, and warm and cool colours, that gives a sense of form to drawings and paintings of the ear. Look to see where light catches the bony cartilage of the helix and antihelix and at where darker tones indicate the recessed concha, or central cavity.

This demonstration was done in acrylic paint, which looks slightly darker when it is dry than when it is wet – so always wait until the paint is dry before

deciding if you need to adjust the tones. Because acrylic paint is opaque, you can put down dark tones first and then paint highlights on top if you wish, in the same way that you can apply oil

paints or oil pastels. If you were to attempt the same sketch in watercolour, you would have to work from light to dark instead. This sketch took about 45 minutes to complete.

Materials
- *Paper*
- *Acrylic paints: yellow ochre, white, brown oxide, alizarin crimson, cadmium red, vermilion, lemon yellow*
- *Brushes: medium filbert, fine filbert*
- *Stay-wet acrylic palette*

The pose
In this profile view you can clearly see the structure of the ear – the outer fold, or helix, which runs around the outer edge and into the central cavity known as the concha, the antihelix (the inner fold) and the fossa (the 'ditch' or groove between the helix and antihelix).

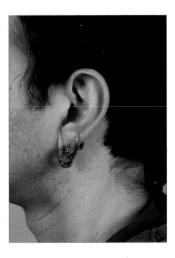

1 Mix yellow ochre and white to form a basic flesh tone and, using a medium filbert brush, scumble it on to the support. Using a fine filbert brush and brown oxide acrylic paint, map in the dark tones on the inside of the ear, looking at the shapes of the shadows in the recesses of the ear.

2 Using a cool purple mix of white, brown oxide and alizarin crimson, put in the curves of the helix and antihelix. Use brown oxide to establish the curve of the outer ear.

3 Add a little ultramarine to the brown oxide and, using vigorous vertical brushstrokes, begin putting in the hair around the ear. Using the same mix, fill in the cool shadows inside the ear; already you are beginning to develop a good sense of the three-dimensional structure.

4 Build up texture in the hair, using brown oxide for the darkest parts and the ultramarine and brown oxide mix for the cooler shadows. 'Draw' the earrings in ultramarine blue. Using varying mixes of brown oxide, alizarin crimson and yellow ochre, put in the flesh tones and adjust the tones inside the ear, adding more alizarin for the area under the ear.

5 Using the same cool purple mix that you used inside the ear, put in the shadow around the jawline. Use pure white to paint the tiny highlights on the earrings and on the inside of the ear.

6 Soften any shadow areas that are too deep, and scumble more colour into the hair, making sure that your brushstrokes follow the direction of the hair growth.

The finished sketch
The contrast between light and dark tones and warm and cool colours has created a strong, three-dimensional sketch. Note, too, how the ear casts shadows on the hair and the nape of the neck, indicating that it does not lie flat against the skull.

The hands, step by step

Hands can be such an expressive part of a portrait that it is well worth devoting lots of time to practising drawing them. The sketch on these two pages took just under an hour to complete and the artist spent as much time measuring and checking as he did drawing.

Hands are quite complicated forms and beginners are often very nervous of even attempting them, but the trick is to start by searching out the overall shape instead of laboriously drawing each finger in turn. When two hands are linked together, as in this sketch, it is often better to think of them as a single form rather than two separate shapes.

When you start putting in details such as creases and wrinkles in the skin, decide which ones are most important structurally and aim for a general impression rather than slavishly copying every single line. If you put in too much of this superficial detail, it can easily detract from the overall shape and structure and dominate the sketch, thus destroying the three-dimensional illusion that you've built up.

Finally – although it sounds obvious – make sure you put in the right number of fingers and that each finger has the correct number of joints!

Materials
- Good-quality drawing paper
- Red Conté stick

The pose
Here we see each hand from a different angle. The sitter's left hand is angled away from us and is therefore slightly foreshortened: the back of this hand looks a lot shorter than the fingers. Note how the shapes of the fingernails appear to change depending on whether they are angled towards or away from our view.

1 Using a red Conté stick, put in faint guidelines to establish the outer limits of the composition. Try to think of the hands as a single unit and start by establishing where the different planes lie. Carefully measure the individual fingers and look at where each one sits in relation to its neighbour.

2 Using light hatching, put in some of the shadow on the underside of the sitter's left arm and wrist. (At this stage, the shading is intended mainly to indicate the planes of the arms, so don't do too much detail.) Begin to delineate the individual fingers, using a light, circular motion around the joints to imply their rounded form.

3 Continue delineating the fingers, observing carefully the shapes of the individual fingernails and where the joints occur. You can also begin putting in some of the more important creases and wrinkles in the fingers. Then put in the shadows on the little finger of the left hand. Using the side of the Conté stick, lightly block in the background.

4 Continue working on the linear detail and the shading on the back of the hand and fingers, using the tip of the Conté stick. (Note how much difference in tone there is.) Try to keep the whole drawing moving along at the same pace, rather than concentrating on one area at the expense of the rest.

5 Adjust the tones as necessary over the drawing as a whole, using the side of the stick to block in large, dark areas such as the jeans and the tip for crisp, sharp detailing.

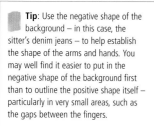
Tip: Use the negative shape of the background – in this case, the sitter's denim jeans – to help establish the shape of the arms and hands. You may well find it easier to put in the negative shape of the background first than to outline the positive shape itself – particularly in very small areas, such as the gaps between the fingers.

The finished sketch
In this sketch the artist has used a combination of sharp, linear detailing (in the fingers and hatched shadows) and broad, sweeping areas of mid and dark tone, allowing the white of the paper to stand for the brightest highlights. He has included just enough of the background to provide a context for the sketch and make it clear that the sitter's hands are resting, with relaxed muscles, on a solid surface.

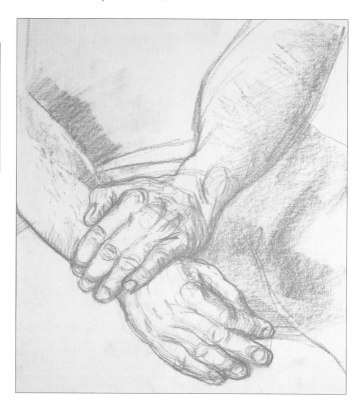

Head-and-shoulders portrait in watercolour

Painting a portrait from life for the first time can be a daunting prospect. Not only do you have the technical aspects to deal with, but you are working with a live model, who will almost certainly fidget and demand to see what you are doing. Before you embark on your first portrait session, practise drawing and painting from photographs to build up your skills and confidence.

This project is done in watercolour, which is the medium of choice for a great number of leisure painters. It is a wonderful medium for painting skin tones, as you can gradually build up layers of soft washes, allowing the paint to merge wet into wet to create soft-edged transitions from one tone to another. Put a lot of care into your underdrawing. If you can get the facial features in the right place and know where the main areas of light and shade are going to be, then you are well on the way to success.

Finally, don't try to do too much. Details like clothing are relatively unimportant in a head-and-shoulders portrait. Instead, try to capture your subject's mood and personality by concentrating on the eyes and expression.

The pose

If you are new to portraiture or to painting with a model rather than from a photograph, a simple pose, with the model looking directly at you, is probably the best way to begin. The eyes are the key to a good portrait, and this pose shows a strong, direct gaze that attracts the attention.

Place a strong light to one side of the model, as it will cast an obvious shadow on the back wall and make it easier for you to assess areas of light and shade on the face, which will assist you with your modelling work. Most importantly, make sure your model is seated comfortably, with good support for her back and arms, as she will have to hold the same pose for some time. You may find it helpful to take photographs for reference so that you can work from these once the model has left.

Select a plain background that does not draw attention away from your subject. You can rig up plain drapes behind the model to achieve this, and choose colours that suit the mood of the portrait or complement the model's skin or hair colour.

Materials

- *HB pencil*
- *300gsm (140lb) HP watercolour paper, pre-stretched*
- *Watercolour paints: light red, yellow ochre, alizarin crimson, sap green, sepia tone, neutral tint, ultramarine blue, ultramarine violet, cobalt blue, burnt umber, cadmium orange, cadmium red*
- *Brushes: large round, medium round, fine round*

> **Tips:**
> • From time to time, look at your drawing in a mirror. This often makes it easier to assess if you have got the proportions and position of the features right. Also hold your drawing board at arm's length, with the drawing vertical, to check the perspective. When you work with the drawing board flat, the perspective sometimes becomes distorted.
> • Over the course of a portrait session, you will probably find that your model will drift off into a daydream, and the eyelids and facial muscles droop, creating a bored, sullen-looking expression. If this happens, ask your sitter to redirect his or her gaze towards you (ideally without moving the head!); this immediately resolves the problem.

1 Using an HB pencil, lightly sketch your subject, putting in faint construction lines as a guide to help you check that the features are accurately positioned.

Resist the temptation to start the face by drawing an outline. If you do this, the chances are that you will find you haven't allowed yourself enough space for the features. Start by working out the relative sizes and positions of the features and then worry about the outline overall.

It is always a good idea to put in faint pencil guidelines – a line down through the central axis of the face and lines across to mark the positions of the eyes, nose and mouth. As a general rule, the eyes are level with the ear tips and approximately halfway down the face. The nose is roughly halfway between the eyes and the base of the chin. The mouth is usually less than halfway between the nose and chin. The sitter in this portrait appears at first glance to have a very symmetrical face, but be aware that most faces are not exactly symmetrical and look carefully at the differences between the left and right side.

2 Begin to put in some indication of the pattern in the model's blouse. You do not need to make it detailed.

3 Mix light red and yellow ochre to make the first warm but pale flesh tone. Using a medium round brush, wash this mixture over the face, neck and forearms, avoiding the eyes and leaving a few gaps for highlights. This is just the base colour for the flesh. It will look a little strange at this stage, but you will add more tones and colours later on.

4 You have to work quickly at this stage to avoid the wash drying and forming hard edges. While the first wash is still damp, add more pigment and a little alizarin crimson to the first skin tone and paint the shadowed side of the face to give some modelling. Add more alizarin crimson to the mixture and paint the lips. Leave to dry.

5 Touch a little very dilute alizarin crimson on to the cheeks and some very pale sap green into the dark, shaded side of the face. Mix a warm, rich brown from sepia tone and neutral tint and start to paint the hair, leaving some highlight areas and the parting line on the top of the head completely free of paint.

6 Mix a very pale blue from ultramarine blue and a hint of ultramarine violet. See where the fabric in the blouse creases, causing shadows. Using a fine round brush, paint these creases in the pale blue mixture.

7 Go back to the hair colour mixture used in Step 5 and put a second layer of colour on the darker areas of hair. Paint the eyebrows and carefully outline the eyes in the same dark brown mixture.

8 Mix a very light green from yellow ochre with a little sap green and, using a fine round brush, paint in the irises, leaving a white space for the highlight where light is reflected in the eye. Strengthen the shadows on the side of the face and neck with a pale mixture of light red and a little sap green.

9 Use the same shadow colour to paint along the edge of the nose. This helps to separate the nose from the cheeks and make it look three-dimensional. Mix ultramarine violet with sepia tone and paint the pupils of the eyes, taking care not to go over on to the whites.

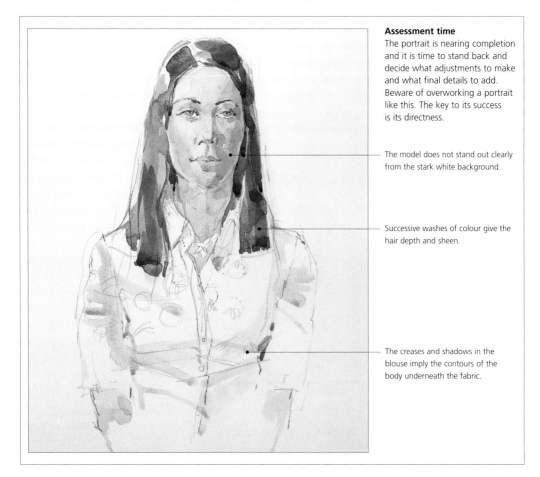

Assessment time
The portrait is nearing completion and it is time to stand back and decide what adjustments to make and what final details to add. Beware of overworking a portrait like this. The key to its success is its directness.

The model does not stand out clearly from the stark white background.

Successive washes of colour give the hair depth and sheen.

The creases and shadows in the blouse imply the contours of the body underneath the fabric.

▶

10 Mix a dark green from sap green, cobalt blue and burnt umber. Using a large round brush, carefully wash this mixture over the background, taking care not to allow any of the paint to spill over on to the figure. (You may find it easier to switch to a smaller brush to cut in around the figure.)

11 While the background wash is still damp, add a little more pigment to the green mixture and brush in the shadow of the girl's head. Mix an orangey-red from cadmium orange and cadmium red and, using a fine round brush, start putting in some of the detail on the girl's blouse.

12 Continue building up some indication of the pattern on the girl's blouse, using the orangey-red mixture from Step 11, along with ultramarine blue and sap green.

Tip: Don't try to replicate the pattern exactly: it will take far too long and will change the emphasis of the painting from the girl's face to her clothing. A general indication of the pattern and colours is sufficient. The face should always be the most noticeable part of any portrait.

The finished painting
This is a sensitive, yet loosely painted portrait that captures the model's features and mood perfectly. It succeeds largely because its main focus, and the most detailed brushwork, is on the girl's eyes and pensive expression. Careful attention to the shadow areas has helped to give shape to the face and separate the model from the plain-coloured background.

Although the hair is loosely painted, the tonal variations within it create a sense of volume.

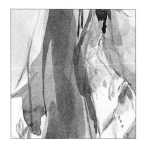

The detailed painting of the eyes and mouth helps to reveal the model's mood and character.

In reality, the pattern on the blouse is much more detailed than this, but a more accurate rendition would have drawn attention away from the girl's face.

The shadow on the wall helps to separate the model from the background and gives the image more depth.

Head-and-shoulders portrait in acrylics

The surroundings and the clothing in this head-and-shoulders portrait have been kept deliberately simple in order to give you an opportunity to practise painting skin tones.

You might think it would make life very simple for artists if there was a ready-mixed skin colour that could be used in all circumstances. However, although you may come across a so-called 'flesh tone' in some paint manufacturers' catalogues, it cannot cope with the sheer variety of skin tones that you are actually likely to encounter.

Even in models with the most flawless of complexions, the skin will not be a uniform colour in all areas. The actual colour (particularly in fair-skinned individuals) can vary dramatically from one part of the subject to another: the cheeks, for example, often look redder than the forehead or chin simply because the blood vessels are closer to the surface. And, just as with any other subject, you need to use different tones to make your subject look three-dimensional. To understand this, look at black-and-white magazine photographs of models

with good bone structure: note how the cheekbones cast a shadow on the lower face. Even though (thanks to make-up) the skin colour may be virtually the same all over the face, in strong light there may be differences in tone.

You also need to think about colour temperature: using cool colours for the shadows and warmer ones for the lit areas is a good way of showing how the light falls on your model. Although cool blues and purples might seem strange colours to use for painting skin, it is surprising how using them with warmer colours can bring a portrait to life.

The same principles of colour temperature also apply to the light that illuminates your subject. Although we are generally unaware of the differences, the colour of sunlight is not as warm as, say, artificial tungsten lighting. It's hard to be precise about the colours you should use for painting skin tones, as the permutations are almost infinite, so the best advice is simply to paint what you can actually observe rather than what you think is the right colour.

Materials
- Board primed with acrylic gesso
- B pencil
- Acrylic paints: Turner's yellow, cadmium red, titanium white, burnt umber, cadmium yellow, lamp black, phthalocyanine blue, alizarin crimson, yellow ochre
- Brushes: large flat, medium flat, small flat

The pose
A three-quarters pose with the light coming from one side, as here, is generally more interesting to paint than a head-on pose, as it allows you to have one side of the face in shadow, thus creating modelling on the facial features. It also means that the sitter can look directly at you, which generally makes for a more dramatic portrait. The lighting also creates highlights in the model's dark eyes, which always helps to bring a portrait to life. Although this model was sitting in front of a very busy background, the artist chose to simplify it to a uniform background colour in the finished portrait to avoid drawing attention away from the face. He also placed more space on the side of the picture space towards which the model is facing: it is generally accepted that this balance of composition creates a more comfortable, and less confrontational, portrait.

1 Using a B pencil, lightly sketch your subject, indicating the fall of the hair, the facial features and the areas of shadow. Put in as much detail as you wish; it is particularly important to get the size and position of the facial features right.

2 Mix a light flesh tone from Turner's yellow, cadmium red and titanium white. Using a medium flat brush, block in the face and neck, adding a little burnt umber for the shadowed side of the face.

3 Add a little more cadmium red to the flesh-tone mixture and use it to darken the tones on the shadowed side of the face, under the chin and on the neck. Mix a red-biased orangey mix from cadmium red and cadmium yellow and paint the cheek and the shadowed side of the neck as well as the shaded area that lies immediately under the mouth. Immediately the portrait is taking on a feeling of light and shade.

4 Mix a pale bluish black from lamp black and phthalocyanine blue and begin putting in the lightest tones of the hair, making sure your brushstrokes follow the direction in which the hair grows. When the first tone is dry, add burnt umber to the mixture and paint the darker areas within the hair mass to give the hair volume. Add more phthalocyanine blue to the mixture and paint the model's shirt.

▶

5 Mix a pale brown from cadmium red, burnt umber, Turner's yellow and titanium white and loosely block in the background, painting carefully around the face. You may find it easier to switch to a larger brush for this stage, as it will allow you to cover a wide area more quickly.

6 Mix a rich, dark brown from lamp black, burnt umber, cadmium red and a little of the blue shirt mixture from Step 4. Using a small flat brush, paint the dark of the eyes and the lashes, taking care to get the shape of the white of the eye right. Use the same colour for the nostril.

7 Use the same colour to define the line between the upper and lower lips. Mix a reddish brown from burnt umber and phthalocyanine blue and paint the shadows under the eyes and inside the eye sockets.

8 Paint the mouth in varying mixes of alizarin crimson, cadmium red and yellow ochre, leaving the highlights untouched. The highlights will be worked in later, using lighter colours.

9 Darken the flesh tones on the shaded side of the face where necessary, using a mixture of alizarin crimson, phthalocyanine blue and a little titanium white, adding more blue to the mixture for the shadow under the chin, which is cooler in tone.

10 Mix a dark but warm black from burnt umber and lamp black and paint the darkest sections of the hair, leaving the lightest colour (applied in Step 4) showing through in places. This gives tonal variety and shows how the light falls on the hair.

11 Add more water to the mixture to make it more dilute and go over the dark areas of the hair again, this time leaving only a few highlights showing through as relatively fine lines.

12 Mix a dark blue from phthalocyanine blue and lamp black and paint over the shirt again, leaving some of the lighter blue areas applied in Step 4 showing through. Your brushstrokes should follow the direction and fall of the fabric.

▶

13 The beauty of acrylics is that you can paint a light colour over a dark one, without the first colour being visible. If you think the background is too dark and there is not sufficient differentiation between the model and the background, mix a warm off-white from titanium white, yellow ochre and burnt umber and, using a large flat brush, loosely paint the background again.

14 Using a small flat brush, cut around individual hairs with the background colour, carefully looking at the 'negative shapes'.

15 Using a fine round brush and titanium white straight from the tube, dot the highlights on to the eyes, nose and lower lip.

The finished painting
This is a relatively simple portrait, with nothing to distract from the sitter's direct gaze. Although the colour palette is limited, the artist has achieved an impressive and realistic range of skin and hair tones. Interest comes from the use of semi-transparent paint layers and allowing the directions of the brush marks to show through.

Carefully positioned highlights in the eyes make them sparkle and bring the portrait to life. The direct, critical gaze is an essential element of the portrait.

Variations in the skin tone, particularly on the shaded side of the face, help to reveal the shape of the face and its underlying bone structure.

The highlights in the hair are created by putting down the lightest tones first and then allowing them to show through subsequent applications of paint.

Portrait in oils on a toned ground

This portrait was painted from a photograph – you cannot expect a model to hold an expression as animated as this for any length of time.

Here, the artist opted for a head-and-shoulders portrait. Your most important decision when setting up a portrait is how much to include. If you leave out the shoulders, you will end up with what looks like a disembodied head; if you include much more of the torso than shown here, emphasis will be drawn away from the face and the balance of the portrait will be wrong.

In order to be able to start from a mid tone, the artist began by toning the canvas using a rich, warm mix of Venetian red and yellow ochre. Working on a white ground can be too strong a contrast. The artist was able to leave some of the ground showing through in the final painting for the brickwork and the mid tones of the model's skin.

The next stage was to make a thin underpainting in order to map out the basic pose. The advantage of using very thin paint for the underpainting is that if you make a mistake you can easily wipe it off with an old rag that has been dipped in turpentine.

In all portraits, it's important to continually refer back to your original points of reference – the width of the eyes, or the distance between the tip of the nose and the chin, for example – to check that your measurements and the proportions of the face are still correct. Be prepared to make adjustments as your work progresses.

Materials
- Stretched oil-primed linen canvas
- Oil paints: Venetian red, yellow ochre, terre verte, burnt umber, titanium white, ultramarine blue, alizarin crimson, lemon yellow, lamp black, cadmium red
- Turpentine
- Old rag
- Brushes: selection of filberts in various sizes

The pose
The model was posed in front of a brick wall, which provides texture and interest without detracting from her expression and features. The photograph was taken in late afternoon, so the sunlight that streams in from the left is both warm in colour and low in the sky, providing good modelling on the face.

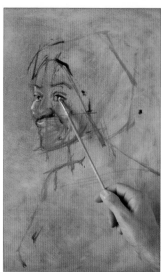

1 Tone the canvas with a dilute mix of Venetian red and yellow ochre and leave to dry. Dilute terre verte oil paint with turpentine to create a thin mix. Using a fine filbert brush, map out the overall structure of the portrait. Start by putting in the shoulder line (which in this case forms a strong diagonal through the composition), neck, facial area and the approximate area occupied by the hair. Then put in the facial features in burnt umber.

2 Put in more lines that you can use as a point of reference, such as the central line through the head. Begin putting in some of the mid tones, such as the bridge of the nose, with a yellowy mix of yellow ochre and terre verte. Mix titanium white with a little yellow ochre and put in 'markers' that you can refer back to later in the painting for the highlights – on the edge of the right cheekbone and top lip, for example. Carefully touch in the whites of the eyes.

> **Tip:** The exact colour of your reference marks is not critical – but varying the colours a little makes it easier for you to differentiate these new marks from the previous ones and keep track of where you are in the portrait.

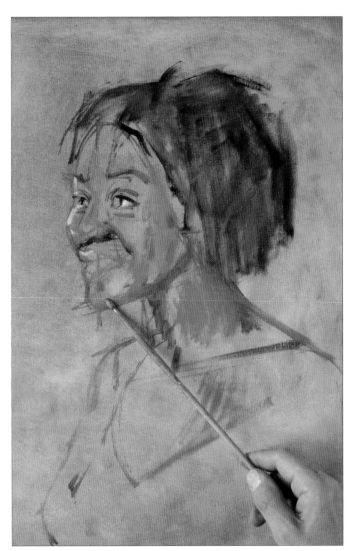

4 For the mid- to dark tones on the face – for example, down the centre of the brow and the bridge of the nose – use a mix of Venetian red, yellow ochre and burnt umber. Add white to this and put in some of the light highlights – on the left cheek and around the mouth, for example. Add ultramarine blue to the original mix for the shadow under the chin, and scumble a little of the same blue mix into the hair to create tonal variation.

3 Scumble burnt umber over the hair, allowing some of the toned ground to show through in places. Roughly scumble the yellowy green mix used in Step 2 on to mid-toned shadow areas such as the neck and the side of the face. Mix a reddish brown from Venetian red, yellow ochre and a little titanium white and apply this on top of the earlier mix, allowing the colours to mix optically on the surface of the canvas. This generally creates a much more lively mix than physically mixing the same colours in the palette.

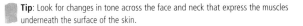

Tip: Look for changes in tone across the face and neck that express the muscles underneath the surface of the skin.

5 Paint the dark tones on the chin with a mix of Venetian red and yellow ochre. Using the brush tip, put in some light marks for the teeth and paint the gums in alizarin crimson. On the model's right shoulder and chest, scumble on a light mix of white and yellow ochre for the highlight areas.

▶

6 Refine the shape and position of the teeth. Mix a yellowy green from lemon yellow, a little terre verte and white and scumble it on to the background, leaving spaces for the mortar lines of the bricks. Looking at the negative spaces around your subject makes it easier to see the positive shapes.

7 Continue to build up the modelling on the face, alternating between warm and cool mixes and light and dark tones. Remember that warm colours tend to advance, while pale ones recede – so if you want an area such as a cheekbone to come forward, use a warm tone.

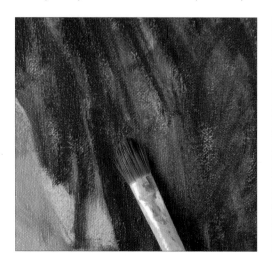

8 Put in the darkest tones in the hair, using a relatively thin mix of lamp black and ultramarine blue. Allow some of the canvas texture to show through.

9 Put in the white of the left eye with a mix of white with a hint of lemon yellow, and the white of the right eye with a cooler mix of white and ultramarine, so that it appears to recede slightly. Reassess the facial highlights and adjust if necessary. Begin blocking in the camisole in cadmium red.

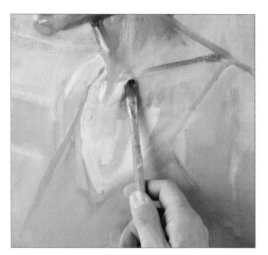

10 Now look at the highlights on the chest and shoulder. The collar bones are very prominent and catch the light, so use a warm mix of white and lemon yellow.

11 Scumble a mix of lemon yellow and white over the brick background, toning it down with a little terre verte in places and leaving the yellowy-green mix from Step 6 showing through for the mortar between the bricks.

12 Add more terre verte to the mix and scumble it over the bricks on the right-hand side. Block in the shape of the model's red top more precisely with cadmium red, adding white to the mix in parts so that the colour is not flat. As you improve the modelling on the chest, look for the highlights.

13 Build up the modelling on the arm, using the same mixes as before. Put in the dark crease under the arm in a mix of burnt umber and terre verte.

Assessment time

When you feel you're getting near the end of any painting, it's important to take time to look critically at what you've done and see what changes, if any, are required. Here, although the modelling on the face is virtually complete, there are a few gaps remaining – particularly around the hair line – where the toned ground shows through. The arms and shoulders almost merge into the background and need to be brought forward. Some of the skin tones are a little too dark in places and need to be toned down; the shadow under the chin and around the jawline, in particular, is both too dark and too heavy, but this is easy to rectify. In oils, you can apply a lighter colour on top of a dark one. You can even wipe off colour using a rag dipped in turpentine if necessary.

This shadow is too dark and heavy.

The arm is too pink and requires more modelling.

The model's top is too light and patchy in colour.

14 There are places on the head that have received no paint, allowing the toned ground to show. Block these in using the same skin tones as before. Strengthen the shadow on the back of the neck; because of the way the light falls, this area is quite dark. Lighten the shadow under the chin using a mix of Venetian red, yellow ochre and terre verte, and soften the edges.

15 Cover any gaps and build up more texture in the hair with a deep blue-black mix of burnt umber and ultramarine blue.

> **Tip**: Don't try to put in every strand of hair, but make sure your strokes follow the direction of growth.

16 Using cadmium red paint, darken the red top. Note, however, that the colour is not totally uniform: creases and folds in the fabric create slight shadows that reveal the form beneath.

The finished painting

This is a lively portrait that perfectly captures the model's expression and personality. The artist began by toning the canvas with a mix of Venetian red and yellow ochre, which was similar in colour to both the mid-tones of the model's skin and the brick wall in the background. This enabled him to allow some of the ground to show through in his finished painting, unifying the surface. Although the colour palette is relatively restricted, the bright highlights and the white of the eyes and teeth really sing out and help to bring the portrait to life. Note, too, the effectiveness of the contrasts in texture – the smoothness of the skin, achieved by blending the paint wet into wet, versus the roughly scumbled paint on the background and the short, spiky brushstrokes used for the hair.

Paint has been lightly scumbled on to the brick wall, exploiting the texture of the canvas.

Because the light is so bright, the highlighted skin areas are paler than you might expect.

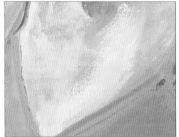

Energetic, spiky brushstrokes capture the texture of the hair.

Young child in acrylics

There are several things to remember when drawing or painting a child. The first is that children are very active and have a short attention span: you cannot expect them to sit still for hours while you work on your portrait, and for this reason you will probably find it easiest to work from a photograph.

Second, in children the head is much larger in relation to the overall body size than it is in adults. Although the human race is infinitely varied, as a general guideline the head is about one-seventh of the total height of the body in adults – but in babies it may occupy almost as much as one-third of the total. The little girl in this portrait is about two years old: her head represents approximately one-quarter of her total height.

This project starts with toning the support – a classic technique that was much used by some of the great portraitists such as Peter Paul Rubens (1577–1640). This provides the advantage of starting to paint from a mid-tone background, rather than a stark white ground, which makes it easier to judge the subtle flesh tones and the effects of light and shade cast by the sun. It also establishes the overall colour temperature of the portrait from the outset. In this instance, burnt sienna gives the portrait a lovely warm glow, which is appropriate to the dappled sunlight that illuminates the scene.

Materials
- *Board primed with acrylic gesso*
- *Acrylic paints: burnt sienna, ultramarine blue, titanium white, cadmium red, lemon yellow, alizarin crimson, phthalocyanine green*
- *Brushes: small round, medium flat, small flat*
- *Rag*
- *Matt acrylic medium*

The pose
Relaxed and informal, this child's attention is occupied by something that we cannot see. Note that she is positioned slightly off centre. If a figure in a portrait is looking off to one side, it is generally better to have more space on that side, as this creates a calmer, more restful mood. Placing a figure close to the edge of the frame creates a feeling of tension.

Preliminary sketch
Flesh tones can be tricky, and you may find it useful to make a quick colour sketch experimenting with different mixes, such as the one shown on the left, before you start painting.

1 Tone the primed board with burnt sienna acrylic paint and leave to dry. Mix a dilute, warm brown from burnt sienna and a little ultramarine blue. Using a small round brush, make a loose underdrawing, concentrating on getting the overall proportions and the angles of the head and limbs correct.

2 Mix a darker, less dilute brown, this time using more ultramarine blue. Using the small round brush, put in the darkest tones of the hair, the shadows on the face and under the collar of the girl's dress, and the main creases in the fabric of the dress. These creases help to convey form.

3 Mix a very pale pink from titanium white, cadmium red and a little lemon yellow and paint the palest flesh tones on the face, arms and legs, as well as some highlights in the hair. Add more water and put in the lightest tones of the girl's dress. Note how the colour of the support shows through.

4 Mix a warm purple from ultramarine blue and alizarin crimson. Using a medium flat brush, block in the dark foliage area to the left of the girl. Add more water and ultramarine blue to the mixture and paint the darkest foliage areas to the right of the girl and the shadows under the stool.

▶

5 Mix a bright green from phthalocyanine green, lemon yellow, titanium white and a little cadmium red. Block in the lawn and background foliage. Use less lemon yellow for the shaded grass and more white for the brightest parts.

6 Mix a very pale green from titanium white and phthalocyanine green and brush it loosely over the child's sun-bleached cotton dress.

7 Mix a dark brown from burnt sienna and ultramarine blue and start to put some detailing in the hair and on the shadowed side of the face. Mix a warm shadow tone from alizarin crimson and burnt sienna and build up the shadow tones on the left-hand (sunlit) side of the face, alternating between this mixture and the pale pink used in Step 3.

8 Add titanium white to the purple mixture from Step 4 and paint the stool to the right of the child. Paint the stool on which she is sitting in a mixture of brown and titanium white, with brushstrokes that follow the wood grain. Mix a rich brown from burnt sienna and alizarin crimson and, using a small round brush, paint the shadows at the bottom of her dress.

9 Dab some of the purple mixture (the stool colour) over the foliage in the background. Using the same colour in this area establishes a visual link between foreground and background; the light colour also creates the impression of dappled light in the foliage. Mix a dark, bluish green from ultramarine blue and phthalocyanine green and paint the shadow under the dress collar and any deep creases and shadows in the fabric of the dress.

10 Using the pale pink mixture from Step 3 and a round brush, go over the arms and legs again, carefully blending the tones wet into wet on the support in order to convey the roundness of the flesh.

Assessment time
The blocks of colour are now taking on some meaning and form: for the rest of the painting, concentrate on building up the form and detailing.

The tonal contrasts on the face are too extreme and need to be blended to make the skin look more life-like.

The hands and feet, in particular, need to be given more definition.

The child is not sufficiently well separated from the background.

Tip: To make flesh look soft and rounded, you need to blend the tones on the support so that they merge almost imperceptibly; it is rare to see a sharp transition from one colour to another. Working wet into wet is the best way to achieve this, gradually darkening the tone as the limb turns away from the light. With acrylic paints, you may find that adding a few drops of flow improver helps matters: flow improver increases the flow of the paint and its absorption into the support surface.

▶

11 Mix burnt sienna with a tiny amount of titanium white. Using a small round brush, paint the dark spaces between the fingers and the shadows between the feet and on the toes. Try to see complicated areas such as these as abstract shapes and blocks of colour: if you start thinking of them as individual toes, the chances are that you will make them bigger than they should be.

12 Refine the facial details, using the same mixes as before. Put in the curve of the ear, which is just visible through the hair, using the pale pink skin tone. Mix a reddish brown from alizarin crimson, ultramarine blue and burnt sienna. Build up the volume of the hair, looking at the general direction of the hair growth and painting clumps rather than individual hairs.

13 Using the purple shadow mixture from Step 4 and a small flat brush, cut in around the head to define the edge and provide better separation between the girl and the background. Mix a dark green from phthalocyanine green and ultramarine blue and loosely dab it over the dark foliage area to provide more texture. Using cool colours here makes this area recede, focusing attention on the little girl.

14 Add a little matt acrylic medium to the pale pink flesh tone and go over the light areas of the face, working the paint in with the brush to ensure that it blends well and covers any areas too dark in tone. The matt medium makes the paint more translucent, so that it is more like a glaze. Do the same thing on the arms, adding a little burnt sienna for any areas that are slightly warmer in tone.

15 Make any final adjustments that you deem necessary. Here, the artist felt that the girl's hands were too small, making her look slightly doll-like; using the pale flesh colour from previous steps, she carefully painted over them to make them a little broader and bring them up to the right scale.

The finished painting

This is a charming portrait of a toddler with her slightly chubby face and arms, rounded mouth, big eyes and unselfconscious pose. There is just enough detail in the background to establish the outdoor setting, but by paying very careful attention to the tones of the highlights and shadows, the artist has captured the dappled sunlight that pervades the scene.

Although no detail is visible in the eyes, we are nonetheless invited to follow the child's gaze.

The subtle blending of colour on the child's arms and face makes the flesh look soft and rounded.

There is just enough background to give the scene a context without distracting from the portrait.

Brushstrokes on the stool follow the direction of the woodgrain – an effective way of conveying both pattern and texture.

Grandmother and child in soft pastels

Family portraits, particularly of very young children, are always popular – and a project like this would make a wonderful present for a grandparent. Soft pastels capture the skin tones beautifully, and you can smooth out the marks with your fingers or a torchon to create almost imperceptible transitions from one tone to another. Build up the layers gradually. You can spray with fixative in the later stages to avoid smudging the colours, but be aware that this could dull or darken the colours that you've already put down. Soft pastel is also a lovely medium for drawing hair, as you can put down many different colours within the hair mass to create depth and an attractive sheen. When drawing hair, look at the overall direction of the hair growth.

Young children have very short attention spans and they certainly can't hold the same pose for the time it takes to draw a detailed portrait. You'll be lucky if they sit still for long enough for you to do anything more than a very quick sketch – so working from a photograph is probably your best option. Even then, it's very hard to get a young child to do exactly as you want if you tell them what to do. Often you either get a shot with the child staring grumpily at the camera, or he or she will wriggle, making a good shot impossible.

One simple solution is to make the photo session into a game by pulling faces, clapping your hands, holding up a favourite toy and generally interacting with the child so that he or she forgets all about the camera. Above all, take lots of shots so you have plenty of reference material to choose from. Then you can combine material from several shots – invaluable if you can't get a shot in which both sitters are smiling at the same time.

Materials
- *Pale grey pastel paper*
- *Soft pastels: pinkish beige, white, dark brown, mid-brown, orangey beige, pale yellow, pinkish brown, reddish brown, dark blue, red, pale blue, grey, pale pink, black*

The pose
This is a happy pose, with both child and grandmother smiling broadly. To help them relax for the shot, the photographer got them to make a little game out of clapping their hands which, in addition to helping them forget that they're having their photo taken, imparts a sense of movement to the pose.

1 Using a pinkish beige soft pastel map out the basic shapes – the heads of the two sitters and the position of the arms. Draw the sleeves and neckline of the grandmother's sweater in white pastel, putting in the most obvious creases in the fabric, and put in the slant of the little boy's shoulders in white, too.

2 Using the pinkish beige pastel again, indicate the position of the facial features by marking a central guideline with the eyes approximately halfway down. The grandmother's head is tilted back, so her eyes are a little above the halfway point. Roughly block in the child's hair and the shadows in the woman's hair in dark brown.

3 Still using the dark brown pastel, put in more of the hair, smudging the pastel marks with your fingers. Indicate the darkest parts of the facial features – the recesses of the eye sockets and nostrils. Apply some flesh tone to the child's face, using mid-brown for the darker parts and a more orange version of the beige used in Step 1 for the lighter parts. Using the side of a pale yellow pastel, roughly block in the base colour of the little boy's shirt.

4 Using the side of a white pastel, block in the grandmother's sweater. Apply a pinkish beige to her face and neck, blending the marks with your fingers.

5 The grandmother's neck is slightly warmer in tone than her face. Use a reddish brown for the slightly darker tones in this area, again blending the marks with your fingers. Use the same colour for the child's lips. Using your fingertips, smooth out the mid-brown on the child's face, leaving the orangey beige for the lighter parts. Use a very dark brown for the child's eyebrows and eyes.

6 Using a dark blue pastel, put in the creases in the fabric of the grandmother's sweater. Block in the arms, using a pinkish brown for the grandmother and a reddish brown for the little boy. Overlay various flesh tones – pinkish beige, orangey beige, red – as appropriate, blending the marks with your fingers. Flesh is not a uniform colour; look closely and you will see warm and cool tones within it.

▶

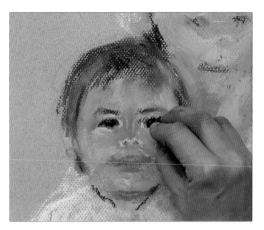

7 With a dark brown pastel, put in the shadow under the child's chin and around the collar of his shirt. Put in some jagged strokes on the hair so that you begin to develop something of the spiky texture. Darken the child's eyes.

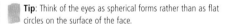

Tip: Think of the eyes as spherical forms rather than as flat circles on the surface of the face.

8 Using the same flesh colours as before, continue building up the modelling on the little boy's face. Add some red to the cheeks, blending the marks with your fingers. Like most toddlers, he has a fairly chubby face, so there are no deep recesses under the cheekbones, but with the mix of light and darker-coloured tones the flesh is starting to look more natural. Using the tip of a white pastel and dabbing on small marks, lightly draw his teeth and apply some tiny, glossy highlights to the lips.

9 Repeat the process of building up modelling on the grandmother's face. Apply pale yellow to her hair.

10 Continue working on the hair, putting in browns and greys to get some tonal variation within the hair. Note, too, how the hair casts a slight shadow on her face. Use a brown pastel to draw in the creases in the little boy's shirt. Draw in the crease lines around the grandmother's nose and mouth with a reddish brown pastel.

Assessment time

The expressions and pose have been nicely captured, but in places the skin tones appear as blocks of colour and need to be smoothed out more. A little more modelling is also needed on the faces and hands. The eyes need to sparkle in order for the portrait to come alive.

The pupils and irises have been carefully observed, but there is no catchlight to bring the eyes to life.

The child's hands, in particular, appear somewhat formless.

11 Continue the modelling on the grandmother's face and neck, gradually building up the layers and fleshing out the cheeks. Use the same colours and blending techniques as before. The adjustments are relatively minor at this stage.

12 Apply more yellow to the boy's shirt, scribbling it in around the dark crease marks. Smudge more brown over the yellow for the stripes in the fabric. A hint of the pattern is sufficient; too much detail would detract from the face.

13 Using the side of the pastel, block in the grandmother's sweater with a very pale blue. Reinforce the dark blue applied in Step 6 to define the folds in the fabric. Apply tiny pale-blue dots around the neckline of the sweater.

▶

14 Draw the little boy's fingernails with a pale pink pastel and apply light strokes of reddish brown between the fingers to separate them. Like his face, the fingers are fairly chubby so you don't need to put too much detail on them. Blend the marks with your fingertips if necessary to create soft transitions in the flesh tones.

15 If necessary, adjust the flesh tones on the boy's arms and fingers. Here, the artist judged that the face was too dark, so she applied some lighter flesh tones – a very pale orangey beige – to the highlights to redress the balance. Apply a range of browns to his hair to build up the texture and depth of colour.

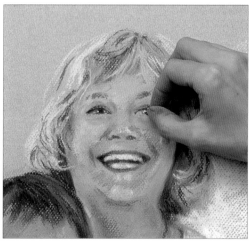

16 Add a thin white line for the grandmother's necklace. Darken her lips and inner mouth; adjust the flesh tones. Redefine the creases around the nose and mouth, if necessary.

17 The final stage is to put in some detail in the eyes – the black pupils and some tiny dots of white for the catchlights.

The finished drawing

This is a relaxed and informal portrait that captures the sitters' moods and personalities. Using soft pastel has allowed the artist to build up the flesh tones gradually, achieving a convincingly life-like effect. Leaving the grandmother's hands slightly unfinished helps to create a sense of movement as she claps her hands together – in much the same way as a blurred photograph tells us that a subject is moving.

In wide smiles, the lips are stretched taut across the arc of the teeth. We see more of the upper teeth than the lower teeth; sometimes only the tops of the lower teeth are visible and almost never the gums.

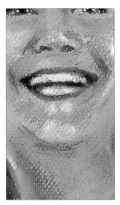

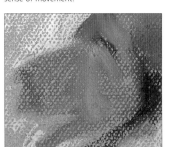

Leaving the hands unfinished creates a sense of movement.

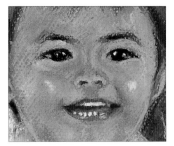

The eyes sparkle: a tiny dot of white is sufficient to bring them alive.

Note how many different tones there are within the hair.

Character portrait in charcoal

Markets are a great place to do quick sketches or take snapshots of people going about their daily business, which you can then work up into more detailed portraits at a later date. People are so engrossed in what they're doing that they're unlikely to take much notice of you – so your photos and sketches may be much more natural.

Here, the artist decided to omit both the background and the woman on the left and to concentrate on making a character portrait of the man – but you could, of course, include the setting, too, provided you kept the main emphasis of the drawing on his face.

This particular portrait gains much of its strength from the fact that there is direct eye contact between the subject

and the artist, which immediately brings the portrait to life and makes the viewer feel involved in the scene. His gaze is quizzical, perhaps even slightly challenging, and even without the inclusion of the market setting, his slightly hunched pose and wrinkled face indicate that he leads a hard life.

Charcoal is a lovely medium for character portraits and, like black-and-white reportage or documentary-style photographs, a monochrome drawing has a strength and immediacy that works particularly well with this kind of subject. The same drawing in colour would have a very different feel – and probably far less impact. Why not try the same project in coloured pencil, too, to see the difference?

Materials
- *Fine pastel paper*
- *Thin charcoal stick*
- *Compressed charcoal stick*
- *Kneaded eraser*

The pose
In this scene two market traders in Turkey were spotted by chance rather than asked to pose formally. So these are character portraits. The artist concentrated on the man on the right, as the three-quarters pose, with direct eye contact, is more interesting than the head-on view of the lady. He has a strong profile, while the woman's face is more rounded and her features less clearly defined. The plastic sheeting could be confusing so it was omitted.

1 Using a thin stick of charcoal, map out the lines of the pose. Look at the angle of the shoulders and back and at where imaginary vertical lines intersect, so that you can place elements correctly in relation to one another. Here, for example, the peak of the man's cap is almost directly in line with his wrist.

2 Still using the thin charcoal stick, lightly put in guidelines to help you place the facial features. Draw a line through the forehead and down to the bottom of the chin, lines across the face to mark the level of the eyes, the base of the nose and the mouth, and an inverted triangle from the eyes down to the nose.

3 Refine the facial features and roughly block in the fur collar on the man's jacket. (It provides a dark frame for the face.)

4 Lightly draw the curve of the top of the skull. Although you can't actually see the skull beneath the cap, you can use the tilt of the head and the features you've already put in to work out where it should be. Remember that the base of the eye socket is generally about halfway down the face, so the top of the skull is likely to be higher than you might think.

5 Now you can draw the cap. Without the faint guideline of the skull that you drew in the previous step, you'd probably make the cap too flat and place it too low on the head. Draw the eyes and eyebrows and the sockets of the eyes. Already you can see how the form is beginning to develop.

▶

Assessment time
The facial features are in place and most of the linear work has been completed, although the details need to be refined and the eyes darkened. Now you can begin to introduce some shading, which will make the figure look three-dimensional and bring the portrait to life.

The jacket looks flat. There is nothing to tell us how heavy it is or what kind of fabric it is made from.

Shading has introduced some modelling on the far side of the face, but more is needed.

6 Sharpen the line of the far cheek and apply loose hatching on the far side of the face (which is in shadow) and on the forehead, where the cap casts a shadow.

7 Using a compressed charcoal stick, which is very dense and black, put in the line of the mouth.

8 Again, using the compressed charcoal stick, put in the pupils of the eyes, remembering to leave tiny catchlights.

9 Using the side of a thin stick of charcoal, very lightly shade the right-hand side of the man's face. The shadow is not as deep here as on the far side of the face, but this slightly darker tone serves two purposes as it helps to show how tanned and weatherbeaten his face is and also creates some modelling on the cheeks.

10 Using the tip of your little finger, which is the driest part of your hand, carefully blend the charcoal on the right cheek to a smooth, mid-toned grey.

11 Using a kneaded eraser, pick out the highlighted wrinkles on the face, and the whites of the eyes. Each time you use it, wipe the eraser on scrap paper to clean off the charcoal and so prevent smudges.

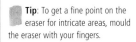

Tip: To get a fine point on the eraser for intricate areas, mould the eraser with your fingers.

12 Block in the dark, shaded side of the cap, using the side of the charcoal stick. Note that the cap is not a uniform shade of black all over: leave areas on the top untouched to show where the highlights fall.

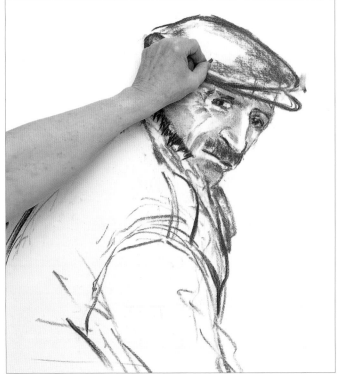

▶

13 Using compressed charcoal, block in the fur collar on the jacket and smooth out the marks with your fingers. By making slightly jagged marks, you can suggest the texture of the fur. Note how the face immediately stands out more strongly when framed by the dark fur.

14 Put in the dark crease lines of the folds in the jacket. The deep creases help to show the weight of the fabric.

15 Using the side of the charcoal, apply tone over the jacket, leaving highlights on the sleeve untouched.

16 Using the side of your hand in a circular motion, blend the charcoal to a smooth, flat tone.

The finished drawing

This portrait is full of character. Note the classic composition, which draws our attention to the face – the overall shape of the portrait is triangular, with the strong line of the back leading up to the face and forming the first side of the triangle, and a straight line down from the peak of the cap to the arm forming the second side.

In addition, the face is positioned roughly 'on the third' – a strong placement for the most important element in the drawing. The three-quarter viewpoint with the sitter's face turned partway towards the viewer, means that there is direct eye contact, immediately involving the viewer in the painting. The sitter's strong profile is also evident from this viewpoint.

Wrinkles in the skin are picked out using the sharp edge of a kneaded eraser.

The crease lines and variations in tone show the weight and bulkiness of the fabric.

The direct eye contact between sitter and viewer makes this a very strong portrait.

Character study in watercolour

A good portrait is about more than capturing a good likeness of the sitter: it should also reveal something of their personality and interests. You can do this by including things that they would use in everyday life as props. You might, for example, ask a keen musician to sit at the piano. Alternatively, you could depict someone at his or her place of work. The sitter for this portrait loves literature and is an avid reader – hence the book that she is holding and the piles of books in the background. Take care, however, not to allow the background and props to dominate. Here the books are little more than simple, graphic shapes. If elements threaten to overpower, reduce their importance in the composition – or even omit them altogether.

As we grow older, we inevitably acquire a few wrinkles and 'laughter lines', all of which give a face character and expression. Here, the artist decided to make a pencil underdrawing and to allow many of the pencil marks to show through in the final watercolour painting. The result is a fresh, lively portrayal that combines the very best characteristics of two very different media – the linear quality of pencil and soft, wet-into-wet washes of watercolour paint in the skin tones. He primed his watercolour paper with an acrylic gesso, which renders any pencil marks softer and blacker than they would otherwise be and creates an interesting, slightly broken texture.

Don't worry about creating an exact likeness of your sitter in the early stages, or you may get caught up in the fine detail and lose sight of the overall composition and proportions. If you get the basics right, the rest will follow.

Materials
- *Heavy watercolour paper primed with acrylic gesso*
- *B pencil*
- *Watercolour paints: raw sienna, cadmium orange, indigo, ultramarine blue, raw umber, black, vermilion, cerulean blue*
- *Brushes: small and medium round*

The pose
This elderly lady's face is full of character and, by including the book that she is reading and the piles of books in the background, the artist has also managed to tell us a little about her interests. However, the television in the background adds nothing to the scene; in fact, it distracts attention from her face. For this reason, the artist decided to omit it.

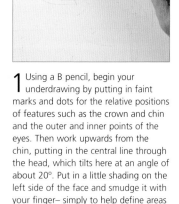

1 Using a B pencil, begin your underdrawing by putting in faint marks and dots for the relative positions of features such as the crown and chin and the outer and inner points of the eyes. Then work upwards from the chin, putting in the central line through the head, which tilts here at an angle of about 20°. Put in a little shading on the left side of the face and smudge it with your finger– simply to help define areas rather than to add tone.

2 Once you've mapped out the position of the features, you can gradually put in more details, such as the spectacles. Loosely hatch shaded areas such as the left cheek; this is simply to delineate the extent of these areas rather than introduce modelling.

3 It's a good idea to lightly hatch or shade part of the area around your subject's head fairly early on in a portrait. Also put in any areas of shade that help you to keep track of where you are in the portrait – for example, in the hair and on the neck.

4 Although you only want to give an impression of the dress fabric, rather than slavishly copy every last detail, you can use elements of the pattern as a guide to the placement of other features. Here, for example, the top of the black pattern just below the neckline is roughly level with the top of the right sleeve. Look, also, for folds within the fabric that cast slight shadows, which suggest the body beneath.

5 Once you've mapped out the figure, decide how much of the surroundings to include and what to change or omit. Although the artist here chose to leave out the television set, he put in a dark background which frames the face and allows the white of the hair to stand out. He also lightly sketched the piles of books, as the sitter's interest in literature is an element of her character he wanted to convey.

6 Begin to define the different planes of the fingers. (Note that the thumb on the right hand is foreshortened: we're looking at the underside of the thumb, with the nail on the very edge.) Put in some shading on the sitter's right arm. There is a strong area of shadow in the underside of the forearm, which clearly shows the muscles of the lower arm. Although you're only establishing the basic lights and darks at this stage, this is the beginning of creating some modelling.

7 To make them stand out more, put in some stronger tones in the facial features – the nostrils, the pupils of the eyes, and the deep creases around the mouth – as well as in the metal rims of the spectacles. Use a kneaded eraser to retrieve any highlights that have been accidentally covered over – for example, on the tip of the nose and within the spectacles. For very fine details, use the sharp edge of the eraser, or mould it to a fine point with your fingertips.

▶

Assessment time

Once you've mapped in the position of the books to the left of the sitter, the pencil underdrawing is virtually complete; now you are ready to begin applying the colour. The underdrawing is relatively detailed and the time and attention you've taken to produce it will pay dividends later, when you come to apply the colour. Although there is not much modelling, you have established the main areas of lights and dark, which you can use as a guide when applying the different tones in watercolour. Most importantly, there is plenty of linear detail in the face, which you will be able to retain in the finished painting.

These pencil lines are strong enough to show through light watercolour washes.

The stacks of books provide a graphic element in the composition without detracting from the figure.

8 Mix a very dilute wash of raw sienna and cadmium orange and, using a small round brush, wash it over the arms and face, omitting only the very bright highlights on the face. Leave to dry. Then mix a blackish blue from indigo and ultramarine blue. Using a medium round brush, wash it over the darkest areas of the background and leave to dry. Note how the brushstrokes of the primer are visible in places, adding texture to the washes.

9 Using a medium round brush, apply a fairly strong wash of cadmium orange over the sitter's dress, leaving a few small areas untouched for the very lightest colours. Leave to dry.

10 Use the oranges from the previous two steps, for the dark and mid tones on the face and neck. The colours are modified a little by the pencil lines that are already there.

11 Mix a warm brown from raw sienna and a little raw umber and put in the pattern of the dress, leaving the underlying cadmium orange showing through where necessary. Leave to dry. Then, using a mix of black and ultramarine blue, put in the darkest tones of the books in the background and the lines of the books behind the sitter's left shoulder, as well as the shadow between the book she is holding and its cover. Allow to dry.

Tips:
• Assess the relative sizes of the various books carefully.
• Leave some of the blue-black mix from Step 8 showing through for pages of the books in the background.

12 Darken the warm brown used for the dress in Step 11 and put in a little more of the mid-to-dark patterning. Continue with the skin tones, using the various tones of the orange and reddish mixes used before and paying attention to the lights and darks. Apply a touch of vermilion to the lips.

13 On the arm and hands, apply dilute washes of vermilion and cadmium orange, singly and together, wet into wet. Using very dilute cerulean blue, 'draw' faint marks on the open book to indicate print and pictures. Wash the same dilute mix over the books to her left.

▶

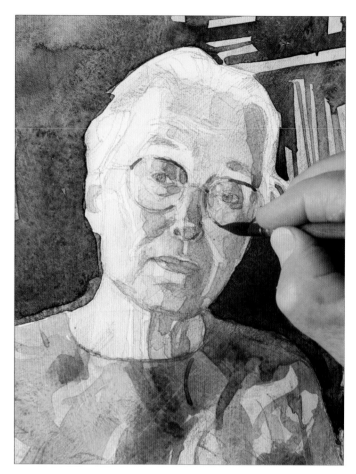

15 Use the same blue-black mix for the very darkest patterning on the dress. Don't try to put in every detail, or the pattern will overpower the painting. A general impression is sufficient. At this point you may find that you need to deepen the very pale orange applied in Step 9; if you do, ensure that all other colours on the dress are completely dry or they will blend wet into wet and ruin the effect.

14 Continue building up the layers on the skin tone, using slightly darker versions of the previous mixes. Brighten the red of the lips with a touch of vermilion. Using the blue-black mix from Step 11 and a small round brush that comes to a fine tip, paint in the metal rim of the spectacles. Darken the pupils of the eyes with the same blue-black mix and wash a very dilute grey into the shaded parts of the hair to create some texture and tonal variation. Be careful not to colour the hair grey, however – your grey shading should, on the contrary, make the white of the hair more striking.

 Tips:
•The spectacle rims catch a lot of reflected light, so the outer edge virtually disappears in places. Observe this carefully and leave gaps where necessary.
• If the hair is to read as white in the finished painting, all of the face – except for the very brightest highlights – must have some tone, however dilute.
• Before you make any last-minute adjustments, make sure that your palette and water jars are clean so that you do not risk muddying your colours in the final stages.

16 You may find that the very dark tones of the dress now dominate and that you need to adjust the skin tones accordingly. Use the same mixes as before, taking care not to lose sight of the overall tonality of the painting.

The finished painting

This is a sensitive portrait that captures the sitter's expression and personality beautifully. Carefully controlled wet-into-wet washes have been used to build up the skin tones and create subtle modelling on the face and neck; the white of the paper has also been exploited to good effect in the highlight areas. The wrinkles and creases in the face, drawn in during the initial pencil underdrawing, add character and expression and show through the later watercolour washes without dominating them. The distracting elements in the background have been reduced to graphic shapes and monochromatic areas of mid and dark tone, against which the figure stands out clearly. The composition and use of light and shade help to convey the lively personality of the sitter.

The patterning of the dress has been subtly painted so that it does not overpower or dominate the portrait.

The wrinkles are conveyed through linear pencil marks.

Note how the very brightest highlights are left untouched by paint.

The background has been reduced to a series of graphic, monochromatic elements.

Seated figure in watercolour

As you have discovered, painting someone in a setting allows you to say much more about them than you can in a straightforward head-and-shoulders portrait. You might include things that reveal something about your subject's interests – a musician with a guitar, perhaps, or an antiques collector surrounded by some of his or her possessions – or their work. In a domestic setting, the décor of the room itself is very often a reflection of your subject's tastes and personality.

The most important thing is not to allow the surroundings to dominate. The focus of the painting must remain on the person. This usually means that you have to deliberately subdue some of the detail around your subject, either by using muted or cool colours for the surroundings, so that your subject becomes more prominent, or, if the setting is very cluttered, by leaving some things out of your painting altogether.

Materials
- *3B pencil*
- *Rough watercolour board*
- *Watercolour paints: raw umber, alizarin crimson, cobalt blue, lemon yellow, phthalocyanine blue*
- *Brushes: medium flat, Chinese, fine round, old brush for masking*
- *Masking fluid*
- *Craft (utility) knife or scalpel*
- *Sponge*

Reference photographs
Here the artist used two photographs as reference – one for the seated, semi-silhouetted figure and one for the shaft of light that falls on the table top. Both photographs are dark and it is difficult to see much detail, but they show enough to set the general scene and give you scope to use your imagination. Instead of slavishly copying every last detail, you are free to invent certain aspects of the scene, or to embellish existing ones.

The highlight on the figure's hair is very atmospheric.

The shaft of bright sunlight illuminates part of the table top while almost everything else is in deep shade.

1 Using a 3B pencil, lightly sketch your subject, making sure you get the tilt of her head and the angles of the table, papers and books right.

2 Mix a warm, pinky orange from raw umber and alizarin crimson. Using a medium flat brush, wash it over the background, avoiding the highlight areas on the window. Add more alizarin crimson to the mixture for the warmest areas, such as the girl's shirt and the left-hand side of the curtain, and more raw umber for the cooler areas, such as the wall behind the girl and the glazing bars on the window. Leave to dry.

3 Mix a very pale green from cobalt blue and lemon yellow and, using a Chinese brush, paint the lightest foliage shades outside the window, remembering to leave some white areas for the very bright sky beyond.

 **Tip**: To enhance the impression of bright sunlight streaming through the window, take care not to paint foliage right up to the edge of the window frame. Instead, allow the white of the paper to stand for the very brightest patches of sky.

Assessment time

Mix a very pale blue from cobalt blue and a touch of raw umber and put in the cooler tones inside the room – the left-hand side, which the shaft of sunlight coming through the window doesn't reach, and the shadows under the table. Leave to dry.

You have now established the warm and cool areas of the painting, which you will build on in all the subsequent stages. Because of her position within the frame (roughly in the first third), the girl is the main focus of interest in the painting, even though she is largely in shadow. Keep this at the forefront of your mind as you begin to put in the detail and as you continually assess the compositional balance while painting.

This area is left unpainted, as it receives the most direct sunlight.

The warm colour of the girl's shirt helps to bring her forwards in the painting.

The shadow areas are the coolest in tone. They recede.

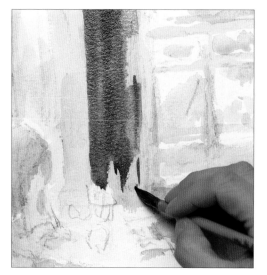

4 Mix a warm brown from alizarin crimson and raw umber and paint the girl's hair. Mix a rich red from alizarin crimson, cobalt blue and a little raw umber and, using a Chinese brush, paint the curtain. Apply several vertical brushstrokes to the curtain, wet into wet, to build up the tone and give the impression that it hangs in folds.

5 Using the same red mixture, paint the shoulders and back of the girl's shirt. Add more raw umber to the mixture and paint the shadow area between the wall and the mirror, immediately behind the girl. Mix a warm blue from phthalocyanine blue and a little alizarin crimson, and paint the dark area beneath the table using loose brushstrokes.

6 Using an old brush, 'draw' the shapes of leaves in the bottom left-hand corner in masking fluid. Leave to dry. Mix a rich, dark brown from raw umber and a little alizarin crimson and, using a fine round brush, paint the darkest areas of the girl's hair.

7 Add a little raw umber to the mixture for the lighter areas of hair around the face. Build up the shadow areas in the foreground of the scene, overlaying colours as before. Darken the girl's shirt in selected areas with the alizarin crimson, cobalt blue and raw umber mixture.

8 Mix a mid-toned green from phthalocyanine blue and lemon yellow and, using a fine round brush, dot this mixture into the foliage that can be seen through the right-hand side of the window. Mix a very pale purplish blue from pthalocyanine blue and a little alizarin crimson and darken the glazing bars of the window.

9 Paint the area under the window in a warm mixture of alizarin crimson and phthalocyanine blue. Mix a dark, olive green from raw umber and phthalocyanine blue and, making loose calligraphic strokes, paint the fronds of the foreground plant. Brush a very dilute version of the same mixture on to the lower part of the mirror. Build up the background tones.

10 Mix a muted green from phthalocyanine blue and lemon yellow. Brush it over the background behind the girl. Because the green is relatively cool, it helps to separate the girl from the background. It also provides a visual link between this area and the foliage on the right.

11 Paint a few vertical strokes on the curtain in a dark mixture of alizarin crimson and phthalocyanine blue. This helps to make the highlight on top of the pile of books stand out more clearly. Mix a warm brown from raw umber and phthalocyanine blue and paint under the window.

12 Rub off the masking fluid from the bottom left-hand corner. Continue building up the tones overall, using the same paint mixtures as before and loose, random brushstrokes to maintain a feeling of spontaneity.

▶

13 Mix a very pale wash of raw umber and lightly brush it on to some of the exposed areas in the bottom left-hand corner. Build up more dark tones in the foreground, using the same mixtures as before.

14 Using a craft (utility) knife or scalpel, carefully scratch off some of the highlights on the bottle on the table. Paint the wall behind the girl in a pale, olivey green mixture of raw umber and phthalocyanine blue.

15 Brush a little very pale cobalt blue into the sky area so that this area does not look too stark and draw attention away from the main subject.

16 Continue building up tones by overlaying colours. Use very loose brushstrokes and change direction continually, as this helps to convey a feeling of the dappled light that comes through the window.

17 Using a 3B pencil, define the edges of the papers on the table. Mix a very pale wash of phthalocyanine blue and, using a fine round brush, carefully brush in shadows under the papers on the table to give them more definition. Dip a sponge in a blue-biased mixture of phthalocyanine blue and alizarin crimson and gently press it around the highlight area on the floor to suggest the texture of the carpet.

The finished painting
There is a wonderful sense of light and shade in this painting, and the loose brushstrokes give a feeling of great freshness and spontaneity. The scene is beautifully balanced, both in terms of its distribution of colours and in the way that dark and light areas are counterposed.

Sunlight pours through the window, illuminating the books and papers. Much of this area is left unpainted.

Pale, cool colours on the wall help to differentiate the girl from the background.

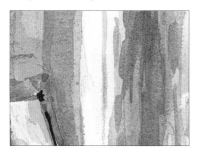

The foreground is loosely painted with overlayed colours, creating a feeling of spontaneity.

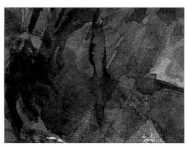

Girl playing on a beach in acrylics

When you include the setting in a painting as well as a person, you need to decide how much of the picture space to allocate to each. If you want to create a character portrait in which the person is the main focus of interest, then you need to make that person a large part of the picture as a whole; a mere hint of the surroundings may be sufficient. If, on the other hand, you want to set the figure in context so that the surroundings become an important part of the overall story, then the landscape or interior may well take up the majority of the picture space. Here, the artist decided to include the wider landscape as a way of bringing back memories of a happy family holiday.

In compositional terms, the position of the figure in a portrait such as this is just as important as the overall amount of space it occupies. Although the girl in this painting takes up only a small part of the scene, it is to her that our eyes are drawn. This is partly because the artist has changed the composition of her reference photo and positioned the child 'on the third' – a classic device for leading the viewer's eye to the main point of interest in a painting – and partly because the beach, sea and headland are painted in less detail.

In situ, you could never do more than make a few quick reference sketches of a scene such as this, as young children never stay still for long. This is where a digital camera can prove invaluable; you can fire off a whole series of shots in a matter of seconds and also play back the images immediately to check that you've got all the reference material you're likely to need before you leave the scene.

The pose
This shot of a little girl playing on a beach is the kind of photo that every parent has in the family album. However, she is positioned so close to the edge of the frame that part of her shadow is cut off. The sea and headland take up so much of the photo that they dominate the composition.

Materials
- *Watercolour board*
- *Acrylic paints: brilliant blue, yellow ochre, lemon yellow, brilliant yellow green, alizarin crimson, cadmium red, phthalocyanine blue, white*
- *Brushes: large round, medium round, fine round*
- *HB pencil*

1 Using an HB pencil, lightly sketch the scene, putting in the lines of balance of the figure (the central spine and the tilt of the shoulders). Note how the artist has changed the composition by positioning the little girl 'on the third', including less of the headland and moving the boat to balance the composition and frame the figure.

2 Mix a thin wash of brilliant blue with a little phthalocyanine blue acrylic paint and, using a large brush, wash it over the sky and sea, making the mix a little darker for the sea. Mix a sand colour from yellow ochre and alizarin crimson and wash it over the beach, adding more yellow ochre for the foreground. Use a redder version of the sand mix for the girl's skin.

> **Tip**: Make sure you leave some space above the little girl's head so that it stands out clearly against the blue of the sea. In the photograph her pale hat is too close to the line of the headland.

3 While the paper is still wet, brush a dilute purple (mixed from alizarin crimson and brilliant blue) over the wet sand, allowing the colour to spread wet into wet. Apply a pale wash of the sand colour over the headland. When dry, mix a dark green from phthalocyanine blue, lemon yellow and yellow ochre and dab in the vegetation. Add a little cadmium red and phthalocyanine blue to a thicker mix of yellow ochre and dot in sand and pebbles in the foreground.

4 Mix brilliant yellow green and brilliant blue to give a vivid blue and brush this colour on to the sea along the horizon. Look for different tones of blue and green in the sea and brush them in, using various versions of the vivid blue mix and adding white to the mix in places. For the wet sand along the shoreline, mix a slightly thicker, pale blue violet from alizarin crimson, white and brilliant blue, and apply using a dry brush.

5 Using a fine round brush, put in the white of the little girl's sun hat, bucket and bathing costume. Mix a warm flesh colour from cadmium red, white and a tiny bit of yellow ochre and put in the shaded tones on the little girl's body – mostly on the left-hand side, but also on the inner edges of her right thigh and calf.

6 Use phthalocyanine blue for the bright blue of the little girl's bathing costume, and a pale purple mix for the shaded side of her sun hat. Continue working on the flesh tones, looking for the light and dark tones within the figure. Use variations of the mixes from the previous step for the darker tones and a mix of lemon yellow, white and cadmium red for the sunlit side of the figure, which is warm in tone.

Tip: You may find it easier to judge the shapes if you turn your painting upside down. This helps you to reproduce how things look, rather than following the way your mind says they should look.

Assessment time
The figure requires very little extra work other than adding the cast shadow on the sand. Although the combination of different colours in the sea works well, there is no real sense of the wavelets breaking on the shore.

The boundary between sea and shore can be made clearer by making more of the breaking waves.

Adding a little more detail and texture to the foreground sand will help to bring it forwards in the picture.

7 Brush more colour into the water, using the same green and violet mixes as before. Mix white and the pale blue-violet mix from Step 4 and, using both your fingers and a relatively dry brush and slightly thicker paint than before, dot in the breaking wavelets along the shoreline.

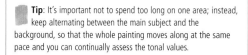

Tip: It's important not to spend too long on one area; instead, keep alternating between the main subject and the background, so that the whole painting moves along at the same pace and you can continually assess the tonal values.

8 Mix a violet shadow colour from the pale blue-violet mix and phthalocyanine blue and, using a fine round brush and fairly thin paint, brush in the shadow that the little girl's body casts on the sand.

9 Using a fine brush, paint the boat in a purplish-blue mix of phthalocyanine blue and alizarin crimson and touch in the light edge of the sail in white.

10 Scumble thicker mixes of yellow ochre and reddish browns into the foreground to create some texture in the sand and pebbles. Paint the sunlit sides of the pebbles in lighter grey-purple mixes.

The finished painting

Acrylic paints are a good choice for a subject such as this as they come in a huge range of colours and can be used very thinly, like watercolour, for delicate areas such as the wet sand, or thickly, like oils, for textural details in the foreground. This painting is full of light and sunshine, and the warm colours on the figure and foreground sand balance the cooler blues and greens of the landscape beautifully, while the composition leads the viewer's eye around the picture, from the figure of the little girl, up to the boat and then across to the headland and back to the girl again.

The modelling on the figure is subtle but effective and conveys the childish plumpness of the figure well.

Note how delicately the reflection in the wet sand has been painted.

Thicker paint, applied both with a brush and with the fingers, is used to give the breaking waves more solidity.

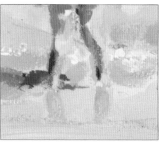

Informal portrait in watercolour

There's no rule that says a portrait has to be formal; a snapshot of a moment in time can be just as effective. Here, the artist took a series of photos of this young couple as they walked along, holding hands, on a sunny autumn afternoon and selected this shot as the one to work from because it was the only one that showed them looking directly at each other, oblivious to the camera. The fact that they are moving also gives the otherwise very static and calm scene more dynamism.

The other thing that makes the scene so appealing is the warm, dappled light. Because of its luminosity and translucency, watercolour is an obvious medium to choose to render the subtle effects of light and shade. Here, you can use wet-into-wet washes to build up the tones of the stonework and create the soft-edged shadows cast on the columns by the leaves. Combine this with wet-on-dry applications for the hard edges of the columns and areas that require more detailing, such as the figures and the foreground leaves. Remember, however, that you cannot apply a dark colour on top of a light one. You have to start with the lightest colour and work up to the darkest.

Materials
- *Heavy HP watercolour paper*
- *Watercolour paints: Prussian blue, raw umber, alizarin crimson, cadmium yellow, cadmium red, Venetian red, yellow ochre*
- *Gouache paint: white*
- *Brushes: large round, medium round, fine round*
- *HB pencil*

The pose
The couple are positioned one third of the way into the picture space – a classic compositional device, as the viewer's eye is immediately drawn to this area. The viewpoint has been chosen so that we are looking back along the row of columns; the line 'linking' the base of the columns seems to slope towards the vanishing point.

1 Using an HB pencil, lightly sketch the couple and their surroundings. Look for anything that you can use as a guide to where things are positioned. Look at the base of the row of columns in particular; as the columns recede into the distance, this line appears to slope upwards towards the vanishing point. Put in the vertical lines of the columns.

2 Continue with the underdrawing until you feel you have put down all the information you may need. The fluted facets of the columns and creases in the young couple's clothing are all things that you can make use of when it comes to doing the painting.

3 Mix a dark olivey green from Prussian blue and raw umber and, using a large round brush, put in the dark tones of the stonework and shadows. Then mix a very dilute reddish orange from alizarin crimson and cadmium yellow and wash it over the sunlit parts of the columns and ground. Use firm, straight strokes for the edges of the columns, otherwise you will get a wobbly effect.

4 Continue painting the columns, with variations on the previous mixes as appropriate. Using a medium round brush, loosely dab in the palest colour of fallen leaves using a dilute wash of cadmium yellow and cadmium red. Mix a flesh colour from Venetian red with a touch of yellow ochre and paint the exposed skin, leaving the highlights untouched. Begin painting their clothes, using Prussian blue with a hint of Venetian red for the jeans and Venetian red for the girl's top.

6 For the darker tones in the girl's hair, use a purplish black mix of Prussian blue and alizarin crimson. Use short, delicate brushstrokes and a fine round brush to build up some texture and detail. Put in the mid-toned leaves using a fine round brush and a reddish brown mix of cadmium yellow and alizarin crimson. Work wet into wet for the background leaves and wet on dry for those in the foreground.

5 Touch raw umber wet into wet on to the denim jeans to create tonal variation, leaving some areas very pale. For the boy's jacket, mix a dark, purplish black from Prussian blue, alizarin crimson and a little raw umber. Paint the girl's hair in an orangey red mix of raw umber and alizarin crimson, and the boy's hair in a mix of olive green and raw umber.

> **Tip:** Having more texture and detail in the foreground than in the background is one way of creating an impression of distance. The viewer's eye assumes that any textured, detailed areas are closer.

7 Apply more warm browns and pinks to the stonework, cutting in around the girl's head to help define her better. Using warmer, slightly darker versions of the previous mixes, begin to build up some modelling on the faces and hair. Darken the clothing, looking for the different tones and creases within the fabric that imply the movement of the limbs beneath.

Tips: Count the columns and their 'flutes' carefully to make sure you put in the right number. Aim for nothing more than a loose impression of the fallen leaves: if you try to put in every single one accurately, your painting will become very tight and laboured.

Assessment time

When you've put in all the basic elements of the composition and established the colours, look for areas that need to be strengthened. This looks a little flat in places, with insufficient contrast between the fore and background. The shadows, in particular, require work. Although the warm and cool colours give an impression of light and shade on the columns, the shadows of the leaves, which add real atmosphere, are missing.

The cast shadows of the leaves, which add real atmosphere to the scene, need to be added.

This highlight area on the girl's neck is too bright.

8 Deepen the shadows on the ground, using dark greys and browns. If you wish you can add a little white gouache to your mixes to create an opaque colour and brush in loose strokes to imply the dappled sunlight on the ground. Using a fine round brush and a range of reddish browns, put in the darkest colours of the fallen leaves.

9 Using short, broken brushstrokes and the same colours as before, build up the tone on the stonework columns. To create a sense of dappled light, add a little white gouache to your mixes for the most brightly lit areas and dab on small randomly-shaped marks for the cast shadows of the leaves.

The finished painting

This portrait exploits the characteristics of watercolour to the full, using wet-into-wet washes of translucent colour while still allowing the white of the paper to shine through. One of the keys to the success of a painting such as this is observing how the figures relate to one another: the time the artist spent on the underdrawing, establishing lines of balance such as the tilt of the shoulders and the angle of the hips, has paid dividends. Although loosely painted, the young couple's animated expressions are clear to see. The beautiful dappled lighting and soft colours give a warm glow to a portrait that is full of charm and life. The diagonal line of the stone columns is a strong compositional device that adds dynamism.

Dabs of opaque gouache, tinted with the appropriate colour, convey the cast shadows on the columns.

The way the light falls across the figures has been carefully observed and rendered, making the portrait atmospheric.

The animated expressions and body language bring the portrait to life, giving it movement and character.

Indian market scene in mixed media

Full of hustle and bustle, often packed with bustling people, colourful displays of fruit, vegetables and other goods, street markets can be a wonderful source of inspiration for artists – but with so much going on, it is often very difficult to work in situ. And even if you do manage to find a quiet spot to set up your easel, the chances are that you will soon find yourself surrounded by curious onlookers, which can be somewhat intimidating.

This is one situation where it is useful to take reference photos, as you can work quickly and unobtrusively, and gather a whole wealth of material to paint from at a later date. Start with distant views and gradually move in closer to your chosen subject – and don't forget about things like advertisements, hand-written signs and unusual produce, all of which can add a lot of atmospheric local detail to your paintings.

If you want to take photographs of people, it is always best to ask their permission, although this does bring with it the risk that your subjects will start playing up to the camera. If this happens, take a few "posed" shots first and then, when they have turned back to their business, take a few more. Another good tip is to set your camera on its widest setting and point it slightly to one side of the person you are photographing. You will appear to be looking somewhere else, but the camera's field of view will be wide enough to include them in the frame, too. Above all, don't stint on the number of shots you take: film is inexpensive and if you've got a digital camera, there are no processing costs at all.

Materials
- *4B pencil*
- *90lb (185gsm) rough watercolour paper, pre-stretched*
- *Watercolour paints: indigo, alizarin crimson, raw umber, cobalt turquoise, cadmium red, Hooker's green, cadmium yellow, burnt umber, cobalt blue*
- *Gouache paints: Bengal rose, permanent white*
- *Brushes: Chinese, fine round*
- *Household candle*

Reference photographs
Here the artist used two photographs. The one on the right shows the corner of the stall and the stallholder selling his wares, and the one below shows the two ladies shopping and rows of colourful bowls of powdered dyes. In her compositional sketch, the artist angled the bowls to provide a more gentle lead-in to the picture.

The stallholder is just visible. He will be more prominent in the painting.

There is nothing of interest in this area.

A more gentle lead-in will be provided if the bowls start in the bottom right corner of the image.

 1 Using a 4B pencil, sketch the subject, taking care to get the perspective right. Note how the bowls of powder get smaller and closer together as they recede into the distance.

> **Tip**: To make it easier to get the shapes of the bowls of powder right, think of them as simple geometric shapes – ovals with rough triangular shapes on top.

2 Mix a warm, greyish blue from indigo, alizarin crimson and a little raw umber and start putting in the cool background colours. Paint the area of deepest shade under the table, adding more raw umber to the mixture for the pavement area. This neutral background will help to unify the painting. With so many vibrant colours in the scene, the overall impact could easily be overwhelming.

3 Add more alizarin crimson to the mixture to make a darker, brown colour and brush in the shadows under the bowls and the wooden vertical supports of the shelves in the background. Use a paler version of the mixture to paint the stallholder's shirt and a darker one to paint the background of the more distant stall and the area immediately behind the stallholder's head. Filling in the negative spaces in this way makes it easier to see what it is happening in such a complicated scene.

5 Using an ordinary household candle, stroke candle wax over the lightbulbs. Press firmly so that enough of the wax adheres to the paper. The wax will act as a resist. The white paper will show through in places, while other areas will take on the surrounding colour, as if that colour is reflected in the glass of the bulb.

4 Mix a warm shadow colour from indigo with a tiny amount of alizarin crimson and paint the shadows under the steel bowls, taking care to leave highlights on the rims. Use the same mixture to paint lines in between the oblong dishes of powder in the background.

▶

Assessment time

Using the same basic mixtures as before, continue putting in some background colours and the shadows under the bowls. The basis of the background is now complete, both tonally and compositionally.

Blocking in the negative spaces makes it easier to see what is happening in the rest of the scene.

We "read" this shaded area as being on a different plane to the stall top, which is in bright sunlight.

Although the bowls are empty at this stage, their shapes and shadows are clearly established.

6 Mix a warm, purplish black from alizarin crimson and indigo and paint the stallholder's hair. Mix cadmium red with alizarin crimson and paint the wooden support on the right-hand edge of the foreground stall. Drybrush a little of the same colour on to the stall top, where powder has been spilt, and start putting the same colour into the bowls of powder. Paint cobalt turquoise on the walls at the far end.

Tip: While you have one colour mix on your palette, see where else you can use it in the painting.

7 Mix a wash of Hooker's green and paint the green plastic that covers the basket on the ground and the mounds of green powder. Mix a warm orange from cadmium red and cadmium yellow and dot the mixture into the background immediately behind the stallholder to indicate the packages on sale. (A hint of the basic shape and colour is sufficient.) Add a little burnt umber to the orange mixture and paint the stallholder's face.

8 Paint the women's skin tones in the same orangey-brown mixture. Mix a strong purple from Bengal rose gouache and cobalt blue watercolour and paint the sari worn by the woman in the foreground, leaving a few highlight areas untouched.

9 Using the same mixture and a fine round brush, paint the creases in the sari, adding more cobalt blue to the mixture for the very darkest creases. By darkening the tones in this way, you will begin to imply the folds in the fabric. Mix a dark purple from Bengal rose, alizarin crimson and a little indigo and dot in the pattern on the sari. Mix Bengal rose with a tiny amount of cobalt blue and paint the mounds of very bright pink powder.

10 Continue painting the powders, mixing cadmium red with Bengal rose for the red powders and using cobalt blue for the blue ones. Don't worry too much about the shapes of the mounds at this stage. This will become clearer as you build up the tones later on.

11 Build up the tones on the powders, using the same mixtures as before. Using a 4B pencil, draw the lines of the plastic-wrapped packages on the corner of the stall. Mix a pale wash of cobalt turquoise and brush over the lines, using a fine round brush.

▶

12 Mix a dark purple colour from Bengal rose, alizarin crimson and a little indigo. Using a fine round brush, accentuate the creases in the sari fabric in the same colour.

13 Using a mixture of alizarin crimson and indigo, paint around the stallholder. Darkening the background in this way helps to make him stand out from his surroundings. Use the same alizarin crimson and indigo mixture to strengthen the shadows on the right-hand side of the stall.

14 By this stage, all you need to do is refine some of the details. Mix a rich, brownish black from alizarin crimson, indigo and cadmium red and darken the stallholder's hair. Darken his skin tones with a more dilute version of the same mixture. Paint the stripes on the colourful woven basket in Bengal rose gouache and darken the tones on the wooden posts of the stall.

15 Tone down the brightness of the paper, where necessary, with very pale washes of the background colours. Paint the highlights on the lightbulbs in permanent white gouache.

The finished painting

Here, the artist has created a lively interpretation of a busy market, packed with colourful sights and people going about their daily business. The composition is much more satisfactory than that of the original reference photographs.

The line of bowls leads diagonally through the image to the two women, while the stallholder is positioned near enough to the intersection of the thirds to provide a secondary focus of interest for the painting.

The contrast between light and dark areas establishes the different planes of the image.

The stallholder's direct gaze encourages us to follow his line of sight across the scene to the two women.

The indentations in the mounds of powder are skilfully conveyed by applying more layers of colour to the darker, shaded areas.

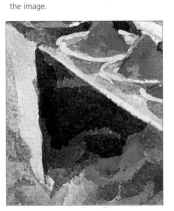

Café scene in acrylics

At first glance, this bustling café portrait looks extremely complicated and full of movement, with a complex play of light and shade across the whole scene. You could be forgiven for wondering how on earth you can capture such a wealth of detail in this busy portrait.

The trick, at least in the initial stages, is to forget about the detail and to concentrate instead on the overall impression. Look for blocks of colour and tone – and try to see the scene as a series of interconnecting shapes, rather than as individual elements. If you get too caught up in details such as a person's hair or the precise pattern on one of the café umbrellas, the chances are that your painting will become tight and laboured.

Remember, too, that the spaces between objects (which artists describe as "negative" shapes) are as important in a painting as the objects themselves (the "positive" shapes). Although the rational part of your brain may be telling you that a person or a solid object such as a table should take precedence over an apparently empty background, in painting terms the two are equally important: one helps to define the other.

The complex pattern of light and shade requires careful treatment, too. There are many shadows here, both in the open foreground and in the dark, narrow street in the background. Shadows are rarely, if ever, black; instead, they often contain colours that are complementary to the main subject. If buildings are a warm terracotta colour, for example, their shadows may contain a little complementary green.

Sketch

Scenes of people can change quickly, so make a quick preliminary sketch to capture the moment.

Materials
- Board primed with acrylic gesso
- Willow charcoal
- Acrylic paints: cadmium yellow, cadmium red, titanium white, phthalocyanine green, alizarin crimson, lemon yellow, ultramarine blue
- Brushes: large round, medium flat, small round
- Kitchen paper

The scene

This is one type of subject in which painting from photographs really comes into its own. There is so much going on that you could do little more than put down the bare bones of the scene on the spot – but a quick reference photo or two will "freeze" the action and provide you with plenty of information on which to base your image.

1 Block in the darkest areas of the background buildings and the shadows on the pavement, using the side of a stick of willow charcoal, as this allows you to cover large areas quickly. Although the charcoal will be covered up by subsequent applications of paint, it allows you to establish the structure of the scene at the outset, and makes it easier for you to find your way around the complex mix of colours and tones.

2 To avoid dirtying your colours when you begin applying the paint, gently dust off any excess charcoal powder using a clean piece of kitchen paper. (Alternatively, you could use a spray fixative.)

3 Mix a warm orange from cadmium yellow and cadmium red. Using a large round brush, brush in the warm colours of background buildings. Paint the café umbrellas and awning in mixtures of cadmium red and titanium white, varying the proportions of the two colours to get the right tones. Putting in these strong tones in the early stages helps give the scene some structure. The order in which you apply them is not terribly important, but while you have got one colour on the palette try to use it everywhere that it occurs.

4 Loosely indicate the café tables in phthalocyanine green. Mix a very dilute green from phthalocyanine green and titanium white and paint the shadow areas in the foreground. (Note that this green is a cool complementary colour to the reds used on the awning and umbrellas.) Add alizarin crimson to the mixture and paint the very dark colours of the buildings in the background. This gives you the necessary darkness of tone without having to resort to using black, which often tends to look flat and lifeless. It also picks up on colours used elsewhere in the painting, creating one of many colour links that will ultimately help to hold the whole image together.

▶

5 Mix a pale yellow from lemon yellow and titanium white and put in the light-coloured buildings in the background. Add more titanium white to the mixtures that you used to paint the umbrellas in Step 3, making the paint fairly thick, and paint the pinkish stripes on the umbrellas.

6 Using the dark mixture from Step 4, begin blocking in the figures sitting at the café tables. Do not try to put in substantial detail at this stage: simply look for the overall shapes. Look at the tilt of people's shoulders and heads and concentrate on getting these angles right, as they will help to make the painting look realistic. Brush more of the dilute phthalocyanine green and white mixture over the street area, particularly at the point just beyond the café where the street narrows and is in deeper shade.

7 Block in the colours of the shirts of the café customers in the foreground, making the colours darker in tone for the creases in the fabric, as this helps to reveal the form of the body and give more of a sense of light and shade.

8 Brush over the highlight areas with titanium white, using the paint thickly in order to create some texture. Deepen the tones of the big foreground umbrella where necessary. Using the same dark mixtures as before, carefully brush around the figures sitting at the café tables; although the figures are little more than blocks of colour at this stage, and very little detail has been put in, defining the negative shapes (the spaces between the figures) in this way helps to separate them from the background so that they stand out more clearly.

Assessment time

Using brilliant blue and alizarin crimson, block in more of the shirt and trouser colours of the passers-by on the left. The main elements are now in place, and the rest of the painting will be a gradual process of refinement: although they may look like fairly abstract blocks of colour at this stage, the subjects will soon start to emerge more clearly. Training yourself to look for blocks of colour, rather than attempting to define every element, is a useful exercise.

The dark blocks laid down in Step 1 provide the structure for the image.

The people are painted as bold blocks of colour; detail can be added later once the basic shapes and colours are in place.

9 Pick out details using a small round brush. Paint the curved chair backs in phthalocyanine green, and the hair of the café customers in various browns mixed from cadmium yellow and cadmium red. Remember to look carefully at the spaces between objects as well as at the objects themselves: going around the figures in a dark tone helps to make them stand out.

10 Continue adding defining details across the painting, again looking at the negative spaces and looking for identifiable blocks of colour on the clothes of the passers-by. Vertical strokes of green on the background buildings are a quick-and-easy way of implying the dark window recesses; the colour also provides a visual link with the green chairs in the foreground.

11 Because it is so bright, the eye is drawn to the paved foreground area in the bottom left of the painting, which looks very empty. Using more of the green mixture from Step 6 and a medium flat brush, make broad horizontal strokes across this area. This enhances the feeling of dappled light playing on the ground and creates texture and interest.

▶

12 Switching to a medium flat brush allows you to shape straight-edged elements, such as the eaves of the roofs (top right) and the table edges (bottom right), more precisely.

13 Using a pale, blue-grey mixture of titanium white and ultramarine blue, loosely indicate the lettering on the café awning. Continue adjusting tones across the whole scene: adding a pale, but opaque yellow to the background buildings reinforces the sense of light and shade, while the shadows on the ground can be made stronger with a bluish-purple mixture as before.

14 Using the flat brush again, block in rectangles of colour on the roofs to define their edges more clearly. The precise colours that you use are not too important: look for the relative lightness and darkness of different areas, as this is what will make the picture look three-dimensional.

15 Using a fine round brush and the same pale blue-grey mixture that you used for the café awning lettering, "draw" in the vertical posts of the awning and the large foreground umbrellas. Adjust the tones on the shaded sides of both awning and umbrellas, if necessary, to reinforce the different planes of the image. If you decide that the bottom left corner is still too bright in relation to the rest of the painting, brush more of the bluey-green shadow mixture across it. Finally, look for any areas that catch the light, such as the edges of the foreground tables and chairs, and lightly touch in the highlights here with a pale mixture of phthalocyanine green and titanium white.

The finished painting

This is a spontaneous-looking painting that belies its careful planning and the meticulous attention to capturing the effects of light and shade. The composition looks informal, like a snapshot of a moment "frozen" in time; in fact, the large, virtually empty space on the left helps to balance the image, while the receding lines of the café tables lead the viewer's eye through the picture to the bustling street and buildings in the background.

Creating the right tonal balance is one of the keys to an image like this; resisting the temptation to put in too much detail, with the consequent risk of overworking the painting, is another. Here, the artist has succeeded on both counts.

Deep shadows reveal the intensity of the sunlight. They are balanced by the large, brightly lit buildings in the background and help to bring the scene to life.

Although there is relatively little detail on the faces, by concentrating on the tilt of the heads and bodies the artist has conveyed a feeling of animation.

The artist has used some artistic licence in choosing the colours for the building in the background, but they complement and balance the foreground colours well.

Dancing couple in pastel pencil

When drawing a moving subject, it's helpful to take a photograph to use as reference. You can use a fast shutter speed to 'freeze' the action and risk losing the sense of movement that you wanted to capture. Alternatively, you can use a slower shutter speed so that there is some blur in the photo – but then you risk not being able to see all the detail as clearly as you would like. Here the artist wanted to see the detail clearly and elected to freeze the movement in the reference photo.

The challenge in this scenario is how to create that all-important sense of movement. Sometimes, even when the action is frozen, we know that the subject must be moving because the 'pose' itself is so precarious that we know it simply couldn't be held for more than a second or two. (Think, for example, of a ballerina in mid-pirouette.) Here the dancers have both feet touching the ground and the movement is not obvious at first glance, so you need to find other ways of conveying a sense of movement.

In this drawing the artist used two techniques to give a sense of movement: a 'ghost' image, indicating the position from which the limbs have just moved, and curved lines in the background, which follow the contours of the bodies. The same techniques could be applied just as well to other moving objects, for instance a horse racing at full stretch, or any sporting action.

Manikin
Also called a lay figure, a manikin (available from art supply stores), is a very handy tool for working out the lines of a pose. Use it to help you to work out the 'ghost' image.

Materials
- *Pastel paper*
- *HB pencil*
- *Pastel pencils: brown, spectrum orange, black, light sepia, pale brown, red, orange, pale blue, cream or pale yellow, red-brown*

The pose
Although the action has been 'frozen' in this photo, the woman's flowing hair and the fact that the right foot of both dancers is in the process of lifting off the ground indicate that they are, in fact, moving.

1 Sketch the scene, using an HB pencil. Imagine guidelines running across and down the image to help you: the man's left hand, for example, is roughly in line with his right heel.

2 Block in the man's flesh tones and hair in brown and emphasize the strongest lines of the pose. Using spectrum orange, block in the woman's flesh tones.

3 Block in both dancers' hair in black. For the shaded parts of the man's trousers and shirt and the woman's dress, apply light sepia. Use the same colour to draw the frill around the bottom of her dress.

4 Using the side of a pale brown pastel pencil, block in the background. Begin to put in stronger, curved lines in the background to emphasize the movement of the figures, echoing the curves of the moving arms.

▶

Assessment time
With the same pale brown pencil, put in a 'ghost' image of the moving legs and arms. This, along with the curved lines in the background which echo the shape of the woman's back, helps to give an impression of movement. Now that the main lines of the drawing have been established, you can begin to refine the detail and add some colour to bring the drawing to life.

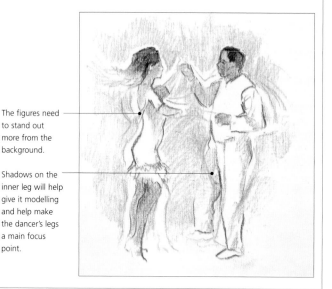

The figures need to stand out more from the background.

Shadows on the inner leg will help give it modelling and help make the dancer's legs a main focus point.

5 Using the same colours as before, darken the flesh tones so that the figures stand out from the background. Block in the woman's dress and the man's waistcoat in red overlaid with orange. (This optical mix of two colours creates a much more lively and interesting effect than a solid application of a single colour.)

6 Using a very pale blue pencil, put in the creases in the man's shirtsleeve and shade his right leg. Block in the shoes in black, leaving the highlights. Working around the 'ghost' image, put in some stronger curved lines that follow the contours of the bodies to enhance the sense of movement.

7 Darken the creases on the trousers and go over the trousers very lightly with a cream or very pale yellow pastel pencil. (Leaving the paper white would look too stark.) Draw the woman's hair, which is streaming out behind her as she moves, with quick flicks of a black pastel pencil.

8 Using horizontal marks, put in the floor. It is on a different plane to the background and using horizontal, rather than vertical, strokes helps to make this clear. Using a red-brown pencil, sharpen the edges of the figures – the hands, faces and the line of the woman's body and legs.

The finished drawing

The sense of movement in this drawing comes as much from the way the background has been handled as from the way the dancing couple has been drawn. The pastel pencil marks are light and free, which gives the drawing a feeling of energy. The synchronized action and engagement of the eyes between the dancers makes this a great study of a relationship. The fact that their whole bodies have been detailed as much (or as little) as their faces is important in a study of a physical activity such as dancing, whereas in a sitting pose the artist may decide to show far less detail in the body than in the sitter's face.

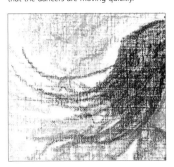

The hair streams out, making it obvious that the dancers are moving quickly.

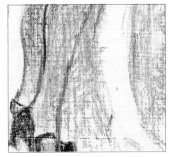

The 'ghost' images imply that this is the position the figure has just moved from.

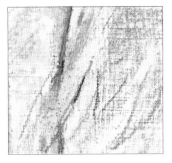

Curved pencil strokes in the background also help to imply movement.

Climber in mixed media

When you're drawing or painting a moving subject, there's obviously a limit to what you can do *in situ*. However, it's always a good idea to try to make a few quick sketches from life, even if you then go home and work up a more detailed drawing and painting later, as it makes you really look at the movements. It also enables you to try out different compositions.

In this project, the artist painted his son practising on an indoor climbing wall. As rock climbers spend time feeling for the next foot- or hand-hold, he was able to make a series of quick sketches and look at the musculature of his subject. He also took a series of photographs to use for reference.

In order to capture something of the energy involved in climbing, he wanted a medium that would allow him to work quickly and vigorously. He drew in the main lines of the body with broad sweeps of oil bar, and then wiped over them with a rag dipped in turpentine to soften the lines and spread the colour. Then he added soft pencil and soft pastel detailing on top, creating lively textural contrasts.

An action scene such as this, where the musculature of the subject is very obvious, is one scenario where a little knowledge of basic anatomy is really useful. You don't need to know the names of the individual muscles, but being aware of where they are and how they contract or extend in order for the limbs to move will make your drawings look more realistic. It also helps if you have some idea of the direction in which the muscles run, as you can imply the muscles beneath the surface of the skin by making your pencil marks or brushstrokes run in the right direction.

Materials
- *Heavy, rough watercolour paper*
- *Oil bars: raw sienna, manganese blue, Naples yellow*
- *Turpentine*
- *Old rag*
- *Graphite pencils: B and 9B*
- *Soft pastels: Naples yellow, burnt sienna, pale blue*

Preliminary sketches made *in situ*
These sketches were all made in around one minute from start to finish so that the artist could work out a composition that appealed to him and get in some practice at looking for the main lines of such a pose.

The pose
This is an extreme and unnatural position, so look for where each limb or feature sits in relation to others. The hands, for example, are positioned one above the other and, if you drop an imaginary line down from them, you will see that they align with the left heel. The shoulder and arm muscles are prominent, revealing the amount of effort required for the climber to cling on. There is a strong diagonal line running from the top of the left shoulder down to the left foot, which creates a dynamic composition.

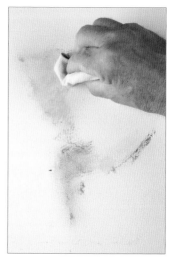

1 Using raw sienna and manganese blue oil bars, put in broad sweeps of colour to represent the climber's back and blue trousers. Dip an old rag in turpentine and wipe it firmly over the oil bar marks to blend them and create the basic shapes.

Tips:
- Tape your paper to a drawing board so that it doesn't slip around.
- Aim for bold, generalized shapes rather than anything precise.

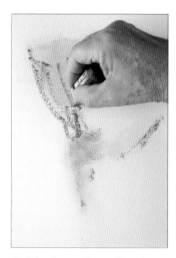

2 Using the raw sienna oil bar, draw in lines to represent the spine, the curve of the shoulder blades, the trapezius (the muscle that connects the shoulders to the spinal vertebrae) and the latissimus dorsi (the muscle that wraps around the sides of the trunk).

3 Wipe over the oil bar lines with a turpentine-soaked rag, as before, but this time do not blend them completely; aim to retain something of the linear quality. Roughly block in the hair with blue oil bar. Using a soft (B) pencil, outline the head and indicate the main muscle masses – for example, around the shoulder blades.

4 Continue using the pencil to put in more detail. Outline the trousers and put in any folds in the fabric that imply the movement of the muscles underneath – for example, under the right buttock and thigh. Use the oil bars to establish the basic shape of the legs, and draw in the feet using the pencil.

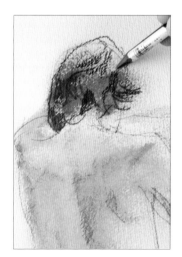

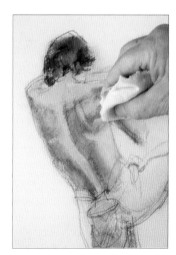

5 Apply raw sienna and a little manganese blue oil bar to the hair and lightly blend on the paper with turpentine to give a dark brown colour. Using a softer pencil (a 9B), put some linear detailing into the hair.

6 Again using the 9B pencil, apply some shading to the back, making closely spaced diagonal lines that follow the direction in which the muscles run. Strengthen the linear detailing on the trousers, again looking for the creases.

7 Use a Naples yellow oil bar to put in the highlights on the back, then blend the marks with a turpentine-soaked rag, as before. The turpentine will also darken and blur any underlying pencil marks.

▶

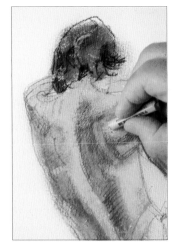

8 Now you can begin using soft pastels to create more texture and variation in the skin tones. Using various shades of Naples yellow and burnt sienna, add more colour and detail to the hair. Apply Naples yellow to the highlit areas of the back, blending the marks with your fingers.

Assessment time
Using a B pencil, sketch in the lines of the climbing wall and the main hand- and foot-holds. This provides a context for the scene without distracting from the figure. All the elements of the drawing are in place and the skin and muscle tones have been nicely rendered, but the drawing could be improved by adding a little more definition and shading over all.

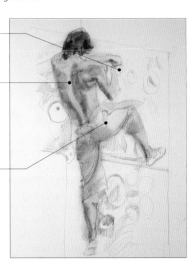

There is very little definition in the right hand.

The skin tones look convincing, but the strong back muscles could be emphasized a little more.

Compared with the rest of the image, the trousers look very pale and washed out.

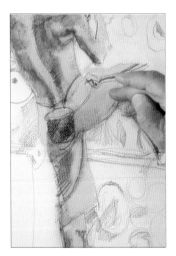

9 Using a 9B pencil, scribble in the chalk bag that the climber has attached to his belt loops. Strengthen the colour of the trousers by applying more blue soft pastel and blending the marks with your fingers.

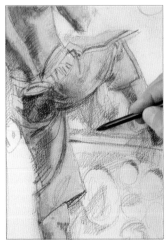

10 Put in a few more lines of pull on the trousers. You can blend the pencil marks into the pastel with your fingers to create a darker tone in this area. Strengthen the cast shadows on the wall behind the climber.

11 Using a red soft pastel, draw in the red lines on the climbing shoes for a final finishing touch. Red is a very strong colour that immediately draws the eye, so be careful not to overdo it.

The finished drawing

This is a quickly executed drawing that nonetheless captures the figure in motion very well. The feeling of movement comes largely from the fact that the pose appears so precarious: our brains interpret the scene and tell us that the figure is moving simply because we know that such a position cannot be held for long. The taut back and shoulder muscles also reveal the amount of physical effort required on the part of the climber. Artistically, the combination of broad sweeps of colour overlaid with vigorous pencil detailing creates a feeling of tremendous energy, while the soft pastel marks on the skin and trousers create a pleasing contrast in texture. Because the climbing wall itself is not particularly worth looking at, it has only been faintly suggested with rough pencil sketching. This means that all attention is on the muscular tension and form of the climber, as well as the unusual angles of his position.

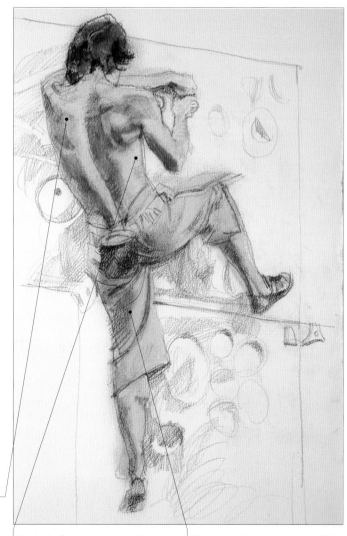

Oil bar marks blended with turpentine create solid areas of tone that are perfect for conveying the dense muscle masses.

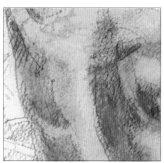

Smudged soft pastel marks create the highlights on the skin and the smooth areas of flesh.

Vigorous pencil marks show how the fabric is being stretched and imply the movement of the limbs beneath.

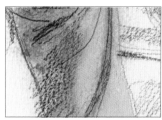

Swimmer in watercolour

Although the subject of this project looks simple enough – a solitary figure swimming underwater, with relatively little discernible detail – the real interest lies in the play of light on the water and the way that shapes are slightly distorted, producing an image that tends towards abstraction. Your task is not only to capture the sleek form of the swimmer and to freeze a moment in time, but also to convey a sense of the dappled sunlight and the movement of the water.

As so often happens in painting, it helps to exaggerate certain elements in order to get across the mood that you want. Distorting the figure of the swimmer slightly in order to make it look more streamlined is one way to do this; making more of the dappled patches of sunlight on the water is another.

Adding a few drops of gum arabic to your paint mixes is a very useful technique when painting water, as it increases the gloss and transparency of watercolour paint. This, combined with the careful build-up of layers of colour, helps to make the water look as if it is shimmering in the sunlight.

Materials
- *2B pencil*
- *200lb (425gsm) NOT watercolour paper, pre-stretched*
- *Watercolour paints: cadmium lemon, alizarin crimson, cerulean blue, cobalt turquoise, cadmium red, cadmium yellow, Payne's grey, ivory black, burnt sienna, burnt umber*
- *Brushes: large round, medium round, small round*
- *Gum arabic*
- *3B graphite stick*

Reference photograph
Fascinated by the way the sunlight played on the water, the artist asked his daughter to dive repeatedly into this brightly tiled swimming pool, so that he could take reference photographs to work on at his leisure. When you are shooting a moving subject, it is hard to predict what you will actually capture on the film, so always take a lot more shots than you think you will need.

There is some dappled light on both the girl and the water, but this can be exaggerated in the painting to increase the feeling of sunlight.

Elongating the legs, arms and hands will increase the sense of movement.

Cutting off the legs at the top of the frame gives a more dynamic composition and allows the figure space into which to move.

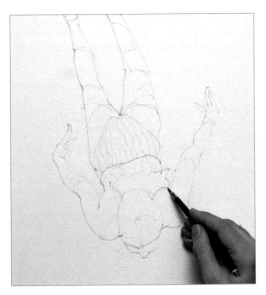

1 Using a 2B pencil, lightly sketch the figure. Note that it is slightly distorted because of the way the light is refracted through the water. In addition, the fingers and legs have been deliberately elongated a little to create a sense of the figure moving through the water at speed.

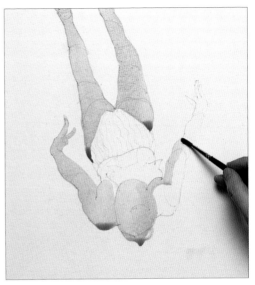

2 Mix a light pink wash from cadmium lemon and alizarin crimson, and a slightly redder version of the same mixture. Using a medium round brush, wash these colours over the whole of the body, alternating between the two mixtures to give some tonal variety. Leave to dry.

3 Mix a strong wash of cadmium lemon and add a little of the lighter pink wash used in Step 2. Using a medium round brush, paint the girl's bikini bottoms in this colour. Leave to dry.

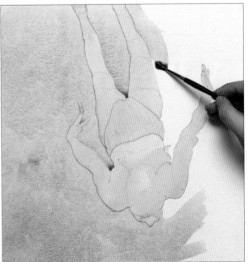

4 Mix a large quantity of a pale blue wash from cerulean blue and a little cobalt turquoise. Wash this mixture over the whole of the background, taking care not to allow any of the paint to go over the figure. (You may need to switch to a smaller brush to "cut in" around the edges of the figure.)

▶

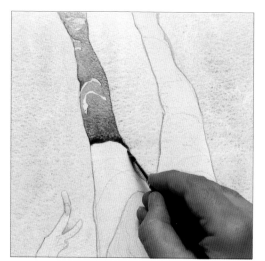

5 Mix three flesh tones from the following colours: alizarin crimson and cadmium lemon; alizarin crimson and a little cerulean blue; cadmium red and cadmium yellow. Dot a small amount of gum arabic into each mixture. Using a medium round brush and alternating between the three mixtures, start to paint over the girl's legs, leaving the base colour showing through in highlight areas. It doesn't matter too much which colour you use where, but try to reserve the darker mixtures for shadow areas.

6 Continue in this way until you have finished painting the legs. Leave to dry.

Tip: Some of the washes may look very dark when you first apply them, but watercolour always dries to a slightly lighter tone. To be on the safe side, test your mixtures on a piece of scrap paper and leave to dry before applying them to the painting.

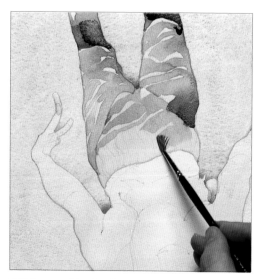

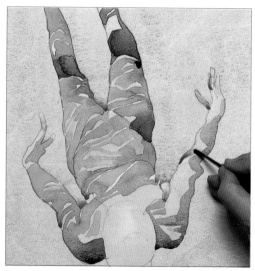

7 Mix a greenish yellow from cadmium lemon with a little Payne's grey. Using a small round brush, paint the ripples of light that run across the bikini bottoms.

8 Using a small round brush and the same flesh tones that you mixed in Step 5, paint the girl's arms and back, leaving some of the underlying wash showing through.

Assessment time
The underpainting is almost complete. The figure stands out well against the pale blue background of the water and is starting to take on a three-dimensional quality. The next stage is to redefine the form by using slightly darker mixtures and to start to put in some of the details.

Varying the flesh tones gives the figure form.

The base colour alone is visible in the most strongly lit areas.

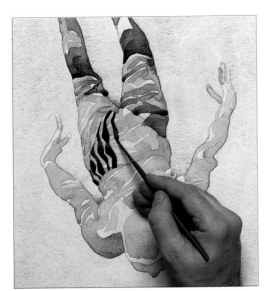

9 Mix slightly darker versions of the flesh tones used in Step 5 and work over the body again, in the same way as before. Mix a warm black from ivory black with a little Payne's grey and paint the stripes on the bikini bottoms. Note that the stripes are not straight lines. This is partly because the pattern is distorted by the way the light refracts from the water and partly because the fabric clings to the girl, helping to indicate the contours of her body.

10 Mix a rich, dark brown from burnt sienna and burnt umber and, using a medium round brush, paint the girl's hair. Leave some areas unpainted and apply a second layer of colour in others so that the hair is not a solid mass of the same tone of brown.

▶

11 Mix a bright blue from cerulean blue and cobalt turquoise and, using a large round brush, begin to wash this mixture over the background. Leave some areas untouched in the top left-hand side, where sunlight dapples the water, and paint ripples in front of the girl's head to show how the water is displaced as she moves through it.

12 Continue working around the figure with the same blue mixture until you have been over the whole of the background. As in Step 4, you may find that you need to switch to a smaller brush in order to paint right up to the edge of the figure, as you must take care not to allow any of the blue mixture to spill over on to the figure. Leave to dry.

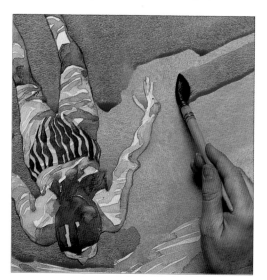

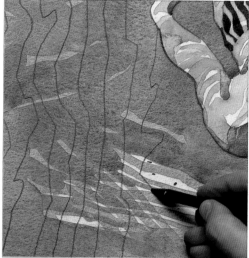

13 Mix a stronger version of the cerulean blue and cobalt turquoise mixture used in Step 11 and add a few drops of gum arabic. Paint over the background again, leaving a few spaces here and there to give the effect of dappled light. Leave to dry.

14 Using a 3B graphite stick, draw the lines of the tiles on the base of the pool. Note that, because of the way the light is refracted and the effects of perspective, the lines are not straight. The lines in the distance slope inwards because this area of the painting is further away from the viewer.

The finished painting

This is a graphic depiction of a swimmer slicing through water, the impression of speed reinforced by a deliberate distortion of her figure and the energetic ripples in front of her head. There is a wonderful feeling of light and warmth in this painting, achieved through the careful build-up of layers of colour.

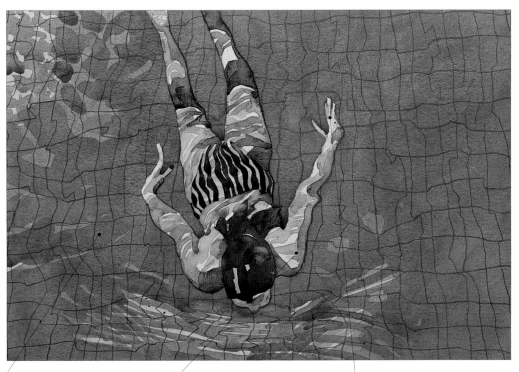

Because of the effects of perspective, the lines of the tiles slope inwards.

The effect of dappled sunlight is created by applying only one or two layers of colour to certain areas.

The swimmer's hands, arms and legs are slightly elongated, which helps to give the impression of movement.

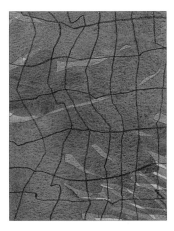

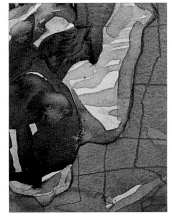

Landscapes and Buildings

Say the words 'landscape painting' and many people's first thought might be a romanticized image of a rural scene untouched by human hand. But of course, human activity plays a crucial role in shaping the landscapes that we inhabit. This chapter demonstrates that the potential for interesting landscape subjects is all around us wherever we happen to live. It begins with a series of lessons on technical aspects and a gallery of drawings and paintings, which gives you the opportunity to see how other artists have tackled a range of landscape challenges. This is followed by a series of quick sketches and finally detailed step-by-step projects, covering topics as diverse as a summer poppy field and a city construction site. Recreate them as practice exercises or use them as a starting point for your own explorations.

Perspective

One of the many challenges in learning how to draw and paint is how to create the illusion of spatial depth on a flat suface. How can you make some objects appear close and others far away? This is done by using a technique known as perspective. At first sight, perspective may seem complex and confusing, but the basics are easy to

understand and even a rudimentary grasp of the fundamentals will enable you to position elements in your work so that they appear to occupy their correct 'space' in the composition.

If you look straight down a road where only one façade of the buildings on each side is visible, the horizontal planes of the upper floors above eye

level will appear to slope down through the length of the street. Horizontal lines below eye level will seem to slope upward. If the viewer of the picture is to be convinced that a road is receding into the distance, then you must reproduce these illusions. With practice, you may be able to do this by eye, but start by taking careful measurements.

Linear perspective

When extended from any receding surface all parallel lines ('perspective lines') meet at the 'vanishing point'. This point is on the 'horizon line', which runs across the field of vision. The horizon line is also known as the eye level, because it always runs horizontally across the field of view at eye level. All perspective lines that originate above the eye level run down to meet the vanishing point and all perspective lines that originate below the eye level run up. Vertical lines remain vertical.

The simplest form of perspective is one-, or single-point, perspective. This occurs when all the receding perspective lines meet at one single point. The vanishing point in one-point perspective always coincides with your centre of vision, directly in front of you.

Parallel lines receding away from the viewer ▼
In this simple illustration of one-point perspective the trees – which, in reality, are all of similar size – appear to get smaller the farther away they are. All perspective lines above eye level run down to the vanishing point (VP) and all perspective lines below eye level run up to the vanishing point.

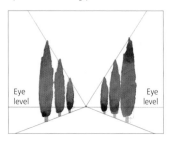

Parallel lines receding to one side ▶
Here, all the elements on the front of the house are on the same plane and so they all meet at the same vanishing point (VP).

Street scene in single-point perspective ▼
In this scene, all the horizontal elements above eye level (for example, the roof lines and the tops and bottoms of the windows) appear to slope down toward the vanishing point, while those below eye level seem to slope up – although, in reality, the planes remain level along the road. If the houses were shown with equidistant planes (that is, without the lines of the roof and road appearing to slope toward the vanishing point), they would not look as if they were parallel to the viewer.

The roofs and many of the windows are above eye level and appear to slope down as the street recedes.

The pavement is below eye level and therefore appears to slope upward as the road recedes.

Two-point perspective

If two sides of an object can be seen at the same time, then two-point perspective comes into play. The principle remains the same, but because two surfaces are visible and both surfaces are at different angles, any parallel lines on those surfaces will eventually join together at their own vanishing point.

In two-point perspective, neither vanishing point falls at your centre of vision. Perspective lines on the right-hand side will converge at a vanishing point off to the right and perspective lines on the left-hand side will converge at a vanishing point off to the left. Even if you move to a position that is higher than your subject, the horizon line on which any vanishing points are situated will still run across your line of vision at

eye level, so all perspective lines will run at an upward angle to meet it. Similarly, if you move to a position below your subject, so that you are looking up at it, all perspective lines will run down to meet the horizon line.

It is very easy to get so caught up in the technicalities of perspective that you lose sight of your drawing as a whole. Once you have mastered the basic principles of perspective, you should

learn to trust your observational skills. Hold a pencil out in front of you to assess the angle of any horizontal lines as they recede toward their vanishing point. Now measure the distances between different elements of your subject carefully, ignoring any preconceptions that you may have about the relative sizes of things.

Two planes visible – two-point perspective ◄
Here we can see two sides of a row of boxes, all of which are oriented the same way. The perspective lines of each side of each box extend to the same vanishing point.

VP Eye level Eye level VP

Multiple-point perspective

When several objects are arranged at different heights and angles, then multiple-point perspective comes into play. It looks a little more complicated, but the rules remain the same. Each object needs to be treated as a separate entity and its vanishing points and perspective lines should be plotted accordingly.

Several vanishing points in the same scene ►
Multiple-point perspective will be used if a building is viewed at a tangent, as the different sides of the building on view will have horizontal planes that extend to different vanishing points. In this example, both vanishing points are out of the picture; the moat façade, diminishing sharply, has a vanishing point close by, but the front elevation with the bridge is viewed at a less oblique angle and has a vanishing point that is farther out, far to the left of the picture area.

Objects at different angles – multiple-point perspective ▼
Here, three box-like shapes are resting on what might be a table top. Each box is facing in a slightly different direction, so each one needs to have separate vanishing points – as does the table, which is oriented differently to the boxes.

This side of the building is viewed from only a slight angle and so the horizontal lines recede only very gradually toward the vanishing points; the vanishing points themselves are far outside the picture area.

This side of the building recedes into the distance; the horizontal lines recede much more steeply, but the vanishing points are still outside the picture area. If you plot the vanishing points on a small-scale preliminary sketch you can then transpose the correct angles on to the full-size support.

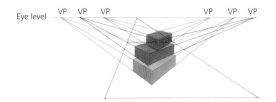

Eye level   VP VP VP   VP VP VP

Aerial perspective

Sometimes known as atmospheric perspective, aerial perspective refers to the way the atmosphere, combined with distance, influences and affects what you see. Being able to identify and utilize these effects will enable you to paint realistic and convincing three-dimensional landscapes.

Four things are directly influenced by distance: these are texture, colour, tone and size. The most obvious of these is size. Objects gradually appear smaller the farther away from you they are. You can see this most clearly by looking along a row of identically sized telegraph poles, fence posts or trees.

Second, detail and textures become less evident with distance. The texture and detail of objects that are nearby, in the foreground of a scene, are often large and in sharp focus; the texture and amount of detail visible in objects that are farther away is vague and less clearly defined. For instance, you could use textural techniques such as sponging or spattering to portray foreground pebbles and sand in a beach scene, or use vigorous brushstrokes to suggest foreground grasses, and reduce the amount of detail in the middle distance and background.

Third, colours seen in the foreground and near distance appear bright and vibrant because the warm colours – reds, oranges and yellows – are in evidence. Colours in the far distance appear much less bright. They are also cooler and contain more blue and violet. So use cool hues toward the horizon and warmer tones in the foreground.

Finally, tonal contrast is reduced with distance. If you were to paint all the trees in a scene the same tone, the spatial relationships would not be clear: it might look as if they were all standing in a row. Make the distant trees paler, on the other hand, and they will appear to recede. Sometimes, tonal contrast disappears completely: distant hills, for example, might appear as one pale mass of land.

The principles of aerial perspective apply not only to *terra firma* but also to the sky. Clouds appear larger when they

are immediately overhead. The sky alters colour, too, being a warmer, deeper blue immediately overhead, gradually becoming paler and often with a cool yellow tinge as it falls towards the horizon and the far distance.

These effects of size, detail and colour are caused by our own visual limitations. They are also caused by the gases, dust and moisture present in our atmosphere, which create a veil through which light has to filter. In addition, all these effects are directly influenced not only by the time of day, but also by the season of the year, the location and the inherent local weather conditions.

As with any endeavour, planning is the key to success. You need to consider any perspective issues from the moment you begin a work and incorporate them from the outset. If you are unsure, make a sketch or working drawing before you begin work on the painting. This will allow you to resolve any possible problems in advance.

The effects of aerial perspective ▶
This simple landscape shows how atmosphere combined with distance influences the way we see things.

Colours in the foreground look warmer and brighter. Shapes are more defined than those in the background.

Detail is more apparent in the foreground, such as the long grasses shown by strokes of green.

A full range of tones can be seen in the foreground. Using very bright and very dark greens gives the effect of a sunny day, with contrasting sunlit and shaded leaves.

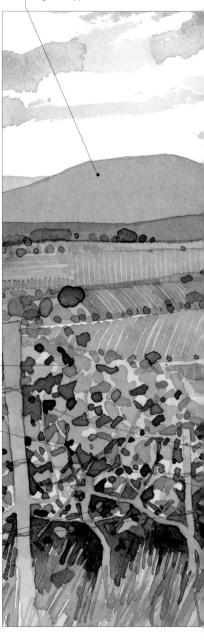

Landforms in the background are flat and uniform, whereas those in the foreground appear to have texture.

Clouds appear smaller the closer they are to the horizon.

Colours in the distance are cooler and less intense.

Clouds appear closer if they have more shape and depth of colour.

Tonal contrast is reduced in the background.

Composing landscapes

Although you may be painting what you can see, you still need to compose your picture. You have to make a decision about what viewpoint to take, which part of the scene to concentrate on, how much of the picture you will devote to the foreground and so on.

Before you start, walk around to find the position that gives you the most interesting angle on the subject. It is a good idea to make a viewfinder, to help you decide how much of the scene to include. Just cut a rectangular aperture in a piece of card; you can then hold it

up at different angles and at different distances from your eyes in order to isolate various sections of the landscape. This can help enormously when you are faced with a wide, panoramic view and you cannot decide which bit to focus on, or where the centre of interest lies.

Choosing a format

The next decision you need to make is which format to use. 'Format' simply means the shape of the painting. The three main formats are horizontal (also known as landscape), vertical (also called portrait) and square. Needless to say, landscapes can be painted on portrait-format supports and portraits on landscape ones. You can also alter the proportions to make what is known

as a 'panoramic' format – that is, a wide-angle view, which extends beyond the field of vision that is normally encompassed by the human eye. Although panoramic formats are often horizontal, particularly when they are of landscapes, they can also be vertical – an approach that might be warranted with a subject such as a dramatic view of a tall cliff.

Your choice of format will be dictated largely by the shape of your subject. A tall subject such as a tree might demand a portrait format. If that tree has a long, horizontal shadow on a sunny day, and the play of light and shadow on the landscape is an important feature of your painting, then a landscape format that fits it all in might be more appropriate.

Landscape format ▲
The image of these cliffs in northern France, painted by Ian Sidaway, sits comfortably in the horizontal format. The curve of the waterline sweeps the eye around to the cliffs and into the painting. At the base of the cliffs, the viewer's attention is caught by the dark ripples and reflections in the water; these in turn bring the eye down to the breaking waves and round again.

Portrait format ▲
The vertical format of this work again suits the subject of this painting by Wendy Jelbert. The viewer's eye is pulled along the length of the craft, which is pointing diagonally into the centre of the painting, and up the steps towards the building. The golden yellow stonework pulls the eye down to the bottom of the picture and the journey begins again.

Dividing the picture area

Over the centuries, artists have devised ways of positioning focal points. The one that is considered to be the ideal division and aesthetically superior to others, is based on the 'golden section', also known as 'divine proportion', in which a line or area can be divided so that the 'smaller part is to the larger as the larger part is to the whole'. A simple grid is made by splitting the picture area into thirds, horizontally and vertically, to give nine sections, with lines crossing at four points. Positioning major elements near these lines or their intersections is supposed to result in a pleasing image.

In landscapes, there is a natural tendency to divide the picture into sky and land. This is not usually the best approach, particularly if it creates a central divide which can make pictures look dull. In a wide landscape you can often increase the sense of depth and space by letting the sky occupy more of the picture area, perhaps two-thirds, or even three-quarters of it. Conversely, with a mountain scene in which you want to express the upward thrust of the land, you could give minimum space to the sky.

Breaking the rules ◀
In this expansive view by Ian Sidaway, the landscape and sky are of equal importance. Placing the horizon on the halfway mark is risky, but the image works because the carefully arranged cloud formations balance the intricate landscape. Note, too, how the path and railings direct the viewer's eye through the scene.

Big sky ▲
In a wide, panoramic landscape, it is important to consider how to divide up the picture space and how much prominence to give to the sky. The area of England in which Geoff Marsters works is very flat, with the great expanse of sky one of its most noticeable features, so in *Fen Landscapes* he has given it three-quarters of the picture.

Divisions on the thirds ◀
The chairs and litter bin are the centre of interest in this painting by Ian Sidaway and are loosely positioned on the intersection grid lines to the right of the image, while the top third of the painting is filled with rows of leafless trees. Together, they balance the empty space in the bottom left of the image.

How much foreground?

A painting can easily be spoiled by a weak or over-dominant foreground. As a general rule, foregrounds should 'introduce' the rest of the picture and lead the eye into it. Too much detail or very strong shapes in the foreground can sometimes have the opposite effect, acting as a block. You can often solve the foreground problem in advance by choosing the best position from which to work – how much of the foreground you see is directly related to whether your viewpoint is high or low. If you look at a scene first standing and then sitting down, you will notice how it changes completely. In a flat landscape, particularly, some feature in the foreground that you may scarcely have noticed suddenly becomes dominant when you view it from low down, while objects in the middle distance are diminished in importance. There is no reason why you should not choose a low viewpoint – for a subject such as mountains, it could be ideal – but it is often better to stand at an easel to paint, or to find a vantage point such as a low wall.

Large foreground ▲

In *The View from Here* by Martin Decent, the foreground occupies roughly two-thirds of the picture space. This is not just empty space, however: the lines of the fence and furrows in the snow curve inward, leading our eye to the focal point of the image, which is placed on the third. In addition, the large foreground adds to the sense of open space, and contributes to the subject of a tough climb uphill.

Curving path ▶

In *Road to Ronda*, Pip Carpenter has organized the picture in such a way that the viewer's eye travels into and around the scene. The area of trees and barely defined grass on the left leads toward the curving path, which the eye naturally follows. The energetic brushwork also gives the painting a wonderful sense of movement and dynamism.

Leading the eye

Most landscapes have a centre of interest, or focal point, to which the eye is drawn. How obvious this is depends on the scene. Examples of an obvious focal point might include a group of buildings in a landscape, a tall tree, or some people sitting down having a picnic – people always grab our attention because we identify with our fellow humans. A less obvious focal point might be a ploughed field making a pattern in the middle distance, a particular hill, a gleam of light on a lake or river, or a light tree set against darker ones. In a successful composition, the viewer's eye should be directed toward the image's centre of interest and encouraged to linger on the picture.

Try to orchestrate the painting so that you set up a series of visual signposts toward the focal point. Diagonal lines or curves invite the eye to follow them, and a device frequently used in landscape is a curving path leading from the foreground in toward the middle distance – where the focal point is often located. A river snaking its way through a landscape, lines of ploughed fields or a line of trees receding into the distance could serve the same purpose.

Pathway into the picture ▲

A common device used to lead the viewer 'into the picture' is to use a path or river travelling from foreground to middle distance, and in *Vineyard in the Languedoc* Madge Bright has used the lines of the vineyard to lead toward the houses.

Trees

When drawing or painting trees, one of the most common mistakes that beginners make is to try to include every detail, without getting the underlying structure in place. Your first step should be to identify the basic shape of the tree. Start by concentrating on the contour or silhouette of the tree shape; it may be helpful to half-close your eyes to avoid the distractions of detail, texture and colour. You might even like to imagine the shapes as flat cut-outs to help see their true outline. Now think about this shape. Is it basically a round shape, such as an oak tree? Cylindrical, like a poplar or cypress? Conical, such as a pine? Once you have identified the basic outline shape, think about the tree's internal structure. Does the main trunk have one or two large branches coming off it or many? Does it split into two or more forks, and if so how far up the tree are they? Whether or not you can see much of the trunk, a knowledge of the tree's structure will make for a more convincing drawing. Remember that without external influences, such as strong winds, disease, or overcrowding, most trees seem to retain a kind of natural symmetry. The trunk of a gnarled fruit tree may lean at a wild angle, but the upper branches may cluster in the other direction.

Cedar tree ◄
This delicate watercolour by Trudy Friend carefully observes the way the branches spread and fall in layers around the thick trunk. Painted using a fine brush and wet-on-dry washes, the foliage colours consist of only three tones of the same silver-green colour.

 Tips: Look at the tree's habit: do its branches spread upwards from the trunk or droop downwards? Lightly put in the underlying structure and make your brush or pencil strokes follow the direction of growth.

Tree shapes

Although tree shapes may look very complex to draw and paint, if you train yourself to view them as simple geometric shapes you will find them much easier to assess. They are actually no more difficult than any other subject. Breaking down complex forms into their most simple shapes is a good principle for any drawing or painting. It is also invaluable when you come to analyse the effects of light and shade.

In these sketches, the basic shape has been very lightly drawn around the outline of the tree. Remember, however, that these are generalizations and that the shape of a tree is often affected by the prevailing weather conditions; for example, on an exposed hillside trees may be lopsided because the wind tends always to blow from the same direction, while trees in poor soil may appear stunted.

Flattened top ▲
This distinctive umbrella pine tree looks as if it has been trimmed to a flattened shape on top.

Cone shape ▲
In many conifers, the branches grow horizontally from the trunk and are shorter toward the top of the tree, creating an overall cone shape.

What about groups of trees within the landscape? Again, try to think not of 'wood' or 'hillside' but instead in terms of abstract shapes – a cluster of flat-bottomed spheres, an elongated diamond shape. Seen from a distance, the base and trunk of trees are often obscured by shadow and perspective, so avoid the temptation, for example, to add neat rows of tree trunks along the edge of a wood. It is more likely that you can see one or two, at irregular intervals, while the rest have been swallowed by shade. From your viewpoint, the foreground fields or grasses may obscure the base of the trees, giving a flat-bottomed appearance to a stand of trees or wood. Having established the general shape of the tree or trees in question, the next stage is to give them three dimensions. As with cloud forms, the key to this is the depiction of light and shade. The shadows beneath a tree are crucial in anchoring it to the landscape so that it looks like it is growing, not floating. Light on the foliage, or bare branches in winter, help give it form. Light hits all objects consistently, but the surface texture and local colour will affect the appearance. Half-shut your eyes once more and think purely in terms of light and shade; you may notice, for example, that a softly rounded tree in the foreground is echoed by a distant stand of the same species.

Cylindrical shape ▲
Poplar and cypress tree branches grow upward and tend to be all the same length, giving a cylindrical shape.

Lozenge shape ▲
Some trees are characterized by a gently tapering, oval shape that narrows toward the top and bottom.

Broken shape ▲
Branches may grow asymmetrically, so that irregular gaps and shapes are created between them.

Rounded shape ▲
Oak trees, as well as beech and maple, have branches that radiate out from the main trunk, and a rounded top.

Gnarled, twisted forms ▲
Wind, harsh conditions or just the nature of the tree may dictate that it grows into twisted forms.

Two trunks ▲
Many shrubs have two or more trunks, with the branches closer to the ground than in trees.

Foliage masses

In depicting foliage, it is not a good idea to attempt to draw every leaf – aim for an overall impression, rather than putting in every detail.

Start by establishing basic facts about your scene. What season is being depicted? What direction is the light coming from, and is it bright or muted? What time of day is it? Low light may result in the undersides of the leaves being lit up, while midday sun will give a dark shadow on the ground. Is it windy, so that you need to show movement? Or rainy, so that the leaves are shiny and highly reflective?

Look for areas of light and shade within the foliage mass, to help create a three-dimensional effect. Study the direction of the light and whether it is hard or soft. Making a tonal study in charcoal or thinned paint can give you an excellent starting point.

Look also for gaps where you can see patches of sky or background colour showing through. These can be wiped out with a kneaded eraser in a drawing or blotted out of a watercolour; or dabs of opaque colour can be laid over existing paint. Few trees are so dense that no such gaps or spots of light are visible, so adding them lends realism.

Think about the way the leaves attach themselves to the branches. Some leaves form close clusters, whereas some spring upward from the branch, while others, such as willows, droop down. These differences can be represented with different marks and mediums. For example, a broad-leafed tree could be expressed by a dabbing movement of a round watercolour brush, while a tree with feathery foliage could be treated with a fan brush.

Finally, analyse the colour. Leaves can range from reddish-black to the palest of creamy yellows; from vibrant, lime green to a dusky blue-grey. Try mixing your own greens rather than relying on pre-mixed greens, which can be harsh. Experiment by mixing ultramarine and yellow ochre, then ultramarine and lemon yellow, for two useful greens. Looking for areas of your foliage colour within the surrounding landscape will also help to ground the tree within the composition and make for a harmonious whole.

Assessing tones ▲
It takes practice to assess tones, particularly when you are dealing with varying tones of the same colour. Try half-closing your eyes, so that you see the subject as a series of shapes. The strong evening sunlight on this loosely described park scene falls on the trees in the middle distance, while the foreground trees are plunged into deep shadow, becoming silhouettes.

Directional brushstrokes ▲
When painting foliage, it is essential to give an impression of the direction of growth. Do the leaves droop down, like willows? Are they grouped in tight, densely packed masses? In this study of a tree in summer, short vertical brushstrokes have been dabbed on to describe the leaves on the overhanging branches, while broad, horizontal strokes represent the shadows on the ground below. Fine vertical strokes are used for the grasses lining the path.

Separate foliage masses ▲
From a distance and, in the strong sunlight, the leaves almost seem to merge. By observing the different tones, colours and textures, the artist has made it clear that it is made up of separate trees and bushes.

Autumn foliage ▲
The rich reds and golds of autumn foliage have always attracted artists. Here, the leaves are an impressionistic mass of colour, with burnt sienna and cadmium yellow merging wet into wet on the paper to create sizzlingly vibrant tones. As the tree is viewed against the light, the detail is subdued, with the dense browns of the trunk and branches providing the structure for the painting. Note how well water-soluble pencils have been used to convey the gnarled texture of the bark.

Practice exercise: **Foliage mass in acrylics**

This is an exercise in assessing and mixing greens, from the yellowy greens of the pathway and grasses to the darker tones of the tree. Practise mixing different greens. You can create warm and cool shades to give the forms an illusion of solidity and depth. Try mixing in a warm yellow such as cadmium and then see how much brighter and more acidic the green is when you replace cadmium with lemon yellow.

Materials
- *Watercolour board*
- *Acrylic paints: cadmium yellow, phthalocyanine blue, yellow ochre, alizarin crimson, brilliant green, titanium white*
- *Brushes: Selection of round and flat brushes in different sizes*

The scene
Shining from the left, the sun clearly shows the spherical form of the tree and its dark interior.

The finished painting
This sketch demonstrates the importance of creating an overall impression of the shape and direction of growth of a foliage mass, rather than attempting to put in every detail. The various tones of green have been carefully observed and the brushstrokes placed to create an impression of the way the leaves are attached to the boughs, hanging downward in loose, heavy fronds.

1 Mix a bright green from cadmium yellow, phthalo blue and a tiny bit of yellow ochre and brush in the main shapes of the composition – i.e., the rounded shape of the tree in the background and the bushes and grasses on either side of the pathway.

3 Paint in the darker bushes in a mix of phthalo blue and a little yellow ochre. Create a thick light green from cadmium yellow, brilliant green and titanium white and, with short strokes and dots, put in the tree's mid-tones.

2 Mix a deep violet from alizarin crimson and phthalo blue and paint in the trunk and main branches. Mix darker green from phthalo blue and a little cadmium yellow and, with a flat brush, block in the mid-tones of the foliage and the shadows under the tree.

4 Vary the proportions of colours in the mixes to get a range of tones in the foliage. Put in dabs for the sky in a pale blue mix of phthalo blue and white. Mix a pink from alizarin crimson and white and dot in the flowers.

Bark

At first glance, bark might seem a rather specific topic for the average landscape painter's consideration, yet as a subject it will appear in most outdoor scenes and is worthy of attention.

Making a study of bark is an excellent way of 'getting inside' your subject, as it helps you to understand the way in which a particular tree grows. The more time you spend observing details of bark, the more the subtleties and nuances of its colour and texture will become part of your artistic vocabulary. Even if you need depict only a small area glimpsed through foliage, the time spent looking at it will ensure that you do not resort to using visual shorthand.

Bark can vary enormously depending on the age and type of the tree. It may be smooth and silky like that of a silver birch, or rough and knotted like an ancient oak; fine in texture like furled sheets of tracing paper or heavy and sculptural like a thick carving. The growth patterns may result in horizontal rings running across the circumference of the trunk or branch, or in deep vertical gouges running up and down it. Some trees, such as the ash, have criss-cross patterns of diamond-shaped furrows, like the opening and closing of a concertina. Some patterns are linear, others knobbly or seemingly random.

Look for the way in which bark expresses the growth of the tree. A twisted tree might have gnarled,

convoluted bark forms; an upright one a more regular surface pattern. Bark patterns are likely to be wide and open on the trunk and older parts, closer and compact on younger branches. The texture of the bark changes where a branch meets the trunk, sometimes forming a cluster of rings like the wrinkles in an old stocking, and thick calluses will form over time around the circular space where a branch has been removed. The tiniest of twigs will have its own textured surface, a mirror of the larger tree in miniature. The perspective of rings around branches and trunks can

help to convey the shape; for example, if a branch is leaning towards you the rings will appear foreshortened.

Think about how to capture these textures in different mediums. Flat washes of watercolour might be appropriate for the mottled layers of a young sycamore. Paint could be dragged or scraped for the ribbon-like bark of a eucalyptus, or laid on with a knife in thick slabs to suggest the patterns on a mature oak. The choice of support can come to your aid: dragging a pastel or dry brush over rough paper can create effective textures. Remember the direction of the light, so that you don't lose form while creating texture.

The colour of bark is rarely uniformly brown; in fact, it may be green or grey, with hints of purple or blue. Lichen or moss can look as if it's been sprayed on. Fungi and the effects of disease may also add their own character to the tree.

Gnarled bark ◀
This pen-and-ink sketch of weathered bark uses both hatching and a pale wash to add tone. The artist felt that relying solely on hatching would detract from the delicate textural forms of the bark. The ridges have been picked out with a variety of dashes and broken lines, which help suggest the organic quality of the natural material. Working in monochrome also seemed to suit the subject matter.

Practice exercise: **Bark close-up in acrylics**

In this exercise, the paint is applied using both a brush and a painting knife. You can create a surprisingly wide range of textures in this way, from delicate overall washes and fine details made with the brush to thin, smooth areas of paint, impasto ridges and jagged lines 'drawn' with the tip of the knife. As in the previous demonstration, it is vital to find points of reference so that you do not lose track of where you are. You will also need to decide whether you want to opt for a photo-realistic portrayal or, as here, exaggerate the colours.

Materials
• Canvas primed with acrylic gesso
• Acrylic paints: burnt umber, naphthol red, yellow ochre, titanium white, ultramarine blue, raw umber, brilliant yellow green, lemon yellow
• Selection of round brushes in different sizes
• Painting knife

The scene
Apart from the occasional splashes of green, at first glance this appears to be an almost monochromatic image of pinky-brown bark. Look closer, however, and you will see tiny paler-toned, almost white areas where the light hits raised patches, hints of a warm yellow ochre, deeper reds, and even dark, cool blues.

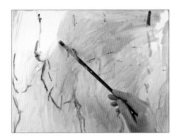  

1 With a thin mix of burnt umber, put in the initial lines. Leave to dry. Mix an undercolour from naphthol red, yellow ochre and titanium white and scumble it over the canvas, varying the proportions of the colours to get some tonal variation. Leave to dry.

2 With a brush, paint over the crevices in the bark in ultramarine blue. Mix a thick but pale purple-pink from burnt umber, naphthol red and titanium white. Smear it over the surface with the back of a small painting knife, then use the tip of the knife to apply strong, thick lines of a rich raw umber.

3 Add more white to the purple-pink from the previous step and, using the back of the knife, smear it over larger areas of the bark to create the basic bark colour, varying the proportions of the colours in the mix as you work so that you do not get a flat expanse of just one tone.

4 For the moss in the crevices, mix a bright green from brilliant yellow green and lemon yellow and apply with a fine brush. Put in other darks as necessary – raw and burnt umbers, and blue-blacks mixed from ultramarine and alizarin crimson.

The finished painting

This is both an experiment in mark making and a lively interpretation of a deceptively simple-looking subject. The underlying colour – various tones of purple-pink – holds the image together, while splashes of bold, acid greens and deep reds on top provide strong complementary colours that play against each other and create a dynamic, contemporary-looking image.

5 Continue in the same range of colours, alternating between the brush, knife back and knife tip, until you have built up the texture and range of tones that you want. Look for both warm and cool tones, as this will give the image a sense of depth.

Bark is not flat: note how the artist has juxtaposed warm and cool tones to convey the different levels of the surface.

Linear marks made using the tip of the brush add texture, and contrast well with flatter applications of colour elsewhere.

Grasses

Whether you are painting a carefully tended park or an expanse of prairie, grass is a major feature of many landscapes. Portraying it convincingly requires a little planning, but can give a scene interest and texture.

Grasslands vary enormously. Vast expanses of rolling savannah, a meadow studded with wild flowers, manicured lawns, grassy sand-dunes, marshes or moorland each have their own character. There may be variations in the same view – scrubby grasses on a mountain slope giving way to cornfields lower down the valley, for example, or simply the contrast between long and mown grass in the more intimate confines of a garden.

In the foreground, a great deal of detail can be used to describe individual stems of grass; in the midground, less detail is visible, but highlights on certain clumps of grass may show the direction of its growth; in the background, one might see some indication of texture, but all detail is lost. By picking out a few foreground stalks and then hinting at others elsewhere, the eye will 'read' the whole area as grassy. This is how we naturally perceive objects.

Sunlight can produce interesting effects on grassland. Wiry grasses can be very reflective and add a silvery sheen to a hillside; long grass under trees makes patterns of light and shade when it catches the sun. Wind creates wave-like ripples and a sense of energy and movement.

Summer grasses ▼
Here, a strong shaft of sunlight falls across a summery garden scene. Softly blended oil pastels have been used on the closely cropped grass of the path, with horizontal strokes. In the long grass, the strokes become vertical with more of a hatching technique. Flower heads are suggested with dabs of horizontal colour. Individual stalks and seed heads have been scratched into the oil pastel, leaving the stained green colour of the paper beneath.

When drawing or painting foreground grass, use rapid upward strokes. The looseness and spontaneity of this approach can help capture the thick, criss-crossing growth without your marks becoming too rigid. Downward strokes can be added for bent stalks, and curls or seed heads added to some blades. Fine brushes or sharp pencils are useful, but you could also try dry-brushing with a brush splayed out between finger and thumb. Scratching through paint or oil pastel can also be effective. On a pencil drawing, an eraser can be used to pick out light grasses.

Echo the patterns for grasses in the background, remembering that clumps will seem small and closer together, and should follow the contours of the land. A smudge of paint may be enough to suggest grasses here. Perspective will give distant areas a pale appearance.

Practice exercise: **Grasses in charcoal**

This exercise gives you the opportunity to practise 'eraser drawing' – using a kneaded eraser to lift off charcoal pigment and imply light grasses growing against a darker background. For a broader line, use the edge of the eraser. To get a very fine tip on the eraser, simply pull it to a point.

Materials
• *Good-quality drawing paper*
• *Charcoal: thick and thin sticks*
• *Kneaded eraser*

The scene
Spiky clumps of grass growing on a sand dune form an interesting contrast in texture to the smooth undulations of the sand, which has been blown into small ridges by the wind. The strong lines within the subject suggested the simple, graphic approach of a monochrome drawing in charcoal.

1 Using the tip of a thick charcoal stick, draw in the base of the top clump of grasses. Wipe the side of the stick over the sand area and smooth out the charcoal marks with your fingers. Use the edge of a kneaded eraser to wipe off pigment to create light-coloured lines of sand, where the sun lights one side of the sand ridges.

2 Using thin charcoal, scribble in the dark areas within the grasses (the shaded area underneath) and draw in the blades of dark grass. For the lighter, yellowy grasses, pull the eraser to a fine point and wipe off charcoal. Also block in the underlying patches of earth.

3 Continue the process of putting in the grasses, alternating between drawing thin, curving marks and wiping off charcoal with the eraser. Draw in the foreground clump, again using a combination of positive marks with the thin charcoal stick and wiping off with the eraser.

The finished drawing
By carefully observing the different tones within the subject and using the eraser to pick out the brightest highlights, the artist has created a convincing portrayal of clumps of grass. This sketch demonstrates the versatility of charcoal. A fine layer smudged with the fingertips represents the sand, while crisp, sharp lines are used for the grasses themselves. The medium allows the artist to work at speed, which helps convey the windswept, natural energy of the scene.

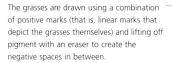

The grasses are drawn using a combination of positive marks (that is, linear marks that depict the grasses themselves) and lifting off pigment with an eraser to create the negative spaces in between.

Note how shadows cast by the grass are not straight lines but are broken by the undulations in the sand.

The use of light and dark tones suggests ridges and makes the sand look realistic.

Rocks and stones

When drawing rocks or stones it is easy to be immediately seduced into trying to describe textural details, but it is important first to get a firm foundation. Try to think of rock shapes at their most basic, blocking in the largest shapes as roughly square or rounded forms. The light source is very important to give these complicated structures a sense of volume, so you may want to add tone at this stage. Remember to include shadows thrown by the rocks on to surrounding surfaces. Next the more complicated outlines and contours within the blocked-in shapes can be described – but keep thinking about light and shade. Finally, when you are happy with the shapes of the rocks, you can add colour and texture.

Many different mark-making techniques come into their own when describing the texture of rocks and stones. Pen-and-ink drawing, with different pressures applied to vary the strength of line, can be useful in suggesting lines of slate. Dry brushwork can create jagged or swirling patches of broken colour to denote craggy surfaces or the tracery of fossils within the rock. A palette knife can be used with thick paint to show stepping levels of stone. Torn paper can be used like a stencil, with paint spattered over, to give character to rock shapes while keeping unwanted paint off adjoining areas. There are numerous texture pastes and additives that can be used with oils or acrylics to give a sculptural effect.

Whatever your chosen techniques, think about applying them sparingly; one well-observed area of a cliff face may have more impact if the rest of the picture is treated more simply. The eye is grateful for a resting space within the picture when confronted by a complicated area of detail.

Light on rock and stone affects its colour enormously. Broad expanses of rock often reflect light, particularly when near the sea, so a shaded area can have warm or cool colours within it. Play around with different ways of creating colour mixes. Alizarin crimson and ultramarine blue with a touch of raw umber gives an interesting neutral that can veer toward warm or cool depending on the proportions in the mix; as can

Boulder ▼
Here, the artist experimented with watercolour and gouache to create texture. To the left, salt crystals were sprinkled over a purplish wash, then shaken off when completely dry to leave shapes that resemble pitted rock. Elsewhere, tonking (printing with scrunched-up paper dipped in paint) has been used. Sponging and dry-brushing add further texture.

alizarin and viridian. Aerial perspective will soften shadows on any object, and cause colours to become cooler and paler as they recede. Think about how much prominence to give them to enhance your chosen subject. When portraying large rock faces or cliffs, a sense of scale can sometimes be achieved by including a figure, or a man-made structure.

Practice exercise: **Slate with lichen in soft pastels**

Soft pastel is great for capturing textures such as those on this lichen-covered slate as you can use the tooth of the paper. Once you study a subject like this in detail, you will be amazed at all the colours and differences in tone.

Materials
- *Dark blue pastel paper*
- *Charcoal*
- *Soft pastels: pale green, permanent yellow light, pale blue-grey, dark blue, yellow ochre, pale blue*
- *Pastel pencils: red violet, blue violet, black*

The scene
Here, the lichen and striations within the slate make a diagonal, which creates a dynamic composition.

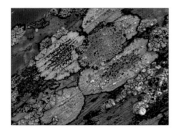

1 Using thin charcoal on dark blue pastel paper, map out the main shapes and striations. Begin putting in some lichen, using pale green and permanent yellow light soft pastels.

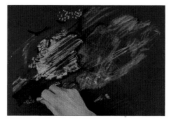

2 Hatch the two violet pastel pencils over the purple-tinged area to the right of the yellow lichen. Using a pale blue-grey pastel, put in more of the lighter patches of lichen, varying your pressure and making range of marks from dots to small squiggles to get some textural variation.

3 Apply the base colour of the slate in pale blue-grey and dark blue, as appropriate, using the side of the pastels and making your marks follow the natural striations in the stone. Dot in yellow ochre for the darker yellow patches of lichen. Reinforce the very dark markings on the slate and within the patches of lichen with a black pastel pencil. These linear marks contrast well with the small dots used for the lichen.

4 Scribble in various pale blues and blue-greys for the lichen, using the tips of the pencils and a range of marks from dots to tight squiggles. Try not to be too literal in your depiction and attempt to put in every single element – an overall impression is what you should be aiming for.

The finished drawing
In this simple drawing, the texture of the paper has been used to good effect, in combination with an impressive range of pastel marks, from crisp dots and linear dashes to broad sweeps of colour made using the side of the pastel. The artist has carefully matched the pastel colours to those in the reference photograph, taking some time before commencing drawing to get this right. The choice of paper colour has a big effect on the end result, as patches of paper are showing through. The result is an interesting study in texture and a great exercise for observing colour in detail.

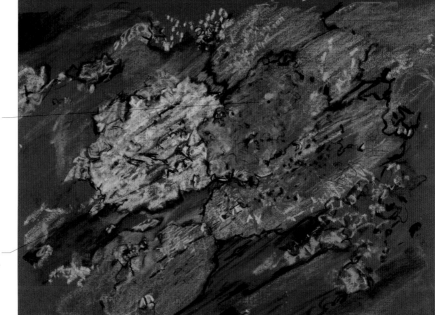

Soft, loosely blended areas of pastel are used to describe the underlying colour of the slate, with the texture of the support also contributing to the overall effect.

Carefully observed linear marks denote the striations and tiny undulations in the surface of the stone.

Bright sunlight

When judging how to depict a sunny scene, it helps to imagine a series of graded tones, with pure white at one end through a deepening range of greys to black at the other. In flat, overcast light conditions you might just use the middle tones; in bright sun, the top and bottom tones are used too.

It might be tempting to think that a light, sunny picture will use mainly light tones or colours, but this can end up looking insipid; it is only when dark tones are introduced that the contrast is created to make the highlights really jump out. When you look at the proportion of light and dark areas within a composition, a painting might on balance be fairly dark, and yet still manage to convey a strong impression of light and heat. An evocative image in Mediterranean countries, where light conditions are strong, is the cool dark alleyway or doorway leading out onto the sunny square.

Very bright sunlight can affect our perception of colour within a scene, particularly on flat or reflective surfaces where it has a bleaching effect. An object can seem to lose its 'local' or actual colour; for example, a cafe awning that you know to be bright orange may appear to be almost white in strong sun. In watercolour this can be conveyed by using just a little pigment in a wash, so that the luminosity of the white paper shows through. In an acrylic or oil painting, you can simply mix plenty of white with the local colour, or alternatively use a scumbling technique, dragging a dry white or yellow-white mix over dry paint – useful when conveying textures.

Shadows play a crucial part in helping to depict sunshine. They shift position with the time of day, so you may need to take a decision on where they fall and block them in quickly. Remember that those closer to you will seem darker than those farther away. Shadows are not simply grey: they are usually affected by some reflected colour from nearby objects. Often they may appear to contain a hint of the complementary colour of the object: and even if this is not obvious, it can be a good idea to add a little for contrast.

Strong light ▼
The strong, clear light in this landscape gives dark shadows to the trees and highlights to the foreground stones and grasses. Aerial perspective gives the far hillside a softer green, and the receding shadows are a cool purple.

Practice exercise: **Alla prima landscape in oils**

In alla prima, the paint is applied in a single layer rather than waiting for successive layers to dry. The artist worked wet into wet and blended tones on the canvas, which often creates more energetic mixes than physically blending colours on the palette. The colours that you get depend on whether the underlying colour is warm or cool. It is this constant interplay of warm and cool, lights and darks, that is the key to an image such as this one, which celebrates the relationship of light against shadow on a furrowed hillside.

Materials
- Canvas primed with acrylic gesso
- Oil paints: ultramarine blue, raw umber, yellow ochre, Venetian red, chrome green deep, lemon yellow, Winsor emerald, titanium white, cadmium yellow deep
- Brushes: selection of filberts in different sizes
- Turpentine/white spirit (paint thinner)

The scene
Strong, low, late-afternoon sunlight illuminates the patch of ground in the centre of the image and casts long shadows across the field. The golden colours give the image a wonderful warm glow.

1 Tone the canvas in a pale blue-grey mixed from ultramarine blue and raw umber. Mix a brown from yellow ochre and Venetian red and, with a large brush, sketch in the fields. Map out the clump of trees in olive green mixed from chrome green deep and yellow ochre. Add a little of this mix to lemon yellow for the sunlit furrow tops.

2 Scumble a warm blue-green mixed from Winsor emerald, ultramarine and yellow ochre over the dark field in the background. Add more blue to the mix and put in the very darkest tones of the trees. Mix a light green from lemon yellow, Winsor emerald and yellow ochre and put in the light foliage tones and the brightest patches of grass.

3 Put in the long shadows with a mix of ultramarine, white and Winsor emerald. Build up the lights and darks, using lemon yellow with varying amounts of white for the lightest tones and an orangey mix of cadmium yellow deep and white for the next brightest. For the darks, use the same green and blue-green mixes as before, alternating for the warm or cool tones you need.

4 Alternate between lights and darks, and warm and cool tones, as you work across the painting, blending the colours wet into wet. Block in the long, cast shadows with the blue-green mix of ultramarine, white and Winsor emerald from Step 2.

5 Roughly scumble on the dark blue-green mix with vigorous, up-and-down brushstrokes for the straggly foreground bushes, for texture.

The finished painting
This contrast of light, bright yellows and oranges with dark, warm blue-greens makes an effective portrayal of sun on the landscape. The low, raking sunlight picks out texture in the furrows and casts long, deep shadows that form an integral part of the composition.

Although the sunlight is strong, note how dark the shadows are: the contrast is dramatic and atmospheric.

Bright, acidic yellow mixes convey the intensity of the sunlight.

Dappled light

An ordinary scene viewed in dappled light can be truly transformed by sparkling contrasts of light and colour. Sometimes a mysterious mood is evoked, as details are lost in shadows. The play of light and shade is a unifying element, bringing together the components of a scene. It can also give a work an abstract quality, as the subject may seem to become less important than the description of the light itself.

The very appeal of dappled light is that it forms a web of complicated patterns. This can be hard to replicate, even when seen upon a flat surface. Adding perspective and different textures to the equation requires further thought. Imagine, for example, a courtyard with a stairway and trees, and light filtering down. Perspective dictates that pools of light closer to you will have a rounded appearance, whereas those farther away will seem to flatten out into elongated shapes, as well as growing smaller. The shadows falling across the vertical sides of the steps will glance down diagonally, according to the direction of the sun, whereas those on the treads will be horizontally distorted. Further distortion would occur on a curved surface, such as a pillar or urn. Rather than getting bogged down in the detail, it can help to look through half-closed eyes, at blocks of light and shade. If you draw the shapes and the spaces around the negative shapes as you see them, you will achieve a surprisingly accurate result.

Textures will bring particular effects. On grass, for example, patches of sunlight may appear to be framed by a fringe of darker grasses in the foreground and lighter ones at the back.

Another point to note is that shadows will be stronger the closer they are to the object casting the shadow.

Once you are aware of these considerations, you are in a better position to use the effects of dappled light to your advantage. If you stick to the basic principles, you can play around with composition a little, perhaps leading the viewer's eye toward areas of interest or even adding contrast to a scene sketched or photographed on an overcast day.

Woodland light and shade ▼
In this lively study, oil pastels were used to create the impression of a low winter sun shining through trees on to the undergrowth of the woodland floor. The artist chose a dark brown oil pastel paper the same colour as the branches of the trees against the light, and scratched off pigment to reveal the colour of the support. Dashes of yellow were applied to depict leaves or grasses caught by the sunlight, and vertical strokes of reddish brown show the foreground foliage.

High noon sunlight ▲
In this acrylic study, the artist studied the way the play of light and shade created a pattern of abstract shapes. The strong contrasts on the stones and paving at the base of the foreground tree are balanced by the sunlight on the buildings and awnings at the back of the square. Note the shape and direction of the light patches on the floor, as opposed to those on the vertical sides of the statue and tree trunk. The shadows also alter in density, from the deep shade on the right-hand side of the painting to the left-hand side, where the trees are more open and there is more reflected light.

Practice exercise: **Dappled sunlight in soft pastels**

Soft pastel is a lovely medium for drawing the transient effects of light, as you can put down both broad areas and tiny, precise details and allow the colours to mix optically on the paper. It is a good idea to use a paper that is similar in colour to the mid tones in your subject. Here the artist selected a pale to mid beige.

Materials
- *Buff-coloured pastel paper*
- *Soft pastels: Dark brown, dark grey-green, white, bright yellow, mid green, very pale green, dark green*

The scene
Light filtering through the trees casts dappled shadows on the ground below, creating interesting patterns on what would otherwise be a bland area.

1 Using the side of the pastels, roughly block in the tree trunks in dark brown and the horizon and perspective lines in dark grey-green. Use white for the patches of sunlight on the ground and the sky visible through the trees. You do not need to be too precise at this stage – just map out the light areas. Using the dark grey-green again, put in the largest shadows and smooth the marks with your fingers.

2 Block in the leaves that are being hit by sunlight with a bright, acid yellow, then scribble in darker patches of foliage in a mid green. Using dark brown, strengthen the shaded side of the tree trunks and smooth out the marks with your fingers. Note how much more substantial the trees look now. Strengthen the shadows too, again smoothing out the marks with your fingers.

The finished drawing
This atmospheric, expressionistic study relies on careful assessment of tones and on seeing the areas of light and dark as shapes, or blocks, of colour.

3 Using the tip of a dark brown pastel, loosely scribble in the dark shapes of the smaller shadows on the ground, then blend the marks. Add the blue-green area beyond the lowest branches, at eye level; this helps to give a sense of distance. Sharpen up the shapes of the patches of sky with a very, very pale green (so pale that it's almost white), then use the same colour for the corresponding patches of sunlight on the ground. Finally, use a dark green to sharpen up and give some definition to the shapes of the darkest patches of foliage.

The use of light and dark greens in the foliage gives this area depth and texture.

Foliage shadows are loose, generalized shapes: do not get caught up in details!

Snow and ice

For artists, the delight of snow is that it can transform a scene. Everyday objects lose their usual outlines and unexpected shapes appear; local colour is removed and new patterns of light and dark emerge. Sometimes the ground is lighter than the sky: normal rules seem to be suspended. With so few familiar features in evidence, you must analyse the scene accurately, so that the viewer is given sufficient clues to 'read' the landscape. Judgements about tone and colour are crucial in establishing a sense of form and distance.

At first glance, a snow scene may seem to be almost monochrome, but careful observation and faithful rendering of cool and warm colours will add depth and interest. Snow, sky, rocks and trees that look white or grey will all, on closer inspection, have subtleties of colouring. The snow itself may look white, but in fact it will contain warmer and cooler tones, depending on the light, as well as textural patterns where it has fallen on intricate forms such as hedgerows.

In watercolour painting, it might seem simpler to leave the white of the paper to suggest snow-covered areas, but applying even the most delicate of washes will bring the painting to life: for example, a pale warm wash on the side of a hill facing the light, and a cool wash on the side in shade.

Subtle shadows on the snowy surface of a field can hint at the forms lying beneath it – a ditch or furrowed track, a series of undulations, a frozen pond. Shadows on snow are full of interest due to the reflective surrounding surfaces. Like any shadows, they are not usually a flat, uniform tone or colour but carry touches of other colours within them. On a sunny day they often look bright blue or mauve against the brilliant white of the snow; as the sun moves lower in the sky, the snow takes on a warm, golden hue and shadows have a blue-green tint; by dusk the snow may look pink and the shadows a soft blue-grey. Shadows on ice are more reflective still. Look out for different characteristics that describe the snowfall in question. Perhaps the snow has been drifting; sometimes a

tree trunk can look as if it has been sprayed from one side. Footprints can look crisp-edged or rounded depending on whether snow has begun to melt. Ice creates strange textures, making grass wiry and giving twigs a crystalline coating.

Ice takes its colour from the object beneath or behind it, for instance it may appear pale green on a mossy rock or clear and sparkling against the sky. A frozen lake loses most of its reflective qualities and becomes a solid mass. Try laying semi-opaque layers of white paint, thinned with water or medium, over a darker colour, to capture this effect; or use a scumbling technique with dryish paint over dark areas.

Snowy bank ▲
In this watercolour study white areas of paper have been saved where needed. The warm yellow of the backlit leaves makes a pleasing contrast to the blues of the snow in shadow. A warm wash has been applied to the top right-hand area of snow, to show the warmth of the sun.

Sunset on snow ◄
The artist made a quick, almost abstract watercolour sketch of the colours of the snow toward the end of a sunny day. A warm-coloured wash was applied first, to capture the pinky-orange colour of the winter sun on buildings and hillsides in the middle distance. A cooler wash added afterward allows some of that warmth to show through, suggesting reflected light on the snow and warm hazy clouds above. The foreground marks are only loose squiggles but the artist has made them convey a strong perspective. If the artist wished to work the piece up further in the studio, these marks are a good basis for foreground detail.

Practice exercise: **Winter scene in oil pastels**

Here, you can try out two ways of depicting snow. For the snow on the ground, block in the colour, looking for cooler, bluer tones that reveal hollows and dips in the land. Blend with a rag dipped in white spirit. On the branches, use the sgraffito technique to scrape off pigment and create thin lines of white.

Materials
- *Mountboard or acrylic board*
- *Oil pastels: pale peach, mid-grey, pale blue, raw sienna, white, dark grey, black, pale violet*
- *White spirit (paint thinner)*
- *Old rag or absorbent kitchen paper*
- *Scraperboard tool*

The scene
Skeletal trees, with their thin covering of snow, give the image a really interesting texture and an almost black and white tonal contrast.

The finished drawing
By using predominantly cool tones – white, pale blues and greys – this image has a wintry feel that is entirely in keeping with the subject. Using a scraperboard tool to reveal the 'snow' on the branches has enabled the artist to create thin, delicate lines far more easily than she could have done with a chunky oil pastel.

The scraperboard tool allows you to create flowing, twisting lines that would be difficult to achieve with the oil pastel.

Slight ripples in the water, created using horizontal dashes of oil pastel, add a hint of movement to an otherwise static scene.

1 Block in the sky with a pale peach oil pastel, then blend the marks with a rag dipped in white spirit. The colour gives a warm overall tone. Draw in the trees and the stream banks in a mid-grey then, using the side of the pastel, put in the darker patches of the water.

3 Block in the background, picking out the sky with peach and white and blending with your fingers. Use a mid-grey pastel for the branches over the stream and a darker grey for those in the foreground. Having more detail and warmth in the foreground is a way of creating depth.

2 Using a very pale blue, put in the shaded snow on the left-hand bank and the snow on the branches, blending with a rag dipped in white spirit. Outline the foreground tree trunks in black, then go over the left-hand side in raw sienna. Strengthen the right-hand bank with mid-grey.

4 Put in the reflections in the water, using white, pale blue, pale grey and pale violet. Using a scraper tool, scrape along the top edges of the branches to reveal the underlying white pastel and create the impression of a thin layer of snow on the branches.

Collecting visual material

Given the vagaries of the weather and how little free time we all have at our disposal, it is often not practical to draw and paint landscapes outdoors. Many landscape artists make preliminary sketches in situ, or take reference photographs of things that catch their eye, which they then work up into a finished piece back in their studio.

Sketches

The more you sketch, the more reference material you will have – and sketching also helps to polish up your observational skills. Making sketches for a painting, as opposed to simply sketching for the fun of it, is rather a special skill, as you must learn to provide yourself with sufficient visual information from which to work at a later date, bearing in mind that a considerable amount of time may elapse between your initial sketches and a more detailed work.

Depending on the kind of work you are planning, you may need sketches in colour, as well as in line. Trying to make a painting from a line sketch in pencil or pen and ink is virtually impossible; you will have no idea what colour the sky was or which areas were dark and which ones light. Get into the habit of including all the information possible on your sketches; it is better to have too much information than too little.

If you do not have time to sketch in colour, make written notes about the colours. Do not simply write 'blue' or 'green', but try to analyse the colours; as long as you can understand your notes, this can be more valuable than sketching in colour, particularly if you intend to use one medium for your sketches and another for the painting. A sketch in coloured pencil, for example, would be very difficult to translate into watercolour or oils.

Choosing a sketchbook ▲
The kind of sketchbook you require depends on your method of working and the kind of visual notes you wish to make. Some artists have two or three sketchbooks in different sizes and formats. John Townend uses a large book for coloured-pencil drawings like the one shown above, and a smaller one for quick pen and ink drawings.

Sketching for painting ◄
This sketch by Stephen Crowther was made as the first stage in planning an oil painting, and the artist has made copious written notes to remind him of the colours. Using a large spiral-bound sketchbook enables him to remove the sheet and pin it up near his easel to refer to when painting.

Materials for sketching

For sketching you can use any drawing media with which you feel comfortable. Pencil is a good all-rounder, as it allows you to establish tone as well as line. Pen and ink is useful for small sketches, but less so for tonal studies.

Coloured pencils are tailor-made for colour sketches, and so are pastels and oil pastels, although neither of the latter is suitable for small-scale work. Moreover, both soft pastels and oil pastels are quite messy media, so remember to take some rags or, better still, a packet of moistened hand wipes to clean your hands. For oil pastels, you will need paint thinner and rags to clean your hands, plus brushes if you intend to spread the colours. You will not need fixative for oil pastels, but you will for soft pastels, as it is easy to smudge work when you are carrying it.

If you prefer to paint your sketches, both watercolours and acrylics are quick drying and relatively easily portable, although you will also need a water container and a selection of brushes.

For supports, you can buy large sketching pads of drawing paper, pastel paper and watercolour paper, or clip individual sheets to a drawing board. Sketchbooks of all these kinds of paper are available in a wide range of sizes but, unless you like to work small, do not be tempted by a tiny address-book size, as you may find that it restricts and frustrates you.

You might also like to consider investing in a portable sketching easel and stool. And do not forget how easy it is to get sunburnt when you are engrossed in sketching outdoors, even on what might appear to be a dull day.

Choosing the medium ◄
When you are out sketching it is wise to take a selection of different drawing media, as you may find that a particular subject is better suited to one than another. John Townend likes coloured pencil for landscapes, but prefers pen and ink for architectural subjects, where colour is less important than line.

Making colour notes ►
Gerry Baptist works mainly in acrylic, using vivid colours, and his watercolour sketches reflect his artistic preoccupations; a monochrome pencil sketch would therefore not provide the information that he needs for his paintings.

Collecting ideas ▲
David Cuthbert does not make sketches with a specific painting in mind, but he has several sketchbooks in which he notes down anything he sees, often taking photographs at the same time so that he has a 'library' of possible ideas.

Taking reference photographs

Some purists might say that artists should never work from photographs, but this is a not realistic demand. Most painters have limited time at their disposal and the weather can make outdoor work impossible, so it is better to paint from photographs than not to paint at all. There are a few things to bear in mind when you take your photographs, however:

• Cameras cannot always capture very subtle nuances of colour. Dark colours, in particular, are often reduced to a formless mass with no detail. If possible make colour notes in the medium in which you plan to work, noting the colours you mixed to make shades.
• Remember that photographs tend to flatten out perspective and to reduce the feeling of three-dimensional space.

• Use your digital camera in situ as a compositional aid: you can review the image immediately and make minor adjustments to your viewpoint to see what effect they have.
• Take as many shots as you can, from different angles and viewpoints; close up and at a distance. With the advent of digital cameras, processing costs are no longer an issue.

Gallery

In this gallery, you will find landscape drawings and paintings by professional artists in all the main media. Study them carefully to see what you can learn from their composition, use of colour, and technical approaches to painting this most fascinating of subjects. Many different forms, natural and man-made, are featured, and it may surprise you where inspiration can be found.

Line and wash ▶

In *White Village, South Spain*, Joan Elliot Bates has combined linear pen-and-ink work with light washes of watercolour. The paint has spread the ink in places, so there is no obvious boundary between line and colour. When you combine different media, it is important that they work together, or the drawing will lack unity.

Luminous colours ◀

In this pastel painting, *Window in Provence*, Patrick Cullen has built up the colours thickly, using short pieces of pastel to make broad marks. To create the gentle but luminous colours, he has restricted himself to light and mid tones, controlling them carefully and changing the direction of the strokes to give variety to the different surfaces that he is depicting.

Restricted colour palette ▼

In Patrick Cullen's atmospheric *Casa de Lido*, the pastel is again applied thickly and layered in places. Again the colour palette is restricted to mostly light and mid tones. Cullen usually works either on sandpaper or on heavy watercolour paper on which he first lays a ground of paint.

Man-made landscape ▶

In her oil painting *East End Pipes*, Karen Raney has found an exciting and unusual subject which has allowed her to explore strong contrasts of tone and the relationships between shapes and colours. This painting demonstrates that potential landscape subjects can be found everywhere, not just in conventionally 'pretty' rural settings. Note how the pipes on either side of the painting point inward, directing the viewer's eye into the painting. The patch of sky is relatively small, but it prevents the image from being too oppressive.

Watercolour plus soft pastel ▼

Hazel Harrison's unnamed painting combines watercolour (applied initially as an underpainting) with soft pastel. Some artists use a watercolour underpainting in much the same way as they would a coloured ground, covering most of it with pastel. Here, however, the two media work together, with the watercolour playing an important part in the overall effect. The brush marks of the watercolour show through in places – for example, in the foliage, where they are used to suggest the movement of the trees in the breeze – while the pastel is used to build up texture and create areas of broken colour.

Dramatic colour ▼

Oliver Bevan paints scenes using colour in a way that is not strictly naturalistic but which evokes a powerful atmosphere. In this oil painting, *Sharp Corner*, strong contrasts of tone and colour produce a highly dramatic effect, with a slight sense of menace reinforced by the two dark figures and the gravestone-like shapes in the foreground. Note how well the dark, silhouetted patches are balanced by the areas of light.

▶

Bold brushstrokes ▲
This unnamed oil painting of a Mediterranean landscape by Karen Raney illustrates what is meant by creating a sense of movement in a composition. The eye is led into and around the painting by the wing-like shape of the foreground roof and the directional brushwork. The bold brushstrokes also create a feeling of tremendous vibrancy and energy that is perfectly in keeping with the subject.

Landscape in close-up ◄
One of the most difficult decisions to make is how much to include and focus on. You can often make a more expressive statement by moving in close, as Doug Dawson has done in *The Edge of the Meadow*. The strong diagonal of the tree is balanced by the horizontal bands of colour formed by the foreground and by the light field in the middle distance.

Delicate brushstrokes ▶

The textures in this watercolour, *Birch Trunks* by Juliette Palmer, have been described with great care, with a succession of small, delicate brushstrokes used for the trunks and distant clumps of twigs.

Energetic pastel strokes▼

Pastel is often associated with delicate colours, but this powerful landscape, *Summer Hillside* by James Crittendon, shows that considerable depth of tone can be achieved by laying one pastel colour over another. The pastels have been applied vigorously, giving the painting a lovely feeling of energy; in the trees, particularly, the effect is very much like brushstrokes in an oil or acrylic painting.

▶

Precision strokes ◄
There is a luminous quality in Maureen Jordan's pastel painting, *Bluebells at Isabella*: one can almost feel the warmth of the sunlight. In a landscape setting, flowers usually need to be treated more broadly and simply than they would in an indoor group: the important features are the overall colour and the growth habit of the flowers. Here, even the flowers in the foreground are no more than dashes of pastel, the marks have been carefully placed and the flowers are immediately recognizable to anyone who has seen a bluebell wood.

Spontaneous use of line and wash ►
Mike Bernard rarely uses one medium on its own; in *Cow Parsley and House*, he has combined watercolour with pen drawing. This has allowed him to introduce touches of detail into the foreground while keeping both the drawing and the watercolour washes free and unrestrained. The heads of the cow parsley are ink blots dropped from the pen, which have spread in places into the surrounding colours. The linear highlights were achieved by scratching into dry paint.

Complementary colours ▼
In *Pines on Beauvalla*, Gerry Baptist has controlled the juxtapositions of colour carefully, using complementary colours such as yellow and mauve to create maximum impact while giving a realistic account of the landscape.

Thick and thin paint ▲

Brushwork is an important element in David Curtis's oil painting, *Red Lane, near Dromfield*. The brushstrokes follow the direction of the tree trunks and branches, describing them with great economy. Depth and recession are suggested by the contrast between thick and thin paint: on the right-hand tree the paint is thick, while for the area of blue distance it has been brushed lightly over the surface. The effect is an energetic rendering of a very static scene.

Cool colours ▶

The colour scheme in Ted Gould's *Snow Scene* is cool throughout; the yellow of the hat and scarf provides the only touch of contrast for the blues, blue-greens, greys and grey-browns. The painting is in acrylic, used thickly on canvas.

Quick sketches: Complex shapes

Trees can be a delight to draw – particularly old trees that have gnarled bark and twists and splits in their trunks – as they allow you to explore a wide range of textural techniques and approaches. Monochrome sketches are perhaps the most satisfying of all as, without the distraction of colour, the textures and shapes really come into their own.

However, trees are complicated forms and can be one of the biggest challenges to the inexperienced landscape painter. To get used to looking at them as simple shapes and assessing their growth patterns, practise making quick sketches. Set yourself a strict time limit – anything from 5 to 30 minutes – and, before you put pencil to paper, really look at your subject and analyse its structure. Look in particular at the way the branches grow out of the main trunk: do they spread out straight, veer upward in a v-shaped pattern on either side of the trunk, or droop down? Sketching deciduous trees in late autumn or winter, when they've shed their leaves, is a particularly useful exercise, as it allows you to become familiar with the underlying shape.

Once you have got the basic shape right, you can move on to adding tone so that your sketch takes on more of a three-dimensional feel. Experiment with different media, too – pencil, charcoal, pen and ink and even the humble felt-tip pen all create different moods and qualities of mark.

The scene
This tree was badly damaged in a winter gale. The artist came across it when she was out for a walk in the country and was attracted by the many shapes made by the broken and contorted branches and by the gnarled texture of the bark.

5-minute sketch: graphite pencil ▼
After putting down the outline with slightly jagged pencil strokes, the artist then scribbled in the darkest areas of tone, such as the undersides of the branches and the shaded interior of the split in the trunk. Even in a quick 5-minute sketch such as this, you can begin to capture something of the form of the tree.

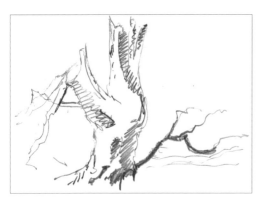

10-minute sketch: graphite pencil ▼
In a slightly longer sketch, you can begin to refine the detail, putting in tones that range from a mid-grey on the shaded parts to a much denser black in the hollowed recess near the base. In addition to providing information about the light and shade, the tone is applied in such a way as to hint at the pattern of the bark.

15-minute sketch: graphite pencil ▶
The shading is more highly developed in this sketch and the tree looks more three-dimensional. Although the background is not drawn in detail, putting in the horizon and blocking in generalized shapes for the trees and bushes in the distance sets the tree in a recognizable context.

25-minute sketch: graphite pencil plus pen and ink ▼
Confident, scribbled pen lines over an initial pencil sketch give this drawing a real sense of energy and capture the character of the tree very well. Note the use of a wide range of marks, from simple hatching on the trunk to tiny flecks and dashes for the small leaves.

Quick sketches: Finding a focal point

When you are sketching on location, particularly when you have faced with a panoramic view, it is very easy to get carried away by the grandeur of the setting and lose sight of the fact that your image needs to work as a composition. Always look for something that you can use as a focal point, such as a large boulder or a tree, and place it at a strong point in the picture space so that the viewer's eye goes immediately to it. Placing the focal point 'on the third' almost always works well.

Look, also, for lines (real or imaginary) that lead the viewer through the scene – maybe a wall or a fence, a line of bushes or, as here, a stony track leading into the distance.

When you are out for a walk, take a sketchbook with you and spend a few minutes making quick sketches to improve your ability to compose a scene. After a while you will find that looking for a focal point and devising ways of directing the viewer's eye around the picture becomes second nature.

The scene
The track directs our attention to the mountains in the distance, while the rocks on the left provide a much-needed focal point.

5-minute sketch: charcoal ▼
Compositionally, the track is a way of drawing our attention to the backdrop, as are the wedge-shaped slopes on the left and right. Once she had worked out the composition, the artist scribbled down some very rough, linear marks for the pebbly track and rocks, and smudged charcoal to create broad areas of dark and mid-tone. The mountains were largely left untouched, so that they are paler than the foreground areas, which helps to create a feeling of recession.

15-minute sketch: chisel-tip pen ▶

You may never have thought of using a chisel-tip marker as a drawing tool but, although it is not the most sophisticated of implements, it can be very useful for making quick sketches on location as it is easily portable and clean to handle. By adjusting the angle at which you hold it and by applying differing amounts of pressure, you will also find that it can make a surprisingly varied range of marks. Here, the artist used spiky vertical marks to convey the texture of the grasses, while rough circles describe the pebbles on the track and wispy curves imply the fluffy clouds overhead. The chisel-shaped tip of the pen was used to block in larger elements such as the trees, bushes and boulders, creating a convincing sense of solidity in these areas. Note how the amount of visible detail decreases with distance: apart from a few sketchy lines to indicate the contours, the distant mountains are left blank.

30-minute sketch: soft pastels ▼

A cream pastel paper gives an underlying warmth to the image; the tooth of the paper also has an effect, as it helps to convey the texture of the pebble-strewn ground. Note how many different greens and yellows the artist has used. She has overlaid them to create lively colour mixes and blended them in parts so that areas of soft grass contrast effectively with the hard texture of the rocks.

Rolling hills in acrylics

Sometimes when you are painting a landscape, one element – a lone tree, a waterfall, a farm building, for example – attracts your attention; at other times, it's the sheer scale and drama of a broad panorama that draws you. In the latter case, it can be hard to evoke the same feeling of awe in the viewer that you felt on beholding the scene; more often than not, the reason for this is that you have failed to provide a focal point in your image.

In the landscape shown here, gently rolling hills sweep far away into the distance in an idyllic rural setting. But even in the most rural of settings, evidence of former industries can often be seen. Although the quarries in which they were cut have long since ceased to operate, these abandoned millstones provide the artist with a focal point for his painting. Without them, the scene would look like an empty stage set, with nothing to hold the viewer's interest.

This project uses acrylic paint in a similar way to traditional watercolour, with the colours being built up gradually in thin glazes, so that each layer is modified by the underlying colours. It also incorporates a wide range of textural techniques, from drybrush work to less conventional methods such as pressing bubble wrap into the paint and dabbing on paint with your fingertips. There is no 'right' or 'wrong' way to apply paint to the support: use whatever tools you have to hand to create the effect you want.

Materials
• Card primed with acrylic primer
• B pencil
• Acrylic paints: cadmium yellow, cadmium red, phthalocyanine blue, burnt umber, magenta, titanium white, cobalt blue, cerulean blue
• Brushes: medium round, small round
• Rag
• Bubble wrap

1 Using a B pencil, make a light underdrawing of the scene, taking care to get the ellipses and angles of the millstones right.

The scene
The millstones are the focal point of the painting. Note how they form a rough triangle, positioned just off centre at the base of the image, leading the viewer's eye up the line of the hill and back down again to the foreground. When you paint a scene like this, make sure you spend time selecting the best viewpoint.

2 Using a rag, spread cadmium yellow acrylic paint straight from the tube over the support, leaving a few gaps in the sky area for clouds. Drop a little cadmium red over the centre left of the image and blend it into the yellow paint with the rag so that the two colours merge on the support, creating an orange, wedge-like shape. Leave to dry.

3 Mix a dark green from cadmium yellow and phthalocyanine blue. Using a medium round brush, scumble the mixture over the wooded hillside in the middle distance to give a generalized impression of trees. While the first green is still damp, add a little more blue to the mixture and dot this in for the darkest areas of green.

4 Mix a dull but warm orange from cadmium yellow, cadmium red and a little burnt umber and brush it over the distant escarpment on the left of the image and over the fields in front of the wood. The warm colour helps to bring this area forward in the image.

5 Using a medium round brush, apply a thin glaze of magenta in a broad stroke over the slope of the hill on the left. Add a little phthalocyanine blue to the mixture and paint the crest of the escarpment behind it. While the paint is still wet, gently press bubble wrap into it to create some texture.

▶

6 Add a little burnt umber to the warm orange mixture from Step 4 and brush it loosely over the bottom left corner of the painting, where the grasses and underlying soil are much darker in tone. While the paint is still wet, lift off some of the colour by 'drawing' the shapes of the light-coloured grass stems in the foreground with the tip of a paintbrush to reveal the colour of the support beneath.

7 Darken the hillside, using the same colours as in Step 5. Press bubble wrap into burnt umber paint and then press the bubble wrap across the bands of orange and magenta on the left to create loose, textured dots that echo the growth pattern of the vegetation. Paint the fence posts using a dark, reddish brown mixed from phthalocyanine blue and burnt umber. Mix a dark purple from cadmium red and phthalocyanine blue and brush it over the shaded sides of the millstones. For the darkest stones, use phthalocyanine blue.

8 Dot in the shapes of the isolated trees in the middle distance, using the same warm orange that you used to paint the fields. Following your initial pencil marks, mark out the field boundaries in burnt umber. Roughly block in the buildings in the middle distance in magenta. Brush a broad sweep of magenta over the hill to the right of the buildings and wipe a rag over it to blur the colour.

9 Brush titanium white over the sky area, allowing a hint of the underlying yellow to show through to maintain the overall warm colour temperature of the scene. Re-establish the highlight areas on the ground by smearing on titanium white paint with your fingertips, which gives a more spontaneous-looking and random effect than applying the paint with a brush.

Assessment time
It is becoming clear which parts of the scene are in shadow and which are brightly lit, and the underlying yellows and oranges give a warm glow to the whole scene. Now you need to concentrate on putting in the greens and browns of the landscape and on building up the textures so that the spatial relationships are established more strongly. Having more texture in the foreground than in the background is one way of creating a sense of scale and distance.

Note how the colours become paler in tone the farther away they are, which helps to create a feeling of distance and recession.

The yellow used as a base colour on these sunlit fields will modify any glazes that are applied on top.

More texture is needed in the grasses in the immediate foreground.

10 Reduce the starkness of the white areas by brushing over them with a thin glaze of the appropriate colour – cobalt blue over the wooded area, burnt umber over the shaded parts of the hillsides, and various yellow-orange mixtures over the sunlit fields. Note how the scene becomes more unified as a result.

11 Mix a bright green from cadmium yellow and cerulean blue and, using a medium round brush, paint over the mostly brightly lit fields in the middle distance. Note that some of the fields contain crops, so leave the underlying orangey-brown colour in these areas and take care not to go over the field boundaries.

12 Add a little more titanium white to the mixture to lighten it and paint the most distant fields. Mix a neutral brown from cadmium yellow, cadmium red and phthalocyanine blue and use it to tone down the reddish areas on the hill to the left, which look too harsh.

13 Mix a slightly darker green from cadmium yellow and phthalocyanine blue and paint the green grass in the immediate foreground. The use of a darker tone pulls this area forward and makes it seem closer to the viewer. The shaded sides of the millstones look too red in tone and jump forward too much. Mix a neutral brownish grey from cadmium yellow, cadmium red, cobalt blue and titanium white and paint over these areas, reinforcing the cast shadows with a slightly darker version of the same mixture.

14 Using a very small round brush, carefully paint a thin line of titanium white around the top edge of the millstone that is lying on its side, so that it appears to be rim-lit by the sun, keeping your hand as steady as possible.

15 Using a small round brush, dry brush thin strokes of burnt umber over the foreground to the left of the millstones to add texture and create the impression of grass stems blowing in the breeze.

The finished painting

Finally, put in the sky using a bright blue mixed from cerulean blue and titanium white. This tranquil landscape simply glows with sunlight and warmth. The scene covers a wide area but the millstones in the foreground, which are positioned slightly off centre, provide a strong triangular shape at the base of the image and a much-needed focal point. Although they occupy only a small part of the frame, the buildings in the middle distance provide a secondary point of interest, to which our eye is drawn by the gently sloping diagonal lines of the hills and fields.

Strong textures in the foreground help to pull this area forward and imply that it is closer to the viewer.

The sloping line of the hills leads our eye down toward the buildings, which form a secondary point of interest.

The greens and browns of the fields are modified by the underlying yellow, adding warmth to these rather subdued colours.

Rocky canyon in soft pastels

This is one of the best-known and most distinctive of all landscapes in the USA – Bryce Canyon in south-western Utah. The colourful rock formations, a series of eroded spires, are best viewed in early morning and late afternoon, when they glow in the sunlight.

When you are drawing formations such as these, look for tonal contrast within the rocks as this is what shows the different planes and makes them look three-dimensional. If a rock juts out at a sharp angle, there is a clear transition from one plane to another and the difference in tone between one side and another is very obvious. If the rock is smooth and rounded, the transition in tone is more gradual.

Drawing the many fissures and crevices also shows the form of the subject. If the shadows in these crevices are very deep, you might be tempted to draw them in black – but black can look very stark and unnatural. Instead, use a complementary dark colour for the shadows – so if the rocks are a reddish-brown, as here, try opting for a purple-based shadow colour.

Materials
- *Pastel paper*
- *Thin charcoal stick*
- *Soft pastels: pale blue, grey, violet, dark blue, browns, cadmium orange, pale pink, greens, yellow ochre*
- *Clean rag or paper towel*
- *Kneaded eraser*
- *Conté stick: brown*
- *Blending brush*

The scene
Trees in the foreground provide a sense of scale: without them, it would be hard to estimate how tall the rocks are.

> **Tip**: If you are working from a photograph, you may find that it helps to grid up both the photograph and your drawing paper and then work systematically on one square at a time until all the elements are in place.

1 Using a thin charcoal stick, draw the rock formations and lightly indicate the main areas of shade. Using the side of a pale blue pastel, block in the small patch of sky that is visible above the rocks.

2 Using a cool grey pastel on its side, block in the darker, shaded areas of the rock formations. This gives the rocks some form and establishes the direction from which the light is coming.

3 Using a violet pastel on its side, put in the strata of the background rock-face. Note how the diagonal lines within this rock-face reveal the structure and add drama to the composition.

4 Again using the side of the pastel, strengthen the horizontal strata on the background rock, applying light shade of blue at the top of the rock and a darker blue at the base.

5 Begin applying colour to the rock formations, using brown and dark violet in the shadow areas, using the edge of the pastel to define the divisions between the sections. The crevices between the rocks are dark and deep: a deep violet provides the necessary dark tone and is a warmer and more lively colour than black.

6 Apply cadmium orange to the rock formations. On the shaded facets, where the orange is overlaid on the violet, a rich optical colour mix ensues. On the more brightly lit parts of the landscape, the orange represents the naturally warm, sun-kissed colour of the rock. The colour combination is sympathetic but striking.

▶

Assessment time
The structure of the rock formations is beginning to emerge, but the contrast between the shaded and the more brightly lit facets is not yet strong enough: the tonal contrasts need to be much stronger and this is something that you can build up gradually, continually assessing the lights and darks as you work. The rock formations also need to be brought forward in the scene, so that they stand out clearly from the cliff in the background.

The main rock formations look rather flat and need more modelling.

It is hard to tell that this cliff is some distance behind the main rock formations. It looks as if it is joined to the foreground rocks, so the perspective needs work.

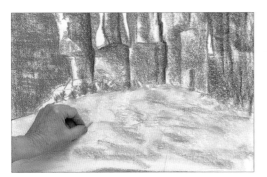

7 Lightly apply pale grey and pink over the foreground scrubland. Use grey for the shaded areas and pink for those illuminated by the late-afternoon sunlight.

8 Apply touches of pale green to the scrubland, then soften the whole area by blending the colours with a clean rag or piece of paper towel, using a gentle circular motion.

9 Using a kneaded eraser, wipe off the shapes of the trees in the foreground. If you accidentally wipe off too much, simply repeat Steps 7 and 8 for the right background colour.

10 Draw the trees, using a brown Conté stick for the trunks and their shadows, and bright green to roughly block in the masses of foliage.

11 Wipe a clean rag or a piece of paper towel over the top of the background rock-face and the sky to lift off excess pastel dust and soften the colour.

 Tip: Turn the rag around in your hand so that you do not smudge violet over the sky.

12 Soften the violet on the lower part of the background rock-face by using a blending brush, brushing it both horizontally and vertically. If you have not got a blending brush, you could use your fingers or a torchon, but the bristles of the brush create very fine lines in the pastel dust, which are perfect for the striations in the rock. Although this rock-face is in the distance, it is important to create some subtle texture here.

▶

13 Add more detail to the main rock-face, using the side of the deep violet pastel to overlay colour and the tip to draw on short horizontal and vertical lines to emphasize the different facets within the rock.

14 Now start working on the foreground scrubland. Using a pale green pastel on its side, roughly scribble in the base colour of the scrubby bushes that cover the ground immediately below the rock-face.

15 Build up the foreground foliage, using a range of pale and mid-toned greens and grey-greens. A general impression of the shapes is all that is required. Put in the roadway with a warm yellow ochre pastel.

16 Define the edges of the roadway in brown. Also add a range of browns to the scrubland, using jagged, vertical strokes of dark brown for the thickest stems and branches. Make sure your pastel strokes follow the direction of growth.

The finished drawing

This colourful drawing captures the heat and the mood of the scene very well. Warm oranges and purples predominate and are perfectly suited to the arid, semi-desert landscape. The artist used bold linear strokes to capture the striations and jagged texture of the rocks and the drawing is full of energy. Although some texture is evident on the background cliff, blending out the pastel marks in this area has helped to create a sense of recession. For the foreground scrubland, the artist opted for an impressionistic approach, describing the overall shapes and textures with dots and dashes of greens and grey-greens. This contributes to the liveliness of the scene and concentrates attention on the rocks, which are the main point of interest.

As the background cliff is less textured, it appears to be farther away.

The trees are dwarfed by the rocks that tower above, and give a sense of scale.

Tonal contrasts reveal the different facets of the rocks.

Craggy mountains in watercolour

In this exercise in aerial perspective, although the scene is very simple, you must convey a sense of the distances involved in order for it to look convincing. Tonal contrast is one way of achieving this: remember that colours are generally paler toward the horizon, so the mountains in the far distance look paler than those in the foreground. Textural contrast is another way to give a sense of distance: details such as jagged rocks and clumps of snow need to be more pronounced in the foreground than in the background.

The use of warm and cool colours to convey a sense of light and shade is important, too. Cool colours, such as blue, appear to recede and so painting crevices in the rocks in a cool shade makes them look deeper and farther

away from the viewer. Warm colours, on the other hand, appear to advance and seem closer to the viewer. These should be used for the areas of rock that jut upward into the sunlight.

Although you want the painting to look realistic, do not worry about getting the shape of every single rock exactly right, If you try to put in every crack and crevice that you can see, you will get so bogged down in detail that you will lose sight of the images as a whole and your painting may become tight and laboured. It is more important to convey an overall impression.

Use short, jagged brushstrokes that follow the direction of the rock formations to convey the craggy texture and, above all, try to work freely and spontaneously.

Materials
- *2B pencil*
- *Rough watercolour board*
- *Watercolour paints: ultramarine blue, burnt sienna, cobalt blue, phthalocyanine blue, alizarin crimson, raw umber*
- *Brushes: large round, old brush for masking*
- *Sponge*
- *Tissue paper*
- *Masking fluid*
- *Scalpel or craft (utility) knife*

The scene
These craggy peaks make a dramatic image. The drama is enhanced by the billowing clouds, set against a brilliant blue sky, and the last vestiges of snow clinging to the rocks in the late spring.

Textural detail is most evident in the foreground; this also helps to create a sense of distance.

Note how the colours look paler in the distance, due to the effect of aerial perspective.

1 Using a 2B pencil, lightly sketch the scene, indicating the main gulleys and crevices and the bulk of the clouds in the sky. Keep your pencil lines loose and fluid: try to capture the essence of the scene and to feel the 'rhythm' of the jagged rock formations.

2 Mix a pale, neutral grey from ultramarine blue and burnt sienna. Using a large round brush, wash this mixture over the foreground mountain.

3 Mix a bright blue from cobalt blue and a little phthalocyanine blue. Using a large round brush, wash it over the top of the sky. While this is still wet, dampen a small sponge in clean water, squeeze out the excess moisture, and dab it on the sky area to lift off some of the colour. This reveals white cloud shapes with softer edges than you could achieve using any other technique.

> **Tips:** The sponge is used in this project to lift off paint colour applied to the sky area, and to apply paint. The surface of the sponge leaves a soft, textured effect.
> • Each time you apply the sponge, turn it around in your hand to find a clean area, and rinse it regularly in clean water so that you do not accidentally dab colour back on to the paper.

▶

4 Mix a neutral purple from alizarin crimson, ultramarine blue and a little raw umber. Using a large round brush, dampen the dark undersides of the clouds and touch in the neutral purple mixture. While this is still damp, touch in a second application of the same mixture in places to build up the tone. If necessary, soften the edges and adjust the shapes of the dark areas by dabbing them with a piece of sponge or clean paper towel to lift off colour.

5 Study your reference photograph to see exactly where the little patches of snow lie on the foreground mountain. Using an old brush, apply masking fluid to these areas to protect them from subsequent applications of paint. Use thin lines of fluid for snow that clings to the ridges and block in larger areas with the side of the brush. Wash the brush in liquid detergent and warm water. Leave the masking fluid to dry completely before moving on to the next stage.

6 Mix a dark blue from cobalt blue and phthalocyanine blue and paint the distant hills between the two mountains. Dilute the mixture and brush it over the background mountain. Leave to dry. Mix a dark brown from burnt sienna with a little alizarin crimson and ultramarine blue, and wash this mixture over the background mountain. Add a little alizarin crimson and begin painting the foreground mountain.

7 Using a large round brush, continue to paint the foreground mountain. Use the same dark brown mixture that you used in Step 6 for the areas that catch the sun, and phthalocyanine blue for the areas that are in the shade. Paint with relatively short and slightly jagged vertical brushstrokes that echo the direction of the rock formations. This helps to convey the texture of the rocks.

Assessment time
Because of the careful use of warm and cool colours, the painting is already beginning to take on some form. Much of the rest of the painting will consist of building up the tones you have already applied to enhance the three-dimensional effect and the texture of the rocks. At this stage, it is important that you take the time to assess whether or not the areas of light and shade are correctly placed. Note, too, the contrast between the foreground and the background: the foreground is more textured and is darker in tone, and this helps to convey an impression of distance.

The rocks that jut out into the sunlight are painted in a warm brown so that they appear to advance.

The crevices are in deep shade and are painted in a cool blue so that they appear to recede.

The background mountain is painted in a flat colour, which helps to convey the impression that it is farther away.

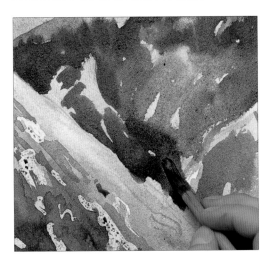

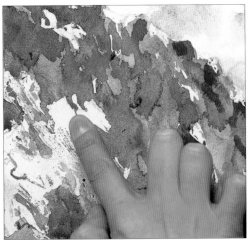

8 Mix a deep, purplish blue from alizarin crimson, phthalocyanine blue and raw umber. Brush this mixture along the top of the background peak, leaving some gaps so that the underlying brown colour shows through. Using the dark brown mixture used in Step 6, build up tone on the rest of the background mountain, applying several brushstrokes wet into wet to the darker areas.

9 Continue building up the tones on both mountains, using the same paint mixtures as before. Leave to dry. Using your fingertips, gently rub off the masking fluid to reveal the patches of white snow. (It is sometimes hard to see if you have rubbed off all the fluid, so run your fingers over the whole painting to check that you have not missed any.) Dust or blow all dried fluid off the surface of the painting.

▶

10 Using the tip of a scalpel or craft knife and pulling the blade sideways so as not to cut through the paper, scratch off thin lines of paint to reveal snow in gulleys on the background mountain.

11 Apply tiny dots of colour around the edges of some of the unmasked areas to tone down the brightness a little. Continue the tonal build-up, making sure your brushstrokes follow the contours of the rocks.

12 Dip a sponge in clean water, squeeze out any excess moisture and dampen the dark clouds. Dip the sponge in the neutral purple mixture used in Step 4 and dab it lightly on to the clouds to darken them and make them look a little more dramatic.

13 The final stage of the painting is to assess the tonal values once more to make sure that the contrast between the light and dark areas is strong enough. If necessary, brush on more of the purplish blue mixture used in Step 8 to deepen the shadows.

The finished painting

This is a beautiful and dramatic example of how contrasting warm colours with cool colours can create a sense of three dimensions. Although the colour palette is restricted, the artist has managed to create an impressively wide range of tones.

Jagged brushstrokes that follow the direction of the rock formations create realistic-looking textures on the foreground mountain and the white of the paper shines through in places, giving life and sparkle to the image.

The white of the paper is used to good effect, implying patches of snow clinging to the rocks.

The soft-edged clouds and brilliant blue sky provide a perfect counterbalance to the harshness of the rocks below.

The background mountain is painted in flat washes, with far less textural detail than the foreground.

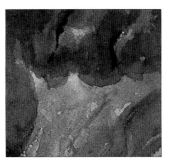

Flower garden in water-soluble pencils

This scene was invented entirely from the artist's imagination, using quick sketches of flowers in her own garden and photographs from a garden centre catalogue as reference. When you are combining material from several sources, take the trouble to check a few basic facts. Make sure that the flowers you've selected really do bloom at the same time, and check the relative sizes, so that you don't make a ground-hugging plant appear taller than a small tree.

The project gives you the chance to combine classic watercolour techniques with the relatively modern medium of water-soluble pencils. The characteristics of water-soluble pencils are exploited to the full here. The pencil marks are used dry, to create fine linear detail, particularly in the foreground. They are also covered with watercolour washes, so that the colours merge. You can control the amount of blur to a certain extent: if you wet the tip of the pencil before you apply it, the pencil marks will blur less, allowing you to hold some of the detail and texture in these areas.

Materials

- *140lb (300gsm) NOT watercolour paper, pre-stretched*
- *Water-soluble pencils: dark blue, light brown, cerulean blue, light violet, dark violet, blue-green, olive green, red, yellow, orange, deep red, green*
- *Watercolour paints: cerulean blue, rose doré, Linden green, dark olive, olive green, cobalt blue, cadmium yellow, Naples yellow, burnt sienna, vermilion, alizarin crimson, Payne's grey*
- *Brushes: medium round, fine round*
- *Ruling drawing pen*
- *Masking fluid*

> **Tip**: Changing from a horizontal to a vertical format may alter other elements as well. In the final composition, the path still runs from the bottom right to the top left but the artist made the foreground flower border more prominent.

Reference sketches

Look closely at detailed sketches, illustrations or photographs of individual flowers before you embark on your full-scale painting. Although a massed clump of foliage and flowers may look like an indistinct jumble, knowing the shape and colour of an individual bloom will help you capture the essential features of the plant.

Preliminary sketch

The artist invented a garden scene and made a small sketch to try out the colours and the composition. To begin with, she opted for a horizontal format. Then she decided that this placed too much emphasis on the pathway and that a vertical format, with the rose arch as the main feature, would have more impact.

1 Using a dark blue water-soluble pencil, sketch the main shapes of your subject. Dip a ruling drawing pen in masking fluid and mask the lightest parts of the flowers.

2 One of the advantages of using a ruling drawing pen is that it holds the masking fluid in a reservoir. A range of marks is used to convey the different textures of each of the massed clumps – flowing lines for the poppy heads and little dashes for the daisy petal in the foreground. It would be more difficult to achieve this with a dip pen as the nib would block up, leaving blobs and blots on the paper.

3 Shade in the trunk of the tree with loose pencil strokes, using a light brown water-soluble pencil. (This makes the marks more permanent.) Dip the tip of the pencil in clean water and draw the branches. Draw the wooden rose arch in the same colour. Colour in the individual delphinium blooms with small dots of cerulean blue, changing to light and dark violet for the stems that are in deeper shade. Dip the pencil tip in water to make some of the marks.

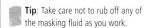

Tip: Take care not to rub off any of the masking fluid as you work.

Assessment time
Continue with these dots and dashes of pencil work until you have established the general colour scheme of the garden. Don't be tempted to do too much or the pencil work might begin to overpower the picture: this is a painting, not a drawing, and it is the watercolour paint applied in the subsequent stages that will give the work its character.

Blue-green for the foliage.

Olive green and light violet for the iris leaves.

Yellow, red and orange for the poppies.

The negative spaces between the clumps of flowers are as important as the flowers themselves.

▶

4 Dampen the background with water. Wash a pale mix of cerulean blue watercolour paint over the sky, brushing around the branches. Dot rose doré over the rose arch: the paint will blur, suggesting full-blown blooms. Brush Linden green under the arch and dot a mixture of dark olive and cerulean blue into the background and between the delphiniums. While the paint is still damp, add bright olive green with cerulean blue and brush over the first blue wash.

5 Dampen the middle distance with clean water. Dot cerulean blue, rose doré and cobalt blue on to the delphiniums. Both the paint and the initial water-soluble pencil marks will blur and spread, causing the flowers to look slightly out of focus. Mix a neutral brown from olive green and rose doré and brush it into the negative spaces between the iris stems. The flowers will begin to stand out more against this dark background.

6 The distance and middle ground have now been established. Note how the soft tones and lack of clear detail help to imply that these areas are further away from the viewer.

7 Mix a bright green from cerulean blue and cadmium yellow and dot it loosely into the pathside area for the hummocks of low-growing ground-cover plants that spill over on to the path.

8 Dampen the path. Starting near the arch, brush pale Naples yellow over the path, adding burnt sienna towards the foreground. Brush clean water over the tip of a brown water-soluble pencil and spatter colour on to the path, using the brush. Start spattering in the foreground and work towards the rose arch. As the brush dries, the drops of water – and the dots of colour – get smaller, and this will help to create a sense of recession.

9 Note how effectively the curved path leads the eye to the focal point of the painting – the rose-covered arch. The spattered drops of colour provide important texture in what would otherwise be a large expanse of flat brown.

10 Brush cadmium yellow and then vermilion over the red poppy heads, allowing the colours to blend on the paper, and brush a tiny bit of alizarin crimson over parts of the foreground poppies to give added depth of tone.

11 Mix Payne's grey with olive green for some of the background poppy leaves and stems. Add a little cobalt blue to the mixture for the foreground poppy leaves. Dot cadmium yellow in the centre of the daisy flowers.

▶

12 Finish the bottom left-hand corner, using the same green mixture as before.

13 Using your fingertips, gently rub off the masking fluid to reveal the white parts of the flowers.

14 Some of the exposed white areas now look too stark – particularly in the background. Mix a very pale wash of cerulean blue and brush it over some of the iris stems to tone down the brightness – otherwise the viewer's eye will be drawn to these areas, which are not the most important parts of the scene.

15 Now go back to the water-soluble pencils to add sharper details in the foreground. Use a deep red pencil to delineate the petals and frilly edges of some of the larger poppies, and draw a green pencil circle around the yellow centres of the poppies. Darken the spaces between the daisy petals with a dark blue pencil.

The finished painting

This painting is a romantic, impressionistic portrayal of a traditional flower garden. Softly coloured poppies, irises, daisies and delphiniums line the winding path, which leads to the focal point of the image – the rose arch. There is a hint of mystery in the painting, too: what lies on the other side of the archway?

Flowers in the background are more blurred than those in the foreground, but some linear detail is still visible.

The poppies are painted with a number of different techniques – masking for the twisting stems, wet-into-wet washes for subtle colour blends, and fine pencil detail.

Reserving the white of the paper for the daisy petals adds sparkle to the image.

The textured path provides subtly coloured but necessary foreground interest.

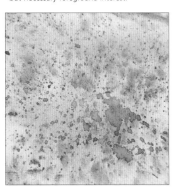

Poppy field in watercolour

Lush expanses of wild flowers are always attractive, and when those flowers are a rich and vibrant red, like this stunning array of poppies, the subject simply cries out to be painted.

This project presents you with several challenges. First and foremost, it is an exercise in painting spontaneously and in creating an impression rather than trying to capture each individual flower. Work quickly and freely, and focus more on the overall tones than on specific details. Make sure you do not make the poppies look as if they have been planted in neat, straight rows. It is surprisingly difficult to position dots of colour randomly, but unpredictable techniques, such as spattering, can help.

Second, remember that this is not a botanical study: what you are trying to create is an overall impression of the scene, not an accurate record of how the flowers are constructed. You really do not want a lot of crisp detail in a scene like this, otherwise it will look stilted and lifeless. This is where watercolour really comes into its own. Wet-into-wet washes that merge on the paper create a natural-looking blur that is perfect for depicting a mass of flowers and trees swaying in the breeze.

Finally, take some time considering the tonal balance of the painting. Red and green are complementary colours so they usually work well together, but if the greens are too dark they could easily overpower the rest of the painting. On the other hand, if they are too light they will not provide a strong enough backdrop for the flowers.

Materials
- 2B pencil
- 140lb (300gsm) rough watercolour paper, pre-stretched
- Watercolour paints: cobalt blue, alizarin crimson, gamboge, raw sienna, sap green, Delft or Prussian blue, viridian, burnt umber, cadmium orange, cadmium red, Payne's grey
- Brushes: large mop, medium mop, fine rigger, old brush for masking fluid, medium round, fine round
- Masking fluid

The scene
This field is a blaze of red poppies as far as the eye can see, counterbalanced by a dark green background of trees. Although the horizon is very near the middle of the picture, which can sometimes makes an image look static, this effect is offset by the fact that the top half of the image is divided more or less equally into trees and sky. However, the sky is very bright, and this detracts from the poppies; so using artistic license with the colour here will improve the overall effect.

The sky lacks colour and needs to be made less dominant.

The dark trees provide a neutral background that makes the red of the poppies all the more vibrant.

1 Using a 2B pencil, lightly sketch the outline of the trees and some of the larger foreground poppies. Don't attempt to put in every single flower – a few of the more prominent ones are all you need as a guide at this stage. Using an old brush, apply masking fluid over the poppies in the foreground. In the middle ground and distance, dot and spatter masking fluid to create a more random, spontaneous effect. Draw some thin lines of masking fluid for the long grasses in the foreground. Clean your brush thoroughly and leave the painting to dry.

2 Using a medium round brush, dampen the sky area with clean water, leaving a few strategically placed gaps for clouds. Mix up a strong wash of cobalt blue and drop this on to the damp sky area, so that it spreads wet-into-wet up to the gaps left for the cloud shapes. The colour is more intense than it was in reality, but the sky needs to look dramatic and it is perfectly acceptable to use artistic licence and alter aspects of the scene in this way. Leave to dry.

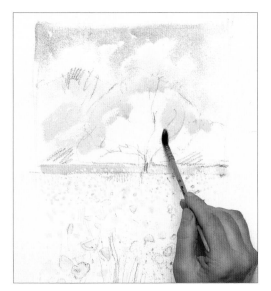

3 Apply a strong wash of gamboge to the tree tops. Add raw sienna and brush over the base of the trees and the horizon. Touch raw sienna into the clouds. While this is still damp, touch a purplish-blue mixture of cobalt blue and alizarin crimson on to the underside of the clouds. Leave to dry.

4 Mix a dark green from sap green, raw sienna and a little Delft or Prussian blue. Using a medium round brush, brush this mixture over the trees to create dark foliage areas, allowing some of the underlying gamboge to show through in places.

5 Continue building up the foliage on the trees, leaving a few gaps. Mix a mid-toned green from gamboge and sap green and, using a large mop brush, brush this mixture over the lower part of the painting – the poppy field. Leave to dry.

6 Mix a darker green from viridian and cobalt blue and apply this mixture to the foreground, using a large mop brush. Use the same colour to touch in some dark lines for the long shadows under the main tree. Leave to dry.

7 Mix a dark green from sap green, raw sienna and burnt umber and, using a fine rigger brush, brush thin lines on to the foreground. Leave to dry. Spatter the same mixture over the foreground to represent the grass seed heads and add texture. Leave to dry.

▶

Assessment time

Cool greens and yellows have been put in across the whole painting, establishing the general tones of the scene. As you continue to work, you will probably find that you need to darken some of the background colours to maintain a balance between them and the foreground. This kind of tonal assessment should be an ongoing part of all your paintings. Now it is almost time to start putting in the bright red poppies in the foreground, the finishing touches that will bring the scene to life. Try above all else to maintain a feeling of spontaneity in the painting as you work: the poppies must look as if they are randomly distributed over the scene.

The dark tonal masses of the background have been established.

Spattering in the foreground gives interesting random texture.

8 Mix a dark green from Delft or Prussian blue, viridian and burnt umber and, using a medium mop brush, darken the trees, leaving some areas untouched to create a sense of form. Add a little more burnt umber to the mixture and, using a fine rigger brush, paint the tree trunks and some fine lines for the main branches. Leave to dry. Using your fingertips, gently rub off the masking fluid.

9 Mix an orangey red from cadmium orange and cadmium red. Using a fine round brush, start painting the poppies in the background.

10 Continue painting the white spaces with the red mixture used in Step 9, leaving a few specks of white to give life and sparkle to the painting. Apply a second layer of colour to some poppies while the first layer is still wet; the paint will blur, giving the impression of poppies blowing in the wind, and the tone will deepen.

11 Using a fine, almost dry brush and the same dark green mixture used in Step 7, paint in the exposed foreground stalks and grasses. Finally, using a fine rigger brush, touch in the black centres of the poppies with a strong Payne's grey.

The finished painting

This is a loose and impressionistic painting that nonetheless captures the mood of the scene very well. It exploits the strong effect of using complementary colours (red and green), but the density of colour has been carefully controlled so that the whole painting looks balanced, with no one part dominating the rest.

The sky is darker than in the original photograph, which helps to maintain the tonal balance of the scene.

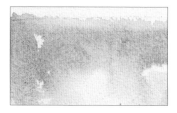

The shadow under the tree is painted with short brushstrokes that echo the direction in which the grasses and flowers grow.

Only the foreground poppies have painted centres. Those in the background are so far away that a blur of colour suffices.

Wisteria-covered archway in acrylics

Using an archway as a frame for a view is a classic compositional device, drawing the viewer's eye through the scene to linger on what lies beyond. Here, however, the view through the arch is little more than a soft, out-of-focus blur: the main interest lies around the arch itself, in the form of the old and somewhat worn brick wall and the violet-coloured wisteria flowers that cascade over it.

In this project, acrylic paint is used both in thin glazes to build up the colour and more thickly, mixed with white, for the mortar lines in the brickwork and the wisteria flowers.

Contrasts of texture are important in building up the image, and a range of techniques is used to achieve this. Spatters of paint in the foreground convey the gravelly texture of the path; fine texture paste on the wall gives a sense of the worn, crumbling brickwork; and different brushstrokes, from flowing curves to short dabs and dashes, capture the textures and shapes of the foreground plants.

Materials
- *300gsm (140lb) NOT watercolour paper*
- *HB pencil*
- *Painting knife*
- *Fine texture paste*
- *Ruling drawing pen or fine-nibbed steel dip pen*
- *Masking fluid*
- *Acrylic paints: light blue violet, vermilion, Hooker's green, yellow ochre, titanium white, violet, burnt sienna, cadmium orange, cadmium yellow, ultramarine blue*
- *Brushes: medium chisel or round*
- *Waterproof sepia ink*

The scene
Although this viewpoint shows the arch and pathway well, there is no real focus of interest and the detail of the flowers is indistinct.

The wisteria flowers
By moving around to the right, the artist was able to see more clearly the colours in the petals and how the flowers hang in clusters. Taking reference photographs or making quick sketches of details such as this will prove invaluable.

1 Using an HB pencil, lightly sketch the scene. Using the tip of a small painting knife, dab texture paste randomly over the brickwork and the path. Leave to dry. Dip a ruling drawing pen or fine-nibbed steel dip pen in masking fluid (frisket) and mask out the lightest parts of the wisteria and the other foreground flowers, and the mortar lines around the archway and in the brick wall. Leave to dry.

2 Mix a very dilute wash of light blue violet and, using a medium chisel or round brush, apply it over the sliver of sky that is visible at the top of the image and through the archway. Brush dilute Hooker's green over the foliage that can be seen through the arch. Mix yellow ochre with a little vermilion and titatnium white and brush this mixture over the path on the far side of the arch.

3 Mix separate washes of violet and light blue violet. Alternating between the mixtures, brush these colours over the flowers. For the deepest-coloured flowers, drop more violet, wet into wet, into the first wash. Leave to dry.

4 Brush a dilute wash of burnt sienna over the brick wall, changing to very pale yellow ochre for the lower part of the wall, and a mixture of burnt sienna and cadmium orange over the archway.

▶

5 Mix a warm brown from burnt sienna, Hooker's green and vermilion and, while the brickwork is still wet, drop this mixture into it in places to deepen the colour. Brush in the general shapes of the wisteria foliage and the foliage above the wall in Hooker's green. Using various mixtures of Hooker's green and Hooker's green plus cadmium yellow, start painting the spiky foliage of the foreground plants.

> **Tip**: When painting the foliage, match your brushstrokes to the shape of the plant – curving, calligraphic strokes for long-leaved plants, short dots and dashes for round-leaved plants.

6 Brush the warm brown colour from Step 5 over the foreground and the darkest parts of the wall to build up the colour. While it is still wet, add more burnt sienna to the mixture and spatter it over the first brown. Mix a dark blue-green from Hooker's green and ultramarine blue and paint the foliage to the left of the arch, adding cadmium yellow to the mixture for the grass at the base of the image. Leave to dry.

7 Using the blue-green mixture from the previous step, continue painting the foliage to the left of the arch, noting the spiky shapes of the leaves. Mix a dark brown from violet and burnt sienna and brush this mixture over the wall and path, so that the colour is gradually built up in thin glazes. Apply the colour unevenly to create some tonal variation and texture.

8 Using a technical drawing pen or fine-nibbed steel dip pen loaded with waterproof sepia ink, draw the wrought-iron gateway. (Black ink would look too harsh: sepia is a much more gentle colour.)

Tip: The ink must be waterproof, otherwise it will smudge if any paint is applied on top of it.

9 The wisteria flowers look a little flat; build them up by brushing on pure violet in the darkest areas. Leave to dry.

Assessment time

Rub off the masking fluid with your fingertips; sometimes it is hard to see whether or not you have removed all the fluid, so run your fingers over the whole painting to make sure no lumps of fluid are left. Blow or shake off any loose, dried fluid before you continue painting.

Although the painting is nearing completion, it needs a little more "punch" and contrast. Take some time at this stage to assess where more work is needed: by glazing selected areas with thin layers of acrylic paint, you can build up the colours to the required density while at the same time adding much-needed texture on areas such as the path and brickwork. The adjustments that you make in these final stages of the painting will be relatively small, but they make an important contribution to the overall effect.

The areas previously covered by the masking fluid are too stark and need to be knocked back.

More detail is required in the foreground foliage.

10 Apply a thin glaze of light blue violet over the exposed parts of the wisteria flowers. Mix a dilute yellowy green from Hooker's green and cadmium yellow and brush it over the wisteria trunk and the foliage at the base of the right-hand wall. Mix a blue-green from ultramarine blue and Hooker's green and brush it over the plants to the left of the gate to tint the exposed areas and deepen the foliage colour.

11 Mix a pale, yellowish brown from yellow ochre and green and paint some of the exposed mortar lines in the brickwork. Do not worry if you go outside the mortar lines as it will simply serve as a glaze, enhancing the texture of the crumbling brickwork. Dot violet paint into the wisteria flowers to give more contrast between the light and dark flowers. Paint the shaded interior of the arch in the same colour.

12 Dotting the paint on the tip of the brush, paint the lightest wisteria flowers in a pale, opaque mixture of white and light blue violet. This points up the contrast between the lightest and darkest areas and gives the flowers more depth.

The finished painting
This is a soft, romantic painting of part of an old walled garden. The plants are painted in a fairly loose, impressionistic way rather than as highly resolved botanical studies, but they are nonetheless recognizable from their general shapes and colours. The path draws our eye through the scene to the flower-covered wall and archway; the arch itself is positioned slightly off centre, which adds interest to the composition and prevents it from looking too static.

The blue-green colour of the plants in this area balances the blues and violets of the wisteria.

Although no detail is visible, the garden beyond the archway is implied through the use of soft, muted colours.

The artist has paid careful attention to the different colours within the flowers and to the overall shapes of the flower clusters.

Snow scene in charcoal

Here is an interesting challenge: how do you draw a bright, white subject such as snow using charcoal, which is one of the densest and darkest drawing mediums available? The answer is not to attempt to draw the snow at all: allow the white of the paper to stand for the brightest parts of the snow and use the charcoal for the mid- and dark tones. Focus your attention on the clumps of earth that poke up above it and the thicket of trees on the right, rather than on the powdery, white covering on the ground.

Also, note that the snow is not a uniformly pure, unsullied white. The ground undulates, forming little peaks and shaded troughs. Tones of grey are required to make this distinction – smooth, pale tones without any sharp edges. To give the drawing impact, you also need to contrast the heavy, solid forms of the trees and background ridge with the much softer and less substantial shapes of the clouds and shadows. Use all the blending techniques at your disposal: smudge lines with your fingers or the side of your hand, or blend marks with a torchon, a sponge or tissue paper, as this allows you to build up areas of tone without creating a hard line.

If you get accidental smudges, do not worry. This is an unavoidable part of charcoal drawing and you can always wipe off powder with an eraser. A kneaded eraser gives a soft, smooth finish; for sharp edges, cut a plastic eraser or pull a kneaded eraser to a fine point. For an cheaper alternative, try small pieces of soft white bread.

The scene
Here is a typical winter scene across a ploughed field. The thicket of trees on the right provides a focal point while the clumps of earth poking up through the snow form diagonal lines across the field that lead the viewer's eye through the composition.

Materials
- *Smooth drawing paper*
- *Willow charcoal sticks – thin and medium*
- *Kneaded eraser*
- *Compressed charcoal stick*
- *Large torchon*
- *Plastic eraser, cut to give a sharp edge*
- *Small sponge*

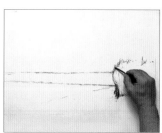

1 Using a thin charcoal stick, map out the proportions of the scene. Look for specific points from which you can measure other elements. Here, the artist used the clump of trees as a starting point. When he measured it, he discovered that the distance from the base of the clump to the base of the ridge in the distance is roughly the same as the distance from the base of the trees to the base of the image.

2 Using the side of the charcoal, roughly block in the wedge-shaped area of land in the middle distance and the thicket of trees on the right. Make jagged, spiky marks for the top of the thicket to convey the texture of the trees. Note also that some areas are darker in tone than others; although you will elaborate this later, it is a good idea to get some tonal variation into the drawing even at this early stage.

3 Using the tip of a medium charcoal stick, draw the darkest areas within the thicket of trees. Look for the negative shapes – the spaces between the branches rather than the branches themselves. Switch to a thin charcoal stick for the branches that stick out at the sides and top of the main mass. Using a kneaded eraser, lightly stroke off charcoal for the lighter-toned branches within the clump.

4 Start to introduce some form into the wedge-shaped area of land in the middle distance. The trees at the front of this area are very dark in tone, so build up the tone with heavy, vertical strokes. Use a thin charcoal stick to start dotting in the exposed clumps of earth peeping up above the snow in the field and make thin vertical strokes for the grasses on the right-hand side of the image.

5 Using a stick of compressed charcoal, put in some very dark blacks in the trees in the middle distance so that you gradually begin to build up texture and tone. Also use the compressed charcoal to draw more of the exposed clumps of earth that run across the field, making small, dotted marks of varying sizes and making the marks darker as you come toward the foreground.

6 Rub some charcoal on to a scrap piece of paper and press the end of a large torchon into the resulting powder. Gently stroke the torchon over the snow that leads down to the clump of trees to create soft shadows.

Assessment time
The main elements of the composition are in place, but the contrast between the sky (to which no charcoal has been applied so far) and the dark, dense tones of the trees is too extreme. This balance needs to be corrected. Even so, the thicket of trees on the right still needs to be darkened in places. Your task now that the essentials of the composition are all in place is to develop texture and tone across the image. In order to do this, you will need to continually assess the tonal balance of the drawing as a whole, to ensure that no one part becomes too dominant.

7 Using a plastic eraser, wipe off some of the charcoal to create the effect of snow on the edges of the fields in the middle distance. By carefully cutting the eraser down with a razor you can make it produce a crisp, sharp-edged line.

As yet there is no detail in the sky, which forms roughly half the image.

With the exception of a few foreground shadows, there is no texture or detail in the snow areas.

▶

8 Wipe the side of a medium stick of charcoal over the sky area. Note how the coverage is uneven, creating lovely dappled marks.

9 Using a circular motion, vigorously rub a small sponge over the sky to smooth out the charcoal marks.

10 There is a band of blue in the sky above the land and below the mass of clouds. Block this in using the side of a medium charcoal stick and blend it to a mid-grey with a torchon, making it darker in tone than the rest of the sky. Using a kneaded eraser and a vigorous circular motion, lift off shapes for the looming storm clouds. Do not worry about the tones within the clouds at this stage; just try to get the approximate shapes. Note how putting some detail in the sky has changed the mood of the drawing from a tranquil winter scene to something much more dramatic, in which the threat of a storm is imminent.

11 Put in some very dark storm clouds and blend the charcoal with your fingertips or a sponge. Immediately, the scene looks much more dramatic; note how the dark areas of sky balance the thicket of trees on the right of the image. Scribble some charcoal on a piece of scrap paper to get some loose powder, as in Step 6. Dip a torchon in the powder and gently stroke it over the sky to create softly blended areas of mid tone between the clouds. This allows the white areas of the clouds to stand out more clearly.

12 The sky is now quite dark, so you may need to darken the land mass to make it more dominant. Compressed charcoal gives a very rich, intense black. Note how the snow also seems to sparkle and stand out more once the land mass has been darkened.

13 Using a thin charcoal stick, put in any remaining exposed clumps of earth on the field. Re-assess the whites in relation to the rest of the image. You may need to use a kneaded eraser to lift off some charcoal in the grasses on the right.

The finished drawing

This drawing demonstrates the versatility of charcoal. It can be blended to give a smooth, even coverage, as in the mid-toned areas of the sky, or used to create bold, highly textured marks, as in the clump of trees. The success of the image is due largely to the contrast between the very light and the very dark areas. In scenes like this, the key is often to darken the dark areas rather than to lighten the lights.

Charcoal is softly blended with a sponge to create the clouds.

The exposed clumps of earth are paler in the distance, creating a sense of recession.

'Drawing' some of the branches with an eraser creates fine, crisp-edged lines.

French vineyard in watercolour

This deceptively simple-looking scene is a useful exercise in both linear and aerial perspective. Take care over your underdrawing, as it underpins all the rest of the painting: if the rows of vines appear to be going the wrong way it will look very strange. It is worth taking plenty of time over this stage.

You also need to mix tones carefully. Note how the dark green vine leaves in the foreground give way to a much paler, yellower green in the distance – and then see how these pale greens gradually darken again above the horizon, shifting from a mid green to a

very bluish green on the distant hills. Remember to test out each tone on a scrap piece of paper before you apply it.

Materials
- *2B pencil*
- *140lb (300gsm) rough watercolour paper, pre-stretched*
- *Watercolour paints: cerulean blue, Naples yellow, gamboge, light red, sap green, ultramarine violet, cobalt blue, viridian, Payne's grey, burnt umber*
- *Brushes: large mop, medium mop, fine round*

The scene

Sometimes one reference image simply does not give you enough information to create the painting you want. Do not be afraid to combine elements from several photos or sketches to create the desired effect. Here, the artist referred to the long panoramic-format photograph for the close-up detail of the vine leaves and the farm buildings, but based his composition on the larger photograph, in which the rows of vines are angled in a more interesting way.

1 Sketch the outline of the hills and vines, then dampen the sky with clean water, leaving some gaps. Mix a wash of cerulean blue and drop it on to the damp areas. Leave to dry.

2 Mix a pale wash of Naples yellow and touch it into the dry cloud shapes and along the horizon line. Leave to dry.

3 Darken the top of the sky with cerulean blue and leave to dry. Mix gamboge with light red and brush over the vines. Paint light red on the foreground and in between the vines.

4 Using a medium mop brush, loosely paint strokes of sap green into the foreground, heading along the perspective lines toward the vanishing point on the horizon, to indicate the rows of vines. Leave to dry.

5 Mix a deep blue from ultramarine violet, cobalt blue and viridian and wash it over the hills. Put a few dots along the top edge to break up the harsh outline and imply trees.

6 Mix a mid-toned green from viridian with a little cobalt blue. Using a medium mop brush, brush this mixture over the lower part of the hills. Mix a dark blue from cobalt blue, ultramarine violet and viridian. Using a large mop brush, darken the shadows on the distant hills. Use the same colour to stipple a few dots on the green hills to imply trees on the horizon.

Tip: It is often easier to assess colours if you turn your reference photo upside down. This allows you to concentrate on the tones without being distracted by the actual subject matter.

Assessment time
Once you are happy with the general lines and colours of the scene, you can start thinking about adding those all-important touches of detail and texture. Do not be tempted to do this too early: once you have painted the detail, it will be much harder to go back and make any tonal corrections to the background or the spaces between the rows of vines.

The perspective of the foreground has been established, leaving you free to add detail and texture.

The background is virtually complete, with darker shadows on the hills providing a sense of light and shade.

▶

7 Mix a dark green from sap green, Payne's grey and a little burnt umber. Using a large mop brush, wet the foreground with clean water, leaving gaps for the vines. Using a medium mop brush, brush the dark green mixture on to the damp areas and let it flow on the paper to define the general green masses of the vines and their leaves. Paint the dark shapes of the foreground vine leaves.

8 Continue painting the vine leaves, as in Step 7. Do not try to be too precise or the painting may easily start to look overworked: generalized shapes will suffice. Mix a warm but neutral grey from ultramarine violet and burnt umber and, using a fine round brush, paint in the stems of the vines and the posts that support them, taking care to make the posts smaller as they recede into the distance.

9 Mix a dark shadow colour from ultramarine violet and a little burnt umber and brush this mixture across the ground in between the rows of vines. Again, take care over the perspective and make the shadows narrower as the vines recede into the distance.

10 Mix a warm, reddish brown from light red and a touch of Naples yellow and use this to paint the buildings in the background. This warm colour causes the buildings to advance, even though they occupy only a small part of the picture area. Using a fine brush and the same dark green mixture that you used in Step 7, touch in some of the detail on the vines.

11 Using an almost dry brush held on its side, brush strokes of light red in between the rows of vines. This strengthens the foreground colour but still allows the texture of the paper to show through, implying the pebbly, dusty texture of the earth in which the vines are planted.

12 Using a fine brush, brush a little light red on the top of the roofs. This helps the roofs to stand out and also provides a visual link with the colour of the earth in the foreground. Add a little burnt umber to the light red mixture to darken it, and paint the window recesses and the shaded side of the buildings to make them look three-dimensional.

The finished painting

Fresh and airy, this painting is full of rich greens and warm earth colours, providing a welcome dose of Mediterranean sunshine. Note how most of the detail and texture are in the foreground, while the background consists largely of loose washes with a few little dots and stipples to imply the tree-covered mountains beyond. This contrast is a useful device in landscape painting when you want to establish a sense of scale and distance.

Cool colours in the background recede.

Simple dots and stipples are enough to give the impression of distant trees.

Note how the rows of vines slant inward and converge toward the vanishing point.

Warm colours in the foreground advance.

Sun-bleached scene in acrylics

It could be said that contrast is the key to depicting bright sunlight in a work of art. In this scene of the landscape around a ruined temple in Sicily, the sunlight has the effect of bleaching out colour from all the pale-coloured stones and worn pathways – but unless you make the shadows really dark, the whole painting will look too pale and insipid. So it is the contrast that counts.

The key is to work gradually, building up the density of colour in stages. Even though this demonstration is in acrylics it's a good idea to leave the brightest highlights unpainted to begin with, just as you would in watercolour. Once you have put in the mid tones, it is much easier to judge how far you need to darken or lighten everything else. Keep assessing the darks and lights in relation to each other as you go: you may be surprised at how dark the deepest shadows turn out to be.

Another thing to remember when you are painting a deep panorama such as this one is the effect of aerial perspective. Colours look paler with distance, so this is one way of creating a sense of recession. Note, too, how the sky pales toward the horizon.

Texture is also less evident in things that are farther away, so concentrate on the textural detail in the foreground. There are a lot of trees and scrubby bushes in this scene that give you the chance to exploit dry brush and other textural techniques. However, beware of putting in too much detail. An impression of the shapes and textures will be sufficient, as it is really the intensity of the light and its effect on the landscape that are the subjects of this atmospheric painting.

Materials
- *Heavy watercolour paper*
- *HB pencil*
- *Acrylic paints: brilliant blue, alizarin crimson, cadmium yellow, yellow ochre, ultramarine blue, titanium white*
- *Brushes: Selection of rounds and filberts in different sizes*
- *Absorbent paper towel*

The scene
There is so much of interest in this scene that the artistic possibilities are huge. You might choose to walk along the path and paint the temple itself; you might decide that the twisted olive trees and dramatic shadows are to be the subject of your painting; or you might, as the artist has done here, elect for a broad panorama that concentrates on the play of light and shade. The dramatic shadows cast by the trees are counterbalanced by the patches of brilliant sunlight, lending a semi-abstract quality to the rocky forms. Whatever you choose, remember that a strong composition is essential; the viewer's eye has to be directed thorough the image in some way, particuarly when there is so much visual information to take in. Here, our attention is directed via the path to the ruined temple which, although it occupies only a small part of the picture space, is a strong focal point.

1 Using an HB pencil lightly sketch in the horizon, the square shape of the temple, and the main lines of the walls leading up to it. Wash a dilute mix of brilliant blue over the sky and then, using a paper towel, dab off some of the colour near the horizon to suggest a heat haze. Turn the work upside down to make it easier.

2 Mix a dilute, pale wash of alizarin crimson with a little cadmium yellow. Using a large round brush, wash it over the land in the background and over the parched earth on the left. Mix an earthy brown from yellow ochre with a touch of both ultramarine blue and alizarin and wash it over the land on the right for a warm undertone.

3 Mix a blue-green from ultramarine and yellow ochre and block in the dark foliage in the foreground, varying the proportions of the colours as necessary. Roughly put in the large foreground in a purple mix of alizarin and ultramarine. Touch in the blue of the distant hill in a mix of ultramarine and white.

4 Mix an olivey yellow from ultramarine, cadmium yellow and white and touch in the trees on the right – just the basic shapes. Mix a pinky white from alizarin crimson and white and block in the shapes of the temple. Add yellow ochre to the mix and scumble it on for the scrubland.

5 Continue putting in blocks of colour across the landscape, using the same pink- and ochre-based mixes as before. Remember that colours appear paler with distance, so add more white to your mixes for the background areas. Leave the brightest patches of earth in the foreground untouched for now.

6 Mix white, alizarin and cadmium yellow and put in the sun-bleached stones and earth in the foreground. Make this mix slightly thicker, for texture. Block in more shadows with a deep purple mixed from alizarin and ultramarine. With a fine brush, refine the temple in purples and pinks.

▶

Assessment time
The artist has built up a good feeling of recession in the landscape, with darker tones in the foreground and lighter, paler ones in the middle distance and background. This could be improved by increasing the amount of textural detail in the foreground. However, the image is still lacking in form: the land in the middle distance, in particular, looks rather flat and it is hard to make sense of the different planes. To enhance the bright, sunny feel, the shadows need to be intensified for more contrast between them and the bright patches of ground.

This area is lacking in form.

There is insufficient contrast between the lights and the darks.

Although the foliage masses have been put in, these blocks of colour do not yet 'read' as trees.

7 Using a very fine brush, put in the trunks of the trees in a very dark purple. Define the shapes and tones of the foreground blocks of colour more clearly, so that the image becomes more three-dimensional. Look, in particular, at the purple-pink shadows the trees cast on the ground. Observe the shaded sides of the ruined walls in the foreground, which have a very dark tone compared to the sunlit patches.

8 Create more modelling on the left-hand side of the image, in the tussocky scrubland. By using different tones of purple-pink here, you can create a sense of light and shade and the undulations in the land. Dot in some darker trees and shrubs, too, remembering to keep the tone lighter than that used for the blue-green foreground foliage so that you create an impression of distance.

The finished painting

The heat and intensity of the bright summer sunlight is captured here. The piece is loosely painted, relying on blocks of colour and the interplay of light and shade. Very little detail is evident, but by carefully setting down the different tones the artist has created a convincing impression of depth and three-dimensional forms. The effects of aerial perspective have been well observed and the bold brushstrokes and dabs of colour give the painting energy.

Note how the land is paler and bluer in the distance than it is in the foreground.

The strong contrast between light and shade enhances the feeling of bright sunlight.

The different tones in the foliage masses make them appear three-dimensional.

Impasto landscape in oils

Impasto means thicker-than-usual paint. For some artists, one of the main attractions of oils and acrylics is that they can be built up thickly to create a range of exciting surface textures.

Impasto techniques are far from new. Both Rembrandt and the great 19th-century landscape painter J.M.W. Turner used thick, solid paint in some areas of their paintings, contrasting this with thinner applications elsewhere. Van Gogh was the first artist to use uniformly thick paint, applied in swirling or jagged brushstrokes; since then many artists have exploited the expressive and dynamic qualities of thick paint, sometimes squeezing it on to the canvas straight from the tube and then modelling it with a brush, or applying it with a painting knife or even using their fingers to create the right effects.

Impasto work of this nature requires a great deal of paint, so it is a good idea to bulk it out with one of the special media sold for impasto work in both oils and acrylics. This is particularly necessary if you are working in acrylics, as the paint is slightly runnier than oil paint. Adding an impasto medium enables you to produce two or three times the amount of paint, without changing the colour of the paint in any way.

With its scrubby vegetation and pebbly path, this Mediterranean cliffside scene provides many opportunities for working impasto. In a landscape such as this, however, it is generally helpful to include some quieter, flatter areas, such as the sea and sky, for the viewer's eye to rest on. This exercise is painted entirely with a painting knife.

Materials
- *Canvas-covered board primed with acrylic gesso*
- *HB pencil*
- *Oil paints: phthalocyanine blue, titanium white, ultramarine blue, alizarin crimson, cadmium lemon, sap green, burnt sienna, raw sienna*
- *Rag*
- *Small painting knife*

The scene
This is a classically composed scene, with the main cliff falling at the intersection of the thirds and the path leading our eye through the picture. The contrasting textures – the relative smoothness of the sea and sky versus the pebbly path and dense vegetation – make a picture that is full of interest.

1 Using an HB pencil, lightly sketch the scene so that you have a rough guide to where to place the different elements.

2 Mix a pale blue from phthalocyanine blue and titanium white. Using a rag, smear it across the sky. Add more phthalocyanine blue and, using a small painting knife, put in the sea in the distance, smoothing the paint out so that the coverage and density of colour are fairly even.

3 There are some deep shadows on the sea; paint these in using ultramarine blue. Still using the painting knife, apply strokes of thick titanium white for the clouds. The rough impasto work helps to give a sense of volume to the clouds.

4 Mix a dark purplish blue from alizarin crimson and ultramarine blue and smear it over the rocky, exposed area of cliff on the right, adding some sap green to the mixture as you work down toward the path. To capture the jagged feel of the rocks, pull the paint up with the tip of the knife to form small peaks. Mix a bright green from cadmium lemon, sap green and a little burnt sienna and begin putting in the lightest parts of the foreground vegetation on the left, dabbing in a more yellow version of the mixture in parts.

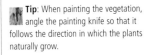 **Tip**: When painting the vegetation, angle the painting knife so that it follows the direction in which the plants naturally grow.

5 Mix a pale brown from raw sienna and white and paint the rough-textured ground to the right of the path.

▶

6 Add more raw sienna to the mixture and include some darker browns in the vegetation.

7 Mix a pale purple from ultramarine blue, titanium white and a little alizarin crimson and use this to put in the shaded sides of the foreground rocks to the right of the path. Paint bright highlights where the sun hits the tops of the rocks in titanium white.

Assessment time

The impasto work has created bold, dynamic textures in the dark cliff and path, but the foreground of the image looks rather flat and featureless in comparison. Increasing the texture in the foreground plants and rocks will also help to create more of a sense of scale and distance in the painting.

The vegetation is little more than splashes of colour, with virtually no texture or detailing.

The path is distractingly bright.

8 Mix a very dark green from ultramarine blue and sap green and put in the very darkest areas of the plants that are growing on the cliff side, dabbing the paint on with the tip of the painting knife. Add some alizarin crimson to the mixture and put in some slightly curved strokes, using the side of the knife, for the taller stems and branches.

9 Continue to build up textures, using the same colours as before. Vary the way that you apply the paint, sometimes using the side of the knife and sometimes the tip. Paint the tall, thin grass on the right-hand side of the painting using a mixture of raw sienna and white, and dab on brownish stones on the path in mixes of cadmium yellow and raw sienna.

The finished painting

Impasto work adds great vitality to this image: you can almost reach out and feel the texture of the rocks and plants. The artist has also made full use of the range of marks that can be made with a knife, from smoothing out the sky and sea areas with the flat of the knife to dabbing on small blobs of paint with the tip, and even dragging the side of the knife over the canvas to create long, flowing marks for the thinnest stems and branches.

Note how the knife marks echo the direction in which the plants grow.

A flatter application of paint over the sea makes a calm area. The lack of texture here also helps to create a sense of distance.

Thick oil and acrylic paint can be pulled up with the tip of the knife to form small peaks, as here.

Woodland path in gouache

This project is about interpreting what you see and conveying the mood of the scene, rather than making a photo-realistic rendition. That does not mean that observation is not important. When you are painting a scene like this, look at the overall growth patterns. Are the tree trunks tall and straight or do they lean at an angle? Do the branches droop and spread on either side of the trunk, like weeping willows, or is the foliage weighted toward one side, like maples and Scots pines? Is the shape of the tree conical or rounded?

Look at where the shadows fall, too – and remember that the shape made by the shadows should match the shape of

the objects that cast the shadows. Above all, make sure that the shadows are dense enough, as the contrast between the dark and the brightly lit areas is what gives the work a three-dimensional quality.

This scene gives you the opportunity to explore many different textures – the tangled undergrowth and criss-crossing branches, the rough texture of the path and the peeling bark on the trees. Again, do not try to place every detail precisely. Spatters of paint convey the rough texture of the ground, while the colour of the tree trunks and the patterning of the bark call for more carefully placed brushstrokes.

Here the artist also added a few small pieces of collage in the final stages. This is optional, and you may think that the image does not need it; however, provided you do not overdo things it is well worth experimenting with simple techniques like this, as they can bring an added dimension to your work.

Materials
• *Watercolour paper primed with acrylic gesso*
• *4B pencil*
• *Masking fluid*
• *Medium-nibbed steel dip pen*
• *Gouache paints: phthalocyanine green, brilliant yellow, raw umber, raw sienna, zinc white, scarlet lake, jet black, phthalocyanine blue*
• *Brushes: large wash, small round, old toothbrush*
• *Newspaper*
• *Gum arabic*

The scene
Although there is no real focus point of interest in this scene, the textures and the contrasting shapes (the sweeping curve of the path against the strong vertical lines of the tree trunks) make it very rewarding to paint. The shadows and bright sunlight over the foreground also add interest.

1 Using a 4B pencil, sketch the scene, putting in as much detail as you feel you need. Your underdrawing will help you to keep track of where things are once you start applying the paint.

> **Tip**: You do not need to get all the branches in exactly the right place in your underdrawing, but you should try to be faithful to the general patterns of growth and the rhythms of the scene. Although this is a fairly loose, impressionistic painting, it must look convincing – but it is also important to try to capture a sense of spring-like growth and energy in the scene.

2 Using a medium-nibbed steel dip pen and masking fluid mask the lightest trunks and branches. Also mask any branches that are lighter than their immediate surroundings, even if they are brown in colour rather than a light, silvery grey. Using an old toothbrush, spatter some masking fluid over the undergrowth. Leave to dry: this will not take long, but it is essential that the masking fluid is completely dry before you apply the first washes of colour.

3 Before you begin the painting stages, take some time to make absolutely sure that you have masked all of the light-coloured areas of branches and foliage that need to be protected. Even though gouache is opaque and it is perfectly possible to paint light colours over dark ones, such corrective measures should only be used as a last resort – otherwise you run the risk of losing some of the freshness and spontaneity of the painting.

4 Mix a dilute, bright green from phthalocyanine green and brilliant yellow. Using a large wash brush, put in broad horizontal strokes for the band of undergrowth that runs across the centre of the scene. Mix a duller green from phthalocyanine green and raw umber and repeat the process in the foreground. For the tree trunks in the background, put in vertical strokes of raw sienna and raw umber, occasionally adding some green to them.

5 Mix a dilute yellowish brown from zinc white and raw umber and brush the mixture lightly over the earth in the foreground, allowing some of the support to show through to create some texture in this area. The earth on the far right, behind the band of undergrowth, is warmer in tone, so paint this in raw sienna. While the paint is still wet, touch a little scarlet lake into it so that it spreads of its own accord.

▶

6 Mix a very dark greenish black from jet black, phthalocyanine blue and phthalocyanine green and paint the little stream in the background. Add raw umber to the mixture and paint the cast shadows on the ground.

7 Add more phthalocyanine green to the mixture and paint the shapes of the trunks in the background. Using the bright green mixture from Step 4, spatter colour over the foreground for the low-growing plants alongside the path.

8 Roughly cut masks from newspaper the same shape as the largest cast shadows on the ground and lay them in position. (There is no need to stick them down.) Mix brilliant yellow with white, load an old toothbrush with this mix, then spatter it over the foreground, pulling the bristles back with your fingertips.

9 Repeat the spattering process with a mixture of white and raw umber to create the rough, pebbly texture of the path in the foreground. When the paint is dry, remove the newspaper masks: the scene is now beginning to take on more depth and texture.

10 There are some warm, pinkish tones on the path, so mix scarlet lake and white and lightly spatter a little of the mixture over the foreground. Leave to dry completely, then rub off all the masking fluid.

Tip: When you have removed a little of the masking fluid, squash it into a ball and rub it over the surface of the painting like an eraser. Any remaining fluid will stick to it.

Assessment time
Now that you have removed the masking fluid, it is easier to see what must be done to complete the painting. Although the general shapes are all there, at this stage you can see that the painting lacks depth: you need to increase the density of the shadows to resolve this.

The exposed areas are too stark and bright and contain no detail.

Overall, the colours are too light; the image does not have the feel of dense, dark woodland.

11 Mix a pale brown from raw sienna and white. Using a small round brush, paint the shaded sides of the exposed tree trunks. Add raw umber to the mixture and paint the shadows cast on the tree trunks by other branches.

12 Mix brilliant yellow with a little phthalocyanine green and, using a small round brush, dot in the yellow flowers in the undergrowth, making the distant dots slightly smaller than those in the foreground.

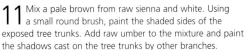

13 Using various versions of the dull green mixture from Step 4, paint the exposed grasses on the bottom right of the painting, keeping your brushstrokes loose and flowing.

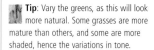

Tip: Vary the greens, as this will look more natural. Some grasses are more mature than others, and some are more shaded, hence the variations in tone.

14 The yellow flowers in the centre look a little too vibrant, so tone them down by dotting some of the dull green mixture from the previous step into this area. Put in some solid areas of green, too, obliterating the exposed whites and re-establishing any shadow areas that have been lost on the grasses. Using mid-toned browns, reinforce the lines of trunks in the background.

15 You might consider the painting finished at this point, but here the artist decided to enhance the three-dimensional quality of the upper part of the image by incorporating a little collage. If you do this, take care not to overdo it, or the result could end up looking messy and overworked.

16 Paint strokes of branch-coloured paint on a piece of scrap paper and leave to dry. Cut out curving, branch-shaped pieces and brush a little gum arabic on to the reverse side. Position the pieces on the painting and brush gum arabic over the top to fix them in place. Leave to dry. (The advantage of using gum arabic is that, unlike ordinary glue, it can be painted over if necessary.) The collage element adds depth and texture to the image.

The finished painting

This is a lively and atmospheric painting of a woodland path in dappled sunlight. The strong vertical lines of the tree trunks and the diagonal lines of their shadows give the picture a feeling of energy that is echoed by the textural details and bold applications of colour. The palette of colours chosen by the artist is muted but natural looking. Although the scene looks deceptively simple, there is much to hold the viewer's attention.

Spatters and dots of colour convey the texture of the path and the tiny flowers.

The use of collage on some of the branches is subtle but effective.

Carefully placed brushstrokes are used for the grasses and tree bark.

Miniature landscape in coloured pencils

On a cold autumn or winter's day, you could be forgiven if the idea of taking your sketch pad and drawing tools and working outdoors for several hours did not seem very appealing. So why not bring the landscape (or at least a small part of it) indoors? This project combines a reference photo of a tiny area of woodland floor with a real leaf to create a delicate but beautifully observed nature study.

This is a miniature in several senses of the word: the finished drawing measures only 10.5 x 7.5cm (4¼ x 3in.), and the subject itself is tiny.

Despite its size you do not need to depict every twig and particle, or worry if pieces appear in different places to where they are in reality.

With this kind of detailed coloured-pencil work, you need to put down a number of very light layers of pigment. If you apply too heavy a layer, the wax in the pigment clogs up the tooth of the paper, and subsequent layers will not go on as smoothly or as evenly. The key to success is to work slowly, building up the tones and textures gently. Try to maintain an even pressure, using the side of the pencil so that the coverage is smooth and there are no obvious pencil marks. Even an experienced artist could easily take a whole day to produce a work as detailed as this, so do not be tempted to rush things.

Materials

- *Smooth illustration board*
- *HB pencil*
- *Coloured pencils: Pale grey, light yellow, black, mid grey, reddish brown, light yellow ochre, raw umber*

The scene

On a walk through her local woods, the artist spotted this patch of ground covered in twigs and leaf litter, with delicate fronds of bracken in the top right corner adding an inviting splash of colour. She thought it would make an interestingly textured background for a small nature study and took a photo to use as reference in her studio, planning to incorporate a natural object such as a leaf, pine cone or feather to complete the composition. This is an interesting approach to composing an image, as it allows you to play around with the scale of your subject for artistic effect.

1 Make a frame from two L-shaped pieces of card and move them around over your reference photo until you see a composition you are happy with.

2 Place your chosen leaf, or other natural object, in position on the photo. Note how the artist has placed the leaf on the diagonal, to create a more interesting composition.

3 Draw the frame size you have created on smooth illustration board, then sketch in the shape of the leaf in HB pencil. Block in the base colours for the ground and the green leaves, using a pale, cool grey for the lightest colour on the ground (the twigs) and a light yellow for the leaves. The colour should be barely perceptible at stage, as you will be building up the layers of colour very gradually.

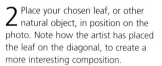

Tip: Do not apply the colours too strongly at this stage. If you do, dab at the surface with a kneaded eraser twisted to a point.

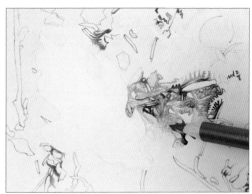

4 Now preserve the light, bright areas of the picture by drawing in the various pieces of woodland debris – the positive shapes of small twigs, pieces of leaves and small pebbles – in a cool grey. Begin drawing in the negative shapes, too – the dark areas of earth in between – in black. This helps the eye to flow from one shape to another.

5 Start building up the layers of colour. Use a combination of linear strokes (for the debris, such as twigs) and squiggles for the mottled texture of the earth, alternating between mid and dark greys and a reddish brown.

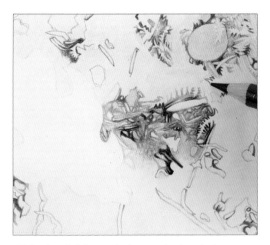

6 Continue building up the layers and colours in the background, alternating between greys and browns as before. Use a dark grey pencil to reinforce the edges of the tiny leaves. Effectively, you are repeating Step 3 – but this time, you will be using colour and refining the edges of the shapes.

7 Apply light yellow ochre to the leaf, leaving the highlight edges of the main vein uncoloured, as this is the very lightest part. Apply raw umber over the darker parts of the leaf, blending the colours very gently so that you do not get any harsh edges and allowing the underlying yellow ochre to show through to give a warm, golden glow. Draw in the dark edges of the other veins in raw umber.

Tip: It is important to keep your pencils very sharp for detailed work such as this. Keep a pot beside you for the shavings and sharpen often, using a razor or a pencil sharpener. Rotate the pencil as you work to keep the point for as long as possible.

Tip: With such a jumbled background, it is very easy to lose track of where you are in a drawing. Keep one finger of your non-drawing hand on your reference photo as you work, so that you can easily refer back to the right area.

▶

8 Add shadows to the leaf in raw umber and darker reddish brown, so that it takes on a three-dimensional feel. Leave the highlight light.

9 Continue applying colour to the background. When you have put in the underlying moss, make tiny flicks of grey over the edge to create texture.

10 Redefine the leaf edge and darken the shadows within the leaf in the reddish brown.

Assessment time

The leaf (the main subject) has been left relatively light, with no more than a couple of layers of soft colour. When you have applied an initial layer of colour to the whole image, you will be able to assess how the leaf relates to the background. This allows you to build up the tones gradually, continually assessing each part of the drawing in relation to the rest and slowly refining the shapes which, at this stage, are not yet sufficiently well defined.

The initial colour needs to be strengthened.

The edges of the leaf are not yet clearly defined.

The leaf looks flat and one-dimensional and does not stand out from the background.

11 Some of the very brightest areas of the leaf may now look too pale in relation to the rest, so darken them if necessary, using the same colours as before. Using very sharp grey and reddish brown pencils, go over the edges of the leaf veins to really define them. Continue putting in the background, continually assessing the leaf in relation to it.

12 Using a black pencil, put in a small shadow under the leaf to help lift it away from the background and appear more three-dimensional.

The finished drawing

Although this is an impression of the scene rather than a very literal interpretation that includes every single twig and pebble, the amount of detail and the subtlety of tone that can be achieved using coloured pencils are very well demonstrated. Pencils are perfectly suited to this type of 'busy' subject. Within the leaf, the transitions from one shade to the next are virtually imperceptible. The background, drawn from a reference photo rather than from life, is muted in colour, allowing the leaf to stand out, while the tiny splashes of green moss add freshness and sparkle.

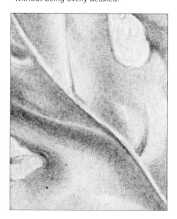

Crisp, linear detailing on the veins and subtle shading within the leaf make it look three-dimensional. It is realistically shaped without being overly detailed.

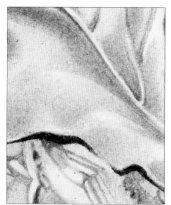

The shading under the leaf helps to 'lift' it from the background.

The bright yellows and greens of the moss add freshness to an image that is otherwise made up primarily of muted, earthy shades.

Landscape detail in gouache

Don't assume that landscapes have to be on a wide, panoramic scale. Little details that you come across – an old tree stump covered in fungi, a stretch of a mountain stream, or pebbles on a beach, as here – provide just as much scope for interesting compositions.

Here, a random arrangement of pebbles in a small fishing harbour, which the artist came across quite by chance, has been transformed into a colourful painting that is full of texture and interest.

Of course, subjects like this require careful planning on the part of the artist. You have to decide how much of the scene to include, and where to place the edges of the painting. You may even have to move things around a little to get the effect you want, just as you might when painting a still life indoors, although beware of doing too much as this can ruin the spontaneity.

In this project, the pebbles are painted more or less life-size. Painting a smaller subject than normal is a useful exercise, as you will have to look at things in a different way. Your normal tendency when painting a landscape might well be to scan the scene rapidly to gain an impression of the key elements; you will probably then decide how to make these elements stand out. When you concentrate on a small area everything counts; you need to look at how the parts relate to one another in terms of their size, shape and colour, and adjust your position until you have the best viewpoint. Moving a step to your left or right, backward or forward, can make a big difference.

Materials

- *Illustration board*
- *B pencil*
- *Gouache paints: cadmium yellow deep, cadmium orange, burnt umber, phthalocyanine blue, ultramarine blue, zinc white, ivory black, mid green, flame red, lemon yellow, cerulean blue*
- *Brushes: large wash, small round, fine round; old toothbrush*
- *Rag or absorbent paper towel*
- *Small painting knife*
- *Acrylic gold size*
- *Gold leaf*

The scene
Pebbles in a harbour, glistening with water left by the retreating tide, present an interesting challenge. When painting a subject like this, look for contrasts of size and colour.

1 Using a B pencil, mark a grid of squares on your paper. Many of the pebbles are similar in size and shape, so the grid will help you to keep track of which pebble you are painting. Again using the B pencil, make a light underdrawing.

2 Mix separate washes of cadmium yellow deep and cadmium orange. Wash cadmium yellow deep over the whole paper. While it is still wet, brush in cadmium orange, leaving some areas as pure yellow. Press a clean rag or absorbent paper towel over the top right of the paper, to lift off some of the orange. Leave to dry.

3 Load an old brush or toothbrush with burnt umber and any other colours that you can detect in the sand, and drag a painting knife through the bristles to spatter paint over the paper, creating a background of large-grained sand. (If you do not have a painting knife, an ordinary kitchen knife will work just as well.) Leave to dry.

4 Mix various blues and greys from phthalocyanine blue, ultramarine blue, zinc white and ivory black. Using a small round brush, begin putting in the pebbles. Note that you are simply placing the pebbles at this stage; although they look like flat circles and ovals, you will begin to build up the form later.

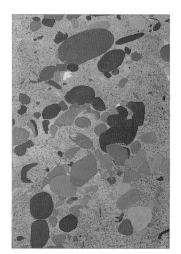

5 Continue putting in the pebbles, varying the colours. Some have a purple undertone; others have a greenish tinge, created from a base colour of mid green plus zinc white or ivory black, as appropriate. Leave to dry.

6 Load the toothbrush with cadmium yellow deep. Drag a painting knife through the bristles, as in Step 3, to spatter both the pebbles and the sand with yellow paint. Repeat the process using flame red and lemon yellow.

Tip: To get the size of the spatters right, try practising on a piece of card, holding the toothbrush at different distances from the painting.

▶

7 While the yellow spattering is still wet, drag a rag or a piece of absorbent kitchen towel over the spatters on some of the larger and darker pebbles to create streaked marks. On other pebbles, simply dab off any excess paint with a damp cloth to reveal the underlying colours, so that the spatters look like mica or other mineral crystals lodged within the stone, rather than lichen growing on top.

Assessment time

The initial blocking in of colours is complete, and the sand (which contains spatters of several different colours) looks convincingly textured, but at this stage the majority of the pebbles simply look like circles or ovals of dark colour positioned within the sand, rather than three-dimensional objects. The lighting is fairly flat and uniform, so there are no clearly defined shadows to help you, but if you look closely at the original you will see differences in both tone and colour temperature, with the sides of the pebbles that are turned away from the light being cooler (bluer) in colour. As you complete the painting, you should concentrate on reinforcing these tonal contrasts and on giving the pebbles more texture.

Smudging wet paint over dry has created streaks of paint that provide a good basis on which to build up more texture.

The shape of the pebbles is clear, but so far they all look flat and one-dimensional.

The texture of the sand has been built up well by blending colours wet into wet and by spattering.

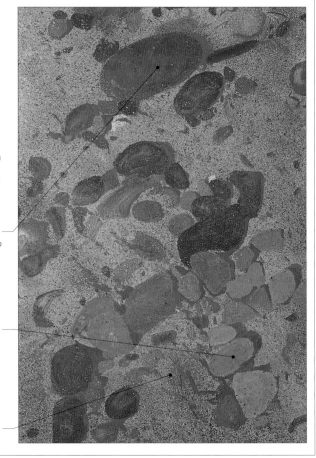

8 Mix a bright but chalky blue from cerulean blue and a little zinc white. Using a small round brush, brush this mixture over the brightest parts of any blue-grey pebbles. Mix a pale yellow from cadmium yellow deep, lemon yellow and zinc white, and a pale pink from flame red and white, and dab these mixtures over the large, pale pebble near the top of the painting, using short horizontal brushstrokes. Mix a dilute, neutral shadow colour from phthalocyanine blue and a little burnt umber. Paint the small shadows to the right of the largest pebbles; they immediately look much more three-dimensional.

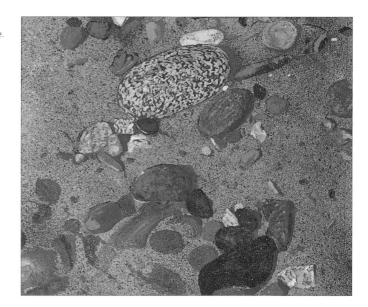

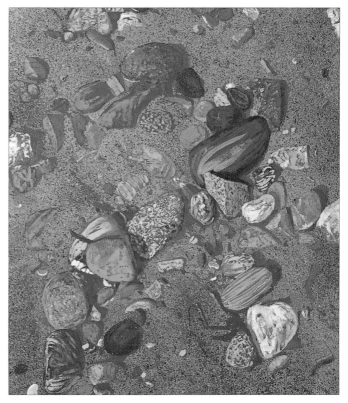

9 Continue to build up the texture and tonal contrasts within the pebbles, using all the colours on your palette – pale yellows and pinks, blue-greys, and almost pure white for the very lightest pebbles.

10 Vary your brushstrokes, stippling the paint in some places and using short strokes in others, but always allowing some of the underlying colours to show through.

11 Using a very fine brush, stipple all the colours on your palette on to the sand to create the appearance of large grains of sand or very tiny pebbles. Stand back from your work at regular intervals in order to see how the whole painting is progressing.

12 Many different colours have now been spattered and stippled on to the sand, creating a suitably granular-looking background for the pebbles. Take time to assess whether or not the texture of the sand is complete before you move on to the next stage.

13 If some of the stones look too dark in relation to the rest of the image, stipple or dab on some of your very pale yellow mixture. Use artistic licence where necessary in your choice of colours and keep looking at the balance of the painting as a whole.

 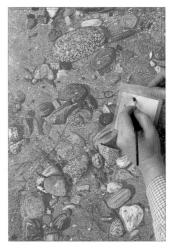

14 Now for the final touch – the twine that twists and turns its way through the pebbles, creating a dynamic diagonal line that draws our eye through the composition. Using a fine round brush, 'draw' the line of the twine in acrylic gold size. Leave the size until it is tacky to the touch, following the manufacturer's instructions.

15 Lift a small piece of gold leaf by the backing paper and position it on the sized surface. Brush over the backing paper with a soft brush. Press a piece of kitchen towel over the gold leaf to ensure that it adheres firmly. Brush off any excess gold leaf with a clean, dry brush.

The finished painting

This is a deceptively simple-looking still life, but the gradual build-up of tones and textures makes it very convincing. A number of textural techniques have been used, and the artist has exploited the chalky consistency of gouache paint to give the pebbles solidity. The use of gold leaf for the twine is an imaginative touch that adds yet another texture to the image.

The trick with a painting like this is not to overwork it. Try to build up the image as a whole, rather than trying to finish one small area before you move on to the next. Taking time out at regular intervals, so that you can stand back and assess whether or not you have built up the textures to the degree that you want, is also important.

Just a hint of a shadow under the right-hand edge of the largest pebbles is enough to make them look three-dimensional.

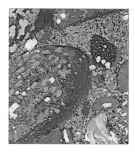

The different facets of the stones have been carefully observed.

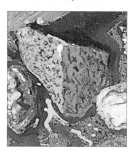

The twine, created by applying gold leaf, snakes its way through the image in a diagonal line.

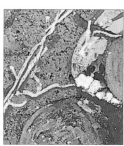

Large-scale landscape in charcoal

Drawing on a large scale is very liberating, both physically and mentally. Physically, it allows you to use the full stretch of your arm and hand to make bold, sweeping marks that are full of energy. Mentally, you have to simplify things and stop yourself getting bogged down in unnecessary detail. Try to return to the essence of the scene – the aspects that made you want to draw it in the first place.

Charcoal is the perfect medium for a project such as this, as it is so versatile and easy to apply. You can drag the side of the charcoal across the support to cover large areas quickly, blend it using a variety of techniques, or use the tip to make expressive, linear marks.

If you cannot find sheets of purpose-made drawing paper large enough, a roll of lining (liner) paper from a DIY store makes an inexpensive alternative. Pin it to a drawing board (or attach it with masking tape), and then place the drawing board on a studio easel or hang it on a wall.

The composition of large-scale drawings needs careful thought and planning. Before you embark on the actual drawing, it is a good idea to make a schematic sketch of the composition, working out where the centre of interest falls and making sure that the viewer's eye is led to that point.

Materials
- *Drawing paper 1 x 1.25m (3 x 4ft)*
- *Charcoal: thick and thin sticks*
- *Kneaded eraser*

The scene
The rocky escarpment is surmounted on the left by a wooded area that echoes the bands of trees at the base of the escarpment and in the fields below. A narrow track leads the eye into the scene along the line of trees and up to the rocks. There are a range of shapes and textures in the grasses, trees and rocks that make the scene interesting.

1 First, decide how much of the scene you want to include in your drawing and map out the positions of the main elements. To make this process easier, divide the scene into quarters (either mentally or by making light marks at the edges of the paper) and mark out where things fall in each square. Use light marks at this stage, just to establish where everything goes. Lightly block in the slope of the cliff to give yourself a visual guide to where to position the trees that stand at its base.

2 Work out where the darkest areas of tone are going to be and roughly block them in with a thick charcoal stick. The wooded mass on the top of the cliff is very dark, so you can apply a lot of pressure to the charcoal for this area. However, it is not a solid, straight-edged wedge shape: look closely and you will see that the tops of the trees are gently rounded. Observe shapes closely at this stage, to bring together a convincing and realistic composition. Outline the trees at the back of the fields with light dots and dashes, then block them in with the side of the charcoal stick.

3 Turn your attention back to the cliffs and look for differences in tone: the contrasts between dark, shaded gullies and crevices and the more brightly lit areas that are in full sunshine give the cliffs some sense of form. Block in the larger areas of tone using the side of the charcoal stick and moving your whole arm, not just your hand, keeping the coverage fairly uneven so that some of the paper texture shows through. Note that the brightest areas are barely touched by the charcoal. Continue blocking in the band of trees at the back of the fields, putting in nothing more than generalized shapes at this stage.

4 Outline the trees at the base of the cliff, then sketchily develop some tone within them. Note the number of different shapes – the tall, elongated cypress trees and the more rounded shapes elsewhere. Start to put in some jagged, linear marks on the cliff to create some texture.

> **Tip:** Continually check the size of the trees and the distances between them and other elements of the scene. It is very easy to make the trees too big and destroy the scale of the drawing.

5 Finish outlining the shapes of the band of trees that runs across the middle of the drawing. Now you can begin to develop the foreground a little. Put in the foreground grasses, using both the tip of the charcoal and the side.

> **Tip:** Work across the drawing as a whole, rather than concentrating on one area. This makes it easier to get the tonal balance of the drawing right.

6 Continue working on the trees in the middle of the drawing, concentrating on the overall shapes. Add more tone to the trees at the base of the cliff so that they begin to stand out more. Using the tip of the charcoal, put in more jagged, linear marks on the side of the cliff. These dark fissures help to create a sense of form and texture.

▶

Assessment time
Details in the image are taking shape, but it requires much more tonal contrast and texture. The trees are little more than generalized shapes at this stage and do not look truly three-dimensional; you need to develop more tone within them and also to put in the shadows that they cast. We are beginning to see the different facets of the cliff, but the darkest marks are not yet dark enough to give us any real sense of form.

Very little work has been done on the foreground. It is too bright in relation to the rest of the image.

The linear marks on the cliff need to be developed further to create a sense of form.

The foreground grasses are too indistinct. More texture is needed here.

7 Very gently stroke the side of a thin charcoal stick over the foreground to create some tone and texture. Note how using the charcoal in this way gives a slightly uneven coverage. Press slightly harder on the charcoal to put in the sides of the track that zigzags its way through the scene. Also indicate the shadows cast by the trees.

Tip: Smooth out the long cast shadows with your fingertips, in order to make them less textured than the trees themselves.

8 Very gently make a series of horizontal marks over the fields immediately below the cliff, pulling the full length of the charcoal stick over the paper to create the effect of ploughed furrows. Using the tip of the charcoal and pressing down firmly, put in the dark trunks of the trees in the centre of the image.

9 The trees are now taking real shape. Look at how the light catches them. Darken the shaded sides, using the side of the charcoal to create broad areas of tone. Immediately the trees begin to look more three-dimensional as you add the shadows they cast. Developing this tone takes them away from generalized shapes.

10 Using a kneaded eraser, gently lift off some of the charcoal from the side of the trees that catches the light. If you lift off too much, simply go over the area in charcoal again. Using the tip of a thin charcoal stick, introduce more texture into the foreground grasses by making crisp, dark, vertical marks.

The finished drawing

Working on a large scale has allowed the artist to use the full stretch of his arm to make bold, sweeping marks that give the drawing a very energetic, lively feel. He has concentrated on the essentials of the scene, rather than trying to put in every single detail, but his clever use of tonal contrasts gives the image a convincing sense of form. The foreground track leads our eye through the scene to the trees and cliff beyond – a classic compositional device.

Note how the contrasts between light and dark areas reveal the different facets of the cliff-face.

Detail diminishes with distance; the amount of detail that we can discern in the grasses tells us that they are in the foreground.

Lifting off charcoal from the most brightly lit sides of the trees shows us which direction the light is coming from.

Hillside town in mixed media

Line and wash is the perfect technique for this brightly coloured lakeside town, where you need fine detailing in the buildings and soft wet-into-wet washes in the surrounding landscape.

This project uses both waterproof and soluble inks, as they bring very different qualities to the image. Waterproof ink must be used in areas where you want the pen lines to remain permanent, such as the skyline and the wrought-iron balconies. Soluble ink, on the other hand, blurs and runs in unpredictable and exciting ways when you brush water or watercolour paint over it. Before you embark on any pen work, therefore, you need to think carefully about what kind of ink to use where.

In this scene, the tree-covered background is darker than the foreground. (Often in landscape paintings, you find that things in the background appear paler because of the effect of aerial perspective.) This helps to hold the image together, as it provides a natural frame around the focal point – the colourful buildings and their reflections.

Materials
- *HB pencil*
- *120lb (220gsm) good-quality drawing paper*
- *Art pen loaded with waterproof sepia ink*
- *Art pen loaded with water-soluble sepia ink*
- *Watercolour paints: ultramarine blue, cobalt blue, sap green, yellow ochre, phthalocyanine green, cadmium orange, cadmium red, burnt sienna, cadmium yellow, alizarin crimson, deep violet*
- *Brushes: medium round*

> **Tip**: If you are working from a reference photograph in which the light is very flat and bland, imagine how the light would fall on the scene on a bright sunny day. Where and how long would the shadows be? Make sure you keep your imaginary lighting consistent over the whole scene.

The original scene
This photograph was taken on a very overcast day, simply as a reference shot for the architectural details. As a consequence of the weather, the colours are dull and the light is flat and uninteresting. In situations like this, feel free to improve on what you saw at the time by making the colours brighter in your painting.

The composition pulls your eye to the edge of the picture, out into the centre of the lake.

The boat is a very stark white and detracts from the bright colours of the buildings.

The light is very flat: more contrast is needed to make the buildings look three-dimensional.

Preliminary sketch
Here the artist decided to crop in to make the composition tighter than it was in the original photograph. He also moved the boat further into the picture.

1 Using an HB pencil lightly sketch your subject, taking plenty of time to measure the relative heights and angles of the buildings carefully and making sure that you keep all the many vertical lines truly vertical. You can work much more loosely for the background hillside and trees, which will form a much softer, impressionistic backdrop to the scene.

2 Using waterproof sepia ink, put in the skyline. Using water-soluble sepia ink, put in the roofs and background trees, loosely hatching the trees to indicate the tones.

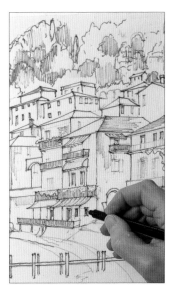

3 Continue with the line work, hatching the darkest areas of the trees in water-soluble ink, which you want to blend with paint in the later stages, and drawing the railings on the balconies in waterproof ink, so that the lines are permanent.

4 Using waterproof sepia ink, block in the windows on the shaded sides of the buildings.

▶

Assessment time

The pen work is now complete and will underpin the whole of the painting. If you have planned it properly, the lines drawn in waterproof sepia ink will be permanent, while those drawn in water-soluble ink will blur and run when washed over with watercolour paint. You cannot predict exactly how the lines will run, but this unpredictability is part of the fun and will impart great liveliness and spontaneity to the finished work.

Hatching in water-soluble ink indicates the areas of light and dark on the trees.

Waterproof ink is used for all the lines that need to be retained in the final painting.

Loose scribbles indicate the ripples in the water.

5 Mix a bright blue from ultramarine blue and cobalt blue watercolour paints. Using a medium round brush, wash this mixture over the sky, leaving some gaps for clouds. Mix a pale wash of sap green and brush it over the trees. Note how the soluble sepia ink blurs, giving the impression of the tree branches. Add a little yellow ochre to the mixture for the trees on the right-hand edge of the painting. Leave to dry.

6 Mix a dark green from ultramarine blue and phthalocyanine green and paint the tall cypress trees that stand along the skyline. The vertical lines of the trees break up the horizon and add interest to the scene. Use the same dark green mixture to loosely brush in some dark foliage tones on the trees, taking care not to allow any of the paint to spill over on to the buildings below.

7 Mix a terracotta colour from cadmium orange, cadmium red and burnt sienna. Using the tip of the brush, paint the roofs, adding more burnt sienna for the shaded sides of the roofs. Note how the whole picture begins to take on more form and depth as soon as you put in some shading.

8 Use a slightly paler version of the mixture used for the roofs to paint the shaded sides of some of the buildings. Work carefully so that you retain the sharp vertical lines of the buildings. This is an important aspect of making the buildings look three-dimensional.

9 Mix a very pale wash of yellow ochre and brush it on to the front of some of the houses. Paint the shaded sides of the terracotta-coloured houses in a mixture of yellow ochre and burnt sienna.

10 Finish painting the façades of the buildings. Mix a light green from sap green and cadmium yellow and dot in the foliage on the balconies. While this is still damp, dot on dark phthalocyanine green to build up some tone and depth.

▶

11 Paint the striped awnings in dilute washes of alizarin crimson and cobalt blue (but don't try to make the stripes on the awnings too precise and even, or the work will start to look stilted). Paint the window shutters in cobalt blue and phthalocyanine green.

12 Mix a pale but warm purple from ultramarine blue, deep violet and burnt sienna and paint the shadowed sides of the buildings and a narrow strip under the awnings. This reinforces the three-dimensional effect and separates the houses from each other and from the background.

13 Using the same colour, continue putting in the shadows on the houses and on the shoreline promenade and jetty. Paint the reflections in the water, using watered-down versions of the colours used on the buildings. Leave to dry.

14 Mix a deep blue from ultramarine blue, cobalt blue and a little deep violet. Carefully brush this over the water area, working around the boat and the posts of the jetty and leaving some gaps for broken ripples and highlights.

The finished painting

With the addition of a few final details (the jetty, painted in a mixture of burnt sienna and ultramarine blue; the upturned boats in very pale washes of alizarin crimson and ultramarine blue, and the boat on the lake in alizarin crimson), the painting is complete. Precise pen work in both water-soluble and waterproof ink has combined with loose brushstrokes and wet-into-wet washes to create a lively rendering of this charming lakeside town.

The blurred, wet-into-wet trees focus attention on the sharply defined buildings.

Loose strokes of colour are used to depict the awnings.

Precise pen lines set down in the very earliest stages remain in the finished work.

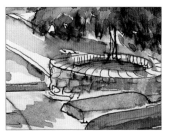

Church in snow in oils

Buildings are an integral part of many landscape paintings. Even when they are not the prime focus of attention, they add an element of human interest by implying the presence of man, and they also help to give a sense of scale.

In this project, the church in the background brings another dimension to a tranquil rural setting. Its solid form, positioned roughly on the third, contrasts well with the surroundings.

Begin by establishing the basic shape of the building and painting it as a flat area of tone. You can then develop this, creating contrasts of light and shade that reveal the different sides of the building, and finally putting in just enough detailing to tell us about the architectural style and period. The human brain is amazingly adept at interpreting a few general indications of shape and texture, and too much information can actually destroy the balance of the painting as a whole – particularly when the building is in the background, as here. The farther away something is, the less detail is required.

For this project, the artist began by toning the canvas with dilute olive green oil paint. The cool colour suits the wintry scene and gives a good, neutral mid tone from which to start painting.

Just like water, snow reflects colour. Where the sun strikes, the snow may be tinged with warm yellows or even pinks, depending on the time of day, while shadows will contain shades of blue and violet. Do not paint everything as a brilliant white: shadowy areas contrasting with small patches of bright, sunlit snow will have far more impact. The shadows in the snow also reveal the contours of the land beneath.

Materials

- *Stretched and primed canvas*
- *Oil paints: olive green, permanent mauve, titanium white, cobalt blue, raw sienna, viridian, burnt sienna, Indian yellow, cadmium red, lemon yellow*
- *Turpentine*
- *Brushes: selection of small and medium filberts*

The scene

Although the church is far away and relatively indistinct, it is still the main focus of the scene. Along with the trees, it provides a strong vertical element on which the viewer's eye can alight, while the curve of the water leads us around the scene.

1 Make an underdrawing of the church, main trees and water area, using a small brush and thin olive green paint. When you paint buildings it is particularly important to get the proportions and angles right, so measure carefully and take your time over this stage. Also indicate the shadows on the snow in the foreground and roughly scumble in the largest reflections in the water.

2 Block in the trees on the far bank, using a mid-toned purple mixed from permanent mauve, titanium white, cobalt blue and raw sienna, and a blue-green mixed from olive green, viridian and a tiny amount of burnt sienna. Using a small brush, begin putting in the cool shadows on the snow on the far bank, using a blue-grey mixed from cobalt blue, titanium white and permanent mauve.

3 Continue putting in the shadows on the snow on the far side of the water. Block in the reflections of the trees in the water, using olive green for the darkest trees and lighter olive green and purple mixes elsewhere, and leaving gaps for the brightest areas of water.

4 Mix a pinkish brown from burnt sienna, titanium white and cobalt blue and paint the walls of the church. Paint the snow-covered roof, which is in shadow, in a cool blue-grey. Overlay some pale blue on the purple trees in the background; this helps to link the trees with the snow.

Assessment time
Lively scumbles are a quick way of establishing basic shapes and tones in the early stages of a painting, and are particularly useful when you are painting outdoors. The underpainting is now virtually complete. For the rest of the painting, concentrate on texture and detailing, checking periodically to ensure that you maintain the tonal balance.

The church, which has been roughly blocked in, adds solidity to the scene.

Lively scumbles establish the basic shapes and tones.

▶

5 Indicate the grasses on the near bank by scumbling on a little of the dark green mixture from the previous step and raw sienna. The warmth of the raw sienna helps to bring them forward in the painting. Brush on more blue for the shadows in the foreground snow, using horizontal strokes that follow the direction of the shadows. For the unshaded areas of snow, use a warm off-white colour mixed from titanium white and a tiny amount of Indian yellow.

6 Using a fine brush and the purplish-grey mixture from Step 2, put in the bare branches that poke up from the ivy-covered trees in the background. Do not try to put in every single detail or the painting will start to look overworked and fussy; you can create a general impression of the shape and texture of these thin branches by means of a series of short parallel lines. Reserve the main detailing and texture for the foreground of the scene.

7 Put in the thin saplings along the bank, as well as their reflections. Darken and strengthen the colours of the reflections: once you have established the general area, you can smooth out the brushstrokes, blending the colours together on the canvas.

8 There is an overly bright and distracting area of water near the centre of the image, which needs to be toned down in order to blend in with the rest of the painting. Leaving the brightest areas untouched, lightly brush a very pale purple over this area.

9 Mix a warm but pale yellow from Indian yellow and titanium white. Lightly touch it into the sky, where the winter sun shines through from behind the clouds.

10 Continue with the linear, dry brush detailing on the bare branches of the trees, as in Step 6, again resisting the temptation to put in too much detail.

11 Using a fine sable brush and a pale blue-grey mixture, put in the branches of the young saplings on the bank. Adjust the proportions of the colours in your mixture: the shaded branches are bluer in tone, while those branches to which the snow is clinging are whiter.

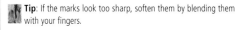
Tip: If the marks look too sharp, soften them by blending them with your fingers.

12 Strengthen the colours of the low bushes on the far side of the water, using short vertical strokes of reddish browns and dark olive greens. The warm colours help to bring this area forward in the painting.

▶

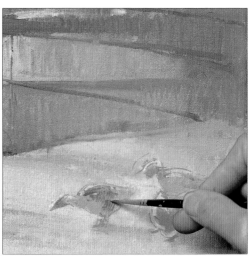

13 Using thin paint, draw the shapes of the box topiary and geese on the near bank. Roughly block in the shapes of the topiary with a pale blue-green mixture, adding more white on the side that catches the light. Using the same colours as before, brush in the shadows cast by the topiary and the geese.

14 Warm up the foreground snow by scumbling the off-white colour from Step 5 over those areas that are not in shadow. Paint the geese in a blue-tinged white, adding more blue to the mixture for the markings on the feathers. Paint their feet, legs and beaks in cadmium red mixed with white and a little lemon yellow.

15 Using a paler version of the pinkish brown from Step 4, paint the sunlit sides of the church so that the building looks three-dimensional. Paint the lines on the tower in a blue-grey, adding more white where the snow clings to the ridges. Paint the castellations on the turret by overpainting some of the sky colour. Use the brush handle to blend colours around the edge of the church and create a crisp outline.

16 Paint the windows of the church in a dark brown, leaving the underlying colour showing through for the stonework.

The finished painting

This is a muted scene that nonetheless captures the feeling of thin, early-morning winter sunlight very well through its use of pale blues and pinks. The church is rendered indistinctly and almost appears to be seen through a haze, but there is enough detail to tell us about the architectural style. The geese in the foreground are painted in more detail and add life to what might otherwise be a rather static scene. Note how many different tones there are within the snow.

The brushstrokes in the reflections have been softly blended.

Warm but pale yellow in the sky lightens the scene.

The geese and their shadows enliven the foreground.

Window in mixed media

Many people would have passed by this little window in favour of something with more obvious appeal, such as brightly painted shutters or a courtyard filled with colourful blooms. The beautiful proportions of this old window, however, with its worn stonework and row of empty terracotta pots, struck an instant chord with the artist. It is proof, if proof were needed, that you can find a subject to paint wherever you go.

Why not try this approach for yourself? Instead of looking for the picturesque, deliberately set out to find a subject that most people would consider to be unsuitable for a painting – the contents of a builder's skip, perhaps, or battered tin cans in the street. Even graffiti on a brick wall or a rusting padlock on a rickety old wooden gate can be turned into intriguing, semi-abstract studies.

From a pictorial point of view, one of the most fascinating things about old, worn subjects like this is that they have wonderfully subtle colours and textures, which makes them ideal candidates for the whole spectrum of watercolour textural techniques. Spattering, sponging, stippling and a whole range of additives can all be incorporated to good effect.

This project starts by using oil pastels as resists, revealing both the texture of the paper and underlying colours. Remember to press quite hard on the oil pastels, otherwise there won't be enough oil on the paper to resist the watercolour paint applied in subsequent stages.

Materials
- *2B pencil*
- *140lb (300gsm) NOT watercolour paper, pre-stretched*
- *Soft oil pastels: light green, dark green, pale yellow, terracotta, bright orange, pink, light grey, mid-toned grey, olive green*
- *Watercolour paints: cerulean blue, dioxazine violet, Payne's grey, olive green, burnt sienna, cadmium orange, leaf green, phthalocyanine blue, cobalt blue*
- *Brushes: medium round, fine round*
- *Ruling drawing pen*
- *Masking fluid*

Preliminary sketch
This scene contains relatively few colours and lots of dense shadows. The only way to make it look realistic is to work out in advance where the darkest and lightest tones are going to be, as the artist has done in this quick tonal sketch.

1 Using a 2B pencil, lightly sketch the outline of the window with its row of terracotta flowerpots, the main blocks of stone that surround it, and the mass of plants growing on the left-hand side.

2 Dip a ruling drawing pen in masking fluid and mask the glazing bars on the window frame, the highlights on the rims of the terracotta flowerpots and the little yellow flowers on the bush on the left. Note the differing types of marks: thin straight lines for the highlights and short dots and dashes for the individual flower petals. Leave to dry.

3 Now start to put in colour and texture with soft oil pastels, pressing quite hard to ensure that enough oil is deposited on the paper to act as a resist when the watercolour paint is applied. Roughly dash in the leaf shapes, using light green for the tallest bush and a darker green for the one in the foreground. Drag pale yellow streaks across the stonework under the window. Put in some terracotta pastel on some of the bricks and the flowerpots. Draw the orange and pink flowers on the bush. Put in some light- and mid-toned grey on the worn stonework under the window.

Assessment time
With the addition of a few more pastel marks – more green on the leaves, orange on the terracotta pots, and a dark olive green in the spaces between the pots – the oil pastel stage is now complete. Oil resists water, so these colours will show through any subsequent watercolour washes. Because you are using a rough paper, some of the oil pastel lines will be broken and the texture of the paper will also be visible. Take time to check that you have included all the areas where you want texture.

Short dots and dashes convey the shapes of the leaves and flowers.

Long, broken strokes are used for the worn stonework.

▶

4 Now for the watercolour stages. Dampen the stonework with clean water. Mix a very pale greyish blue from cerulean blue and a little dioxazine violet watercolour paints and brush this mixture over the stonework, adding a little Payne's grey for the shadowed areas and a little more violet for the foreground. Brush very pale olive green over the shadowed stonework beneath the window ledge. Applied wet into wet, the colour blurs and looks like soft lichen.

5 Mix a very pale wash of cerulean blue and paint the white woodwork of the right-hand window frame. (Leaving the frame as white paper would look too stark in relation to the rest of the image.) Mix a warm brown from burnt sienna and dioxazine violet and carefully paint the window panes, leaving some gaps for highlights reflected in the glass.

6 Mix an orangey brown from cadmium orange and dioxazine violet and paint the first terracotta flowerpot. Add Payne's grey to the mixture for the second pot in the row, which is in shadow, and burnt sienna for the third and fourth pots.

7 Note how the oil pastel marks that you applied in the early stages resist the watercolour paint, creating very realistic-looking but subtle texture in the stonework under the window and the flowerpots. The texture of the paper plays a part in this, too.

8 Mix a pale but warm grey from cerulean blue and a little dioxazine violet and wash this mixture over the stonework under the window. While the wash is still damp, brush burnt sienna over the terracotta pastel of the bricks. Allow the paper to dry slightly, add dioxazine violet to the burnt sienna wash and paint the cracks in the stonework.

9 Mix dioxazine violet with a little olive green and spatter this mixture lightly over the foreground to create some texture on the path and wall. These spatters of dark colour look like clumps of moss or small pebbles – both of which are in keeping with the somewhat derelict and dilapidated nature of the subject.

10 Mix a fairly strong wash of leaf green (which is a bright, yellowy green) and brush it over the lightest areas on the tops of the bushes. Add cerulean blue to the mixture and use this colour to paint the mid-toned leaves, taking care not to obliterate all of the light green.

11 Mix a dark green from olive green and phthalocyanine blue and dot in the darkest tones of the leaves on the background bush, making sure your brushstrokes follow the direction in which the leaves grow. You are now beginning to establish the form of the bushes.

▶

12 Add cobalt blue to the dark green used in Step 11. Paint the spaces between the leaves of the foreground bush.

Tip: Using a range of contrasting greens like this makes it clear that there are two very different bushes in this picture. You may find it easier to assess the tones if you half close your eyes.

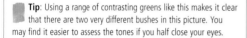

13 Mix a very pale wash of cerulean blue and brush it over the white spaces to the left of the bushes, which look very stark in relation to the rest of the image. Mix a very dark green from burnt sienna, olive green and a little phthalocyanine blue. Stroke this mixture on to the very darkest leaves on the foreground bush, taking the colour across the front of the window to imply overhanging leaves and branches. Leave to dry.

14 Gently rub off the masking fluid. Mix a dark purple from cobalt blue, violet and a little burnt sienna and darken some of the shadows around the window.

15 Mix a very pale wash of cerulean blue and tone down the starkness of some of the revealed whites.

The finished painting

This is a beautifully controlled study in texture, painted using a relatively subdued and limited palette – proof that simplicity is often the most effective option. The empty flowerpots are what really make the picture: they provide visual interest in the foreground to hold the viewer's attention and also imply a human presence in the scene.

Using a range of greens both gives depth and indicates that there is more than one type of plant in this area.

Leaving tiny areas of window pane unpainted conveys the impression of light being reflected in the glass.

Two textural techniques, spattering and the use of resists, have been combined to good effect here.

Moroccan kasbah in watercolour

The location for this striking project is the World Heritage site of Ait-Ben-Haddhou, in southern Morocco. It is a traditional-style village made up of several earthen fortresses, each one some 10m (30ft) high.

With its straight-edged buildings and clean lines, the scene looks deceptively simple, but it demonstrates well how important it is to train yourself to assess tones. The earthen buildings are all very similar in colour (predominantly ochre and terracotta), so without strong contrasts of tone you will never succeed in making them look three-dimensional.

If you are painting on location, you may find that the light, and therefore the direction and length of shadows, changes as you work. It is a good idea to make light pencil marks on your paper, just outside the margins of your painting, indicating the angle of the sun. This makes it easier to keep the lighting consistent when you are painting over a period of several hours.

Materials
- 2B pencil
- 140lb (300gsm) NOT watercolour paper, pre-stretched
- Watercolour paints: cerulean blue, yellow ochre, light red, vermilion, mauve, white, alizarin crimson, Hooker's green, Winsor yellow, Payne's grey, ultramarine blue, burnt umber
- Brushes: large wash, medium round, medium flat, fine filbert

> **Tip:** Use a pencil to measure the relative heights of the buildings. Hold the pencil out in front of you and align the tip with part of your subject (say, the top of the tallest building), then run your thumb down the pencil until it aligns with the base of the building. You can transfer this measurement to your watercolour paper, again holding the pencil at arm's length. It is important to keep your arm straight and the pencil vertical, so that the pencil remains a constant distance from the subject.

The original scene
The artist took this photograph around midday, when the sun was almost directly overhead. Consequently, the colours looked somewhat bleached out and there were no strong shadows to bring the scene to life. She decided to use a little artistic licence and enhance what she saw by intensifying the colours in order to make her painting more dramatic.

The sky looks pale and does not have the warmth that one associates with hot African countries.

Here, the mud-brick buildings look pale and bleached out; in the right light, however, they glow a warm orangey-red.

1 Using a 2B pencil, lightly sketch the scene, taking careful note of the relative heights of the buildings and their angles in relation to one another.

3 Mix a pale but warm terracotta colour from yellow ochre, light red and a tiny amount of vermilion. Using a medium round brush, wash this mixture over the buildings, working around the fronds of the foreground palm trees and adding a little more yellow ochre as you work across from right to left.

2 Using a large wash brush, dampen the sky area with clean water, brushing carefully around the outlines of the buildings to get a neat, clean edge. Mix a wash of cerulean blue. After about a minute, when the water has sunk in but the paper is still damp, quickly brush on the colour. (You may want to switch to a smaller brush to paint up to the edge of the buildings. Use the side of the brush and brush the paint upward, to avoid accidentally getting any of the blue colour on the buildings.)

Tip: Vary the tone of the buildings. If they are too uniform in tone they will look newly built and mass produced.

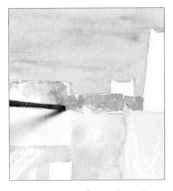

4 Add a little mauve to the mixture to make a deeper tone. Paint the wall at the base of the picture, painting around the trunks of the palm trees. Hold the brush at an angle as you do this and make jagged marks, as this helps to convey the texture of the trunks and shows that they are not straight-edged.

5 Continue working across the painting until you have put in all of the lightest tones of the buildings.

6 Mix a mid tone from yellow ochre and a tiny amount of mauve and, using a medium flat brush, stipple this mixture on to the buildings in the centre of the painting to give them some texture as well as tone. Add more mauve to the mixture for the darker left-hand side.

▶

7 Brush white watercolour over the top edge of the building in the centre. This reduces the intensity of the yellow and makes it look as if it has been bleached by the sun.

8 Mix a dark terracotta from light red, yellow ochre and a touch of alizarin crimson and start painting the darkest tones – the sides of the buildings that are in deepest shade.

Assessment time

The light, mid and dark tones are now in place across the picture and, although the tones have not yet reached their final density, we are beginning to get a clear sense of which facets of the buildings are in bright sunlight and which are in shade. From this stage onward, you need to continually assess the tonal values as you work, because even slight changes in one area will affect the balance of the painting as a whole. Take regular breaks, propping your painting up against a wall and looking at it from a distance to see how it is developing.

Stronger contrasts of tone are needed in order for the buildings to look truly three-dimensional.

Details such as the recessed windows and doors will help to bring the painting to life.

9 Mix a very dark terracotta colour from light red, yellow ochre and a touch of alizarin crimson, and begin putting in some of the fine details, such as the door in the exterior wall and some of the small windows. You are now beginning to establish a feeling of light and shade in the painting.

10 The right-hand buildings, which are in the deepest area of shade, look too light. Darken them as necessary by overlaying more washes of the colours used previously. Also darken the mid-toned wall in the centre of the picture and put some dark windows on the light side.

11 The lightest walls now look too light in relation to the rest of the painting, so darken them with another wash of the pale terracotta mixture used in Step 3. Build up the tone gradually. You can apply more washes if necessary, but if you make things too dark there is no going back.

12 Mix a yellowy green from Hooker's green and a little yellow ochre and, using a fine filbert brush, start putting in the green palm fronds in the foreground. Make short upward flicks with the brush, following the direction in which the palm fronds grow.

▶

13 Continue painting the palm fronds, adding a little Winsor yellow at the point where the fronds spring out from the trunk. Paint the shaded sides of the palm trunks in Payne's grey, using short, broken strokes to indicate the knobbly surface texture of the trunks.

14 Lighten the grey by adding a little yellow ochre. Using the side of the brush, dab this mixture on to the left-hand side of the painting to indicate the scrubby texture of the bushes that grow in this area. Mix a very pale green from Payne's grey, yellow ochre and Hooker's green and dot in the sides of the palm trunks that catch the light. Mix a grey-green from Payne's grey and Hooker's green and dot this mixture into the foreground shrubs. Mix a pale purple from alizarin crimson and ultramarine blue and paint the dry earth and the shadows around the base of the palm trees.

15 Mix a pale wash of alizarin crimson and darken the wall in the foreground. Feel free to use some artistic licence in your choice of colours. Although the wall is, in reality, more terracotta than pink, you are trying to put colour into a subject that does not have much in order to create some drama and variety in your image. Adjust the tones over the painting as a whole if you feel that it is necessary.

16 Mix a dark brown from light red and Payne's grey and put in the dark details, such as the windows. Dry brush a pale mixture of Hooker's green over the foreground to give it some tone. Mix a dark brown from burnt umber and Payne's grey and dab it on to the palm trunks to give them more tone and texture. Paint the shadows of the palm trees on the wall in a pale tone of Payne's grey.

17 Mix a dilute wash of white watercolour paint and brush it over the tops of the highest buildings. Because the paint is transparent the underlying colour shows through, creating the effect of strong sunlight shining on the buildings and bleaching out the colour. Do not worry if the white looks too strong when you first apply it to the paper as it will quickly sink in and look natural.

The finished painting

The artist has managed to create a surprisingly wide range of tones in this painting, and this is one of the keys to its success, as the variety helps to convey not only the weathered textures of the mud bricks but also that all-important sense of light and shade. Rich, warm colours – far warmer than in the original reference photograph – help to evoke the feeling of being in a hot country. The foreground trees and bushes contrast well with the buildings in both colour and shape.

Transparent white watercolour paint allows some of the underlying colour to show through, and this creates the impression of sun-bleached brick.

In reality, this wall is the same colour as those behind. Painting it a warm pink brings it forward in the picture and helps to create an impression of distance.

Note the use of complementary colours – the orangey ochres and terracottas of the buildings against the rich cerulean blue of the sky.

Arch and balcony in gouache

In the eighteenth and early nineteenth centuries, it was common practice for members of the aristocracy to undertake a grand tour of the major cities of Europe in order to complete their education. In those days before the advent of picture postcards and easy-to-use cameras, sketches made *in situ* were, for many, the only means of recording the wonders that they saw. As a consequence, watercolour paintings abound of the sites that they visited: great palaces and chateaux, romantic vistas and ruined follies were all captured on paper to show to admiring friends and relations.

In some respects this project, which relies on careful observation and measuring to record the detail of the building, is very much in the same tradition. However, it also goes beyond that, seeking as it does to capture the spirit of the place and the quality of the light. Attempting to create a sense of atmosphere is one of the things that will lift your work above the level of a technical exercise and turn it into a painting. Moreover, whether you are painting close to home or in a land far away, the very act of consciously examining your subject over an extended period of time somehow seems to imprint the scene in your memory in a way that taking a photograph can never do.

The building that features in this project is the Royal Pavilion, in Brighton, in the south of England, commissioned and closely overseen by the then Prince Regent (later King George IV), who confessed that he cried for joy when he contemplated the Pavilion's splendours.

Often when you are painting buildings – particularly ones such as this, which are rendered in stucco or plaster or constructed from smooth stone – you are dealing with very subtle differences in tone. You need to observe your subject and assess the tonal differences very carefully, as this is what conveys the three-dimensional nature of the building.

Remember, too, that gouache paint always looks slightly darker when it is dry than it does when it is wet. Make sure you test your mixtures on a scrap piece of paper or board and allow them to dry thoroughly before you apply them to your painting, as this is the only way to judge whether or not you have got the mix right. Although it is possible to paint over areas if you find you've made them too dark, it is far better to get the tone right first time – particularly when you are using the gouache in the form of thin washes, as here – otherwise your painting may start to look heavy and overworked.

The scene

Many people might have been tempted to select a viewpoint that included the whole of the arch and window, with the arch symmetrically positioned, but this could lead to a very static composition. This viewpoint is much more interesting: it allows us to see the form of the arch, rather than just a flat façade, while the turret on the edge of the balcony is positioned "on the third".

Materials

- *Watercolour paper*
- *Acrylic gesso*
- *HB pencil*
- *Illustration board*
- *Gouache paints: raw umber, zinc white, jet black, ultramarine blue, brilliant yellow*
- *Brushes: small round*

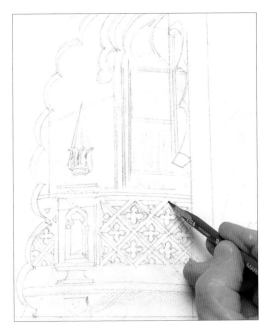

1 Using a sharp HB pencil, make an underdrawing on watercolour paper primed with acrylic gesso. It is important to measure everything carefully. Pay particular attention to the shape, size and number of the quatrefoil shapes in the tracery of the limestone balcony.

2 Mix a dark brown from raw umber, zinc white and jet black and, using a small round brush, paint the dark spaces around the quatrefoil shapes on the balcony. In some areas light is reflected back: paint these shapes in a blue-grey mixture of zinc white and ultramarine blue.

3 Using the dark brown mixture from Step 2, paint the shaded side of the foreground arch. Add more white to the mixture and paint the dark cast shadows on the right-hand side of the scene, making sure you paint them with crisp edges.

4 Paying careful attention to where the light falls and alternating between the brown and blue-grey mixtures used in the previous steps, paint the scallop shapes on the left-hand side of the foreground arch.

▶

5 Mix a warm stone colour from zinc white, brilliant yellow and a litle raw umber and paint the lightest area of wall behind the balcony. Add ultramarine blue to the dark brown mixture and paint the shaded area above the turret and the edge of the stuccowork to the left of the window.

6 Paint the shaded left-hand side of the foreground arch, using the same dark mixtures as before. Although bright highlights are visible through gaps in the stonework, it is too difficult to try to work around them at this stage: you can reinstate them later using pure white gouache.

7 The blue sky reflected in the window can be seen behind some of the cut-out shapes in the balcony: paint these in a bright blue mixed from ultramarine blue and zinc white. Complete the dark shadows behind the quatrefoil shapes on the balcony; note that the colour changes should not be uniform in tone.

8 Mix a light brown shadow colour from raw umber and zinc white and paint the unpainted stonework on the right of the foreground arch. Scumble a little ultramarine blue over the cast shadows that you painted in Step 3 to make the colour look less flat and create some variety of tone.

9 Add ultramarine blue to the warm stone colour that you mixed in Step 5 and paint the shadow areas on the balcony. Paint the lightest areas of stone on the balcony in a pale mixture of brilliant yellow and zinc white; you will need to look very carefully to see where the tone changes.

10 Add raw umber to the stone colour and paint the area under the overhang of the balcony, which is in shadow and therefore darker in tone. Using a mid-tone brown, put in some of the dark detailing and the most deeply shaded side of the turret.

11 Put in the mid-toned areas of the glazing bars on the window, using a slightly paler version of the stone colour used earlier. Mix ultramarine blue, zinc white and a tiny amount of yellow and paint the reflections of the sky in the window, painting around the very lightest areas, where the curtain hangs in folds.

Tip: To avoid dirtying the white on your palette when mixing it with other colours, use a clean brush and add white to the colour you have already mixed rather than vice versa.

Assessment time
Now that the painting is almost complete, spend some time assessing the tonal values. Is the difference in tone between the light and dark areas strong enough? Any adjustments that you make in the final stages will be very slight.

This dark mass tends to overpower the image; the highlights should be reinstated.

The unpainted white areas are too stark; they leap out from the image and demand attention.

12 Using the stone colour, reinforce the shadows on the underside of the glazing bars. Mix a pale blue from ultramarine blue and lots of zinc white and paint those highlight areas of the curtain that are unpainted. Paint the scalloped edges that jut out from the right-hand side of the arch and scumble a little blue over the darkest part of the arch in order to create some texture and variety of tone in the stonework.

13 Dot in some pure white highlights on the left-hand side of the arch, where light shines through the tracery of the stonework.

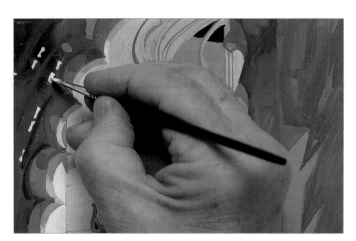

Tip: Keep the paint mix quite thick when you are putting in highlights. If you use very watery paint, it is harder to control and may run. Touch the tip of a fine brush into the paint so that there is very little paint on the fibres, and hold the brush almost vertical to the support so that you can make very small, tightly controlled marks.

The finished painting
This is a considered painting of an interesting architectural detail. However the bold shadows and sense of light and shade lift it beyond being a mere record of the building. The arch frames the view, but the fact that it is off-centre creates a more dynamic and interesting composition. The colour palette is limited, but the subtle differences in tone have been carefully observed to create a scene that really looks three-dimensional.

Using gouache enables you to paint highlights over dark paint without any of the underlying colour showing through.

Note how the subtle differences in tone convey the feeling of strong sunlight and the form of the turret.

Scumbling different colours over the darkest area prevents it from looking flat and creates texture and variety in the stonework.

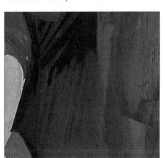

Venetian building in pen and ink

This project is an exercise in perspective. The bottom of the balcony is more or less at the artist's eye level – so this is the horizon line. If you look at the initial pencil sketch in Step 1, you will see that the artist has drawn the bottom of the balcony to form a straight, horizontal line across the centre of the image. Any parallel line above this point (such as the line of the roof) will appear to slope down toward the vanishing point, while anything below it (such as the base of the building) appears to slope upwards. Take time over your initial pencil sketch to make sure you get the angles and proportions right. Texture is important, too, and the rough texture of the ancient brickwork is very pleasing to the eye. Do not try to draw every single brick, as this would make the image too 'busy' and detract from the overall effect. Leaving some areas empty gives a much-needed contrast of texture and implies the smooth render that would once have covered the whole façade.

Pen and ink is an ideal medium for architectural drawings, as it allows you to make very precise marks. Here, both permanent and water-soluble inks are used, creating a combination of crisp, linear details and ink washes, which soften the overall effect. For this project, the artist chose to use sepia ink, rather than black, as it is a much softer colour and helps to give the drawing a rather nostalgic, old-fashioned feel.

Materials
• *Heavy drawing paper*
• *HB pencil*
• *Permanent and water-soluble sepia inks*
• *Steel-nibbed pens*
• *Fine paintbrush*
• *Gouache paint: white*

The scene
Old buildings such as this one, with the canal lapping at its foundations, are common in Venice, and can evoke a strong sense of the past. The decorative lines of the balconies are not overly ornate, but they hold our interest, and the beautiful arched doors and windows form a repeating pattern that runs through the whole image.

1 Using an HB pencil, make a light, detailed sketch of the scene, making sure you measure all the different elements.

Tip: The buildings are receding. Put in the perspective sight-lines as a guide; you can erase them later.

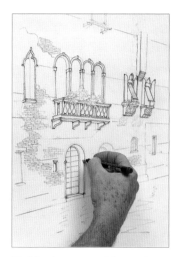

2 Following your pencil lines and using permanent sepia ink, carefully ink in the windows and balconies. It is very important not to use water-soluble ink here, as you want to retain all the crisp detail of these lines in the finished drawing.

3 Continue with the ink work, using water-soluble sepia ink for the foliage and brickwork. Also hatch the windows behind the open shutters on the top right of the drawing in water-soluble ink, drawing the lines close together as this area is very dark.

4 Continue working on the brickwork, alternating between permanent and water-soluble sepia inks. Put in the lines of the Venetian blinds in permanent ink. Here the artist has put the blinds in at different heights to add interest.

5 Using water-soluble ink, put in some light hatching around the window recesses, in the windows below the blinds, and under the balconies to introduce some shading. (The ink will be washed over at a later stage, so that the hatching marks blend together to create an area of solid tone.)

Assessment time
The main lines are now in place. However, although there is some indication of the shading around the windows and balconies, the image overall looks rather flat and two-dimensional. From this point onward, concentrate on creating more depth and texture.

Although there is some texture and detail, the image as a whole is rather lifeless. Washes of colour will help to counteract this.

▶

6 As the light is coming from the right of the scene, the balconies cast oblique shadows on the façade of the building. Put them in lightly, using an HB pencil. (The pencil lines act as a positional guide – they should be covered up by washes of ink later.)

7 Using permanent ink and zig-zagging vertical lines, draw the ripples in the water. Hatch the darkest areas of the water, using water-soluble ink. The ripples will remain visible when a wash is applied, while the hatching will blend to an area of solid tone.

8 Erase all the remaining pencil lines, apart from the cast shadows that you put in in Step 6. Load a paintbrush with water and brush over the shaded parts of the building. The lines drawn in water-soluble ink will dissolve, allowing you to create areas of solid tone.

9 Continue brushing water over the water-soluble ink, including the canal. Brush colour over the doors, darkening them with more ink if necessary. Dilute some sepia ink (or use sepia watercolour paint) and brush it over the cast shadows on the building, keeping within the pencil marks.

10 Using a fine paintbrush and white gouache, paint in the reflections of the doors in the water. Gouache paint used straight from the tube can be quite thick so only dip the tip of your brush into it.

The finished drawing

This is an evocative and elegant pen-and-ink study of a classic Venetian building. Permanent ink was used for the linear details in the most important areas, while brushing water over the water-soluble ink has helped to create areas of tone that soften the harshness of the pen work, transforming an architectural study into something much more picturesque. Although only one colour of ink was used, a good range of tones was created by washing water over different densities of hatched marks.

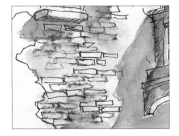

Both permanent and water-soluble ink have been used here, creating a combination of linear detail and soft tonal washes.

The linear detailing of the building, as in the balcony, has been drawn using permanent ink.

White gouache paint, which is opaque, is used to paint the light reflections on top of the dark patches of water.

Washing water over hatched lines produces an area of solid tone – the closer together the lines, the darker the tone.

Moorish palace in acrylics

Small details can often sum up the character of a building far more effectively than a view of the building in its entirety – particularly when, as here, there is an abundance of decorative detail in the form of beautifully shaped arches and mosaic tilework.

This scene shows part of a fourteenth-century Moorish palace in Andalucia, in southern Spain. The view is painted from the central courtyard, which is surrounded by a cool, shaded gallery of the horseshoe-shaped arches that are so typical of this area and period. An arched doorway on one side of the gallery leads into a beautiful walled garden resplendent with splashing fountains.

Try to respect the architect's intentions when you are painting buildings of any kind. Symmetry was an important consideration in Moorish architecture and a symmetrical composition will help you to capture something of the formality of this particular building. Remember, however, that you are making a painting, not an architectural plan: you also have to take into consideration things like the play of light and shade and the contrast between the heat of the garden and the coolness of the gallery.

Materials
- *Acrylic paper*
- *Acrylic paints: phthalocyanine green, phthalocyanine blue, cadmium red, titanium white, lemon yellow, alizarin crimson, ultramarine blue, brilliant yellow green*
- *Brushes: large round, medium flat, medium round, small flat*
- *Charcoal pencil*

The courtyard and gallery
From this angle, the arch creates a "frame within a frame", leading us through to the garden and fountains. We can also see the gallery surrounding the courtyard, which tells us more about the building as a whole, and there is an interesting and atmospheric contrast between the brightly lit garden and the cool, shaded gallery.

The garden and fountains
Here, you can see the garden and fountains clearly. Architecturally, however, it is not as interesting as the view from the courtyard.

> **Tip**: Always spend time exploring your subject from different viewpoints before you start painting; even a slight adjustment to your position can make a substantial difference. Instead of trying to capture the whole scene, decide what elements appeal to you most – and make quick compositional sketches to decide which viewpoint works best.

1 Mix a bright blue from phthalocyanine green and phthalocyanine blue. Using a large round brush, lay a flat wash over the paper. Leave to dry. Using a charcoal pencil, sketch the scene, observing the perspective carefully to ensure that all the lines run at the correct angles.

2 Mix a warm, off-white stone colour from cadmium red, titanium white and lemon yellow. Using a medium flat brush, paint the lightest tones of the vertical columns and foreground arch. Add a little more red to the mixture and paint the arch into the garden and the line of bricks above the foreground arch.

3 Add more water to the mixture and paint the shaded tiled area of floor beyond the arch. Because the paint is very dilute, it serves as a glaze, allowing some of the colour of the support to show through.

4 Mix a purple shadow colour from alizarin crimson, ultramarine blue and a little lemon yellow and, using a medium round brush, paint the huge wooden doors on each side of the arch leading into the garden. Use a dilute version of the same colour for the tiled courtyard floor.

5 Mix a pale, bright green from brilliant yellow green and titanium white and paint the lightest foliage. Add more brilliant yellow green and a little ultramarine blue and dot in some darker foliage. Paint the pool surround in the stone colour from Step 2, adding more white for the side in sunlight.

▶

6 Mix a warmer stone colour from cadmium red, lemon yellow and titanium white and, using a small flat brush, paint the darker-toned bricks that run around the top of the arch.

7 Paint the fountain base in the same colour and the interior of the fountain bowl in the initial pale stone colour. Add more water to the pale stone colour and scumble it loosely over the ground inside the archway. Reinforce the shadows at the top and base of the supporting columns. Brush a little very dilute lemon yellow over the wooden doors.

Assessment time

Although the dark wooden doors give some indication of perspective and distance, the image looks very flat and one-dimensional. There is some detailing on the brickwork of the arches, but the garden in the background consists of little more than a few blocks of colour. The next stage is to reinforce the sense of depth. More foreground details, suggesting the intricacy of the carved arches, would help to bring the arches forwards in the scene. Introducing some reflected light into the glazed tiles of the gallery floor would help to connect this area with the sunlit garden that lies beyond.

Indistinct masses of green imply the garden beyond, but more definition is needed.

The sloping line of the door gives some indication of depth and perspective.

8 Mix a dark green from phthalocyanine green and brilliant yellow green, and a lighter green from brilliant yellow green and lemon yellow. Using a small round brush, dot these two mixtures over the foliage to give it more form, using the lighter colour higher up, where the sun catches the trees.

9 Mix a dull red from cadmium red, titanium white and a little phthalocyanine blue. Using a medium flat brush, put in the terracotta tiles of the courtyard, leaving lines of the blue glaze showing through. Darken the shaded edge of the step leading into the garden with the same colour.

10 Mix a greenish black from phthalocyanine green and a little ultramarine blue. Block in the dark leaves of the potted plant to the left of the foreground arch and dot the same colour into the foliage in the garden; again, this helps to link the inner and outer courtyards.

11 Add a little cadmium red and some titanium white to the pale stone colour and, using a small flat brush, put in the pink-coloured tiles around the top of the archway. Paint the small blue tiles in this area in a mixture of phthalocyanine blue and titanium white. Darken the shaded edge of the step.

▶

12 Add a little titanium white to the pale stone colour and, using the tip of a small flat brush, paint mortar lines around the top of the arch. Using the same colour, paint the highlit side of the column that separates the central arch from its neighbour.

13 Using a small round brush and the terracotta mixture from Step 9, paint the plaster above the tiles. Paint the decorative tiles above the arch using the same colour and phthalocyanine blue. Interpret the pattern loosely. Add the mortar lines that separate the tiles, as you did in Step 12.

14 Paint the water splashing from the fountain in titanium white. Mix a pale ochre from lemon yellow and brilliant yellow green and paint the back wall of the garden, allowing some of the foliage colour to remain visible.

15 Mix a very dilute, dull purple from alizarin crimson and phthalocyanine blue and paint the shadows cast by the heavy wooden doors on the tiled floor with smooth, even brush strokes.

The finished painting

This painting is all about contrasts: contrasts of light and shade and of warmth and coolness. The colour palette is beautifully balanced: the colour of the blue-toned ground is picked up in the tilework and the water, while terracotta and ochre complement the blue and bring added warmth to the scene. The arch in the foreground acts as a frame for the arched doorway and the garden beyond – an established compositional device that draws the viewer's eye through the picture.

The soft colours of the tiles, brickwork and plaster look faded, as befits the age of the building.

Pale yellows and greens are used to show how strongly the sunlight is hitting the tops of the trees.

The splashing water of the fountain is painted with energetic, curving brushstrokes.

The original blue-toned ground shows through the thin terracotta glaze, creating a feeling of coolness in this shaded area.

Cityscape in oil pastels

A construction site might not seem the most obvious subject for a drawing project but, if you choose your viewpoint carefully, the bold colours and graphic shapes can give you the chance to create a modern-looking, semi-abstract drawing. It will also test your ability to work with straight lines – always important when drawing buildings, whatever era they date from.

Scenes such as this can be found in towns and cities all over the world and recording a new building at all stages of its construction, from site clearance through to completion, makes an interesting long-term project. Moreover, many companies are waking up to the investment potential of buying original art – so who knows? If there is a prestigious building project going on near your home and your work is good enough, you might even be able to sell it to the owners to display in the reception area or to use in promotional literature.

Oil pastels are not renowned for their subtlety of colour, but for a subject such as this, which relies on the bold, primary colours of the building cranes for much of its impact, they are ideal. You need to press quite firmly on the oil pastels, so use a heavy drawing paper or an oil-painting paper for this project to avoid the risk of tearing the support.

Materials
- *Heavy drawing paper or oil-painting paper*
- *4B pencil*
- *Oil pastels: pale greys (warm- and cool-toned), bright blue, red, yellow, white, lilac, Naples yellow, black*
- *Scraperboard tool or craft (utility) knife*

The scene
The brightly coloured cranes stand out dramatically against the cloudless blue sky, while the straight lines of the cranes and the buildings under construction create a graphic, almost abstract composition. The diagonal lines of some of the cranes make the composition more dynamic.

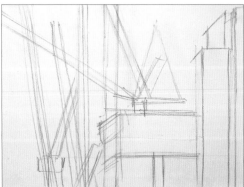

1 Using a soft pencil, mark out the lines of the cranes and the buildings under construction. There is no need to put in any of the internal lines at this stage, but do make sure you measure all the angles and distances carefully.

2 Using pale grey oil pastels, block in the building on the right. Note that the shaded sides are cooler in tone than those in full sunlight, so alternate between warm- and cool-toned greys as required.

3 Block in the sky, using the side of a bright blue oil pastel and making sure you do not go over the lines of the cranes. Putting in the negative shapes of the background sky at this early stage makes it easier to see any thin lines of the cranes that you have not yet drawn.

> **Tip**: It is easy to lose track of where you are in a complicated drawing such as this, so refer continually to your reference photo to make sure you don't apply the sky colour over any of the lines of the cranes.

4 Begin putting in the red lines of the cranes, using bold, confident strokes and pressing quite hard on the tip of the pastel. Lightly stroke the side of the pastel over the warm-toned shadow areas of the buildings.

5 Now put in the bright yellow of the cranes, filling in the spaces between the rungs with blue. Work white oil pastel over part of the sky and blend it with your fingers.

6 Using the side of a lilac oil pastel, roughly block in the shaded sides of the buildings on the right. (Note, in particular, the shadow cast on the building on the far right of the image.) Apply the same colour to some of the shaded interior floors of the building on the left. Work Naples yellow, which is a pale, warm yellow, over the warm-toned area of the building in the centre and add small dashes of red on the tall foreground building.

7 Using the tip of a black oil pastel to make strong, bold marks, draw the reinforced steel joists of the building in the background. Establish the different storeys of the building on the left, using a range of shadow colours (blue, lilac, black) as appropriate. Use the side of the pastels to make broad, lightly textured marks; you can then go over them with other pastels to blend the colours optically and create a more interesting shadow colour.

▶

Assessment time

The drawing is nearing completion and only a few minor adjustments are needed. In places, the cranes are lost against the building or the sky and need to be more sharply defined. Some of the shadows need to be darkened slightly.

This crane merges into the building behind it and needs to be a little more clearly defined.

The lines of the white crane are quite delicate and will be hard to draw with a thick oil pastel.

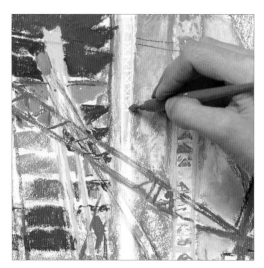

8 Using a scraperboard tool or the tip of a craft knife, scratch off blue oil pastel to create the lines of the white crane in the centre of the image.

9 Scratch into the red crane on the left to create some highlight areas, and strengthen the red diagonal line so that the crane really stands out against the building.

The finished drawing

This artist has matched the medium to the subject beautifully. The bold, vibrant colours of oil pastels, which might be too brash and unsubtle for many subjects, are perfect for the bright, primary colours of the cranes and sky. Although it is difficult to draw fine details with oil pastels, they are the ideal drawing tool for the solid, graphic lines of this scene. Using the side of the pastels for the façades of the buildings brings another quality to the image and creates a lighter texture. Overlaying one colour on another, particularly in the shadow areas, has created interesting optical colour mixes that are much more lively and interesting than a flat application of a single colour could ever be.

Allowing colours to mix optically on the paper creates lively shadow effects.

The sgraffito technique allows you to scratch off the pastel and create fine lines.

Finger blending in the sky softens both the colour and the texture.

Water and Sky

The sky provides the source of light in a landscape painting and is a
major factor in establishing the atmosphere of a scene. Making
studies of skies, in their many moods, is something that all
landscape artists are advised to do. This chapter looks at a whole
range of skies and cloud conditions, from turbulent, storm clouds
to a tropical sunset that is saturated with reds, oranges and pinks.
Another major element of landscapes is water – both naturally
occurring features such as seas and rivers, and man-made structures
like ponds and canals. As water provides a critical feeling of
movement in scenes that might otherwise be static, it presents
its own challenges and deserves special consideration.
This chapter begins with a series tutorials explaining the technical
aspects, which is followed by a gallery of drawings and paintings
that you can study. Then there are step-by-step projects that you
can use as practice exercises and as a source of inspiration when
devising your own sky- and seascapes.

Clouds

The sky often makes up the largest area of a landscape painting, and can be vital in creating atmosphere, as well as in adding a sense of scale and perspective. At its simplest, a sky can be expressed by leaving the white paper, or laying a flat or graded wash of colour. More often it will include clouds, so it is worth exploring their characteristics and thinking about how to tackle them in different media.

Have a look at the clouds in your chosen scene. Are they light and wispy, large and heavy, high or low-lying? Do they blend softly into the sky or are the edges crisply backlit against the sun? There may be different cloud forms in the same vista: do you wish to describe them all, or would a simplification best suit your composition? Clouds are changing all the time, sometimes very rapidly, and you may need to work quickly or partly from memory if you are painting from nature. If you are working from photographs, you may find that you can be selective or inventive with your cloud shapes, so long as you have enough visual reference material to help you to convey them convincingly.

Remember that clouds follow the same rules of perspective as the rest of the landscape. They will appear not only smaller in size but also cooler in colour as they recede toward the horizon. Having said that, an interesting phenomenon is that clouds tend to look soft-edged when they are near to you, with crisp edges only taking shape when seen over greater distances, contrary to the usual way that objects lose their sharpness as they recede.

When choosing which medium to use, you may find that particular cloud forms suggest different materials. For example, the soft, fluffy forms of cumulus might be best handled in soft pastels, while higher streaks of cirrus clouds could work well with a wet into wet watercolour treatment. A dramatic sky or a vivid sunset might suit heavy impasto in oils or acrylics. Charcoal can be blended with the fingers or used on a textured ground to capture the graininess of stratus or rain-clouds, or lifted off with a kneaded eraser to convey complex shapes or light effects.

Colour is another factor in deciding your medium. Clouds are seldom a uniform grey, but often contain hints of violet, peach or ochre, depending on the time of day and conditions. Light from the landscape below can reflect colour up into the clouds, particularly in seascapes. Would these subtle variations be captured best in careful layers of watercolour wash, softly scumbled acrylics or swirling soft pastel? Try a few interpretations of the same clouds using different media. Becoming confdent with your materials will give you more options when you plan how to treat the sky within a landscape painting.

Giving clouds volume ▲
Clouds need to be given tonal value in order to create the illusion of three dimensions. When you identify the direction of light falling on the clouds and the shape of shadows (top), you might find it useful to think of clouds in terms of a cluster of spheres. Now the actual shape of the cloud can be described, and further shading added. The water vapour that makes up clouds gives soft outlines to shadows, so to create a convincing effect, avoid crisp or sharp edges (bottom).

Cirrus clouds ◄
Tending to be high, cirrus clouds are somewhat wispy and often stripy or linear in appearance. In this quick watercolour sketch, the paint has been applied mainly wet into wet, with a little sponging off toward the middle of the sky. Note the sense of perspective created by the larger cloud masses in the foreground giving way to flatter forms toward the horizon. The grey of the clouds is created with a mixture of alizarin crimson and phthalocyanine blue, with a touch of yellow ochre.

Stormy clouds ▲

The artist began this study by dampening the paper with water and dropping in a very pale grey, allowing it to spread of its own accord. She then blotted off paint in some areas with a paper towel to reveal the white paper, before adding the mid- and dark greys and the blue of the sky, wet into wet.

Cloudy sunset ▶

Here, thick acrylic paint was applied with a palette knife. The sketch aims to capture an atmosphere, rather than a realistic visual record. Note the limited range of greys and golds used here. It is a good idea to keep to a restrained colour palette when painting dramatic skies, to avoid a garish result.

Passing rain-clouds ▼

Charcoal has been applied swiftly to the dark areas of the foreground, and the paper allowed to show through in the middle distance and background. Blending has softened the texture and tonal contrast. The artist has used a kneaded eraser to suggest light breaking through and detail below.

Skyscapes

Having spent some time looking at clouds and how to portray them, you are better prepared for tackling the sky as a whole. Learn to think of the sky as an integral part of the composition, by including it in the planning stage rather than adding it when the rest of the painting is complete, which can leave it looking a little like an afterthought. Forward planning will also give you the practical advantage of being able to work out the best stage in the painting at which to tackle it. It can be difficult to work around complicated shapes with 'sky colour' and risks spoiling a picture you are otherwise happy with.

The sky can be vital in creating an atmosphere, as well as adding a sense of scale and perspective. As you have seen, clouds play an important part in establishing mood: billowing clouds in a bright summer sky, for example, evoke a different feeling to storm clouds. Clouds can be used as an aid to composition in various ways: the shapes and direction of them may lead the eye toward the focal point of the picture or a flat, uniform sky may act as a restful back-drop to a complicated scene below it.

Your viewpoint will dictate how much of the sky appears in your chosen scene. The same landscape will look vastly different when seen from a high viewpoint as opposed to a low one. In the first, you might see a large expanse of ground rolling away to a thin sliver of sky at the top of the picture. With a low viewpoint this area of land becomes compressed, foreground features loom large against the sky and the horizon line is near the bottom of the picture.

A conventional composition places the horizon line somewhere near a third or two-thirds of the way down the picture, but you may decide otherwise depending on your aims. You also need to think about how the sky relates to the rest of the image: is it the main subject or an adjunct to something else? This will help you decide where to put the horizon line.

Breezy sky ▼

This pastel drawing has a lovely sense of space and movement. The fluffy qualities of the cirrus clouds have been captured using blended soft pastels. Note small areas of blue breaking through the edges, giving a more natural outline. This view is a good illustration of the shadows of low clouds on a landscape, a device that helps to unify the land and sky within a painting, as well as being an interesting subject in itself. The tonal contrast is strongest near the centre of the picture, leading our eye toward the silhouetted trees and blueish hillsides beyond.

Glowing sunset ▲

A gradated pale blue wash provided the foundation for this sunset in watercolour. The pale orange strip of light on the horizon takes on an added brilliance against the dark landscape and the deep grey clouds above.

Big sky ▶

In this oil painting (*The Ploughed Edge* by Timothy Easton), the sky occupies just over two-thirds of the picture space and is crucial in creating a feeling of space and openness. The billowing clouds give a sense of movement and contrast well with the calm, still landscape below. Note how the artist has created a sense of distance through the converging perspective lines of the ploughed furrows and the use of paler, slightly cooler colours in the distance, along the horizon line.

▶

Practice exercise: **Simple sunset using a variegated wash**

One of the best things about learning to paint is that it does not take long before you are able to produce something that will look great hanging on your wall. For any budding landscape painter, a simple skyscape is a good, confidence-building first project. The technique used in this exercise is a variegated wash; this demonstration was done using watercolour, but the same method can be used with acrylics. This exercise works 'on the third' and is good practice for using aerial perspective, so it puts two important 'basics' into practice immediately. It is an excellent introduction to the study of light and movement in water, as well as light in the sky against the very dark buildings. The exercise also shows you how a silhouette can turn a simple variegated wash into an attractive landscape painting – relying on the eye to 'trick' the mind into seeing a landscape rather than actually putting in all the detail.

Some artists find it easier to dampen the paper first, using either sponge or a mop brush dipped in clean water. This allows the colours to blend and merge, without any risk of hard lines appearing between one colour and the next, because paint spreads more evenly on damp paper. When it is properly done, the transition from one colour to another in a variegated wash should be almost imperceptible.

You may need to allow the paper to dry slightly before you apply any paint. This is something that you will learn with practice. Equally, if you prefer, you can work on dry paper.

Make your initial pencil marks as light as possible so that they do not show through and spoil the end effect. If you are wetting the paper, do this after you have made your pencil marks. You will probably need to tape the paper firmly on to your table or easel with masking tape to prevent it from buckling. Apply the water sparingly with long smooth strokes of a clean, flat brush for very even coverage.

The scene

Striking colours, shimmering reflections and a bold silhouette – this picture has all the ingredients for a sunset with impact. Working quickly on dampened paper injects a lively quality into the work that complements the transience of the light and the movement of the water. The horizontal ripples in the water add a sense of depth and calm to the composition. Learning the effects of light is essential – a scene such as this provides excellent practice in observing where light catches and how you can use reflection.

Materials
- 2B pencil
- 140lb (300gsm) rough watercolour paper, pre-stretched
- Watercolour paints: ultramarine blue, cadmium orange, cadmium red, ultramarine violet, alizarin crimson, sepia
- Brushes: large round, small round

Damp versus dry paper

Variegated wash on damp paper
In the finished wash, the colours merge together almost imperceptibly, with no obvious division between the two.

Variegated wash on dry paper
Here, the division between the two colours is slightly more obvious. The pink and yellow are bolder.

1 Using a 2B pencil, lightly sketch the outline of the silhouetted trees on the skyline. Using a large round brush, dampen the paper with clean water. Mix a wash of ultramarine blue and, again using the large round brush, lay a gradated wash over the top half of the paper, adding more water with each brushstroke so that the blue colour pales to almost nothing just above the horizon.

2 Mix an orangey red from cadmium orange and cadmium red. While the paper is still damp lay this colour over the lower half of the paper, allowing it to merge wet into wet into the very pale blue around the horizon line. Leave to dry. Dampen the paper again very slightly. Brush a broad stroke of the same orangey red mix across the middle of the painting (this will form the basis of the silhouetted land area) and dot it into the sky. Leave to dry.

3 Mix a warm purple from ultramarine violet and a little alizarin crimson. Using a large round brush, brush this mixture on to the sky to represent the dark cloud shapes. Add a little more pigment to the mixture to make a darker tone and paint the outline of the silhouetted trees. Using the same mixture, paint a few broken brushstrokes on the water for the dark reflections of both the trees and the land area.

4 Mix a dark violet from ultramarine violet and sepia and darken the silhouetted area, adding a few fine vertical lines for the boat masts that stick up into the sky.

The finished painting
A two-colour variegated wash forms the basis of this colourful sunset, while a bold silhouette gives the viewer a strong shape on which to focus. Although the painting itself is very simple, the choice of rich colours and the careful placing of both the silhouetted land form and the reflections in the water combine to make an atmospheric little study.

The initial blue wash merges almost imperceptibly with the rich, warm colours of the sunset.

The white of the paper shows through in places – a simple but effective way of implying water sparkling in the last rays of the setting sun.

Still water

The smooth quietness of still water often gives tranquillity to a scene. We are all drawn to it visually, and it is a popular artists' subject. Still water takes its colour from surrounding objects, so any discussion of how to draw or paint it is primarily about reflections.

You need to be aware of three planes – the objects above the water, the reflections on the water's surface, and what can be seen beneath the surface. The interplay of these three worlds can be a fascinating subject in itself.

The direction of light on an object affects its reflection. For example, a sunlit tree produces a brightly coloured, sharp reflection on the surface of the water, whereas a tree silhouetted against the light produces a dark reflection, through which the third plane – the reeds or silt or whatever is beneath the water – can be seen clearly.

When water is completely still, the reflection is almost a mirror image of the objects above it. However it is very rare that there is no movement at all. Consequently, reflections are more often portrayed as a slightly less substantial version of the real world. This can be achieved by using less detail and tonal contrast to paint the reflected image; simply painting a paler version often looks amateurish. One or two horizontal lines of ripples or leaves floating on the surface of the water may be enough to convey its surface. Be careful to keep lines of ripples parallel to one another, and to the edge of the paper or canvas, or you may end up with a curved-looking surface to your pond.

It is crucial to keep reflections directly under the shape above the water. A tree trunk, for example, should mirror exactly the same angle in its reflection.

A reflection coming toward you over the horizontal plane of the water will appear longer than the real object. If the reflection is broken by ripples, they will elongate it, mainly vertically, toward the viewer.

Your viewpoint affects reflections. Only if your viewpoint is down at water level will you see the same above the water as on the surface.

Gently rippling water ◀
Wet-into-wet washes lay the foundation and general shape of these riverside trees. Wet-on-dry washes define the shapes further, while linear brush and coloured pencil work hint at a slight breeze rippling the almost still surface. The size of the ripples increasing as they come toward us is loosely but effectively described. Note that the reflections have less textural detail than the willows themselves, but retain the same strength of colour. Because of the artist's viewpoint we glimpse sky between the reflected willows, rather than the distant trees in the background.

Practice exercise: **Reflection in charcoal**

It's important to establish the surface of the water in a subject like this. Here, small ripples in the water help to create a sense of movement, which prevents the image from looking flat and bland.

The scene
Bare, skeletal trees and their reflections seemed to suit a treatment that is graphic and monochromatic – hence the choice of charcoal for this exercise. Note how some of the reflections of the branches are broken up by tiny ripples in the water.

Materials
• *Good-quality drawing paper*
• *HB pencil*
• *Charcoal*
• *Dark grey Conté stick*
• *Kneaded eraser*

1 Carefully map out the scene, using an HB pencil. Using a dark grey Conté, draw in the branches and their reflections. Put in faint zigzag marks for the ripples. Use the Conté for the mid to dark tones in the grass and along the water's edge.

2 Use the side of the charcoal to put in the dark tones in the water. These negatives spaces help to define the shapes of the reflected branches. With a kneaded eraser, wipe out the highlight areas in the water, to show how the light catches the ripples.

3 Use the side of the charcoal to block in the hillside behind the trees and the dark reflections near the bank. Continue putting in the branches and their reflections in charcoal. Do not put in every single branch, otherwise the drawing may lose spontaneity.

4 Using the tip of the charcoal stick, make spiky lines for the thinnest branches. Check that you have put in all the reflections correctly – have you drawn in the same number of reflected fence posts as there are posts on the land, for example?

The finished drawing

In this monochrome study, the artist has taken great care to relate the reflections to the objects; careful measuring of the different elements in relation to one another has paid off. Note, too, how the water is darker than the sky: it takes its tone from the objects that are reflected in it – the bank and the trees. Note the variety of textural marks that can be achieved with charcoal.

Short, spiky marks describe the thinnest branches.

More flowing, linear marks are used for the bigger branches and trunks.

Bold 'scribbles' suggest the darkest tones under the grasses that grow along the water's edge.

In charcoal, particularly for small highlights, it is often easier to block in large areas and wipe out the highlights than to leave the white of the paper to stand for the brightest areas.

Moving water

Moving water is a challenge for the artist: how can one capture the energy of a force that is constantly changing? Photographs of water can look rather static – so if you use them for reference, try to take a series over the course of a few minutes.

When looking at waves on the beach, spend some time absorbing the scene and you might be able to detect a rhythm within the movement. Note how high the waves get, where they break on the shoreline, whether they unfurl in the same manner each time. Perhaps they crash attractively over a particular rock only once every few waves; make a few more marks in your sketchpad whenever that happens.

Aerial perspective is important in seascapes to create depth and distance. Think also about light on sand, pebbles and rocks, and how much detail is needed to enhance the composition.

The same principle applies when describing a cascading waterfall, rushing stream or gently flowing river. Look for the larger shapes that are created and use marks that best express their movement. The force of the waterfall might suggest an energetic approach with palette knife and oils. The stream might best be captured in loose pen and ink overlaid with washes.

Waterfall ▶
In this watercolour sketch, white body colour was applied using a mixture of fluid wash and dry brush to capture the light catching on the falling water as it tumbles over rocks and boulders. The boulders were painted using a texture paste to give them added form.

Rocks and branches interrupting the flow of water can help suggest the force of the flow.

If you are working in watercolour, plan whether you need to leave white areas for surf or foam. Masking fluid can be spattered over the white paper to suggest spray, which may give a more effective result than using opaque gouache or Chinese white over your coloured washes. Resists of candlewax or oil pastel under watercolour can be an appealing way of conveying colours within the water or sunlight sparkling on the surface.

Remember that water gains its colour by reflecting its surroundings. A stream might look peaty-brown until it splashes over rocks, when it will reflect the sky. Cresting waves sometimes look green when seen against the light, blending back to a dark turquoise against the deeper water. Purples, yellows and greys may also find their way into water.

Practice exercise: **Crashing waves in acrylics**

In this demonstration acrylic paints are mixed with acrylic gloss medium, which increases the transparency of the paint and allows you to build up several thin glazes relatively quickly. When two colours are glazed over one another, the integrity of both remains intact – a perfect method for conveying the many different blues and greens that can be seen in the sea. Gloss medium also enhances the depth of colour. The white foam of the waves is created by applying the paint thickly, using a painting knife. When you are painting a scene such as this, describe one area in a spontaneous manner and keep the rest simple. This will often give more impact than a meticulous approach.

Materials
• *Watercolour board*
• *HB pencil*
• *Acrylic paints: phthalocyanine blue, brilliant green, cadmium yellow, alizarin crimson, titanium white*
• *Acrylic gloss medium*
• *Selection of round brushes in different sizes*
• *Small painting knife*

The scene
Waves break around the foreground rocks in foamy spurts of white, revealing the energy and force of the sea, while in the water itself can be seen myriad shades of blue and green. Note the way that these different tones within the water – dark blues and green on one side of the waves, lighter ones on the side that catches the light – give the sea dynamic form and show the movement and energy of the waves as they crash on the rocks.

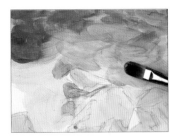

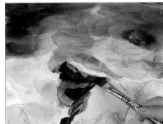

1 Lightly sketch the shape of the rocks in HB pencil, putting in just enough detail to give yourself a guide to the different planes. Use a large round brush and short, slightly curved brushstrokes to imply the swirling waves. Apply dilute phthalocyanine blue over the sea, with a little brilliant green near the rocks, where the water is shallow. Leave to dry (acrylic paint dries quickly, especially when used thinly like this). Mix a pale brown from cadmium yellow and alizarin crimson and wash it over the rocks. Mix in some acrylic gloss medium and brush more phthalo blue over the darker parts of the sea to build up the intensity of colour.

2 Darken the sea with more phthalo blue and gloss medium, adding a greener mix of phthalo blue and brilliant green just above the rocks. Mix a dark violet from phthalo blue and alizarin crimson and, using a smaller brush, paint in the shaded sides of the foreground rocks.

3 Continue building up the form on the rocks, using various browns (mixed from cadmium yellow, alizarin crimson and a little phthalo blue) and purply greys as appropriate, mixing the paints with gloss medium as before. Brush phthalo blue over the sea at the base of the rocks to build up the density of colour.

The finished painting

With bold, confident strokes that echo the shape and direction of the waves, the artist has created a colourful sketch that captures the energy of the waves and the colours of the sea very effectively. The thicker, impasto work on the foam of the sea and on the sculptural quality of the marks on the rocks contrast well with the flatter glazes of colour on the water.

4 Using a small palette knife and a thick mix of titanium white, apply the white 'foam' of the sea. Aim for a combination of broad, flat strokes made using the flat of the knife, and short flecks and linear marks made using the tip. Mix some white with the gloss medium to keep it translucent, so that the underlying sea colour still shows through – in the slightly calmer water to the right of the rocks, for example.

Using a small round brush and thicker versions of the brown- and purple-based mixes used before, continue building up the form on the rocks and add any linear detailing that you feel is necessary.

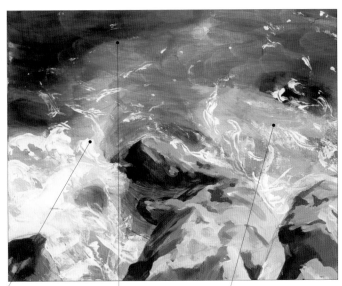

The marks used for the foam range from thick strokes made with the side of the painting knife to lines made using the tip.

Varying the tones conveys the swell of the waves – dark blue farthest from the light, lighter blue on the side that catches the light.

With thin, transparent glazes, the integrity of each colour remains intact: both green and blue are clearly discernible.

Rain and mist

Unlike a sunny scene, where contrasts are strong and colours vibrant, in rain the scene is much more low-key. In overcast conditions the light is flat and muted, creating few sharp shadows. Colours are soft and subtle, with lots of grey tones, and may tend to merge together. The edges of shapes become blurred and ill defined. Rainy landscapes may also be quite dramatic.

Most painters portray rain by the general visual effect that it has on a scene. Perhaps the most obvious point to note is that many surfaces become reflective when wet. What light there is will be reflected back, creating unusual juxtapositions and a play of lights and darks. Puddles and other flat surfaces have an almost mirror-like quality, although the lack of light in the sky usually means that reflections are dark.

One of the most dramatic, if fleeting, visual effects is when a break in the clouds lights up part of the scene, resulting, for example, in sunlit foliage against heavy dark rain-clouds.

If your view includes figures, adding them huddling under umbrellas or hurrying from a downpour can give an element of charm.

Misty views have always attracted artists, lending as they do a romantic, mysterious atmosphere. Misty weather shares some of the visual characteristics of rain, without the reflective surfaces. Your approach will be influenced by the nature of the mist or fog: is it of a uniform thickness and likely to remain where it is, or is it broken and shifting around, in which case you might make notes in the same way you would with moving cloud formations. If it is static and uniform, it is simpler to portray.

Whether you are looking at an enclosed space such as a garden or out over a whole valley, the principles will be the same. Objects very close to you will appear normal, but as they become more distant, the water vapour in the air will flatten out the appearance of colours, texture and detail to the extent that they lose their three-dimensionality. Portraying this is a case of managing the decrease in tonal contrasts as shapes recede into the distance. If the mist is more broken, the challenge is to capture the effect of objects looming in and out of view, creating 'lost and found' edges, which can be immensely atmospheric and visually appealing.

Shanghai downpour ▲
The colours of the umbrella are the focus of this simple composition of an alleyway in Shanghai, China. They are framed by the buildings' muted colours, typical of rainy scenes. Note the shiny surface of the pathway and the dry brushwork that gives it texture. Leaving patches of white paper showing through helps to lighten the scene.

Practice exercise: **Misty scene in acrylics**

The challenge here is to control the decrease in tonal contrast as the shapes recede into the distance. Note how the colours become muted with distance; textural detail, too, is less evident.

Materials
- *Watercolour board*
- *Acrylic paints: yellow ochre, burnt umber, ultramarine blue, alizarin crimson, yellow-green, cadmium yellow, titanium white, turquoise*
- *Brushes: Selection of round and flat brushes in different sizes*

The scene ▶
Although this photo was taken as a portrait-format shot, the artist decided to make a landscape-format painting. Note how the sweeping curve of the path leads our eye to the bridge.

1 Establish the main shapes and structure. Apply a dilute wash of yellow ochre over the foreground path, dropping in a little burnt umber at the edges. Mix a pale purple from ultramarine and alizarin crimson and map out the shape of the bridge. Use the same colour for the left bank and any darker patches in the water. Leave space for the patches of sky.

2 Add more ultramarine to the purple mix, and darken the top of the bridge. Use the same colour for the brick edge of the towpath. Apply a very dilute wash of ultramarine over the foliage area on the right. Loosely 'draw' the trunks in burnt umber and a mix of burnt umber and yellow ochre. Using a range of greens (yellow-green on its own, mixes of ultramarine plus yellow-green and ultramarine plus cadmium yellow) begin to dot in some of the greens of the foliage, splaying out the bristles of the brush to create generalized shapes.

3 Use the same purple mix as before to put in the lines of the trunks on the left bank, in front of the bridge; these trunks are much less distinct in tone than those in the foreground. Put in the sharp line of the canal edge in the same colour. Dot in some greens, using paler, more muted versions of the foreground foliage colours.

> **Tip**: It is generally better to mix greens than to rely on palette greens, as it gives you more control over the tones.

4 Mix a very pale, thin blue from turquoise and titanium white, then paint in the sky above the bridge and the light patches of water. Darken the underside of the bridge by glazing burnt umber over the previous colour. Dot in some greens for the fallen leaves in the foreground. Using a mix of burnt umber and purple, dot in the darker tones in the foreground towpath. If the tree trunks near the bridge are merging into the stonework, as here, strengthen them a little so that they come forward and the spatial relationships of the different elements become clearer.

The finished painting
This sketch captures the effects of mist well. All the detail is concentrated in the foreground, with the background being painted as indistinct shapes.

5 Having more texture and detailing in the foreground helps to create an impression of distance, so continue building up the foreground, using the same mixes as before. Brush a very pale, dilute turquoise and white mix over the misted area to knock it back a little and make it appear less distinct. Vary the direction of your brushstrokes to convey the way the leaves are scattered over the ground and experiment with different techniques, such as spattering and stippling, to create texture.

The diagonal lines of the brick towpath edging draw the viewer's eye deeper into the scene.

Mist obscures the detail of distant objects; this area is painted a cool, watery blue.

Gallery

It is always interesting to see how other artists have approached the technical and creative challenges of portraying skies and water. This gallery section contains drawings and paintings by contemporary professional artists working in a range of media and styles, from loose, impressionistic studies in watercolour to bold, vigorous pastels and finely detailed oils. Study them carefully and see what lessons you can apply to your own work.

Unblended colour ▶
Pastel need not be a soft and delicate medium; it is extremely versatile and responsive to the artist's visual interests and ways of working. In *Swans on the Thames*, Pip Carpenter has created energetic and exciting effects in the picture by laying heavy strokes of unblended colour, using the tip of the pastel stick.

Human interest ▲

You can often give additional interest to a landscape, or stress a centre of interest, by including one or two figures. In Ronald Jesty's *A Wild Day*, the men shielding their heads against the spray from the breaking wave and the woman pointing her hand introduce a narrative, and both these and the surrounding dark rocks provide contrasts of tone which draw attention to the picture's focal point.

Tinted ground ▶

Using a tinted ground is a standard oil-painting practice that is just as applicable to acrylics. Here, the artist used a deep blue ground; the subsequent painting was done quite thinly, so that it modifies the blue without completely obscuring it and it contributes to the overall colour temperature. Note that the horizon line is placed in the centre of the image – something one is generally advised not to do, as it can make an image seem very static, but here it creates a mood of calm.

Sparkling sunlight ◀

8 a.m., Venice Lagoon, made by Ian Sidaway as the early-morning light highlighted the ripples on the water, uses carefully applied wet-on-dry washes. The dappled sunlight on the water surface was created by applying masking fluid prior to making any washes. Colours were kept crisp and clean by using no more than three overlapping washes. Note how the ripples conform to the laws of perspective by getting smaller as they get closer to the horizon.

▶

Flat wash for sky ▲
In David Curtis's study
Sailing Boats, the clear, pale
sky behind the boats is
achieved with a flat wash of
watercolour. This has the
effect of allowing the fine
rigging on the boats to
stand out from the
background.

Light and shadow ◄
Timothy Easton is a master
at capturing the subtle
effects of light in oils. In this
delightful painting entitled
Down to the Sea, the
highlights in the water are
carefully touched in with
white and white tinged with
yellow, while the shadows
on the sand are rendered in
blues and blue-greys. The
diagonal line that runs
through the painting from
top left to bottom right
gives an otherwise tranquil
scene a strong dynamic.

Soft, curving brushstrokes ▲

Paul Dyson's *Floating Leaf* is a simple little scene that many landscape artists might pass by in favour of a grander view. It is a study in contrasts – the softness of the water versus the solidity of the rocks; the vibrant colour of the leaf versus muted tones in the water. The brushwork is controlled, with the brushstrokes in the water following the direction of the water flow to create lifelike ripples. Note how the main centre of interest – the leaf – is positioned slightly off centre and at an angle to add interest to the composition.

Crisp edges ▶

Ronald Jesty achieves his crisp effects and dense, glowing colours by working wet on dry, reserving highlights by painting carefully around them. You can see this effect on the background hills, the dark areas of rock and the water, where small patches of light-coloured paint have been left uncovered by later dark washes of colour. Note how his observation of the rocks beneath the water and the contrast of reflected light and shadow on the surface has helped produce a very realistic impression of a deep pool of clear water. Such elements of realism trick the eye into 'believing' a scene, even when other aspects are fairly abstract or stylized, such as the purple and red colours in the rock.

▶

Colours of water ▲

Many different colours and tones can be discerned in water, particularly in reflections. They must be carefully controlled if the image is to appear convincing. In Jackie Simmond's lovely pastel painting, *Waterlilies and Reeds*, the strongest contrasts of tone are those between the lilies and the foreground water – a deep, rich blue reflected from the sky.

Using paint runs ◄

Watercolours are usually painted with the board held flat or at a slight angle, but in *St-Laurent-de-Cerdans*, Karen Raney has worked with the board upright on an easel, causing the paint to run down the paper at the bottom of the picture. She has left the foreground otherwise undefined – the runs of paint hint at reflections in water.

Textural techniques ▶
This simple watercolour painting by
Albany Wiseman, *Beached Boat at Low
Tide*, is a study in texture, with masking
fluid and paint both being spattered
over the paper to create the shingle-
covered beach. The spattering is subtle
and does not detract from the boat, but
it captures the pebbly beach very well.

Extracting the essentials ▼
Crooked Tree Against the Dazzle, by
Timothy Easton, is, above all, a study of
light and shade; any other elements
have been so simplified that the
painting is almost abstract. Easton has
captured the effect of sunlight glancing
on the water through his short,
carefully blended strokes of white.
The strong diagonal that runs upward
through the painting gives it energy.

Quick sketches: Skies and clouds

The sky is such an integral part of most landscapes that any budding landscape artist would be well advised to spend time practising how to draw and paint it. Get into the habit of making quick sketches whenever you see an interesting sky. Landscape artists have always done this: the British artist John Constable (1776–1837) even described the practice in a letter to a friend as 'skying'. The light can change so quickly that a stunning skyscape can disappear within minutes – so the ability to work rapidly, even if it is just to make a reference sketch that you work on in more detail later, is invaluable.

Clouds almost always add visual interest and character to a sky, whether they be soft, fluffy white clouds in an azure-blue sky at the height of summer, broken cumulus clouds that allow shafts of light to break through and illuminate the landscape below, or heavy storm clouds that impart a brooding, sombre mood. Study the different types of clouds and the moods that they create.

The way that you treat skies and clouds, of course, depends on the medium in which you are working. With powdery mediums such as soft pastel or charcoal, you can blend the marks with your fingers or a torchon to create

smooth areas of tone suitable for cloud-free sections of sky; alternatively, you can allow the texture of the paper to show through in the clouds themselves. In pencil and in pen and ink, you can create the different tones through simple hatching and crosshatching. In watercolour and acrylic paint, delicate washes and glazes allow you to build up the colour and tones layer by layer.

The scene
The glowing colours, both in the sky itself and in the reflections in the gently rippling sea below, were what attracted the artist to this scene. The heavy clouds are lit from above by the setting sun, and it is the contrast between the top-lit sections and the dark underbellies that gives the thick clouds a sense of volume and mass.

5-minute sketch: charcoal pencil ◄
Here, the artist created a range of tones by varying the amount of pressure she exerted on the pencil, with soft, diagonal hatching for the mid-tones and heavier scribbles for the darkest parts of the cloud masses. The white of the paper has been left to stand for the very brightest highlights. The rough texture of the paper also contributes to the overall effect.

**5-minute sketch:
watercolour wash** ▶

By varying the dilution of the paint, you can create a wide range of tones. A light wash was initially applied for the mid tones, leaving the brightest areas untouched. For the darkest tones, a more concentrated mix of the paint was dropped in wet into wet. This creates layers of gradual of tone and soft edges.

**30-minute sketch:
soft pastels** ▼

This sketch is a real explosion of colour! The pastels were applied vigorously, with some marks finger-blended to create smooth patches of blue sky, and other marks being left to pick up the texture of the paper and create texture in the clouds.

Quick sketches: Leading the eye

A riverside setting has lots of potential for interesting landscape sketches. If the river runs swiftly, there will be splashes and swirling eddies as the water breaks around rocks and other objects. Gentle ripples create a different mood, slightly distorting any reflections. Occasionally, you come across a hidden pool in which the water appears to be completely still, where the reflections are sharp and crisp. Each requires a different approach, from dynamic, energetic marks for rapidly flowing water to a more measured, controlled approach for very still water and reflections.

Whatever the mood of the river, it is often a good idea to use it as a compositional device to lead the viewer's eye through the picture. Bear this in mind when you position yourself on the bank to take a reference photo or make a sketch. A view along a river, where you can see how it meanders its way through the landscape, is usually more satisfying in compositional terms than one looking straight across from one bank to the other as, in the latter case, the river will form a broad horizontal band that cuts the composition in two and blocks the viewer's eye from moving any farther through the scene.

When you are drawing water, always remember that it takes its colour from the surroundings – although the colour is generally more muted in the reflection. In a riverside setting the greens and browns of nearby trees may be reflected in the water; alternatively, there may be patches of sky that are so bright that you need apply virtually no colour whatsoever to the support.

The scene
Here, the river forms a gentle curve that leads our eye through the scene to the buildings on the horizon. The sky is very bright and bland, with no dramatic cloud formations to add interest to the scene, so the reflections of the trees along the bank provide a feature in what would otherwise be a completely empty area.

5-minute sketch: sepia water-soluble pencil ▲
Five minutes is plenty of time for you to work out a composition for a larger drawing. Make a quick thumbnail sketch, roughly outlining the shapes of the main elements (including the reflections).

10-minute sketch: sepia water-soluble pencil ▲
A tonal study will require a little more time. Here, the artist lightly brushed a little clean water over some of the pencil marks to blend them to a tonal wash, leaving the brightest areas untouched.

15-minute sketch: sepia water-soluble pencil ▶

In this sketch, more textural detail is evident. It is created by using the water-soluble pencil dry (on the grass on the near bank, for example) and on slightly damp paper, so that the marks spread a little (on the large tree on the far bank).

30-minute sketch: sepia water-soluble pencil ▼

In the longest sketch of the series, the scene is beginning to look more three-dimensional. Note how some elements, such as the large tree on the far bank and the grass in the foreground of the near bank, are given more textural marks, which helps to indicate that they are nearer the viewer and create a sense of recession in the scene.

Cloudscape in charcoal

Charcoal is a wonderful medium for drawing storm clouds, not least because of the intensity of tone that you can achieve with it.

Although clouds look random, your composition needs to be carefully planned. Start by selecting the area of sky that you feel is most dramatic, looking also at what is happening in the land or sea beneath as well as in the sky itself. Begin by establishing the general shape of the cloud mass, paying attention to the individual shapes that are contained within it.

If you find in the later stages that the light and mid tones are merging into the darks, do not be afraid to strengthen the darks still further so that the lighter marks stand out. Work on a heavy, good-quality drawing paper that can withstand quite rough treatment, so that there is no risk of the paper tearing, no matter how hard you scribble. A slightly rough paper is also a good choice, as the texture will show through in the finished drawing, adding another dimension to it.

Above all, do not be tempted to make your drawing too small. A subject like this, particularly in charcoal, demands bold, gestural drawing – and

that is much harder to achieve on a small scale. Give yourself space to work and use your whole arm, not just your fingertips, so that your drawing has a feeling of energy and spontaneity.

The scene

This scene of dark, brooding storm clouds over the sea virtually demands a monochrome treatment. Charcoal seemed the obvious choice, as it allows you to combine smooth, finger-blended passages with more vigorous applications of the pigment. The texture of the paper plays a part, too.

Materials

- *Good-quality drawing paper with slightly rough texture*
- *Charcoal: thin and thick sticks*
- *Kneaded eraser*

1 Using a thin stick of charcoal, put in the horizon line, the dark undersides of the swelling waves and the edges of the main cloud mass. Do not try to put in all the clouds in one go: begin by simply locating different sections of the main cloud mass, so that you have something to use as a guide when you begin to apply some tone to the image.

2 Using the side of a thick stick of charcoal, scribble in the darkest bits of the clouds to help create a sense of their volume. Note how the charcoal picks out some of the paper texture.

3 Continue blocking in the darkest patches, working vigorously and energetically so that the drawing remains quite loose and spontaneous. Blend some of the marks with your fingers to create smooth areas of tone.

4 Apply tone to the sea in the same way and then drag the side of the charcoal down the paper to create the streaks of falling rain. From this point onward you will begin to refine the drawing.

5 Using your fingertips in a swirling, circular motion that echoes the shapes of the clouds, blend the charcoal pigment on the surface of the paper to soften the marks. You can use your fingers to work the pigment.

Assessment time

Only the very brightest patches of the sky have been left untouched, but the clouds themselves still look rather flat and one-dimensional. There is no real sense of volume, nor are the tonal contrasts strong enough – particularly in the sea, where the initial dark marks for the undersides of the waves are now virtually indistinguishable from the rest of the water. Getting the tones right in a drawing like this is always a gradual process of assessment and adjustment, so do not expect to complete this process in one go. Take your time and assess the relative tones carefully and continually.

The sea is almost all a uniform mid-tone.

The sharp band of light along the horizon is not sufficiently well defined; the sky and sea almost merge together.

The brightest patches of sky contain subtle tonal differences: at present, this area is too bright overall.

6 Using the tip of a thin charcoal stick, put in the dark shapes in the water – the undersides of the waves. Use short, scribbly marks that follow the direction in which the waves are flowing.

7 Go over the darkest bits of the clouds again, blending the marks with your fingertips as before to create more rounded, three-dimensional forms. Using the side of a thin stick, reinforce the lines of falling rain at the base of the clouds. You may need to darken the clouds more than you expect, so that the mid tones of the falling rain stand out.

8 Use the sharp edge of a kneaded eraser to wipe out pigment along the horizon line and create the band of light that separates the sea from the sky. Decide where you want to apply a little very pale tone to the very brightest patches of clouds, then dip your fingers in charcoal dust and lightly brush the pigment on to these areas.

9 Using a kneaded or a plastic eraser, carefully wipe off pigment in both the sky and the sea to create more mid tones. If you want to create fine lines to suggest the ripples in the water, use the sharp edge of the eraser, stroking it over the paper in the same way that you would make fine hatching lines with a pencil.

Tip: Scribble some charcoal on to a piece of scrap paper, then gently rub your finger over the scribbles to transfer some of the powdery pigment to them.

Tip: Re-assess the tones continually as you go: you may find that you need to darken some areas still further in order for the highlights to really stand out.

The finished drawing

This is a deceptively simple-looking drawing, but the tones have been carefully assessed and adjusted throughout to capture the dark, oppressive mood of the scene. Note the variety of the charcoal marks: the side of the charcoal has been dragged down the paper to create the bands of falling rain, the tip has been used to create fine, scribbly lines to denote the edges of the clouds, and the pigment has been finger-blended to create patches of soft tone. The white of the paper stands for the very lightest areas and tiny highlights have been created by wiping off pigment with an eraser.

In the sea, the dark undersides of the waves contrast with the tiny, bright patches of light reflected from the sky.

Note the different kinds of mark making – heavy, finger-blended scribbles for the darkest patches, vertical streaks for the falling rain, and a bright highlight created by wiping off pigment with an eraser.

Note the patches of pale tone, even in the very brightest parts of the clouds. These can be created by picking up a little pigment on your fingertips and very lightly stroking it on to the paper.

Stormy sky in acrylics

Although the small strip of land and the high-rise buildings at the base of this picture provide an essential calm, static point on which the viewer's eye can rest, the main interest undoubtedly lies in the dramatic and bleak, stormy sky, with its dark, billowing clouds and the warm glow of the setting sun shining through them.

When you.are painting clouds, remember that you need to make them look like solid, three-dimensional forms, not mere wisps drifting across the sky – you know they are clouds of

vapour but they look like solid objects. You should also follow the rules of perspective and make clouds that are far away smaller than those that are directly overhead.

For this project use acrylic paint thinly, flooding the paper with generous washes of dilute colour. The aim is to create an impressionistic scene, with no hard edges to the clouds and very little detail in the buildings. Let the paint do as much of the work for you as possible, such as puddling at the base of damp areas to form darker tones at the base of the clouds.

Materials
• *Watercolour board*
• *Acrylic paints: cerulean blue, alizarin crimson, burnt sienna, ultramarine blue, lemon yellow, titanium white*
• *Brushes: large round, medium flat*
• *Household plant sprayer*
• *Flow improver*
• *Absorbent paper towel*

The scene
The warm glow of an evening sunset contrasts dramatically with the glowering purple of the storm clouds in this scene. Note the complementary colours – purple and yellow – which almost always work well together. Although the silhouetted buildings along the skyline occupy only a small part of the picture area, they are critical in giving a sense of scale to the image.

1 Using a household plant sprayer, spray clean water on to the board over the areas that you want to remain predominantly blue. (You could brush on water – but the spray gives a more random, less controlled coverage.)

2 Mix a few drops of flow improver into cerulean blue paint. Using a large round brush, drop the paint into the areas that you dampened in Step 1; it will spread and blur to give a soft spread of colour.

3 Scrunch up a piece of clean tissue or paper towel in your hand and carefully dab it on to the blue paint to soften the edges.

Tip: Keep turning the paper towel around in your hand so that you do not accidentally dab paint back on to an area from which you have just removed it.

4 Mix a warm purplish blue from cerulean blue and alizarin crimson and brush it over the land area at the base of the image with the large round brush. Mix a neutral purplish grey from burnt sienna and ultramarine blue. Spray clean water over the left-hand side of the painting and quickly drop in the neutral colour, allowing the paint to pool at the base of the damp area, as storm clouds are darker at their base.

5 Soften the edges of the clouds by dabbing them with a paper towel, as in Step 3. While the paint is still damp, dot in more of the dark mixture in the top right of the painting. The paint will spread wet into wet to form soft-edged patches of colour.

6 Using a watery version of the neutral purplish-grey mixture from Step 4, brush in a dark line above the purplish base, adding more burnt sienna nearer the horizon to warm up the tones. Allow the paint to dry. Mix a warm purple from burnt sienna and ultramarine blue and, using a medium flat brush, make broad, rectangular-shaped strokes for the high-rise buildings along the horizon line, varying the tones so that the nearer buildings are slightly darker than those that are farther away. Use strokes of different thicknesses to create a natural-looking variation in the shapes and sizes of the buildings.

Assessment time
You have now established the basic framework of the image and the main areas of colour – the blue of the open patches of sky, the dark storm clouds that dominate the scene, and the thin sliver of land with its high-rise buildings at the base. However, for the painting to look convincing, the clouds should be made more three-dimensional.

The clouds are soft-edged but do not appear to have volume.

Varying the tones of the buildings helps to create a sense of recession.

▶

7 Mix a pale but warm, yellowy orange from lemon yellow, titanium white and a little burnt sienna. Brush this mixture into the breaks between the clouds, making horizontal brushstrokes that echo the direction in which the clouds are being blown in order to create a sense of movement in the sky. This adds warmth to the horizon and makes the dark storm clouds stand out all the more dramatically.

8 Continue adding this warm, yellowy orange, adding more burnt sienna to the mixture as you get nearer the horizon; the sun is sinking, so the colours are warmer nearer the horizon. Mix an opaque blue from cerulean blue and titanium white, and brush this mixture over the top of the sky, smudging the paint with your thumb to soften the edges and get rid of any obvious brushstrokes.

9 Dip a small piece of paper towel into the warm purple mixture that you used in Step 6 and squeeze out any excess moisture. Lightly stroke the paper towel over the yellow area just above the horizon to create streaks of storm cloud.

Tip: You could apply the paint with a rag or a sponge instead of a piece of paper towel. All these tools create a more random, spontaneous-looking effect than a brush and are very appropriate for a natural scene such as this.

10 Dab light opaque blue into the very dark area at the top of the picture, using your fingertips. Mix a purple from cerulean blue and burnt sienna and swirl it around the light area in the centre of the paper to darken it and give the clouds more of a feeling of depth. Mix a pale, warm yellow from burnt sienna, lemon yellow and titanium white and stroke on shafts of light coming down from the clouds with your fingertips. Using a flat brush, block in the shapes of the nearest buildings on the skyline; using warmer, darker tones in this area will make these buildings look closer to the viewer.

The finished painting

This is a convincing representation of a stormy sky at dusk. The colours are allowed to spread on damp paper and pool naturally, creating soft-edged shapes that are darker at their base and thus appear to have volume. Although the colour palette is limited and based mainly around the complementary colours of purple and yellow, the clever use of different tones of purple in the buildings at the base of the image creates a sense of recession.

The silhouettes of the buildings along the skyline are painted as simple rectangles of colour, exploiting the natural shape of the flat brush.

Purple and yellow are complementary colours and almost always work well together. Here, they create a warm-toned yet dramatic-looking composition.

There are no harsh-edged colours in the sky – dabbing the wet paint with a paper towel helps to remove any potentially distracting brushmarks.

Sunset in oils

This sunset was painted *alla prima* –
that is, in one sitting. This is in stark
contrast to the traditional method of oil
painting, in which the paint is built up in
successive layers, with each layer being
allowed to dry (a process that may take
many days) before the next is applied.
In *alla prima* oil painting, the paints are
applied in a single layer, often thickly.

One of the drawbacks of painting a
sunset – or any fleeting effect of light –
in the field is that the colours change
incredibly quickly. By the time you have
mixed the colour that you see in front
of your eyes, it may already be
disappearing from the sky. To get
around this problem, mix your colours in
advance and try to ensure that you have
a separate clean brush for each one; this
saves time and ensures that your colours
stay fresh. Another option, of course, is
to work from photographs.

It is also a good idea to have two
whites on your palette – one to mix
with warm tones and one to mix with
cool – as this makes it easier to keep the
warm and cool colours clean.

No matter how dramatic the sunset,
it is generally best to include something
other than the sky, simply to set the
scene in context. Here, the palm trees in
the foreground, with their beautifully
curving branches, provide a foil for the
sky behind. The gently rippling sea, too,
adds visual interest and allows you to
explore the effect of light reflected in
moving water.

Note, however, that the trees are not
solid black silhouettes. It is important to
get some variation in tone even in areas
that appear solid, otherwise everything
will look very flat and one-dimensional.
Here, they are painted in various dark,
purply-brown mixes.

The artist began this painting by
toning the canvas with warm pinks,
violets, reds and oranges. The exact
colours are not too important, as they
will probably not show through in the
finished work, but try to ensure they
bear some relation to the final colours –
so think about the colour temperature
and use warm or cool colours as
appropriate.

Materials

- *Primed canvas*
- *Oil paints: violet grey, permanent
  rose, cadmium scarlet, cadmium
  yellow orange, lemon yellow, titanium
  white, Mars violet deep, ultramarine
  blue, cadmium yellow deep,
  cobalt blue.*
- *Brushes: selection of filberts in
  different sizes*
- *Turpentine/white spirit (paint thinner)*
- *Old rag or absorbent paper towel*

The scene

It was, of course, the wonderfully
vibrant colours of the sky that first
attracted the artist's attention, but even
the most dramatic sunset requires some
kind of foreground interest in order to
give it a context. Here, the artist
included the two palm trees. The
shapes form a bold shape at the base
of the image, while the many fronds
break up the silhouette and provide
texture and additional visual interest.

3 Scumble cadmium scarlet, and a mix of cadmium scarlet and white, over the sky, varying the mixes as you see fit. Brush the same colour around the yellow of the sun to define its shape. Mix a vivid orange from cadmium yellow deep and cadmium scarlet and scumble it over the top of the sky, allowing some of the underlying permanent rose applied in Step 1 to show through.

4 Lightly mark out the main lines of the smaller palm tree, as in Step 2, using the very tip of a fine brush. Look at the reflection of the sun in the sea and put in some of the horizontal ripples, using the orange mixture from Step 3 and a mix of lemon yellow and white. You may find that half-closing your eyes makes it easier to see where different colours occur.

5 Mix a deep violet from permanent rose and violet grey and add some of it to the warm dark blue already on your palette. Hold your brush almost vertically, as you would when practising calligraphy, and put in some of the main fronds on the palm trees. To simulate the ripples on the water, dab on some deep violet, using short strokes and an almost dry brush, then repeat with the orange mix from Step 3. The colours blend optically on the canvas, helping to capture the interplay of many different colours as the light shifts.

6 Mix a dark, warm tone from Mars violet deep and ultramarine blue. Using a fine, almost dry, brush, put in more of the palm tree fronds, varying the amount of pressure you apply to create different marks and splaying out the bristles of the brush with your fingertips to create a fan shape reminiscent of the palm fronds. Brush the orange mix over the sea, using short, horizontal brushstrokes as before, then apply the same colour over the permanent rose that lies behind the palm tree.

▶

Assessment time

Putting in the yellow of the sun and its reflection in the sea in the early stages has paid dividends, as the light, bright colour (which was applied very thinly) has a lovely luminosity. Both the sky and the sea lack the intensity of colour that they need and, although we have the beginnings of some broken colour in the ripples on the water, this needs to be taken much further. The shape of the palm trees has been drawn in, but they do not stand out enough against the background; they need to be darkened and more detail added.

Too much of the sky colour shows through behind the palm trees.

The sky needs to be more intense in colour, with a thicker coverage of paint.

The sea looks flat. More short, horizontal brushstrokes of colour are needed here to create the ripples in the water.

7 Apply more of the orange mix behind the palm tree, to cover up most of the initial wash of permanent rose. Using the same dark mixes as before, work on the palm trees. For the fronds, hold the brush almost vertically, about halfway along the shaft, and make a series of short dashes. For the branches, pull the brush over the canvas in sweeping, curving lines.

8 Add cobalt blue to the dark mix to cool it down and continue touching in the dark fronds of both trees. Cut in behind the fronds with the orange mix where necessary, and apply a thicker mix of orange, violet and yellow to the sea, using short horizontal brushstrokes, as before, to strengthen the intensity of the colours reflected in the water.

9 Stand back from your painting and assess the intensity of colour overall. Scumble the orange mix over the sky, allowing some of the earlier colours to show through in parts – particularly on the right-hand side, which is less orange and contains slightly darker, cooler tones than the area to the left of the sun. Skies are rarely, if ever, a flat, uniform colour, and allowing earlier colours to show through adds to the painting's liveliness.

The finished painting

This is a vibrant, colourful painting of a tropical sunset. Note how the horizon line is positioned above the centre of the painting: had it run right across the middle, the image would have had a much more static feel. The colours in the sea have been carefully observed and range from bright, warm yellows and oranges to darker, cooler violets, all of which helps to give the ripples in the water some form. The dark palm trees anchor the painting and provide strong shapes on which the eye can rest, while allowing some of the initial permanent rose wash to show through behind the palms and painting the trees in warm, dark purples rather than solid blacks has enhanced the impression of backlighting.

The thin wash of yellow used for the sun shines through subsequent glazes and gives the painting a lovely luminosity.

Dashes of broken colour capture the mosaic of reflections of the sun in the rippling sea beautifully.

Note the variety of brushstrokes used to paint the thick branches and delicate fronds of the palm trees.

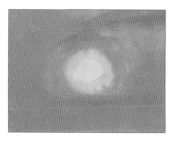

Rainbow in acrylics

A rainbow is a spectrum of light that appears in the sky as a multi-coloured arc when the sun shines on droplets of moisture in the earth's atmosphere. But such a prosaic description does not capture the beauty of the spectacle – nor is it easy to capture it in paint.

One of the most important things to remember is not to make the rainbow too strong to begin with, otherwise it will completely dominate the painting. Start pale and build up the intensity of colour with subsequent layers – and alternate between the rainbow and the rest of the painting, so that you keep the whole painting moving along at the same pace and can continually assess each part in relation to the whole. Although we tend to think of a rainbow as having seven distinct colours – red, orange, yellow, green, blue, indigo and violet – it is, in fact, a spectrum, with no clear line between one colour and its neighbour. 'Feather' your brushstrokes to create smooth transitions.

You also need to think about how you are going to paint the surrounding area of sky. When the sky is very gloomy and overcast there is a temptation to view it as a flat expanse of colour, with little or no tonal variation. Look carefully, however, and you will see that there are many variations in tone. In the demonstration shown here, the artist has deliberately exaggerated this, and even introduced stronger contrasts of colour than are in the original scene for dramatic effect. Even so, he has taken care to blend the colours so there are no obvious brush marks.

When it came to painting the town in the foreground, our artist's approach was to look at things as blocks of colour and tone, rather than attempting to paint individual buildings in detail. The town is some distance away from the artist's viewpoint, but the contrasts of lights and darks, and warm and cool tones, supply enough information for us to be able to interpret the scene. However you could, if you prefer, opt for a more photo-realistic approach and put in lots of fine detail; it all depends on your individual style.

Materials
- *Canvas primed with acrylic gesso*
- *Acrylic paints: Turquoise, white, ultramarine blue, lemon yellow, vermilion, purple red, carmine, emerald green, yellow ochre, brown oxide, cadmium yellow*
- *Brushes: Selection of filberts in different sizes*
- *Absorbent kitchen paper*

The scene
On a murky, rainy day, a dazzling rainbow in the sky illuminates a patch of land in the distance. The curve of the bay draws the eye through the scene, while the town gives interesting foreground detail. There is a large expanse of empty sky, but the rainbow and headland are positioned 'on the third' – a strong compositional device.

1 Using a large filbert brush, wet the canvas with clean water. Brush a very dilute mix of turquoise and white acrylic paint over the sea and sky area, leaving space where the rainbow is going to go. Remember that the colour of the sky is paler near the horizon. The paint will blur and spread over the damp canvas, leaving just a pale wash of colour that you can build up to the desired shade and intensity with subsequent layers.

2 Using the tip of the brush and ultramarine blue, lightly draw in the line of the hill in the foreground that sweeps down to the sea and the distant headland. Brush lemon yellow over the rainbow area.

Tip: If you think you have made the initial wash too strong, dab off paint with a piece of paper towel.

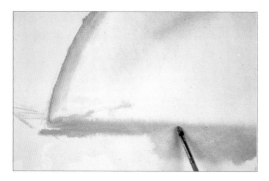

3 Using a fine brush, apply vermilion over the left-hand edge of the rainbow and purple red to the edge of the vermilion, allowing the colours to blend on the canvas so that there are no harsh-edged transitions. Brush turquoise over the sea in the foreground, and then touch in the sandy patches of land on the distant headland in yellow ochre.

Tip: Do not worry if the yellow ochre blurs into the turquoise, giving a greenish tinge, as you can apply stronger, thicker colour later on. The purpose of these early marks is primarily to help you locate where things are in the painting.

4 Using the tip of the brush and purple red, put in the darker patches of land on the distant headland. Keep the paint thin at this stage and use short, tentative marks to search out the shapes. Scrub the same colour into the sky, keeping the coverage quite thin and uneven so that some of the underlying turquoise shows through.

5 Apply a faint line of carmine to the left-hand edge of the rainbow, followed by ultramarine to create a dark purple, and use light, gentle brushstrokes to blend the colours. Mix a bright but relatively dark green from emerald green and yellow ochre and dot in the greens of the headland. Dot in some brown oxide for the darker tones in the town buildings.

Tip: Make tentative marks with the brush to establish lines and shapes.

6 Now apply colour to the sandy beach in the foreground, using a mix of lemon yellow, white and a little vermilion, then add a slightly redder version of the same mix to the part of the sea where the colours of the rainbow are reflected. Begin to define the jetties and the shaded sides of the buildings with yellow ochre, various tones of dark purple mixed from carmine and cobalt blue, and brown oxide. Add white to the purple red on your palette and lightly brush it over the sea, allowing it to blend wet into wet with the colours that are already there.

7 To define the headland, block in light and dark tones as appropriate with mixes of lemon white and yellow in varying proportions for the sunlit patches, vermilion and white for the mid tones and more greens and purples for the darkest areas. Add definition to the foreground buildings by dotting in browns and reds for the roofs, and add cobalt blue as the base colour for the foreground grass. Mix ultramarine blue, white and a little purple red and brush it over the pale part of the sky to the right of the rainbow, 'feathering' your marks to get rid of hard edges.

Assessment time
With the light and dark tones giving some indication of the way the land undulates, the distant headland is beginning to have some sense of form – even though this area of the scene is fairly misty and indistinct. The position of the jetties in the foreground has been put in and the buildings of the town are beginning to take shape. However, both the sea and the sky require several more layers of colour.

More detail is required in the foreground.

The sky needs to look darker and more brooding.

There is no sense of movement in the sea and the colours are too pale.

8 Using a fine brush, touch in a mix of emerald green and white on the right-hand edge of the rainbow. Strengthen the light and dark tones on the headland; you may need to use a stronger, deeper yellow such as cadmium yellow, for the most brightly lit parts. Brush more colour into the sea, using relatively short, horizontal brushstrokes that echo the motion of the waves. Scumble more of the purple red and white mix into the sky, to create some tonal variation, blending the colours on the canvas as before to get rid of any obvious brushstrokes and allowing some of the underlying turquoise colour to show through.

Tip: Look at the lights and darks within the sea: even though the sea is relatively calm, these tonal contrasts reveal the shapes, structure and direction of the waves.

9 Using various mixes and tones of purple red overlaid with ultramarine, yellow ochre, brown oxide, and vermilion, add more definition to the buildings.

10 Apply more colour to the sea, building up thin glazes of turquoise; turquoise and white; purple red and white; white and vermilion as appropriate.

11 Using a fine brush, continue with the buildings in the foreground, alternating between warm and cool tones and lights and darks in order to suggest three-dimensional forms.

The finished painting

This is a lively painting in which the artist has created the effects of a fleeting moment, when colours vibrate and light glistens during a passing storm. The actual colours have been exaggerated for dramatic effect while still retaining the sombre, brooding atmosphere of the stormy sky. The gentle arc of the rainbow draws the eye down to the headland and foreground town, which is painted in just enough detail for it to be clear what is represented. There is a feeling of energy in both the sea and sky, due in part to the way the colours have blended wet into wet on the canvas but also to the way the artist has used horizontal brushstrokes in the sea to capture the direction of the waves.

Even though little detail is present the viewer's eye nonetheless interprets these simple blocks of colour as buildings.

Scumbling the paint on vigorously allows some of the underlying colour to show through, creating interesting mottling.

Applying several layers of thin, semi-opaque colour creates a variety of tones in the water.

Storm clouds and rainbow in watercolour

Watercolour is a wonderful medium for painting clouds. The translucency of the paint enables you to create a feeling of light and air, while wet-into-wet washes are perfect for creating subtle transitions from one colour to another.

One of the most important things to remember is that you need to make your clouds look like solid, three-dimensional forms, not just wispy trails of vapour in the sky. Clouds have a top, a bottom and a side. The top usually faces the sun and is therefore lighter than the side and the bottom. Before you start painting, work out which direction the light is coming from so that you can decide which areas of cloud are in shadow and need to be darker in tone.

Make sure that any changes in tone are very gradual. You can soften colours where necessary by lifting off paint with a piece of kitchen paper or a sponge, but try to avoid hard edges at all costs.

The rules of perspective that apply to painting land also apply to painting the sky, and clouds that are further away will appear smaller than those that are immediately overhead. They will also be lighter in tone.

In this project, dramatic banks of cumulus cloud before an evening storm are the focus of interest and the land below is almost an irrelevance. Although the land is so dark that relatively little detail is visible, it is an important part of the picture, as it provides a context for the scene and an anchor for the painting as a whole. In any landscape, the sky must relate to the land beneath and so you need to continually assess the tonal balance between the two.

Materials
- 2B pencil
- 140lb (300gsm) rough watercolour paper
- Watercolour paints: yellow ochre, cadmium lemon, sap green, raw umber, ultramarine blue, cadmium yellow, Prussian blue, cadmium red, burnt sienna, alizarin crimson, viridian
- Brushes: medium round, fine round, large wash
- Kitchen paper

The original scene
This is a dramatic and unusual sky. Although the clouds and rainbow provide the main focus of interest, the low-angled early evening sunlight picks out enough detail on the land to relieve the monotony of the dark foreground.

Silhouetted tree shapes provide a visual link between sky and ground.

Low-angled sunlight picks out the house and a patch of the foreground field.

1 Using a 2B pencil, outline the tree shapes on the horizon. Mix a very pale wash of yellow ochre and, using a medium round brush, loosely brush it over the sky, leaving gaps for the lightest areas. Mix cadmium lemon and sap green and brush the mixture over the lightest areas of the fields. Mix a dilute wash of dark brown from raw umber and a touch of ultramarine blue and brush it on to the clouds in the top left of the picture. Add more ultramarine blue to the brown mixture and brush loose strokes over the base of the clouds on the right.

2 While the sky is still damp, add more raw umber to the mixture and brush short calligraphic strokes over the clouds to delineate the lower edges, dabbing some of the paint off with kitchen paper to soften the edges. Mix a dark olive green from cadmium yellow and ultramarine blue and block in the dark areas of the foreground and the silhouetted shapes on the horizon.

3 While the foreground is still damp, mix a bluish green from cadmium yellow, ultramarine blue and Prussian blue and brush it over the foreground to darken it. Mix a warm yellowish green from cadmium lemon and cadmium red with a little ultramarine and brush the mixture over the brightest areas of the fields, which are illuminated by shafts of low-angled evening sunlight.

4 Finish blocking in the silhouettes on the skyline. Mix an orangey red from cadmium red and yellow ochre and, using a medium round brush, block in the shape of the distant house.

Tip: The only details you need on the house are the roof and walls. The rules of perspective make further detail, such as windows, unnecessary.

Assessment time
With the addition of a hint of blue sky and the dark hedge that marks the boundary between the house and the field, the painting is really starting to take shape. The foreground is very dark, and so the next stage is to work on the sky so that the picture has a better overall balance.

The sky is too pale to hold any interest.

The foreground is oppressively dark; the sky needs to be much stronger to balance it.

Note how the red house immediately attracts the eye, even though it occupies only a small area.

5 Mix a rich, dark brown from ultramarine blue and burnt sienna. Using a large wash brush, loosely scrub it into the left-hand side of the sky, leaving a gap for the rainbow and dabbing off paint with kitchen paper to soften the edges. Note how this creates interesting streaks in the sky.

6 Using the same colour, make a series of short calligraphic strokes on the sky at the base of the clouds. The clouds are lit from above, so giving them dark bases helps to establish a sense of form. Brush yellow ochre on to the sky above the dark clouds.

7 Again, dab off paint with kitchen paper to get rid of any obvious brushstrokes and create interesting streaks and wispy textures in the clouds. The clouds should look as if they are swirling overhead, their brooding presence dominating the entire scene.

8 Using a darker version of the mixture, darken the clouds again so that the sky has more impact. You need to continually assess the tones in a painting like this, as an alteration to one area can disrupt the tonal balance of the painting as a whole.

9 Finally, paint the rainbow, using a very fine round brush and long, confident strokes. There is no distinct demarcation between one colour and the next, so it doesn't matter if the colours merge. If you do want to boost any of the colours, allow the paint to dry and then strengthen the colours with a second application.

The finished painting

This is a bold and dramatic interpretation of glowering storm clouds. In the sky, the paint is applied in thin, transparent layers, softened in places by dabbing off paint with kitchen paper, and the white of the paper is allowed to show through, creating a wonderful feeling of luminosity. The land below, in contrast, is solid and dark and forms a complete counterpoint to the rapidly moving clouds above.

Successive layers of colour applied quite thickly in the foreground create a feeling of solidity.

The clouds have an airy texture, achieved by applying the paint wet into wet and then dabbing it off with kitchen paper.

A shaft of warm, evening sunlight leads the viewer's eye across the painting.

Seascape in soft pastels

The range of marks that you can make with soft pastels – from soft blends and sweeping strokes made with the side of the stick to sharp, linear marks – is great for matching virtually any effect seen in nature. They are quick to use, allowing you to build up areas of colour rapidly, and are perfect for capturing fleeting effects of weather and light.

This project gives you the opportunity to practise different kinds of blending. A subject such as skies and clouds is perfect for relative newcomers to pastels; because the shapes are not critical, you can practise moving the pigment around on the paper without having to worry about getting the detail exactly right.

Materials
• *Pastel paper*
• *Grey pastel pencil*
• *Soft pastels: mid-grey, dark grey, black, reddish brown, mid-green, pale grey, mid-blue, dark brown, fawn, pale yellow*

The scene
This is a moody and atmospheric seascape, with storm clouds billowing overhead and sunlight glinting on the water. Although the colour palette appears limited at first glance, there are a number of different tones within the clouds and rocks and these need to be blended smoothly. The artist used two reference photos for this exercise – one for the detail of the foreground rocks and one for the stormy sky and sunlight sparkling on the water.

1 Using a grey pastel pencil, outline the headland and foreground rocks. The artist has changed the composition to make it more dynamic: in the photo, the horizon line is in the centre – but here it is positioned lower down.

2 Using the side of a mid-grey soft pastel, block in the darkest tones in the sky and blend with your finger. Allow some areas to remain darker than others, as there is a lot of tonal variation in the clouds.

3 Apply a darker grey pastel for the clouds immediately overhead. (The difference in tone helps to convey a sense of distance, as colours tend to look paler toward the horizon.) Build up the very darkest areas of cloud with more dark grey and black, blending the marks with your fingers as before. Remember to leave some gaps for the white of the paper to show through, to create the impression of sunlight peeping out from behind the clouds.

4 Block in the headland with a dark, reddish brown and smooth out the pastel marks with your fingers. Use the same reddish brown for the foreground rocks, then overlay the brown in both areas with a mid-green, blending the colours partially with your fingers so both colours remain visible.

5 Gently stroke the side of a pale grey pastel across the water area, leaving the central, most brightly lit section untouched.

6 Darken the water by overlaying touches of a dusky mid-blue, green and black. Do not overblend the marks or apply them too heavily: it is important to see some differences in colour within the water and to allow some of the white of the paper to show through to create the impression of light sparkling on the water.

▶

7 Now build up more of the texture on the foreground rocks. Loosely block in the darkest areas (the shaded sides of the rocks) in reddish brown, then overlay dark brown and green and blend the colours slightly with your fingers. For the lighter sides of the rocks, use greys and fawns. Immediately the rocks will begin to look three-dimensional.

Tip: The differences in tone within the rocks are subtle; you may find it easier to assess them if you half close your eyes, as you will then see the blocks of tone and not get distracted by detail.

Assessment time

Stand back from the image to assess what final small adjustments may be needed. Here, for example, the sky requires just a little more work as there are some small patches of cloud even in the very brightest part. The artist also judged that the sea on the far right of the image, which has the dark, brooding storm cloud directly overhead, was slightly too light in tone. In addition, the golden glow of the setting sun on the horizon still needs to be put in.

Without the glow of the setting sun along the horizon, we have no clues as to the time of day.

The addition of a few tiny patches of cloud to this area will add visual interest and prevent this area from looking completely burnt out and featureless.

8 Lightly draw a pale yellow line along the horizon and add touches of yellow in the sky to warm it up, blending the marks with your fingertips or a clean rag.

9 Using the tip of mid-grey pastel, put tiny dashes and dots of colour into the sea on the far right of the image to darken the area slightly and create the impression of wavelets and a sense of movement in the water.

The finished drawing

This drawing uses a number of blending techniques. In the sky, softly blended marks create the impression of swirling clouds. The texture and form of the rocks in the foreground are achieved by overlaying several colours, allowing each one to retain its integrity, and adding a few linear marks as the finishing touch. Our overall impression of the water is that it is a dark blue-grey, but on closer inspection we can see a number of different colours and tones within it – optical mixes that enliven the scene and also imply the movement of the waves in the sea.

The yellow along the horizon contrasts with the cool blues and greys used elsewhere and adds a touch of warmth to the image.

Note how effectively the white of the paper stands for the very brightest areas in both the sky and the sea.

Although little detail is discernible in the distant headland, some tonal variation is essential to prevent it from appearing as a solid silhouette.

Sunlit beach in oils

This simple-looking scene of an almost deserted beach on a bright summer's day gives you the chance to paint two of nature's most fascinating subjects – moving water and sparkling sunlight.

Painting the sea is interesting: how can you capture the constant ebb and flow of the water? The more time you spend in observation the better. Although the movement of the waves may seem random, if you stand still and watch for a while you will soon see a pattern. Look at the shapes that the waves make as they roll in toward the shore and try to fix them in your mind.

One of the risks of painting in bright sunshine is that you can be dazzled by the intensity of the light, with the result that you tend to make the scene too high key. Instead of capturing the brightness of the scene, as you intended, you will find that your work simply looks bleached out. Look for tonal contrasts within the scene and balance bright areas with dark, cooler shadows. The dark passages will make the light areas look even brighter.

When painting highlights, do not try to put in every single one or your work will look fussy. Half-close your eyes: this reduces the glare, enabling you to break down the pattern of light more easily and put in just the key highlight areas.

Finally there is the question of how to paint the sky. If you are painting *en plein air* and the clouds are fleeting, you may want to put them down quickly to capture the effects, whereas with a relatively static scene, you might concentrate on the land first. But remember that clouds have volume: look for the lights and darks within them that make them look voluminous.

Materials
- *Stretched and primed canvas*
- *Oil paints: olive green, cobalt blue, titanium white, alizarin crimson, cerulean blue, burnt umber, Indian yellow, cadmium red, black, lemon yellow*
- *Turpentine*
- *Brushes: small filbert brush, selection of small hogshair and sables*

The scene
The tide has receded, leaving shallow inlets illuminated by bright sunlight and large areas of exposed sand – an interesting contrast of colours and textures.

1 Using a thin mix of olive green, 'draw' the cliffs on the horizon, the lines of the waves and the little channels. At the outset the artist decided to add a small dog to the scene to focus the viewer's attention. Add its outline and shadow now.

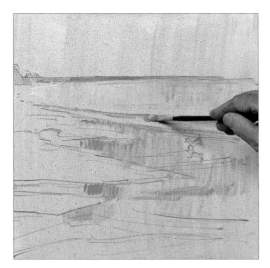

2 Mix a bright, light blue from cobalt blue and titanium white. Using a small filbert brush, loosely scumble the mixture over the shallow areas of water in the foreground of the scene. Add a little alizarin crimson to the mixture to make it slightly more purple in tone, and brush in the line of cliffs along the horizon in the background. Mix a paler blue from cerulean blue and titanium white and use this mixture for the most distant area of sea.

3 Add a tiny amount of burnt umber to the purplish-blue mixture from Step 2 and blend this colour, wet into wet, into the darkest parts of the sea – the undersides of the waves that roll in toward the shore. Mix a rich, dark sand colour from burnt umber and Indian yellow and scumble this mixture over the sand, blending in a few strokes of cadmium red here and there, and adding purple for the very darkest lines along the edges of the water channels.

4 Add a little burnt umber to the bright blue mixture from Step 2, and scumble it over the deepest areas of the foreground water. Using short, vertical brushstrokes, loosely scumble various sand colours over the shallowest parts of the water, where the underlying sand is clearly visible.

5 Continue putting in the sand areas in the middle distance. Note that some areas are pinker and warmer than others; adjust the mixtures on your palette as appropriate. Block in the dog and its reflection in a dark mixture of olive green, black and a little burnt umber.

▶

6 Continue to build up the tones in the water, using the same purplish blues as before to emphasize the darker areas. Overlay pale blue paint over the water-covered sand in the foreground, blending the vertical brushstrokes that you put down in the earlier stages to create the impression of sand seen hazily through shallow water.

7 Now start to work on the sky. Put in the clouds first, using light- and mid-toned greys mixed from burnt umber, cobalt blue and titanium white in varying proportions. Warm or cool the mixtures as necessary by adding a touch of pink or blue. Put in the bright blue of the sky using a mixture of cobalt blue and titanium white.

8 Use a darker version of the olive green, black and burnt umber mixture that you used in Step 5 to reinforce the shape of the dog and its reflection in the wet sand.

9 Now start to put in some of the reflected highlights on the crests of the waves, dotting in little specks of white tinged with yellow to give the impression of sunlight glancing off the surface of the water.

Assessment time

Now that the main elements and colours are in place, take time to assess the tonal balance of the painting as a whole. Although the orange of the sand and the blue of the sea are complementary colours and give the scene a lot of energy, they are both predominantly mid-tones. You need to reinforce the sense of sunlight within the scene – and, paradoxically, the way to do this is to make the dark areas darker, so that they form an effective contrast to the brightly lit parts.

Much of the picture space is empty, and the dog alone is insufficient to hold the viewer's interest More figures paddling in the sea would balance the composition.

You need to create a sense of sunlight sparkling on the water.

The sand is little more than a block of colour at this stage; it needs more texture.

10 Darken the water channels in the foreground, using the same purples and blues as before.

Tip: Do not add any solvent to the paint for this process: using the paint straight from the tube means that it is relatively dry, so the colours do not turn muddy even though you are overlaying paint on a layer that it still wet.

11 Touch some very pale yellow (made by mixing lemon yellow, a little Indian yellow and titanium white) into the top of the clouds to create the effect of warm sunlight.

12 Look at the colours within the sea: it is by no means a uniform blue. Add a little purple to your blue mixes to put in the darkest parts of the small waves as they break on the shore. Loosely block in the figures, using a purplish blue-black. As they are silhouetted, with the sun behind them, little detail is discernible. Add a hint of yellow to titanium white and put in fine lines to create highlights on the foam-tipped wave crests.

▶

13 Continue putting lights and darks into the sea area, using small strokes and dotting in the highlights. In the deeper channels in the foreground water, use loose vertical strokes of a mid-toned blue to create the sense of light shimmering in the water. The brushstrokes will soon be blended out, but their direction is important as it helps to give the effect of sunlight glancing off the water.

14 Continue working on the foreground area, using the sand colour and blue mixes tinged with purple as appropriate. Gently and gradually blend the wet paint on the canvas and smooth out the brushstrokes.

15 Create more variety and texture in the exposed sand area by dotting in other colours – a light yellow mixed from lemon yellow and white, and burnt umber lines and dots. Dot the pale yellow mixture that you used in Step 12 on the wave crests to create the effect of sunlight sparkling over the water.

16 Mix a bright blue from cobalt blue and titanium white and scumble it over the top of the sky to darken it and allow the clouds to stand out more dramatically. The use of a dark colour at the top of the picture holds the viewer's eye within the frame, while the loose brushstrokes help to give an impression of movement in the sky.

The finished painting

This is an attractive painting of an almost deserted beach in summer. Lively brushstrokes convey the dark clouds scudding across the sky, and loose scumbles of colour over the water also help to convey a sense of movement. The viewpoint has been carefully chosen so that the wedge-shaped areas of sand in the foreground balance the composition and lead our eye through the painting. Although the dog and the silhouetted figures in the middle distance occupy only a small part of the scene, their position (roughly on the thirds) means that our eye is drawn to them.

The use of complementary colours (blue and orange) imparts a sense of energy.

Specks of yellow create the effect of warm sunlight glancing off the water.

The dog occupies only a small area, but its position means that our eye is drawn to it.

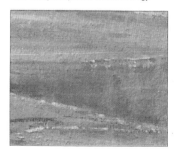

Rocky foreshore in pencil

As this scene has a limited colour palette of predominantly blues, greys and browns, it suits a monochrome medium. Graphite pencil was chosen for its versatility: it can produce fine linear detail with the tip and broad areas of tone using the side, while hatching and smudging increase the range and type of marks that can be made.

If you have good-quality pencils, you will probably be able to get away with using just one or two different grades. A good 2B, for example, can produce a wide range of tones depending on how much pressure you apply, so there should be no need for you to resort to a 5B or 6B for the very blackest tones. The graphite in cheap pencils, however, tends to snap or crumble if you apply a lot of pressure. You may also find that the graphite is bound in poor-quality wood, which simply crumbles away when you try to sharpen the pencil, making it virtually impossible to achieve a fine point. Experiment with different brands until you find one you like.

When you look really closely at a scene such as this, you will see that there is an incredible amount of linear and textural detail. The amount of detail that you include in your drawing is up to you: if you favour a photo-realistic approach, then you may decide to try to capture every single nook and cranny. If you do this, however, you must try to establish some kind of hierarchy in your own mind. If all your lines are the same weight, you may get lost in a plethora of detail in which every line is as important as its neighbour and nothing stands out. Alternatively, you could opt for a looser, less detailed approach that concentrates on the general shapes and lines of the scene and emphasizes the powerful geological forces that shaped the rocks and the landscape. The route that you choose depends on your own emotional response to the scene in front of you.

Materials
• *Good-quality drawing paper*
• *Pencils: F, 2B*
• *Kneaded eraser*

The scene
The stones along the water's edge and the larger boulders on the right point inward on slight diagonal lines, directing the viewer's eye toward the centre of the image – the gently lapping sea and the silhouetted mountains in the distance. The dark, brooding sky holds in the image at the top. This is a classic composition, with the sky and mountains occupying roughly two-thirds of the picture space and the stones most of the remainder.

1 Using a hard pencil (grade F), map out the composition. First, establish the horizon line, the line of the larger boulders jutting in on the right, and the mountains in the background. As you work, look for correspondences between one part and another that you can use as reference points to check that you are locating everything accurately. Drop faint vertical lines down from the tip or base of individual hills to see what they align with on the foreshore. You can erase these construction lines later, once you have sketched out the whole composition and are sure that you've located all the main elements correctly.

2 Continue until you feel you have mapped out all the key elements of the scene and positioned them accurately. Do not try to put in every single stone, but look at the overall shapes of the mountains and the shapes of the largest of the foreground boulders – anything that will help you locate where you are in the drawing as you commence with the more detailed stages. Take plenty of time over this: it is the most critical part of the drawing, because once you have got these major elements right, everything else, such as the shading, textures and tones, will fall into place.

3 Once you have got the main forms, you can begin to put in some of the smaller stones. Keep the drawing very linear at this stage. You can begin to introduce tone and shading later on.

> **Tip:** Remember the rules of perspective: the stones along the water's edge appear smaller as they are farther away. Less texture and detail is evident here, too.

5 Shade the rocks behind the main foreground boulder, which are a mid-tone. Sharpen your pencil to a fine point, then use the side of the graphite to lightly apply tone. Begin applying tone to the foreground rocks on the foreshore in the same way.

> **Tip:** Keep referring back to your source material so that you do not lose track of where you are in the drawing. It is very easy to get so caught up in shading and applying tone to individual stones that you lose sight of the drawing as a whole.

4 Switch to a 2B pencil, which is much softer, and begin putting in some of the darker cracks and crevices in the large boulders on the right, using strong, linear marks for all the crevices and loose hatching marks for the mid tones on the stone. This area is close to the viewer, so texture and detail are more in evidence here than in the background.

▶

6 Put in the very dark shadows under the rocks to help develop a sense of form. At the same time, look for darker tones on the rocks' surface, which are due partly to their natural coloration and partly to the way light hits different planes of the stone, creating shaded and more brightly lit areas.

7 Using the side of the pencil, lightly hatch the mountains in the distance. Some are farther away than others, so look for subtle tonal differences between them to create a sense of distance and recession. Build up the tones gradually. It is easy to darken things later, but if you make the mountains too dark at the start you will destroy the drawing's tonal balance.

8 Using the side of the pencil, lightly hatch the sea with long, horizontal strokes that echo the direction in which the water is flowing. Smudge the pencil marks by rubbing across them with your fingers to create a smoother tone. Mould a kneaded eraser to a peak and gently lift off tiny highlights on the water.

9 Strengthen the darkest tones and continue putting in the mid tones on the foreground rocks, using loose hatching as before. Put in the shadows beneath and within the rocks to establish the different planes of the rocks' surfaces.

10 Add bold linear marks where necessary to delineate the individual rocks and put in the shadows and lines of any deep crevices. These marks will bring the picture together.

Tips: • A 2B pencil is capable of producing a wide range of marks. Vary the amount of pressure you apply to create marks of different densities.
• Do not try to put in every single line. Limit yourself to those that contribute to our understanding of the rock's form and structure.

Assessment time

The drawing is nearing completion and all the main elements except the sky have been put in. All that remains now is to increase the tonal contrast in certain areas and to decide how much textural detail you want to include in the immediate foreground. At this stage, you can decide on the details that will give the drawing atmosphere.

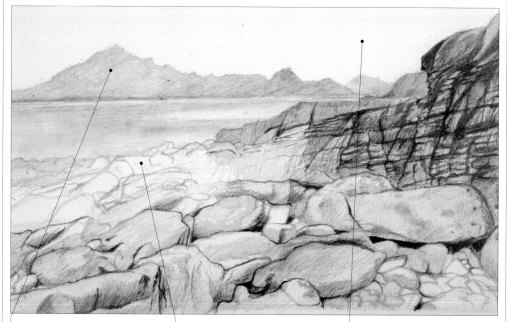

The mountains are similar in tone to the sea and need to be darkened considerably so that they can readily be distinguished from each other.

Virtually no tone or linear detail has been applied to the rocks along the foreshore. Although less detail is required here than in the foreground, at present the viewer's eye is drawn to this area because it is so much brighter than the rest of the drawing.

The sky is bland and featureless: dark, glowering clouds need to be added to complete the drawing and create mood.

▶

11 Using the tip of the pencil, darken the background mountains so that they stand out more. Remember to look for differences in tone between different mountains to imply their spatial relationship to one another.

12 Apply light shading and any linear detail that you feel is necessary to the rocks along the foreshore. Remember that the detail in this area needs to be less evident than in the foreground.

13 Block in the darkest tones of the sky and blend the marks with your fingers to create smooth areas of tone. Use a charcoal-covered kneaded eraser to 'draw' any light-toned wisps of clouds within the very brightest patches.

14 Make light strokes using the side of the pencil to create the mid tones in the sky.

The finished drawing

The versatility of graphite pencil as a medium is well demonstrated in this drawing, with the marks ranging from strong linear strokes to subtle hatching and finger-blending. Although one could choose to add much more texture and detail to the stones than the artist has done here, there is more than enough to convey the three-dimensional nature of the subject. Note, in particular, how careful shading on the foreground rocks captures the undulations on the rocks' surface. Although the mountains in the background are virtually in silhouette, subtle tonal differences reveal that some peaks are farther away than others. The sea and the sky have been put in with light hatching, but again the tones have been carefully assessed in relation to the rest of the image. The light line of the horizon is made with an eraser.

Wispy areas of mid-tone are visible within the clouds, preventing the brightest patches of sky from looking completely empty and bland.

The side of the stone is in shadow, and hence darker than the top. Careful analysis of the tones is essential if you are to make the stones look three-dimensional.

Bold, confident linear marks made with the tip of the pencil are used to convey the deep, angular crevices in the foreground boulders.

Mediterranean seascape in soft pastels

This tranquil scene of waves lapping a Mediterranean shore is full of sunshine and light. Although the composition is simple there is plenty to hold the viewer's attention, from the partially submerged rocks in the foreground through to the town in the distance.

The main interest, of course, is the rippling sea itself, with its myriad tones of blue, green and even violet – and soft pastels are a wonderful medium in which to portray this. It is surprising how many colours you can see in the water. Water takes its colour from objects in and around it – the sky, rocks, seaweed and algae, and so on – so look at the surroundings, as well as at the water, as this will help you assess which colours are required. Half-close your eyes when you look at the scene, as this makes it easier to assess the different colours and tones. It is hard to be precise about which colours to use in this project, as soft pastels are available in such a huge range of colours, but put together a selection of blues, greens, violets and browns, from very pale to very dark.

Remember that the rules of both linear and aerial perspective apply to sea and sky just as much as they do to objects on land. Distant waves, for example, appear smaller than those close at hand. Colours also appear lighter with distance and texture is less pronounced – so smooth out your pastel marks on the sky and the most distant part of the sea by blending them lightly with your fingers or a rag.

Observe your seascape carefully before you draw. You will see that the waves follow a regular pattern, with incoming waves building to a peak and then falling back. Note how high they go and how far back they fall when they break around a rock or crash on the shore.

Materials
- *Cream pastel paper*
- *Neutral brown or grey pastel pencil*
- *Soft pastels: a selection of blues, greens, blue-greens, turquoises, violets, browns, oranges, ochres and white*
- *Soft rag*

The scene
The dark wall on the left forms a diagonal line at its base which directs the viewer's attention towards the town in the distance. The town itself is positioned roughly 'on the third' – a strong position in any composition.

1 Using a neutral-coloured pastel pencil, put in the lines of the headland and horizon and the dark, submerged rocks in the water. Note that the artist decided to make the headland and rocks more prominent in the scene and omitted the light-coloured concrete walkway in the bottom left of the reference photo.

2 Roughly block in the sky using the side of a mid-blue pastel and blend with a clean rag or your fingertips to smooth out the marks.

> **Tips:** • Keep the coverage slightly uneven, to give some texture to the sky. If the colour is completely flat and uniform, it will look rather boring.
> • If you use your fingers to blend the marks, wash your hands regularly so that you do not apply the wrong colour accidentally or create messy smudges. Using a torchon may help you to keep the paper clean.

3 Block in the wall on the left with a mid-brown pastel and smooth out the marks with a rag or your fingers. Scribble in the partially submerged rocks using the same colour.

4 Block in the sea using a turquoise pastel, leaving some spaces for the breaking wavelets. Note that the sea has some areas that are lighter than others, so apply less pressure here.

5 Apply a few light touches of a darker turquoise to the darkest parts of the sea in the background. Loosely scribble jade green over the foreground water to pick up the green tones, varying the amount of pressure you apply to get some variety of tone.

6 Looking carefully at their rough, uneven shapes, apply burnt orange over the tops of the exposed rocks in the sea near the base of the wall, switching to a reddish brown for their bases. Blend the marks gently with clean fingertips.

▶

7 Look at the colours in the water. The underside of breaking wavelets contains some surprisingly dark greens and blues. Stroke these in lightly, making sure your strokes follow the direction in which the waves are moving. Gently smooth the marks a little with your fingertips – but do not overdo the blending, as allowing some of the underlying paper colour to show through helps to create a sense of movement in the water.

8 Continue building up different colours in the water, using dark greens and blues and dots of light spring green.

> **Tip**: Remember to keep referring to your reference photo. It is easy to get carried away with building up the colours and forget to look at the shades that are actually there.

Assessment time

There is a lovely sense of movement in the sea and a good range of different tones and colours. However, the rocks themselves are nothing more than flat blocks of colour and need to be made to look three-dimensional.

The sky is too pale and uniform in colour and needs to be darkened in some areas.

The shape of the town is clear, but there is no detail on the buildings, so it looks flat.

The wall is a flat expanse of brown – it needs to look rough in texture and three-dimensional.

The rocks are little more than patches of colour and lack form.

9 Start to build up some tone and texture on the wall by scribbling on dark greens and browns, making horizontal strokes that suggest the blocks that it is built from. Smudge the colours with your fingers, allowing some of the underlying mid-brown that you put down in Step 3 to remain visible.

10 Repeat the process on the rocks surrounding the partially enclosed still pool, scribbling a reddish brown over the orange to build up the form. On the distant headland, put in the darkest colours of the buildings – the browns and terracottas of the roofs. Apply pale yellow ochre to the white of the headland so the paper does not look so stark.

11 Dot some light and mid-toned olive greens into the headland for the distant trees. Apply pale blue and mid-tone turquoise over the sky to darken it toward the top (because of the effect of aerial perspective, skies generally look paler close to the horizon). Blend with your finger as necessary to soften the effect.

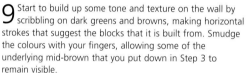

▶

12 Although little detail is visible in the distant town, you need to give some indication of the buildings. Look for the dark tones under the eaves of the roofs. Making small horizontal strokes, apply pale blues and greens over the most distant part of the sea and smooth them out with your fingers. Apply thin lines of dark brown around the bases of the partially exposed rocks.

13 Having now given the rocks some solidity, return to working on the foreground seascape again, and put in the white of the wavelets as they break around the partially exposed rocks. Use the tip of the pastel and dot in white here and there around this area. The softly lapping sea has only a gentle swell, so take care that you do not make the wavelets too big.

14 Continue adding texture to the foreground sea, making sure that the dark greens, blues and purples in this area are dark enough. Do not smooth out your marks too much: it is important to have more texture in the foreground of a scene than in the background, as this is one way of creating a sense of recession.

15 Continue building up form on the exposed rocks, using a range of dark oranges and browns as before. It is now time to put in the final touches – more tiny strokes of white for the breaking wavelets and horizontal strokes of dark greens and blues in the foreground sea, wherever you judge it to be necessary.

The finished drawing

There is a lively sense of movement in the sea: one can almost feel the ebb and flow of the waves and hear them lapping around the rocks. Note how allowing some of the paper to show through the pastel marks creates the effect of sunlight sparkling on the water. There is just enough detail in the distant headland for us to know that there is a town there; more detail, however, would draw the viewer's attention away from the sea in the foreground and destroy the illusion that we are looking almost directly into the sun, our eyes dazzled by its brilliance.

The wall provides solidity at the edge of the picture area and helps to direct the viewer's eye through the scene.

Small horizontal strokes of blues, greens and purples are used to convey the many different shades in the water.

Detail diminishes with distance, and so the pastel marks in this area of the sea are smoothed out to give less texture.

Crashing waves in watercolour

This project depicts a massive sea wave just as it is about to break over craggy rocks. Your challenge is to capture the energy and power of the scene.

Few people would go as far in their search for realism as the great landscape artist J.M.W. Turner, who is reputed to have tied himself to a ship's mast in order to experience the full force of a storm at sea. Fortunately, there are easier and less perilous ways of adding drama to your seascapes.

Construct your painting as if you are viewing the scene from a low viewpoint, so that the waves seem to tower above you. For maximum drama, capture the waves while they are building or when they are at their peak, just before they break and come crashing down. You can gauge the height of the waves by comparing them with rocks or clifftops, while including such features in your painting will provide you with both a focal point and a sense of scale.

Try to attune yourself to the sea's natural rhythms. Watch the ebb and flow of the waves and concentrate on holding the memory of this movement in your mind as you are painting. This will help you to capture the energy.

Finally, remember that water reflects all the colours around it. You may be surprised at how many different colours there are in a scene like this.

The original scene

It is notoriously difficult to photograph a breaking wave at exactly the right moment, and so the artist used this photograph merely to remind herself of the energy of the scene and the shapes and colours.

Reference sketches

Tonal sketches are a very good way of working out the light and dark areas of the scene. You will find that it helps to think of the waves as solid, three-dimensional objects, with a light and a shaded side. Try several versions so that you get used to the way the waves break over the rocks.

Materials
- *4B pencil*
- *140lb (300gsm) NOT watercolour paper, pre-stretched*
- *Watercolour paints: Payne's grey, phthalocyanine blue, cadmium yellow, lemon yellow, Hooker's green, cerulean blue, yellow ochre, raw sienna, sepia, violet, burnt sienna, cobalt blue*
- *Gouache paints: permanent white*
- *Brushes: medium round, fine round*
- *Mixing or palette knife*
- *Fine texture paste*
- *Ruling drawing pen*
- *Masking fluid*
- *Sponge*

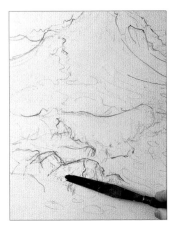

1 Using a 4B pencil, lightly sketch the scene, putting in the foreground rocks and the main waves. Take time to get the angles of the waves right: it is vital that they look as if they are travelling at speed and are just about to come crashing down.

2 Using a palette knife, apply fine texture paste over the rocks. Leave to dry. (Texture paste is available in several grades; the coarser it is, the more pronounced the effect. Here, the wave is more important than the rocks, so fine texture paste is sufficient).

3 Using a ruling drawing pen, apply masking fluid over the crest of the main wave and dot in flecks and swirls of foam in the water. Using a small sponge, dab masking fluid on to selected areas of the sea to create softer foamy areas. Leave to dry.

4 Mix a mid-toned wash of Payne's grey and another of phthalocyanine blue. Dampen the sky area with clean water and brush Payne's grey on to the right-hand side and phthalocyanine blue on to the left-hand side. Leave to dry.

5 Mix a strong wash of cadmium yellow with a touch of lemon yellow. Dampen the waves with clean water and lightly brush the bright yellow paint mixture over the tops of the waves.

▶

6 While the first wash is still wet, brush Hooker's green into the yellow so that the colours merge together. Mix a darker green from Hooker's green, phthalocyanine blue and a little cadmium yellow and brush this mixture into the lower part of the waves, feathering the mixture up into the yellow so that the colours blend imperceptibly on the paper. Brush over this darker green several times to build up the necessary density of tone.

7 Mix a dark blue from phthalocyanine blue and cerulean blue and brush this mixture into the lower part of the large wave, feathering the colour upward. Because the previous washes are still wet the colours spread and merge together on the paper, building up darker tones without completely blocking out the underlying colours. Use loose, swift brushstrokes and try to capture the energy and power of the sea.

8 Mix a mid-toned wash of yellow ochre and brush it over the texture paste on the rocks, adding raw sienna and sepia for the dark foreground.

> **Tip**: Allow the colour to 'drift' into the sea so that it looks as if the sea is washing over the rocks. Unless you do this the rocks will simply look as if they are floating on the water.

9 Mix a greyish blue from violet and Hooker's green. Brush little touches of this colour into the waves and into the pools at the base of the rocks, making swirling brushstrokes to help convey the movement of the water.

10 Using the dark green mixture from Step 6 and the brown used on the rocks, put a few dark accents into the waves. Soften the brushstrokes by brushing them with clean water to blend them into the other wave colours.

11 When you are sure that the paint is completely dry, gently rub off the masking fluid with your fingertips to reveal the foaming crests of the waves and the spattered highlights on the water.

Assessment time

Now that all the masking fluid has been removed, you can see how effectively the white of the paper has been reserved for the swirls and flecks of foam in the sea. However, these areas now look glaringly white and stark: they need to be toned down so that they become an integral part of the scene. However, you will need to take great care not to lose the very free, spontaneous nature of the swirling lines or the water will start to look too static and overworked. The contrast between the light and the very dark areas also needs to be strengthened a little in order to give a better feeling of the volume of the waves.

The exposed areas are much too bright.

The colours work well in this area, but there is not enough of a sense of the direction in which the water is moving.

12 Mix an opaque mauve from permanent white gouache, violet and a tiny touch of burnt sienna. Brush this mixture under the crest of the main wave, so that it looks like shadows under the very bright, white foam.

13 The exposed white areas look too stark against the dark colours of the water and rocks. Mix a very pale opaque blue from cobalt blue and permanent white gouache and cover up the exposed swirls of white in the water.

▶

14 Soften the harsh markings by brushing over more of the cobalt blue and gouache mixture. Paint some swirls of white gouache at the base of the main wave. Putting a little opaque colour into the water helps to give it some solidity.

15 Spatter a few specks of white gouache above the crest of the wave for the flecks of foam that fly into the air. Do not overdo it: too much gouache could easily overpower the light, translucent watercolour washes that you have worked so hard to create.

16 Spatter a few specks of the cobalt blue and white gouache mixture above the rocks. (This area is very dark and pure white gouache would look too stark.)

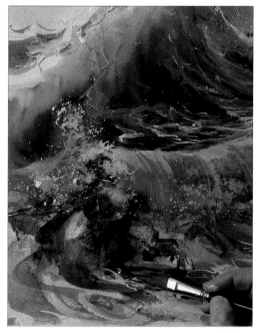

17 Stand back from the painting and assess the tonal values. You may find that you need to darken some of the colours in the centre of the painting.

18 Using the same dark brown mixture as before, build up the tones on the rocks. They need to stand out from the water that surrounds them.

The finished painting

This is a dramatic and carefully observed painting that captures the energy of the scene to perfection. Note the many different tones in the water and the way the brushstrokes echo the motion of the waves. Masking fluid has been used to reserve the white of the paper for the foam of the waves – a simple yet very effective technique for painting moving water. The rocks provide solidity and a sense of scale, but do not detract from the large wave that is hurtling forwards.

Spattering is the perfect technique for depicting foam-flecked waves.

Dark tones in this area contrast with the light edge of the breaking wave and help to give the water volume.

The rocks provide a necessary point of solidity in the scene.

Loose, swirling brushstrokes capture the motion of the sea.

Twilight river in mixed media

This demonstration combines watercolour and soft pastels – lovely for portraying the fleeting effects of light. Start by applying a light watercolour wash for the underlying colour. You can then put either broad strokes of pastel on top and smudge them with your fingertips (creating smooth areas such as the heavy cloud bases in this scene) or apply short dashes of different colours for areas such as the rippling water, allowing the colours to mix optically on the support.

At a glance, you might think that the cityscape along the horizon line is all the same tone. However, look out for those subtle differences in tone that reveal the spatial relationships of the buildings. These tonal differences tell us, for example, that the buildings are behind the bridge (because they are slightly lighter in tone) or that we are looking at the side of a building rather than its façade. If necessary, exaggerate them slightly so that the viewer can 'read' the scene accurately.

As watercolour is the basis for the early stages of this painting, remember the basic principle of watercolour painting, which is to work from light to dark, and put down the very lightest colours (here, the pale, warm yellow of the setting sun) first.

Materials
- Heavy watercolour paper
- Watercolour paints: ultramarine blue, cadmium yellow, Venetian red, alizarin crimson, phthalocyanine blue
- Brushes: Selection of round brushes in different sizes
- HB pencil
- Soft pastels: blue-grey, mid-lilac, warm cream, peachy yellow, blue-violet
- Sponge
- Cotton bud (cotton swab)

The scene
Here, the setting sun casts a wonderful golden glow over the river, while the gentle ripples in the water impart a sense of movement. It is a study of a moment in time. The heavy clouds, lit from behind, add drama to the scene. It is generally not advisable to position your main subject in the very centre of the picture space, but here the silhouettes provide bold, graphic shapes that, along with their reflections, link the sky and water together.

1 Dampen the top third of the paper with a sponge dipped in clean water. Using a large, round brush, lay a wash of dilute ultramarine blue over the sky. Leave to dry. Dampen the lower two thirds of the paper. Mix a very pale yellowy orange from cadmium yellow and a little Venetian red and apply it over this area. Leave to dry.

2 Using an HB pencil, lightly sketch in the shapes of the silhouetted buildings and bridge.

> **Tip**: Shade the undersides of the arches on the bridges to remind yourself that these areas are darker.

3 Mix a dark purple-blue from alizarin crimson and phthalo blue. Using a fine brush, block in the silhouettes and their reflections, adding more water to the mix for the lighter tones.

Assessment time

The watercolour stage is now complete. Although the painting of the buildings is almost monochromatic, by carefully judging the tones, the artist has managed to convey the spatial relationships and give the scene surprising depth and texture. The next stage is to build up the colour and texture in the sky and water.

Paler tones indicate that the buildings are farther away than the bridge.

Pale washes provide the undercolour for both the sky and water.

4 Splay out the bristles on your brush to resemble a fan shape (or use a fan brush) and dry brush on the ripples emanating from the piers of the bridge.

5 Dip a cotton bud in clean water and gently wipe off some small streaks of blue to create lighter cloud patches in the sky. The benefit of using a cotton bud for this, rather than a brush, is that you have more control and can lift off very precise shapes. Dab off any excess water with paper towel or a dry cotton bud if necessary.

6 Block in the heavy clouds with a blue-grey soft pastel, blending it with a mid-lilac for the lighter parts.

▶

7 Put in the golden colour of the sky, using a warm cream for the lighter patches and a peachy yellow for the darker tones, cutting in around the edges of the cloud.

8 Using the blue-grey pastel, lightly put in the dark ripples in the water, making sure you allow both the underlying wash and the texture of the paper to show through.

9 Use the same blue-grey to strengthen the dark reflection of the arch of the bridge.

10 Using a fine brush and the deep purple-blue from Step 3, paint in the boats and their reflections. At the same time, tidy up the silhouetted buildings and their reflections.

11 Using the warm cream and peachy yellow pastels, strengthen the golden tones on the water.

12 Make any final adjustments that are necessary in the sky, darkening the top of the image by just stroking the side of a blue-violet pastel over the paper.

The finished painting

This delicate study exploits the unique characteristics of both watercolour and soft pastels to perfection. The subtle, translucent watercolour washes provide the basic undercolour for the whole painting and give it a wonderful feeling of luminosity, while the broken colour of the pastels captures the effect of light sparkling on gently rippling water beautifully. The slightly rough texture of the paper, too, plays a part in giving the scene vitality.

The bridge is warmer and darker in tone than the background buildings, so it appears closer to the viewer.

There is a lovely interplay of colours on the water, which seems to shimmer in the reflected light of the setting sun.

The pastel marks are softly blended to create the dark, heavy clouds.

Reflections in watercolour

Any artist would be happy to while away a few hours in these tranquil surroundings, sketching the bright, sunny colours of this lakeside scene in the heat of the summer, with the reflections of hillsides covered in trees.

However, straightforward symmetrical reflections can sometimes seem a little boring and predictable, so look out for other things that will add interest to your paintings. Sweeping curves, such as the foreshore on the right in this scene, help to lead the viewer's eye through the picture, while interesting textures such as the stones in the foreground are always a bonus.

This project also provides you with the challenge of painting submerged objects. Here you need to think about the rules of perspective: remember that things look paler and smaller the farther away they are. As an added complication, the way that water refracts lights also distorts the shape of submerged objects. Trust your eyes and paint what you see, rather than assuming that you know what shape things are. Remember to think of light and shade for the submerged stones, too.

Materials
- B pencil
- Tracing paper
- 140lb (300gsm) NOT watercolour paper, pre-stretched
- Watercolour paints: alizarin crimson, Naples yellow, phthalocyanine blue, phthalocyanine green, burnt sienna, French ultramarine, Payne's grey, quinacridone magenta
- Brushes: medium round, fine round, old brush for masking fluid
- Masking fluid
- Gum arabic
- Paper towel

> **Tip**: Leave the tracing paper attached to one side of the watercolour paper, so that you can flip it back over if necessary during the painting process and reaffirm any lines and shapes that have been covered by paint.

The scene
You can almost feel the heat of the sun when you look at this photograph of a lake in southern Spain. The foreshore and hillside are dry and dusty, while the lake itself appears to be slowly evaporating, exposing rocks in the shallows. Because of the angle at which the photograph was taken, the colours are actually less intense than they were in real life. The artist decided to exaggerate the colours slightly to emphasize the feeling of heat.

The distant mountains are muted in colour and will benefit from being made more intense in the painting.

Much of the foreground is made up of submerged stones. You could put some exposed stones in this area to add interest.

1 Using a B pencil, make an initial sketch on tracing paper to establish the main lines of your subject. When you are happy with the result, trace your sketch on to pre-stretched watercolour paper. Using an old brush, apply masking fluid to some of the large foreground stones. Leave to dry.

2 Mix alizarin crimson with a little Naples yellow and, using a medium round brush, brush the mixture over the mountains and up into the sky. Leave to dry. Mix a bright blue from phthalocyanine blue and a little phthalocyanine green. Dampen the sky with clear water and, while the paper is still wet, brush on the blue mixture, stopping along the ridge and drawing the colour down into the mountains. Leave to dry.

3 Mix a mid-toned orangey brown from Naples yellow and burnt sienna, and paint the dry and dusty foreshore of the lake, dropping in more burnt sienna for the darker areas. Leave to dry.

4 Mix a purplish grey from burnt sienna, French ultramarine and alizarin crimson. Using a fine round brush, brush clean water across the mountains and then brush on vertical marks of the grey mixture for the cooler, darker recesses. The paint will blur wet into wet on the damp paper, and spread, leaving no hard edges. Leave to dry.

5 Using the burnt sienna and Naples yellow mix and a medium round brush, paint the arid, sandy background on the top right of the painting. While this area is still wet, mix an olive green from phthalocyanine green, burnt sienna and a little Naples yellow and, using a medium round brush, paint in the loose shapes of trees and bushes. Paint the shadow areas in the trees in the same purplish-grey mix used in Step 4. Leave to dry.

▶

6 Paint more trees on the left-hand side of the painting in the same way. Brush clean water across the sky. Mix Payne's grey with a little phthalocyanine green and, using the tip of the brush, dot this mixture into the damp sky area to denote the trees that stand out above the skyline. The colour will blur slightly. Leave to dry.

7 Using a B pencil, map out a few more stones on the shoreline. Mix a warm brown from burnt sienna and French ultramarine and brush in on to the foreground, working around the stones. Add more French ultramarine to the mixture and paint shadows around the edges of the stones to establish a three-dimensional effect. Leave to dry.

8 Brush clean water over the lake area. Mix burnt sienna with a little quinacridone magenta and, using a medium round brush, wash this mixture loosely over the shallow foreground of the lake, where partially submerged stones are clearly visible.

9 Brush phthalocyanine blue over the lake's centre. Wet the blank area at the top of the lake and brush on gum arabic. Add fine vertical strokes of Naples yellow, burnt sienna, quinacridone magenta mixed with French ultramarine, and the olive mixture used in Step 5. Leave to dry.

Assessment time
With the reflections in place, the painting is nearing its final stages. All that remains to be done is to put in some of the fine detail. Step back and think carefully about how you are going to do this. Far from making the painting look more realistic, too much detail would actually detract from the fresh, spontaneous quality of the overall scene.

This area lacks visual interest. Adding submerged stones here will indicate both the clarity of the water and how shallow it is at this point.

These stones look as if they are floating on the surface of the water.

10 Dip a medium round brush in clean water and gently lift off the flattened, elongated shapes of underwater stones, varying the sizes. You may need to stroke the brush backward and forward several times on the paper in order to loosen the paint.

11 As you lift off each shape, dab the area firmly with clean paper towel to remove any excess water. Turn and re-fold the paper towel each time you use it, to prevent the risk of dabbing paint back on.

▶

12 The submerged stones in the foreground of the lake add visual interest to what would otherwise be a dull, blank area of the scene, but as yet they do not look three-dimensional. The large stones above the surface of the water and on the shoreline also need more texture if they are to look convincing.

13 Mix a dark brown shadow colour from burnt sienna and French ultramarine and, using a medium round brush, use this mixture to loosely paint the shadows underneath the submerged stones. This makes the stones look three-dimensional and allows them to stand out more clearly from the base of the lake. It also adds texture to the base of the lake. Leave to dry.

14 Using a fine brush, wet the area at the base of the reflection and touch in a mixture of French ultramarine and alizarin crimson to soften the edges. Mix burnt sienna with a little French ultramarine and use it to touch in the shadows under the largest rocks on the shoreline. Leave to dry. Using your fingertips, gently rub off the masking fluid.

15 Using a fine, almost dry brush, brush water over the exposed rocks and then drop in a very pale burnt sienna wash. Leave to dry. Dry brush a darker mixture of burnt sienna on to the rocks in places, for dark accents. To make the rocks look more three-dimensional, stroke on a little French ultramarine for the shadow areas.

The finished painting

This is a truly inviting image. The lake looks so realistic that you want to dabble your toes in it, while the feeling of heat is almost tangible. The artist's skilful use of complementary colours (the bright blue of the sky set against the rich orangey brown of the stones and earth) has helped to create a really vibrant piece of art.

Textural details, such as the dry brushwork on the rocks and the distant trees painted wet into wet, are subtle but effective, while the careful blending of colours in the reflections conveys the stillness of the water perfectly. The composition is simple, but the foreshore leads the eye in a sweeping curve right through the painting.

The lake is not a uniform blue throughout, but takes its colour from the objects that are reflected in it, as well as from the visible shallow areas.

A judiciously placed shadow under one edge of the stones helps to make them look three-dimensional.

The easiest way to paint the reflection of the small rocks in the distance is simply to paint a thin line of burnt sienna right through the middle.

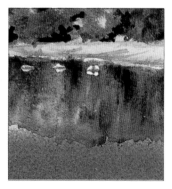

Pond reflections in acrylics

Reflections in water are fascinating – but completely still and perfect mirror images of the nearby landforms or sky do not necessarily make for the most interesting drawing or painting. When the water is moving slightly, reflections are distorted and there is immediately more visual interest. Your challenge is then not only to capture the reflections convincingly, but also to create a gentle sense of movement.

Before you begin drawing or painting, take the time to look at both the shape and size of the ripples in the water. Are the ripples horizontal, caused by a slight breeze blowing over the water? Or are they circular, emanating from a subject moving through the water such as a small boat or water bird? Watch out for these shapes and form your brushstrokes accordingly.

Another useful tip if you are painting in watercolour or acrylics is to brush clean water over the paper before you apply any colour. Then, when you paint in the rippling lines of the reflections, the paint will spread and blur on the surface, wet into wet, creating soft-edged shapes that seem to have a movement of their very own.

Remember, too, the laws of perspective: in order to create a sense of distance, foreground ripples need to be larger and farther apart than those in the background.

Materials
- *Heavy watercolour paper*
- *HB pencil*
- *Acrylic paints: alizarin crimson, ultramarine blue, brilliant green, phthalo blue, yellow ochre, titanium white, lemon yellow*
- *Brushes: Selection of rounds and filberts in different sizes*

The scene
Unusually, the composition is split horizontally into thirds – the bankside area, the dark reflections of the foliage, and all the light, rippling reflections of the bare trees. Although the fisherman crouched on the bank is only a tiny part of this scene, he provides the focal point of the image. The ripples in the foreground water distort the reflections, adding interest.

1 Using an HB pencil, lightly sketch the main elements of the scene, putting in nothing more than generalized outline shapes for the bankside bushes. Take care to get the angles of the fisherman's shoulders and knees right – correctly observing details such as these is the key to the getting the pose right. Put in the main lines of the reflected trees as a guide for when you come to paint.

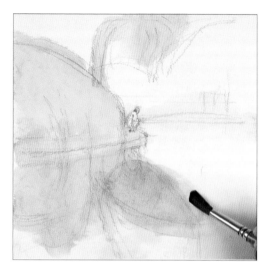

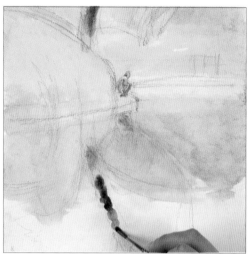

2 Apply a very dilute purple wash mixed from alizarin crimson and ultramarine blue over the reflection of the sky. Strengthen the mix for the tree trunk on the bank and the stonework along the bank edge. Mix a bright, mid-green from brilliant green and phthalo green and loosely wash it over the bushes on the left. Add more phthalo green and a little ultramarine for the dark green reflection in the centre of the image.

3 For the trees on the right-hand side, which are both darker and cooler in tone, add more ultramarine to the dark green mix from Step 2. Put in the fisherman's blue jacket in ultramarine. Wet the water area with clean water. Mix a dark brown from yellow ochre, ultramarine and alizarin crimson and, using a fine brush, put in the reflection of the main tree trunk and branches. The paint will spread on the damp paper, keeping the edges of the reflection soft.

4 Now start to build up some form in the bankside foliage, using mixes of yellow ochre, ultramarine and white in varying proportions. Half close your eyes so that you see the foliage as blocks of colour, rather than as individual branches of leaves.

5 Continue building up the foliage, adding lemon yellow for the lighter areas on the left. Paint the stonework of the banksides in a purple-pink mix of alizarin crimson, ultramarine and white. Begin putting in the dark blue-green reflection in the water with varying mixes of ultramarine and yellow ochre.

▶

6 Work on the reflections, using the blue-green and purple-pink mixes from the previous step in varying proportions. Add white to some of the mixes to make them both lighter in colour and more opaque. Note how the reflections near the bank are broken by small ripples in the water: use short, horizontal brushstrokes to convey this.

7 Add more white to the blue-green mix and dot in the lightest patches in the foliage, varying the proportions of the colours in the mix as necessary. It is through these tonal variations that you will begin to give the foliage a realistic sense of form.

8 Now that the basic colours and shapes are in place, you can begin to refine the detail. Put in the branches and trunks within the foliage mass using the same purple-pink mix as before. Dry brush the grasses on the left-hand bank in a mix of brilliant green, white and yellow ochre. Paint the fisherman's jacket in a mix of ultramarine and white, and his jeans in ultramarine with a tiny amount of alizarin crimson. His skin tones are a mix of lemon yellow and alizarin.

Tip: Note how the fisherman's reflection is slightly distorted by the ripples in the water. It is only in completely still water that a reflection will be a perfect mirror image of the subject.

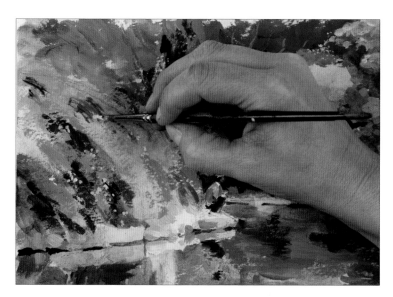

9 Put in the dark tones of the exposed patches of earth on the left bank in reddy browns mixed from alizarin crimson, yellow ochre and a touch of phthalo blue. Dot in the flowers using tiny dots of lemon yellow and lemon yellow mixed with white.

Tip: For really tiny dots such as these, try experimenting with using the tip of the brush handle, rather than the bristles, to apply the paint.

Assessment time

The foliage masses have been put in as generalized blocks of tone, but as they are quite a long way away it would be a mistake to attempt to render them in great detail. Note how the use of brighter, warmer tones in the foreground and cooler, bluer tones in the background helps to create a sense of distance. The painting is virtually complete and only a few finishing touches are needed – mostly in the bottom third of the image, where only the largest of the reflected branches have been painted.

Warm yellows and greens help to bring this area of the painting forward and imply that it is closer to the viewer than the bluer areas.

Cool, blue tones in the background indicate that this area is farther away.

Painting dark tones right up to the edge of the seated figure allows him to stand out more clearly from the background.

The reflections of many of the smaller branches are missing; as a result, this area of the painting is distractingly empty.

The viewer's eye is drawn to this area of the water, as it is so bright and featureless.

10 Wash over the water area with clean water. Using a fine brush and the same olivey, muted green mixes as before, strengthen the reflections of the large tree and put in more of the rippling, reflected lines of branches on the left-hand side. Hold the brush almost vertically, to create flowing, calligraphic marks.

11 Check the shapes and colours of the reflections, and touch in more muted greens on the left-hand side.

12 The reflections of the tower blocks on the right-hand side are very pale, but without the application of a little more colour this area will look very stark and white in relation to the rest of the image. Wash clean water over the area, then, using a neutral grey-brown and a fine brush, put in the rippled lines of the buildings and the lampposts on the bank.

13 Draw in the line of the fishing rod in pencil, then go over it with a dark purple-blue mixed from ultramarine and alizarin. When this is dry, very carefully brush a pale green highlight along the top edge.

The finished painting

This is a fairly loose, impressionistic sketch that is, nonetheless, full of atmosphere. The mood is one of quiet contemplation: the fisherman is positioned centrally on the width of the picture space, which generally creates a sense of calm in a picture, and, although he takes up only a small part of the image, it is to him that the viewer's eye is drawn. The limited palette of (predominantly) blues and greens enhances the feeling of tranquillity. The reflections take up about two-thirds of the image: were it not for the ripples in the water, which add a sense of movement, the painting might well look unbalanced.

The strong curve line of the bank helps to direct our eyes toward the fisherman.

The crouched figure of the fisherman is the focal point, even though he takes up only a small part of the picture space.

The foliage is painted as blocks of different tones of blue-green, creating a sense of depth within the foliage masses.

Note how the reflections blur, wet into wet, creating a sense of gentle movement in the water.

Waterfall in watercolour

Waterfalls offer particular challenges to watercolour artists. Not only do you have to paint a liquid that lacks any real colour of its own, but you also need to make that liquid look wet and convey a sense of how quickly it is moving.

As always, the key is to try to convey an overall impression, rather than get caught up in attempting to recreate life, and paint every single water droplet and leaf. Before you start painting, and even before you make your first preliminary sketch, stop and think about what it is that appeals to you in the scene. Is it the intensity of the rushing water or the sunlight sparkling on the water surface? Is the waterfall itself the most important feature or are the surroundings just as interesting? This will help you to decide on the main focus of interest in your painting – and armed with this knowledge, you can decide how best to tackle the painting as a whole.

In real life, all your senses come into play: you can hear the water cascading down and feel the dappled sunlight on your face. In a painting, however, you have to convey these qualities through visual means alone. Sometimes this means you need to exaggerate certain aspects in order to get the message across – making the spray more dramatic, perhaps, or altering the composition to remove distracting features or make interesting ones more prominent.

Materials
- *B pencil*
- *Tracing paper*
- *140lb (300gsm) NOT watercolour paper, pre-stretched*
- *Watercolour paints: cadmium lemon, phthalocyanine green, Payne's grey, burnt sienna, phthalocyanine blue, alizarin crimson*
- *Brushes: large round, fine round, medium wash, old brush for masking fluid*
- *Masking fluid*
- *Low-tack masking tape*
- *Drawing paper to make mask*
- *Household candle*
- *Gum arabic*

The original scene
Although the scene is attractive, the lighting is flat and the colours dull. Here, the artist decided he needed to increase the contrast between light and shade. To do this, you need to carefully work out which areas will be hit by light from above and which will be in shadow. He also increased the size of the pool below the waterfall: paradoxically, the waterfall itself has more impact if it is surrounded by calmer areas.

The waterfall ends too near the bottom of the frame.

The colours are very subdued. Increasing the contrast between light and shade will make the painting more interesting.

1 Using a B pencil, make a sketch on tracing paper to establish the main lines of your subject and work out the size and shape of your painting. When you are happy with the result, transfer your tracing on to pre-stretched watercolour paper.

2 Place a sheet of white drawing paper between the watercolour paper and the tracing paper and draw around the waterfall area. Cut out the shape of the waterfall and place it in position on the watercolour paper as a mask, fixing it in place with low-tack masking tape. Gently rub a household candle over the area of water below the waterfall, keeping the strokes very loose. This will preserve some of the white of the paper and add an interesting texture.

3 Using an old brush, apply masking fluid over the white lines of the waterfall. Leave to dry.

4 Apply masking fluid to the bright highlight area of sky at the top of the picture area and leave to dry. Using a large round brush, brush clean water over the trees. Mix a strong wash of cadmium lemon and brush it over all the damp areas. Leave to dry.

5 Mask off the water area with paper. Mix a mid-toned green from cadmium lemon and a little phthalocyanine green. Holding a fine round brush at the same angle at which the branches grow, spatter water across the top of the picture. Spatter the damp area with green paint. Leave to dry.

6 Continue spattering first with water and then with the green mixture of phthalocyanine green and cadmium lemon, as in Step 5, until you achieve the right density of tone in the trees. Leave each application of spattering to dry completely before you apply the next one.

Tip: Spattering clean water on to the paper first, before you spatter on the paint mixture, means that the paint will spread and blur on the wet paper. If you spatter the paint on to dry paper, you will create crisply defined blobs of colour – a very different effect.

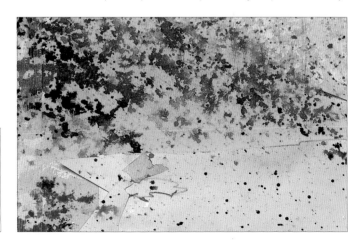

▶

7 Add Payne's grey to the phthalocyanine green and cadmium lemon mixture and, using a fine brush, put in very dark tones along the water's edge in order to define the edge of the river bank.

8 Using a fine brush, brush burnt sienna between the leaves adjoining the dark spattered areas. Mix a rich brown from burnt sienna and Payne's grey and paint the tree trunks and branches. Leave to dry.

9 Using your fingertips, gently rub and peel the masking fluid off the sky area. The sky area is very bright in comparison with the rest of the scene, and so it is important to reserve these light areas in the early part of the painting – even though they will be toned down very slightly in the later stages.

Assessment time

The surrounding woodland is now almost complete. Before you go any further, make sure you have put in as much detail as you want here. The water takes its colour from what is reflected in it. Because of this it is essential that you establish the scenery around the waterfall before you begin to put in any of the water detail.

The line of the riverbank is crisply painted, establishing the course of the river.

The rocks in the waterfall have been marked in pencil, providing an underlying structure for the scene.

10 Using masking fluid, mask the long strokes of white that cascade down from the waterfall into the pool below. Leave to dry. Using a medium wash brush, brush clean water horizontally across the top of the water above the waterfall. Brush a little gum arabic on to the damp area. Keeping the brush fairly dry in order to control the colour, brush vertical strokes of phthalocyanine blue mixed with a little alizarin crimson and burnt sienna on to the damp area.

11 Brush straight lines of Payne's grey across the top of the waterfall to denote the edge over which the water topples. Mix Payne's grey with phthalocyanine blue and brush on to the waterfall itself, using a dry brush technique. On the lower part of the fall, make the marks longer and rougher to indicate the increased speed of the water. Leave to dry.

12 Re-wet the pool above the fall. Using a fine, round brush, touch cadmium lemon into the damp area. Dab on vertical strokes of cadmium lemon, burnt sienna, and phthalocyanine green for the tree trunk reflections. The colours will merge together and the fact that they are blurred helps to convey the wetness of the water.

13 Brush burnt sienna mixed with Payne's grey on to the cascade of water that runs into the pool.

> **Tip:** By applying clean water to the surface before you paint, the strokes diffuse and blur, giving soft blends rather than hard-edged streaks of colour.

14 Working from the bottom of the waterfall upward, brush a mixture of Payne's grey and phthalocyanine blue into the waterfall. Note how the texture of the candle wax shows through. Keep the brush quite dry, dabbing off excess paint on paper towel, if necessary. Add a little alizarin crimson to the mixture for the darker water at the base of the fall.

▶

15 Paint the rocks under the waterfall in a mixture of Payne's grey, phthalocyanine blue and a little alizarin crimson. Use the same mixture to paint more rocks poking up through the foam of the water. Dry brush water along the left and right edges of the painting and apply the rock colour – again with an almost dry brush. The paint will spread down into the damp area.

16 Stipple little dots of masking fluid on to the base of the pool below the waterfall for the white bubbles of foam. Leave to dry. Apply a light wash of phthalocyanine blue mixed with a little Payne's grey over the pool below the waterfall, brushing the paint on with loose, horizontal strokes. While the paint is still damp, run in a few darker vertical lines of the same mixture. Leave to dry.

17 Using a large brush and a darker version of the phthalocyanine blue and Payne's grey mixture, paint the dark area at the base of the pool with bold, zigzag-shaped brushstrokes. Leave to dry.

18 Using your fingertips, gently rub off the masking fluid on the lower half of the painting. Stand back and assess the tonal values of the painting as a whole. If the exposed area looks too white and stark, you may need to touch in some colour in the water areas to redress the overall balance of the scene.

The finished painting

This is a very lively rendition of a waterfall in full spate, which conveys the mood and atmosphere of the scene rather than capturing every leaf and twig in painstaking detail. Much of the paper is left white, in order to convey the full force of the rushing water. The painting has a stronger feeling of light and shade than the original photo, and hence more impact.

The white of the paper conveys the cascading, foaming water.

Skilful use of the wet-into-wet technique has allowed colours to merge on the paper, creating realistic-looking reflections.

Longer brushstrokes in the lower part of the waterfall help to create an impression of movement in the water.

Rock pools in mixed media

Working in mixed media can be an exciting process, as it offers you the chance to combine different kinds of marks and textural effects in the same painting. Before you start, however, think about the character of the landscape and decide which media will best suit your purpose. You can combine as many media as you wish, but think about how they will work together and try to exploit the unique properties of each.

In the rocky seashore scene demonstrated here, the artist used thin, translucent watercolour washes for the sky and background sea, soft pastel for subtle colour blends on the rocks, charcoal for strong, linear detailing, and acrylic paints mixed with modelling paste for the heavier impasto work on the foreground rocks. When you use modelling paste or texture paste, it is better to apply several thin layers rather than one thick one, allowing each layer to dry before you add the next.

It is generally a good idea to start by mapping out the main lines of a relatively complex scene such as this in pencil. Here, the artist used a water-soluble pencil, but you could use ordinary graphite if you prefer. These initial pencil marks may well be covered over by paint in the later stages, but the very act of making them will give you a better understanding of the natural rhythm of the landscape.

Materials
- *Heavy rough watercolour paper*
- *Watercolour paints: ultramarine blue, alizarin crimson*
- *Black water-soluble sketching pencil*
- *Acrylic paints: alizarin crimson, ultramarine blue, titanium white, yellow ochre*
- *High-viscosity acrylic modelling paste*
- *Soft pastels: orange-brown, pink-brown, blue, browns, ochres, bright olive green, bright green*
- *Charcoal: thin stick*
- *Brushes: Selection of rounds in various sizes*
- *Small painting knife*
- *Sponge*

The scene
The rocks lead the viewer's eye through the picture space in a series of diagonal lines to the sea and mountains in the background. The foreground is full of texture and the muted palette of soft blues, browns and ochres provides overall harmony.

1 Wet the paper all over with clean water. Mix a very dilute wash of ultramarine blue watercolour paint with a tiny bit of alizarin crimson and wash it over the support, leaving a few white patches in the sky for the cloud shapes. Dampening the paper first means that the paint will spread wet into wet over the support, leaving no hard-edged brush marks.

2 Using a black water-soluble sketching pencil, put in the main shapes of the rocks in the foreground and middle distance. Keep your marks very loose: do not try to include every crack or crevice, but simply pick out the main directional lines to help you establish the composition of the scene.

3 Mix a thick purple-pink from alizarin crimson, ultramarine blue and titanium white acrylic paints and blend in some acrylic modelling paste. Using a small painting knife, smear the mix over the foreground rocks, adding yellow ochre to the mix for the larger patches of lichen. Vary the texture: keep some areas very smooth and others highly textured.

4 Using orange-brown and pink-brown soft pastels, block in the seaweed-covered rocks in the middle distance. Delineate the darker patches within this area with a thin stick of charcoal.

Tips: • Do not overblend pastel colours – it is important that they retain their individuality, otherwise you will end up with very flat, muddy colours.
• Allow the texture of the paper to show through on the rocks.

▶

5 Mix a cool blue from ultramarine and white acrylic paints with a tiny amount of alizarin crimson. Using a medium round brush, block in the shapes on the mountains in the background, varying the proportions of the colours to get some variation in tone and create a sense of recession.

6 Thin the paint mix by adding lots more water, then brush it over the sea in the background. Continue applying acrylic paint to the rocks, using the same mixes as before. Lightly stroke pink-brown or blue pastels over the foreground rock pools, then blend the marks with your fingers.

Assessment time

The main shapes and structures have been blocked in and we can see the beginnings of some texture and modelling on the rocks. However, many of the rocks still look rather flat and one-dimensional and it is hard to determine exactly which areas in the immediate foreground are water and which are rocks.

The sky looks bleached out, but this is easy to remedy. An initial pale wash often looks too pale once the painting has developed, but it is far better to build up the colour to the required density gradually, by adding more layers, than to make it too dark to start with. The sea in the background is also too pale and flat in relation to the rest of the image.

The initial watercolour wash on the sky is so pale that it is barely visible.

The sea is too pale and there is no sense of movement in the water.

The rocks lack modelling – particularly in the foreground.

7 Overlay various browns, ochres and olive green soft pastels on the seaweed-covered rocks in the background, smoothing the marks with your fingers. To give the rocks more of a sense of form, put in the very darkest patches with strong charcoal marks.

8 Continue using the charcoal to block in the dark, shaded sides of the rocks, as well as for bold, linear marks for the cracks and crevices.

9 Using the small painting knife and the same purple-pink and acrylic modelling paste mixes as before, build up more texture on the foreground rocks. Then, using the tip of the knife, dot in the white foam of the wavelets in the sea so that you begin to create some sense of movement in the water.

10 Add more textural detail to the foreground rocks by dotting and stroking in some bright green pastels, for the lichen.

▶

11 Mix a dilute, pale purple-grey from alizarin crimson, ultramarine and white acrylic paints and, using a fine brush, lightly touch more colour into the sky. Refine the shapes and tones of the mountains, too, using paler tones for the more distant mountains.

 **Tip:** Use thick paint for solid land masses so that they stand out.

12 Apply a thin line of white acrylic paint along the base of the mountains, where they come down to the sea. Use the black water-soluble pencil to put in smaller stones on the spit of land in the middle distance.

13 Dab a small sponge in a blue-grey mix of ultramarine, alizarin crimson and white with a tiny bit of yellow ochre and lightly press it on to the foreground rocks to create a more lichen-like texture.

The finished painting

This is a lively, energetic painting that combines several media without ever allowing the unique qualities of each one to be overpowered by the others. Delicate watercolour washes capture the translucency of the sea and sky, while the solid land masses are conveyed in thicker, opaque acrylics. Soft pastels are applied lightly in the middle distance, allowing the texture of the paper to show through. The addition of modelling paste allows for heavier, impasto applications that perfectly convey the rough texture of the rocks. The colour palette is muted, consisting mostly of soft blues and pink-browns, with sharper touches of yellow ochre and bright olive greens in the lichen and seaweed.

The deep shadows under the rocks, drawn in charcoal, are an important part of the scene as they reinforce the point where the land ends and the water begins.

The solidity of the opaque acrylic paint contrasts well with the translucent watercolour used for the sky.

Combining acrylic paint with modelling paste creates a thick mix that is ideal for capturing the rough texture of these rocks.

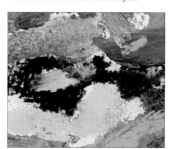

Harbour moorings in watercolour

Ports and harbours are a never-ending source of inspiration for artists. The scene is constantly moving with the tide, and the changing seasons bring different conditions. Reflections in the water, patterns in the sand, and countless details from boat masts to barnacles: there are thousands of things to stir the imagination. The sound of lapping water and squawking gulls, and the smell of seaweed combine to make this one of the most enjoyable of all scenes to paint.

The key is to plan ahead and think about what you want to convey. Harbours are busy places, with lots of things going on and a host of details to distract the eye, and you will almost invariably need to simplify things when you are painting. Decide on your main focus of interest and construct your painting around it. You may find that you need to alter the position of certain elements within the picture space, or to subdue some details that draw attention away from the main subject and place more emphasis on others.

This particular project uses a wide range of classic watercolour techniques to create a timeless scene of a working harbour at low tide. Pay attention to the reflections and the way the light catches the water: these are what will make the painted scene come to life, and there is no better medium for these transient effects of the light than watercolour.

Materials
- *4B graphite pencil*
- *140lb (300gsm) NOT watercolour paper, pre-stretched*
- *Watercolour paints: cadmium orange, Naples yellow, phthalocyanine blue, cerulean blue, permanent rose, raw sienna, ultramarine blue, burnt umber, cadmium red, burnt sienna, light red*
- *Gouache paints: permanent white*
- *Brushes: old brush for masking, 2.5cm (1in) hake, small round, medium filbert, fine filbert, fine rigger*
- *Masking fluid*
- *Masking tape*
- *Plastic ruler or straightedge*

The scene
The tilted boats, wet sand and textures on the harbour wall all have the potential to make an interesting painting, but the sky and water are a little bland and there is no real focus of interest.

The town on the far side of the estuary is a little distracting.

The boats form a straight line across the image; it is unclear where the main focus of interest lies.

Preliminary sketch
The artist decided to make more of the water in his painting, introducing reflections that were not there in real life. He made this preliminary charcoal sketch to work out the tonal values of the scene. He then decided that the boats were too close together and that the scene was too cramped. In his final version, therefore, he widened the image so that the right-hand boat was farther away; he also introduced two figures walking across the sand to provide a sense of scale.

1 Using a 4B graphite pencil, sketch the scene, putting in the outlines of the harbour wall, distant hill, boats and figures. Look for the natural lines of balance of the figures and at how their weight is distributed: this is the key to getting the composition right. Indicate the different bands of sand and water in the foreground.

2 Using an old brush, apply masking fluid over the foreground water and the brightly lit right-hand side of the main boat to protect the highlight areas that you want to remain white in the finished painting. To get fine, straight lines, place a plastic ruler or straightedge on its side, rest the ferrule of the brush on top and gently glide the brush along.

3 Spatter a little masking fluid over the foreground of the scene to suggest some random texture and highlights in the sand and water. Be careful not to overdo it as you need no more than a hint of the sun glinting on these areas.

4 Mix a pale orange from cadmium orange and Naples yellow. Wet the sky in places with clean water. Using a hake brush, wash the orange mixture over the left-hand side of the sky and phthalocyanine blue over the right-hand side, leaving some gaps for clouds.

5 Using the same mixtures, carry the sky colours down into the water and sand, paying careful attention to the colours of the reflections in these areas. The warm colours used in the sky and sand set the mood for the rest of the painting.

▶

6 Mix a dilute wash of pale greyish purple from cerulean blue and a little permanent rose. Wet selected areas of the sky with clean water so that the colours will merge on the paper. Using the hake brush, wash the mixture over the darkest areas of cloud on the left-hand side of the sky and bring the colour down into the background hills and water. Darken this greyish-purple mixture by adding more pigment to it and start putting a little colour on the shaded side of the largest boat in the scene.

7 Using the same mixture of cerulean blue and permanent rose, continue building up washes on the sides of the largest boat. It is better to start light and build up the colour to the correct density by applying several layers than to attempt to get the right shade of blue straight away.

8 Darken the harbour wall with a wash of cadmium orange mixed with Naples yellow. While still wet, drop in a mixture of phthalocyanine blue and a little raw sienna. Paint the reflections of the harbour wall in the wet sand. Apply a little cerulean blue to the main boat and the one behind it.

> **Tip**: Do not make the wall too dark at this stage: assess how strong it should be in relation to the background.

9 Using a small round brush, apply a dark mixture of ultramarine blue, burnt umber and a little cadmium red to the main boat. Mix a purplish grey from cerulean blue and permanent rose and, using a ruler or straightedge as in Step 2, paint the shadow under the main boat. Leave to dry.

10 Using your fingertips, gently rub off the masking fluid to reveal the highlights on the water and sand.

11 Apply further washes, wet into wet, over the hill in the background of the scene so that the colours fuse together on the paper, using ultramarine blue and light red, with a touch of raw sienna for the dark areas in the middle distance. Continue building up the tones of the reflections and intensify the colour of the water by adding a little cerulean blue with a touch of Naples yellow.

12 To add more texture to the ridges of sand in the foreground, apply strokes of burnt sienna straight from the tube, lightly stroking an almost dry medium filbert brush over the dry painting surface. This allows the paint to catch on the raised tooth of the paper, creating expressive broken marks that are equally suitable for depicting the sparkle of light on the water.

Assessment time

The basic structure of the painting is now in place. There are four principal planes – the sky, the landscape on the far side of the river which has put some solidity into the centre of the picture, the boat and harbour wall (the principal centre of interest in the painting), and the immediate foreground, which is structured to lead the eye up to the boat. Now you need to tie everything together in terms of tones and colours.

All the boats need to be strengthened, as they are the main interest in the painting.

The land is not sufficiently well separated from the estuary area.

More texture and depth of tone are needed on the harbour wall to hold the viewer's eye within the picture area.

▶

13 Now you can begin gradually to build up the washes to achieve the correct tonal values. Darken the harbour wall, using the original mixture of cadmium orange and a touch of raw sienna and build up the sandy area immediately in front of the main boat with the same mixture.

14 Using a small round brush and a dark mixture of ultramarine blue and light red, put in some of the detail on the boats. Note that, although the difference is quite subtle, one side of the boat is in shade and therefore darker than the other.

15 Now concentrate on the reflections of the boats, using colours similar to those used in the original washes. Do not make the reflections too opaque. Keep these washes watery and as simple as possible. Use vertical brushstrokes so that they look more like reflections.

16 Mix a warm blue from cerulean blue, permanent rose and a touch of burnt umber and put in the two figures and their reflections.

17 Using a fine rigger brush and resting the ferrule on a plastic ruler or straightedge, as in Step 2, put in the masts on the main boat in a mixture of ultramarine blue and light red and the rigging in a paler mixture of cerulean blue and permanent rose.

18 Using a filbert brush and the original mixture of cadmium orange and a little permanent rose, darken the stonework on the harbour wall. These uneven applications of colour give the wall texture and make it look more realistic.

The finished painting

This project brings together a range of classic watercolour techniques – wet into wet, building up layers of colour, using masking fluid to preserve the highlights, dry brush work – to create a lively painting that captures the atmosphere of the scene beautifully. The background is deliberately subdued in order to focus attention on the moorings. The main subject (the largest boat) is positioned at the intersection of the thirds, with the diagonal line of the sand directing the viewer's eye toward it. The different elements of the scene are perfectly balanced in terms of tone and composition.

The harbour wall is painted wet into wet to create muted but interesting colours and textures.

The town in the original scene has been replaced by an atmospheric blend of colours that suggests wooded hills.

The two walking figures introduce human interest to the scene and provide a sense of scale.

Glossary

Additive
A substance added to paint to alter characteristics such as the paint's drying time and viscosity. Gum arabic is a commonly used additive in watercolour painting.

Alla prima
A term used to describe a work (traditionally an oil painting) that is completed in a single session. *Alla prima* means "at the first" in Italian.

Blending
Merging adjacent colours or tones so that they mix into one another. In dry, powdery drawing media, such as charcoal or soft pastel, blending is usually done with your fingers or by using a torchon.

Body colour
Opaque paint, such as gouache, which can obliterate underlying paint colour on the paper.

Charcoal
This is made by charring willow, beech or vine twigs at very high temperatures in an airtight kiln. Charcoal is available in powder form and as sticks. It can also be mixed with a binder and pressed into sticks of 'compressed' charcoal, creating a form that is stronger than regular stick charcoal and which does not break so easily. Charcoal pencils, made from sticks of compressed charcoal encased in wood, are also available.

Below: Coloured pencils

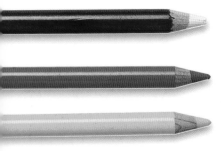

Colour
  Complementary: colours that lie opposite one another on the colour wheel.
  Primary: a colour that cannot be produced by mixing other colours, but can only be manufactured. Red, yellow and blue are the three primary colours.
  Secondary: a colour produced by mixing equal amounts of two primary colours.
  Tertiary: a colour produced by mixing equal amounts of a primary colour and the secondary colour next to it on the colour wheel.

Colour mixing
  Optical colour mixing: applying one colour on top of another in such a way that both remain visible, although the appearance of each one is modified by the other. Also known as *broken colour*. Optical colour mixes tend to look more lively and interesting than their physical counterparts.
  Physical colour mixing: blending two or more colours together to create another colour. Physical colour mixes tend to look duller than their optical counterparts.

Cool colours
Colours that contain blue and lie in the green-violet of the colour wheel. Cool colours appear to recede.

Composition
The way in which the elements of a drawing are arranged within the picture space.
  Closed composition: one in which the eye is held deliberately within the picture area.
  Open composition: one that implies that the subject or scene continues beyond the confines of the picture area.

Conté crayon
A drawing medium made from pigment and graphite bound with gum. Conté crayons are available as sticks and as pencils. They create an

Above: Waterproof ink

effect similar to charcoal but are harder, and can therefore be used to draw fine lines.

Drybrush
The technique of dragging an almost dry brush, loaded with very little paint, across the surface of the support to make textured marks.

Eye level
Your eye level in relation to the subject that you are drawing can make a considerable difference to the composition and mood of the drawing. Viewing things from a high eye level (that is, looking down on them) separates elements in a scene from one another; when viewed from a low eye level (that is, looking up at them), elements tend to overlap.

Fat over lean
A fundamental principle of oil painting. In order to minimize the risk of cracking, oil paints

Below: Oil pastel sticks

containing a lot of oil ('fat' paints) should never be applied over those that contain less oil ('lean' paints) – although the total oil content of any paint mixture should never exceed 50 per cent.

Fixative
A substance sprayed on to drawings made in soft media such as charcoal, chalk and soft pastels to prevent them from smudging.

Foreshortening
The illusion that objects are compressed in length as they recede from your view.

Form
See Modelling.

Format
The shape of a drawing or painting. The most usual formats are landscape (a drawing that is wider than it is tall) and portrait (a drawing that is taller than it is wide). Panoramic (long and thin) and square formats are common.

Glaze
A transparent layer of paint that is applied over a layer of dry paint. Light passes through the transparent glaze and is then reflected back by the support or any underpainting. Glazing is a form of optical (or broken) colour mixing as each glaze colour is separate from the next, with the colour mixing taking place within the eye of the viewer.

Below: Blending watercolour pencils

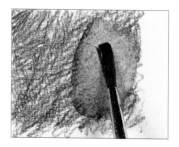

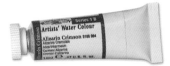

Above: Tubes of watercolour paint

Gouache
Opaque paint which can hide underlying paint on the paper.

Graphite
This is a naturally occurring form of crystallized carbon. To make a drawing tool, it is mixed with ground clay and a binder and then moulded or extruded into strips or sticks. The sticks are used as they are; the strips are encased in wood to make graphite pencils. The proportion of clay in the mix determines how hard or soft the graphite stick or pencil is; the more clay, the harder it is.

Ground
The prepared surface on which an artist works. The same word is also used to describe a coating such as acrylic gesso or primer, which is applied to a drawing surface.

Hatching
Drawing a series of parallel lines, at any angle, to indicate shadow areas. You can make the shading appear more dense by making the lines thicker or closer together.
  Cross-hatching: a series of lines that crisscross each other.

Highlight
The point on an object where light strikes a reflective surface. Highlights can be added by leaving areas of the paper white or by removing colour or tone with a kneaded eraser.

Hue
A colour in its pure state, unmixed with any other.

Impasto
An impasto technique involves applying and building oil or acrylic paint into a thick layer. Impasto work retains the mark of any brush or implement used to apply it.

Line and wash
The technique of combining pen-and-ink work with a thin layer, or wash, of transparent paint (usually watercolour) or ink.

Manikin
A jointed wooden figure that can be moved into almost any pose, enabling the artist to study proportions and angles. Also known as a *lay figure*.

Mask
A material used to cover areas of a drawing, either to prevent smudging, stop marks from touching the paper underneath, or to allow the artist to work right up to the mask to create a crisp edge. There are three materials generally used for masking – masking tape, masking fluid and masking film (frisket paper). You can also simply cover up the relevant part of the drawing by placing a piece of paper over it.

Medium
The term has two very different meanings in art techniques:
(1) The material in which an artist chooses to work – pencil, pen and ink, charcoal, soft pastel and so on. (The plural is 'media'.)

Below: Blending pastel pencils

Above: Liquid acrylic ink

(2) In painting, 'medium' is also a substance added to paint to alter the way in which it behaves – to make it thinner, for example. (The plural in this context is 'mediums'.)

Modelling
Emphasizing the light and shadow areas of a subject through the use of tone or colour, in order to create a three-dimensional impression.

Negative shapes
The spaces between objects in a drawing, often (but not always) the background to the subject.

Overlaying
The technique of applying layers of watercolour paint over washes that have already dried in order to build up colour to the desired strength.

Palette
(1) The container or surface on which paint colours are mixed.
(2) The range of colours used by an artist.

Perspective
A system whereby artists can create the illusion of three-dimensional space on the two-dimensional surface of the paper.
  Aerial perspective: the way the atmosphere, combined with distance, influences the appearance of things. Also known as atmospheric perspective.
  Linear perspective: this system exploits the fact that objects appear to be smaller the further away they are from the viewer. The system is

based on the fact that all parallel lines, when extended from a receding surface, meet at a point in space known as the vanishing point. When such lines are plotted accurately on the paper, the relative sizes of objects will appear correct in the drawing.
  Single-point perspective: this occurs when objects are parallel to the picture plane. Lines parallel to the picture plane remain so, while parallel lines at 90° to the picture plane converge.
  Two-point perspective: this must be used when you can see two sides of an object. Each side is at a different angle to the viewer and therefore each side has its own vanishing point. Parallel lines will slant at different angles on each side, accordingly.

Picture plane
A imaginary vertical plane that defines the front of the picture area and corresponds with the surface of the drawing.

Positive shapes
The tangible features (figures, trees, buildings, still-life objects, etc.) that are being drawn.

Primer
A substance that acts as a barrier between the board or canvas and the paint, protecting the support from the corrosive agents present in the paint and the solvents. Priming provides a smooth, clean surface on which to work. The traditional primer for use with oil paint is glue size, which is then covered with an oil-based primer such as lead white. Nowadays, acrylic emulsions (often called acrylic gesso) are more commonly used.

Recession
The effect of making objects appear to recede into the distance, achieved by using aerial perspective and tone. Distant objects appear paler in colour than those close to the observer.

Above: Gouache paint

Resist
A substance that prevents one medium from touching the paper beneath it. Wax (in the form of candle wax or wax crayons) is the resist most commonly used in watercolour painting; it works on the principle that wax repels water.

Sgraffito
The technique of scratching off pigment to reveal either an underlying colour or the white of the paper. The word comes from the Italian verb *graffiare*, which means 'to scratch'.

Shade
A colour that has been darkened by the addition of black or a little of its complementary colour.

Sketch
A rough drawing or a preliminary attempt at working out a composition.

Below: Gouache paint

Above: A tub of oil paint

Solvent
See **Thinner**.

Spattering
The technique of flicking paint on to the support in order to create texture.

Sponging
The technique of applying colour to the paper with a sponge, rather than with a brush, in order to created a textured appearance.

Stippling
The technique of applying dots of colour to the paper, using just the tip of the brush.

Support
The surface on which a drawing is made – usually paper, but board and surfaces prepared with acrylic gesso are also widely used.

Thinner
A liquid such as turpentine or citrus

Left: Acrylic glaze

solvent which is used to dilute oil paint. Also known as solvent.

Tint
A colour that has been lightened. In watercolour a colour is lightened by adding water to the paint.

Tone
The relative lightness or darkness of a colour.

Tooth
The texture of a support. Some papers are very smooth and have little tooth, while others – such as those used for pastel drawings – have a very pronounced texture.

Torchon
A stump of tightly rolled paper with a pointed end, using for blending powdery mediums. Also known as paper stump or tortillon.

Underdrawing
A preliminary sketch on the canvas or paper, which allows the artist to set down the lines of the subject, and erase them if necessary, before committing to paint.

Underpainting
A painting made to work out the composition and tonal structure of a work before applying colour.

Value
See **Tone**.

Vanishing point
In linear perspective, the vanishing point is the point on the horizon at which parallel lines appear to converge.

Viewpoint
The angle or position from which the artist chooses to draw his or her subject.

Warm colours
Colours in which yellow or red are dominant. They lie in the red-yellow half of the colour wheel and appear to advance.

Above: Three different grades of pencil

Wash
A thin layer of transparent, very diluted watercolour paint.
   Flat wash: an evenly laid wash that exhibits no variation in tone.
   Gradated wash: a wash that gradually changes in intensity from dark to light, or vice versa.
   Variegated wash: a wash that changes from one colour to another.

Wet into wet
The technique of applying paint to a wet surface or on top of an earlier paint application or wash that is still damp.

Wet on dry
The technique of applying paint to dry paper or on top of an earlier paint application or wash that has dried completely.

Below: Bars of oil paint

Index

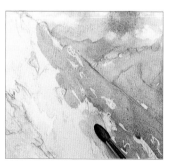

Acknowledgements

The publishers are grateful to the following artists for contributing step-by-step demonstrations: Ray Balkwill: pp498–503; Diana Constance: pp86–9, 194–9, 290–5, 372–7; Martin Decent: pp254, 284–9, 344–9; Joe Francis Dowden: pp474–9, 486–91; Douglas Druce: pp94–7; Abigail Edgar: pp74–9, 90–3, 182–7, 188–93, 206–11, 212–15, 216–19, 220–5, 226–31, 259, 263, 410–11, 269, 271, 296–301, 326–9, 330–3, 388–93, 394–7, 426–9, 442–5, 458–63, 470–3, 480–5, 492–7; Timothy Easton: pp344–9, 446–51; Wendy Jelbert: pp302–7, 312–17, 366–71, 464–9; Beverley Johnston: pp340–3; Vincent Milne: pp176–81, 261, 264–5, 406–7, 267, 410–11, 430–3, 434–7; Melvyn Petterson: pp318–21, 350–3, 422–5, 438–41, 452–7; John Raynes: pp62–3, 66–9, 70–3, 80–5, 98–103, 104–109, 110–15, 200–5, 212–17, 378–83; Paul Robinson: pp354–9, 384–7; Ian Sidaway: pp170–5, 240–5; Albany Wiseman: pp164–9, 404–5, 308–11, 322–5.

The authors and publishers are grateful to the following for permission to reproduce illustrations: Gerry Baptist: pp51 (right), 147 (bottom), 278 (bottom left); Joan Elliot Bates: p274 (top); Mike Bernard: p278 (bottom right); Oliver Bevan: p275 (bottom right); Madge Bright: p255 (top); Bridgeman Art Library: William Etty: p50

(left), 'Study for a Male Nude'; Gerald Cains: p146 (top); Pip Carpenter: pp255 (bottom), 412 (top); Trevor Chamberlain: p150 (top); Patrick Clossick: p151(top right); James Crittendon: p 277 (bottom); Patrick Cullen: p274 (bottom left and right); David Curtis: pp152 (top right), 279 (top), 414 (top); David Cuthbert: p48 (top); Doug Dawson: p276 (bottom); Paul Dyson: p415 (top); Timothy Easton: pp148 (bottom), 403 (bottom), 414 (bottom), 417 (bottom); Abigail Edgar: pp256 (bottom left and right), 257 (all), 258 (left, centre and top right), 260 (top), 262 (top), 264 (top), 266 (top), 268 (all), 270 (all), 336–7, 400 (all), 401 (bottom left and right), 402, 410 (top), 418–19; Trudy Friend: pp401 (top), 403 (top), 256 (top); William Edward Frost: p48 (bottom) 'Life study of the female figure'; Harold Gilman: p50 (bottom) 'Nude on a Bed'; David Gould: pp150 (bottom), 151 (bottom), 279 (bottom); Elizabeth Harden: p49 (bottom); Hazel Harrison: pp42–3, 50; James Horton: p49 (top left and top right), 50 (top); Wendy Jelbert: pp252 (right), 258 (bottom right), 406 (top), 408 (top), 300–1, 420–1; Ronald Jesty: pp413 (top), 415 (bottom); Maureen Jordan: pp52, 278 (top); Geoff Marsters: pp152 (top right), 253 (right); Robert Maxwell Wood: p53; Vincent Milne: pp37–41, 44, 45, 54l, 55, 56–65, 124–6, 128–3, 134–5, 136, 137 (bottom), 138–41, 154–63; Juliette

Palmer: p277 (top); Ken Paine: pp149 (top), 153(top left and bottom); Karen Raney: pp151 (top left), 275 (top right), 276 (top), 416 (bottom); Ian Sidaway: pp248 (top right, bottom left), 249 (top and bottom), 252 (left), 253 (top and bottom left), 412 (bottom); Jackie Simmonds: p416 (top); Effie Waverlin: pp248 (bottom right), 249 (centre); Albany Wiseman: pp250–1, 417 (top).

For permission to reproduce photographs: Jon Hibberd: p260 (bottom), 262 (bottom), 264 (bottom left), 406 (bottom left), 410 (bottom left), 430, 492; Martin Norris: p266 (bottom); Ian Sidaway: pp146 (bottom), 147 (top); Sally Strand: p149 (bottom).